How to Do *Everything* with Your

Visor

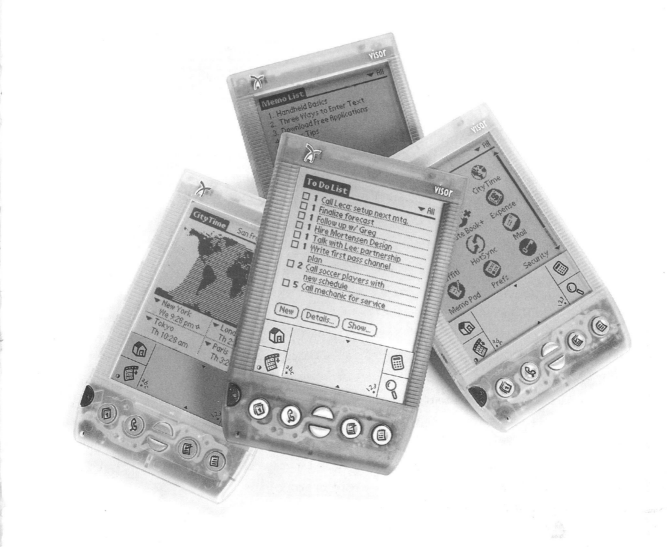

How to Do *Everything* with Your Visor™

Rick Broida
Dave Johnson

Osborne/**McGraw-Hill**

Berkeley New York St. Louis San Francisco
Auckland Bogotá Hamburg London
Madrid Mexico City Milan Montreal New Delhi
Panama City Paris São Paulo
Singapore Sydney Tokyo Toronto

Osborne/**McGraw-Hill**
2600 Tenth Street
Berkeley, California 94710
U.S.A.

For information on translations or book distributors outside the U.S.A., or to arrange bulk purchase discounts for sales promotions, premiums, or fund-raisers, please contact Osborne/**McGraw-Hill** at the above address.

How to Do Everything with Your Visor™

234567890 2CUS 2CUS 019876543210

ISBN 0-07-212696-5

Publisher	Brandon A. Nordin
Vice President and	
Associate Publisher	Scott Rogers
Acquisitions Editor	Jane Brownlow
Project Editor	Janet Walden
Acquisitions Coordinator	Cindy Wathen
Technical Editor	Lisa Lee
Copy Editor	Marcia Baker
Proofreader	Pat Mannion
Indexer	David Heiret
Computer Designers	Lauren McCarthy
	Jani Beckwith
Illustrator	Lyssa Sieben-Wald
	Beth E. Young
Series Design	Mickey Galicia
Cover Design	Dodie Shoemaker

Handspring™, Springboard®, Visor™, and the Handspring logo are trademarks of Handspring, Inc., and may be registered in some jurisdictions.
The Handspring logo and Visor photographs on the cover are used with permission from Handspring, Inc.

This book was composed with Corel VENTURA™ Publisher.

Dedication

For Dottie Klimazewski, Jeff Moskow, Steve Wagstaff, and Barbara Krasnoff,
without whom I couldn't possibly have made it this far.
For Caroline, one of the kindest, coolest, and most gracious people on the planet, and
the best sister a guy could have.
For Shawna, whom I would follow to the ends of the earth, let alone Michigan.
And for my beautiful, amazing, impossibly wonderful daughter Sarah, who brings
me joy every single day.

—Rick

For Paul, who started all this.

—Dave

About the Authors

Rick Broida and **Dave Johnson** are avid Palm-using technology journalists living in Colorado.

Rick Broida has written about computers and technology for over 10 years. A regular contributor to *Computer Shopper*, *Family PC*, *GamePower*, *Home Office Computing*, *Portable Computing* and other publications, he specializes in mobile technology. Along with Dave Johnson, he is the co-author of *How to Do Everything with Your Palm™ Handheld* (Osborne/McGraw-Hill, 2000). Recognizing the unparalleled popularity of the PalmPilot and the need for a printed resource covering the platform, he launched *Tap Magazine* in 1997. Now known as *Handheld Computing*, it remains the only magazine devoted to the Palm OS platform.

Dave Johnson has been writing about computers since his first book, *The Desktop Studio: Multimedia with the Amiga,* was published in 1990. Since then he's written over a dozen books, including *Digital Photography Answers* (Osborne/McGraw-Hill, 1998), *How to Use Digital Video* (Sams, 2000) and *Small Business Office 2000 For Dummies* (with Todd Stauffer; IDG, 1999). Dave is senior editor at *Planet IT*, an online magazine published by CMP, and contributes to magazines like *Home Office Computing* and *Family PC*. In his spare time he photographs wolves, scuba dives, and entertains his cat.

About the Technical Editor

Lisa Lee is an author and engineer from the San Francisco Bay Area. She was the technical editor for *How to Do Everything with Your Palm™ Handheld, Mac OS 9: The Complete Reference, Mac OS in a Nutshell, Complete Idiot's Guide to WebTV, Teach Yourself Mac OS 8.5 in 24 Hours*, and several other Mac books. She has also written about Macintosh computers, Web graphics software, Linux, WebTV, Palm, Pocket PC, and Visor handhelds.

Contents at a Glance

Contents

Acknowledgments

This book was a pleasure to write, in large part because the whole team was so great to work with. We greatly appreciate the efforts of Jane Brownlow, Tara Davis, Janet Walden, and Cindy Wathen. We'd also like to thank Studio B, who brought us the Palm book and therefore made this one possible.

Special thanks to the folks at Handspring and Switzer Communications for their assistance. We'd also like to acknowledge a few other folks.

Rick would like to say:

If Dave thinks I'm going to thank him yet again for helping me realize my lifelong dream of writing a book, he's sadly mistaken. But I would like to thank him for putting up with my occasional tantrums, which, ironically, are usually his fault.

Special thanks to my wife, Shawna, who gave me unyielding support during the tumult of this book. A luckier husband there could not be.

Dave would like to add:

I'd like to thank Rick for not throwing quite as many tantrums as last time. I say I'd *like* to, but I can't, because he was more of a pain to work with this time than last. Sheesh. At least he gave me a really cool poster from *The Matrix*.

Introduction

The Visor is such a great little tool that any book about it runs the risk of reading like a promotional brochure. This much is certain, though—together we have written thousands of pages about the Windows platform and half of it always seems to be apologetic. "If you don't see the File menu, you need to reboot and send $10 in cash to Microsoft, and, well, that's computers for you...." Books about computers are often more about getting it to work in the first place or explaining why it doesn't work right than telling you what you can actually accomplish.

Not the Visor, though. It's one of the most forgiving, user-friendly, and noncrashable computers ever devised. And because it suffers from so few technical glitches, this book is mostly about *doing things* with your Visor—accomplishing stuff and making your life more fun and more efficient. In that sense, this is one of the most enjoyable writing experiences we've ever had.

If it's possible to do something with a Visor, we cover it somewhere in *How to Do Everything with Your Visor*™.

Part I, "Get Started," covers the basics. We talk about the various Visor models and which one you should consider buying. From there, you get a guided tour of your Visor and the desktop software that comes with it. We'll teach you things you never knew about getting around the Visor applications and how to synchronize data with your PC or Macintosh. Having trouble with Graffiti? Be sure to check out Chapter 4, which features tons of Graffiti hints, tips, and shortcuts.

Part II, "Get Things Done," focuses on accomplishing the important tasks you need to do every day. We show you the Visor's core applications and then tell you stuff you'd never think of—like how to get the most out of your Visor when you go on a business trip.

Part III, "Beyond the Box," is where things really get interesting. Read those chapters and you'll learn how to manage your finances, track your stocks, and balance your checkbook. We also delve into the arts, with chapters on creating drawings and music. You might think there's not a lot to say about playing games, but there's a whole world of entertainment hiding out there—and we show you how to tap into it. In fact, you might throw away your Game Boy after reading Chapter 20. And don't forget to check out Chapter 14, where you learn everything you need to know about Visor communications: e-mail, Web browsing, faxing, and more.

We wrote this book so you could sit down and read through it like a novel. But if you're looking for specific information, we've made topics easy to find. Plus, you can find special elements to help you get the most out of the book:

- **How to**   These special boxes explain, in a nutshell, how to accomplish key tasks throughout the book. You can also read the "How to" bullets at the beginning of the chapter for a summary of what the chapter covers.

- **Notes**   These provide extra information that's handy for trivia contests, but isn't essential to understanding the current topic.

- **Tips**   These tell you how to do something a better, faster, or smarter way.

- **Cautions**   These warn you away from something you might regret doing. We hope to save you some headaches with these.

- **Sidebars**   These boxes talk about related topics that are pretty darned interesting, but you can skip them if you prefer. Actually, sidebars often make for fascinating reading. Throughout the book, we've inserted sidebars that pit Dave against Rick to discuss certain Visor topics.

Within the text, you'll also find words in special formatting. New terms are in italics, while specific phrases that you will see on the Palm screen or need to type yourself appear in bold.

Want to talk to us? You can also send questions and comments to us at palmquestions@radioguys.com. Thanks, and enjoy reading the book!

Part I

Get Started

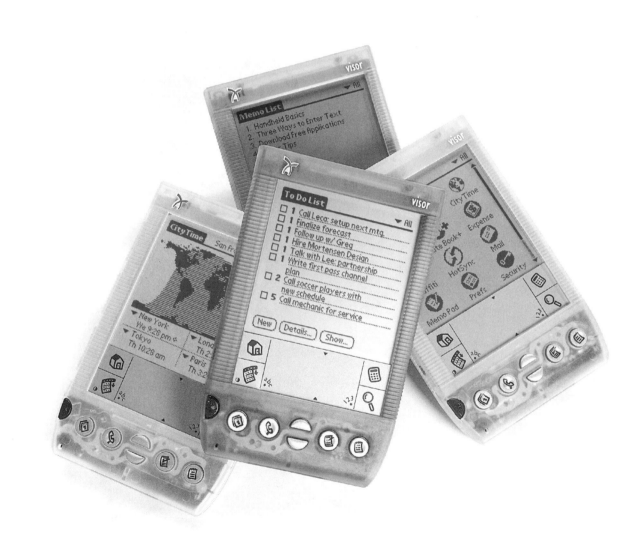

Chapter 1

Welcome to Visor

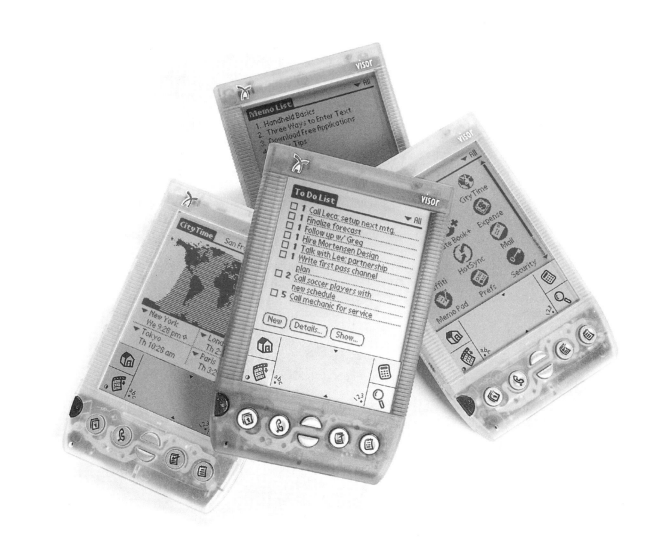

How to...

- ■ Distinguish between Visors and other Palm devices
- ■ Choose one of the three Visor models
- ■ Use Palm OS software on a Visor
- ■ Buy a Visor

It all started with a block of wood. In 1994, Jeff Hawkins, founder of a little-known company called Palm Computing, envisioned a pocket-size computer that would organize calendars and contacts, and maybe let travelers retrieve their e-mail from the road. This idea of a personal digital assistant (PDA) was by no means new, but previous attempts—like Apple's highly publicized Newton MessagePad—had failed to catch on with consumers.

Hawkins knew he'd have a tough time selling the concept, so he decided to convince himself before trying to convince investors. His device would be roughly the size of a deck of cards—much smaller and lighter than the Newton—and would therefore fit in a shirt pocket. But would it be practical even at that size? Would it be comfortable to carry around? Hawkins decided to find out. Before a single piece of plastic was molded, before a single circuit board was designed, the Palm Computing Pilot existed solely as a block of wood.

In his garage, Hawkins sawed a length of 2-by-4 to the size he'd envisioned for his handheld device, put it in his shirt pocket, and left it there—for several months. Although he quickly came to realize that such a form factor made perfect sense, doors slammed whenever he showed the "product" to potential investors. "The handheld market is dead," was the mantra at the time.

Fortunately, modem-maker U.S. Robotics didn't think so. The company liked the idea of the Pilot so much, it bought Palm Computing outright. In March 1996, the company unveiled the Pilot 1000, and the rest is history.

Flash-forward four years. The Pilot—which would eventually be renamed PalmPilot and then just Palm—had become the fastest-growing computer platform in history, reaching the million-sold mark faster than the IBM PC or Apple Macintosh. In the interim, U.S. Robotics had been assimilated into networking giant 3Com, and Palm Computing along with it. The Palm line had grown to include a variety of models, and companies like IBM, Qualcomm, and Symbol Technologies had adopted the Palm operating system for their own handheld devices.

Hawkins himself departed Palm Computing in 1998—not to take up golf, not to delve into a different kind of work, but to reinvent the wheel he'd already invented. In September 1999, his new company, Handspring, introduced the Visor—a licensed Palm clone (see Figure 1-1) that many say is superior to the devices that preceded it.

The Visor made quite a debut. Handspring was so swamped with orders during the first four months, the best it could manage was a four to six week turnaround. Positive press, combined with lower-than-Palm prices, created a kind of buying frenzy that lasted well past the 1999 holiday season. In short, the Visor was an overnight success—much like the Pilot that started it all.

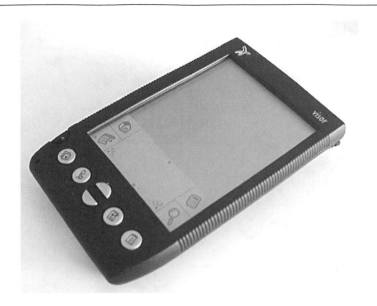

FIGURE 1-1   The Handspring Visor, a Palm clone from the inventors of the original Palm

What Makes the Visor So Unique?

Why all the fuss? What makes a Visor—and, for that matter, any device that runs the Palm operating system—so special? To answer this question, we must first look at what a Visor actually is. Put simply, it's a pocket-size electronic organizer that enables you to manage addresses, appointments, expenses, tasks, and memos. If you've ever used a Franklin Planner or any similar kind of paper-bound organizer, you get the idea.

However, because a Visor is electronic, no paper and ink are involved. Instead, you write directly on the device's screen, using a small plastic stylus that takes the place of a pen. A key advantage here, of course, is that you're able to store all your important personal and business information on a device that's much smaller and lighter than a paper planner.

What's more, you can easily share that information with your Windows-based or Macintosh computer. Visors are not self-contained: they can synchronize with a desktop computer and keep information on both sides up-to-date. This is an important advantage because it effectively turns your Visor into an extension of the computer you use every day. Changes and additions made to your desktop data are reflected in the Visor and vice versa (see Figure 1-2).

Saying that a Visor is an extension of your computer is only a half-truth: in reality, the Visor is a computer in its own right. It is capable of running sophisticated software written by third-party

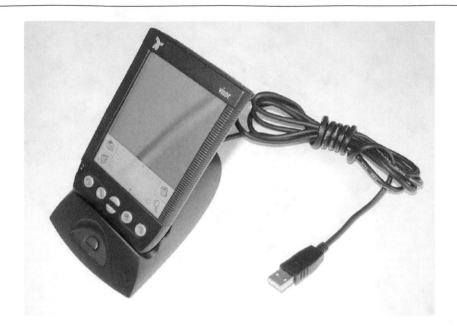

FIGURE 1-2 A Visor connects to your computer via its HotSync cradle, which allows data to be synchronized on both devices

developers, and those developers number in the tens of thousands. There are thousands of programs available that extend your Visor's capabilities, from spreadsheet managers and expense trackers to electronic-book readers and Web browsers. Got five minutes to kill? You can play a quick game of Asteroids. Need to check your e-mail while traveling? Snap on a modem and dial your Internet service provider (ISP).

Simplicity is a major key to the Palm platform's success—and, therefore, the Visor's as well. The devices are amazingly easy to use, requiring no more than a few taps of the stylus to access your data and a little memorization to master the handwriting-recognition software. Most users, even those who have little or no computer experience (like Dave), find themselves tapping and writing productively within 20 minutes of opening the box.

About Springboard Technology

To look at a Visor is to see a device that closely resembles a Palm III. While the two are indeed very similar, the Visor has one significant advantage: its Springboard expansion slot. This rear-facing slot, which makes the Visor look not unlike a Nintendo Game Boy, accommodates special hardware modules that expand the device's capabilities. In fact, the modules work much like Game Boy cartridges: you simply plug one in and start using it.

What can Springboard do for you? Here's a list of some of the modules now available:

- An MP3 music player
- A complete *Merriam-Webster dictionary*
- A voice recorder
- An FM radio (see Figure 1-3)
- A digital camera
- A collection of *Star Trek* novels
- A GPS receiver
- A Tiger Woods golf game

We'll tell you all about these and other modules in later chapters. Suffice it to say, your Visor can go *way* beyond mere information-management.

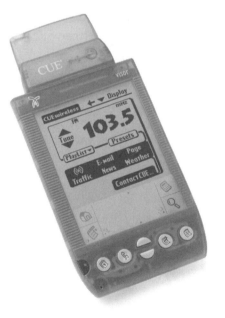

FIGURE 1-3 The CUE Radio, which receives FM stations and weather reports, is only one of the many compelling expansion modules available for the Visor

The Springboard Modules We Really Want

Rick: Let's see, I want a module that gives me a cell phone, a wireless modem, an encyclopedia, every *Star Trek* book ever written, and a Chiclet dispenser. Actually, most of that stuff will probably show up this year, though not all on the same module. In the meantime, I'm enjoying InnoGear's MP3 player and digital recorder. With it, I can enjoy a little Louis Prima while I'm stuck in line at the post office or record a voice note reminding myself to come to the post office in the morning when the lines aren't so long.

Dave: The real technological hurdle in Rick's dream module is, obviously, the Chiclet dispenser. For me, though, the perfect module would provide extensive voice recognition so I could talk, not type. Of course, it would have to record voice notes and convert them into text memos, and play a few hours' worth of MP3 music to boot. If I'm not getting too greedy, it would be cool if the Visor also had GPS satellite navigation and a high-speed wireless modem, too.

An Overview of the Visor Models

Whether you're still shopping for a Visor or you've been fiddling with one for a month, it's good to have an understanding of the three models that are available. Physically, they're identical, although one of the models—the Visor Deluxe—is available in different colors. Here's a quick overview of the three.

Visor Deluxe

This is the top-of-the-line Visor. It comes with 8MB of memory—6MB more than either of its siblings—and is available in five different colors (many of which are reminiscent of Apple's iMac computers). At press time, the Deluxe had a list price of $249.

NOTE   *All prices mentioned in this book are subject—and likely—to change. Fortunately, they'll be going down, not up.*

Visor

The "middle child," the Visor features 2MB of RAM and is available only in the slate-black color. At press time, its list price was $179—definitely a bargain among Palm OS devices.

Visor Solo

The Visor Solo is identical to the Visor, except it comes without desktop software and a HotSync cradle. Aren't these items essential to using the device? Yes and no. For one thing, not everyone owns a computer, and the Visor is a very capable information manager all by itself. In other words, you don't necessarily need a computer connection to use a Visor (although you would miss out on all the great third-party software).

The more likely scenario is using the Solo as a second Visor. Suppose you buy a Visor, fall in love with it, and decide to buy another one for your spouse. You already own the necessary software and a HotSync cradle, so why pay for them again? Because the Solo lists for $149, you can save a few dollars by using the two Visors with one computer. For a small business that wants to deploy, say, a dozen Visors, this approach can add up to considerable savings.

What They Have in Common

Clearly, the differences between the three models are few. Price-conscious buyers will likely choose the Visor, while those seeking extra memory and/or a color shell will "splurge" for the Visor Deluxe.

In the next chapter, we give you a guided tour of the Visor, introducing you to its various features. In the meantime, let's discuss the common thread that links all Visors: the Palm Operating System.

What Is the Palm Operating System?

Windows is an operating system. Mac OS 8 is an operating system. The core software that drives any computer is an operating system. Hence, when we refer to the Palm OS, we're talking about the software that's built right into the device—the brains behind the brawn. The Palm OS itself not only controls the Visor's fundamental operations, such as what happens when you press a button or tap the screen, but also supplies the built-in applications (the Address Book, Memo Pad, Date Book, and so on—all of which we discuss in detail in later chapters).

Why isn't it called the Visor OS? Handspring licensed the operating system from Palm, Inc., much the same way that, say, Gateway licenses Windows from Microsoft. Gateway supplies the hardware, but the software used is Windows. Similarly, the Visor hardware is made by Handspring, but it runs the Palm OS (see Figure 1-4).

The key thing to remember is your Visor can run 99.9 percent of the software that runs on devices made by Palm, Inc. Just as all software written for Windows runs on all computers that use Windows, all software written for the Palm OS runs on Visors. A handful of programs may be incompatible (they're exceedingly rare), but the vast majority work just fine.

NOTE   *The same cannot be said for add-on hardware. That is, most accessories designed for Palm-manufactured devices are incompatible with the Visor, owing to minor but significant differences in their physical design. Thus, if you're shopping for, say, a keyboard, make sure you get one that's made for the Visor, not for the Palm.*

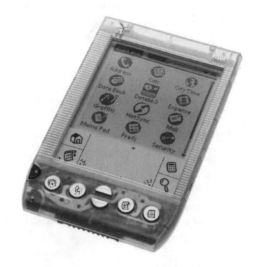

FIGURE 1-4   It may look a little different from Palm-manufactured handheld computers, but the Visor employs the popular Palm Operating System

Visor Advantages

On the off chance you're still trying to decide between a Visor and a Palm device made by Palm (or another licensee), we've outlined a few of the advantages of the Visor line, and why they're important.

- **USB HotSync Cradle**   As noted earlier, the HotSync cradle is used to synchronize your Visor and computer. The cradle included with the Visor employs a USB interface, whereas Palm cradles rely on older serial technology. The latter are more likely to cause setup hassles, whereas USB affords plug-and-play simplicity. It also delivers much speedier synchronization.

- **Macintosh compatibility**   Right out of the box, Visors are compatible with most modern Macintosh systems. That's due in part to the aforementioned USB HotSync cradle, which can plug right into Macs that have USB ports. By contrast, the serial cradles included with Palm models require Palm's MacPac kit, which must be purchased separately. That kit also includes the necessary Macintosh software, which is already bundled with Visors. In short, if you're a Mac user, the Visor is a decidedly compelling choice.

- **Improved software**   Although we said earlier that the Visor uses the same Palm OS as other Palm devices, Handspring added a few minor but worthwhile amenities.

Specifically, the Date Book application included with the Visor is more robust than the one that comes with Palms. (We talk about it in greater detail in Chapter 7.) Also, Handspring supplies a handy bonus application called CityTime, a clock that lets you see the time anywhere in the world. You learn more about it in Chapter 12.

- ■ **Springboard**   Although we already discussed it earlier in this chapter, we can't overstate the importance of Springboard technology. No other Palm device has the same level of expandability—one major reason Visors have sold like hotcakes.

Visor Limitations

Is there any reason *not* to choose a Visor over one of the Palm devices made by other manufacturers? Aside from the obvious (you want something thin and sexy like the Palm V, or a model with built-in wireless communications like the Palm VII), there's only one worth mentioning: Flash RAM.

Flash RAM is a special kind of memory that's used by most Palm devices to store the operating system (not unlike the way your computer's hard drive stores Windows or the Mac OS). Although its contents are "permanent"—meaning they're not erased if there's a loss of battery power—Flash RAM is accessible. Translation: if a new version of the operating system becomes available, you can install it on your Palm device.

Visors don't employ Flash RAM, instead storing the operating system on a non-accessible ROM chip. Translation: you're stuck with whatever version of the OS comes loaded—no upgrades possible.

> NOTE   *At press time, Visors were equipped with Palm OS 3.0. The latest version released by Palm, Inc., is 3.5.*

How important is that? For many users, it's not. While a handful of third-party programs may require the newest version of the OS to run, most software will work fine with any version. What's more, third-party applications and utilities often emerge that emulate improvements to the OS. For instance, in OS 3.5, Palm made it possible to access pull-down menus just by tapping at the top of the screen (instead of having to tap the Menu button). A nice feature, sure, but a little freeware applet called MenuHack does the same thing. Similarly, while OS 3.3 added support for infrared HotSyncs, IS/Complete's IrLink affords the same capability.

While it's regrettable that Visors don't have Flash RAM, we wouldn't let it get in the way of our buying one.

Where to Buy a Visor

At press time, Visors weren't nearly as ubiquitous as Palm-manufactured models. You could buy them directly from Handspring (by calling 888-565-9393 or browsing www.handspring.com), or from one of a few retail outlets: Best Buy, CompUSA, and Staples. You'll pay the same prices at all four locations, so you may as well choose the one that's most convenient for you.

By the time you read this, Visors may be sold at additional Web outlets and retailers. One quick and easy way to find them on the Web is with price-comparison sites like MySimon (www.mysimon.com), PriceScan (www.pricescan.com), and PriceGrabber (www.pricegrabber.com).

Finally, if you're looking to save a few extra dollars and don't mind buying used equipment, check auction sites like eBay (www.ebay.com). Although the winning bids usually don't fall too far below list prices, it is possible to save, say, $15 to $20 on a Visor Deluxe.

Chapter 2

A Guided Tour of the Visor

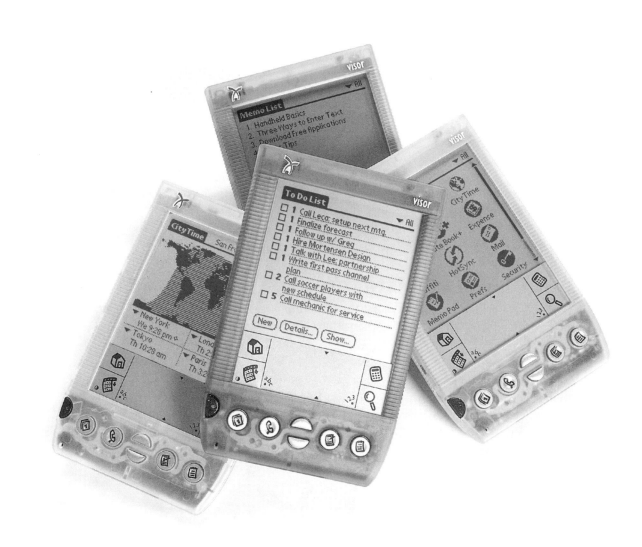

How to...

- Identify the buttons on a Visor
- Identify the infrared transmitter
- Work with the screen and Graffiti area
- Install the batteries
- Turn on the Visor for the first time
- Use the Graffiti tutorial
- Reset the Visor
- Configure your Visor's preferences
- Reset the screen digitizer
- Work with the operating system
- Create and use shortcuts
- Work with Palm Desktop

Okay, enough history—it's time to dive in and start having fun. At the beginning of any lasting and meaningful relationship, you want to get to know the other person as well as possible—find out what makes him tick, what her boundaries are, where they keep their batteries. With this in mind, we tailored this chapter as a kind of meet 'n' greet, to help you overcome that bit of initial awkwardness. Let's turn this blind date into a blissful marriage with two kids, a dog, and a white picket fence!

A Guided Tour of the Hardware

By now your Visor is, no doubt, out of the box and getting the once-over. You're seeing buttons, a screen, some little pictures, and a rear compartment that looks just big enough to hold a pair of batteries. What is all this stuff? What does it do?

The Screen

A Visor screen is capable of displaying roughly 15 lines of text, each about 32 characters across. It can also display graphics with up to 16 shades of gray. The size of the Visor screen is the same as all Palm devices, as is the resolution (160 × 160 pixels).

When you use a desktop computer, you use a mouse to navigate and a keyboard to enter data. When you use a Visor, you use a plastic stylus for both navigation and data entry. That's because the screen is, technically speaking, a *touchscreen,* meaning you interact with it by tapping and writing on it. Should you want to access, say, the Expense program, you'd tap the Expense icon that appears on the screen. If you want to record the price of the dinner you just ate, you'd write the numbers on the screen.

The Difference Between Tapping and Writing

Tapping on the screen is the equivalent of clicking a mouse. You tap on icons to launch programs, tap to access menus and select options in them, and tap to place your cursor in specific places. Writing on the screen is, of course, like putting a pen to paper. Most writing you do on a Visor, however, takes place in a specific area of the screen, which we discuss in the following sections. When you're working in, say, a sketchpad or paint program, you can scribble anywhere on the screen, just as though it were a blank sheet of paper.

NOTE   *Don't press too hard with the stylus. The screen is fairly sensitive, and light pressure is all it takes to register a tap or stylus-stroke. If you press too hard, you could wind up with a scratched screen—the bane of every Visor user.*

The Graffiti Area

As you've no doubt noticed, the bottom portion of the screen looks a bit different. That big rectangular box flanked by two pairs of icons is called the *Graffiti area,* referring to the handwriting-recognition software that's part of every Visor. Graffiti makes it possible to enter information using the stylus, but you can do so only within the confines of the Graffiti area.

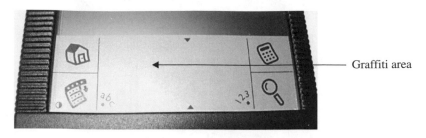

Graffiti area

We tell you more about Graffiti—how to use it and alternatives to it—in Chapters 4 and 21, respectively.

What about those icons on either side of the Graffiti area? They serve some important functions. Here's an overview:

 The Applications button   Represented by a picture of a house and located in the upper-left corner of the Graffiti area, the Applications button is the one you tap more often than any other. From whatever program you're currently running, the *Applications* button takes you back to the main screen—"home base," as it were (hence, the house picture).

 The Menu button   Tapping the icon in the lower-left corner of the Graffiti area—a.k.a. the *Menu* button—gives you access to the drop-down menus that are a part of the Palm operating system. These menus vary somewhat from program to program, as far as the options they provide, but they're quite consistent within the core Palm OS applications.

The Menu button works like a toggle switch. If you accidentally tap it or simply want to make the drop-down menus go away, just tap it again.

 The Calculator button   Probably the most self-explanatory of all the buttons, *Calculator*—located in the upper-right corner of the Graffiti area—launches the built-in calculator.

 The Find button   Finally, we get to the little magnifying glass in the lower-right corner. Because a Visor can store such vast amounts of information, and because sifting through all that information to find what you're looking for can be tedious, there's a handy little search feature called *Find*. We talk more about Find in Chapter 12.

 The Contrast button   Notice the little half-moon icon that's in the lower-left corner of the Graffiti area, near the Menu button. This is the *Contrast* button, used to adjust the screen contrast: tapping it brings up an onscreen slider tool that you move with your stylus until the contrast is to your liking.

2

The Buttons

Below the Graffiti area on every Visor lies a row of buttons, as shown in Figure 2-1. These serve some important functions: to turn the device on and off, to instantly launch the core applications (Date Book, Memo Pad, and so forth), and to scroll up and down in screens of data.

The Power Button

Located on the left side of the Visor and shaped like a half-moon, the *Power* button is self-explanatory. But it serves a second function as well: to activate the screen's backlighting, done by holding the button down for a few seconds. Holding it down again deactivates the backlight, as does simply turning off the Visor.

The Four Program Buttons

So you want to look up a number in your Address Book. You could turn your Visor on, tap the Applications button to get to the Main screen, and then find and tap the Address icon. Or, you could skip all that and simply press the *Address* button, which is represented by a picture of a telephone handset. That serves the dual function of turning on the Visor and loading the Address List program. Talk about a time-saver!

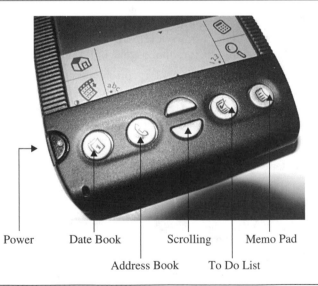

Power   Date Book   Scrolling   Memo Pad

Address Book   To Do List

 The Visor buttons for power, scrolling, and the four core applications

The same holds true for the three other buttons, which launch Date Book, To Do List, and Memo Pad. You can use them at any time, whether the Visor is on or off, to quickly switch between the four core programs.

The Scroll Buttons

Resembling two separated halves of a circle and sandwiched between the two pairs of program buttons, the *Scroll* buttons are used to cycle through multiple screens of data. If you're looking at a memo that's too long to fit on the screen in its entirety, you'd use the Scroll-down button to move down to the next section—not unlike turning pages in a book. The Scroll-up button simply moves you back—or "up"—a page.

NOTE *In many programs, onscreen arrows—usually in the lower-right corner of the screen—serve the same function. Instead of having to press the Scroll buttons, you can simply tap the arrows with your stylus. This is largely a matter of personal preference; try both and decide which method you like better!*

The Back of the Visor

Flip over your Visor. Most of what's back there is self-explanatory, but let's talk about the key areas anyway.

- There's a little hole on the right-hand side that's used to reset the device. Hey, every computer crashes occasionally, and the Palm OS isn't entirely glitch-free. (We talk more about resetting in Chapter 25. For now, however, note that if your Visor locks up, pressing the reset button usually gets it running again.)

- The Springboard socket, shown in Figure 2-2, is currently occupied by a plastic insert, which has no function other than to protect the socket area. Feel free to pop it out and take a look—but try not to lose it. While a Springboard expansion module may soon take its place, you should leave the insert snapped in until then.

- The battery compartment resides near the bottom. We tell you how to install the batteries in "Installing the Batteries" (what else?) a bit later in the chapter.

The Infrared Port

Look at the left-hand side of your Visor and you see a small, dark-red window. This is the *infrared port,* also known as the infrared transceiver or IR port. The infrared port is used to beam data wirelessly from one Visor to another (it also works with other Palm OS devices), and it has a range of about five feet. You learn more about beaming in Chapter 4.

FIGURE 2-2   A plastic insert protects the Springboard socket until you plug in a real module

The Stylus

Next, we come to the stylus. Every Visor has a small plastic pen tucked inside a "silo," which is located along the right-hand side. As you discover in later chapters, a handful of third-party styluses are available—some are made of metal and some are as big as regular pens.

What all styluses have in common is a plastic tip. Under no circumstances should you ever use any kind of ink pen or metal tip on a Visor's screen. That's a sure way to create a scratch, and a scratched screen is a damaged screen.

NOTE *There is one exception. In a pinch, or if you just don't feel like extracting the stylus, you can use your fingernail for light taps on the screen. In fact, many people prefer to operate the calculator this way, as the numbers are large enough for effective finger-taps. We suggest fingernails over fingers, as the latter leave fingerprints— and we like a nice, clean screen.*

The Screen Cover

Each Visor comes with a hard-plastic cover (see Figure 2-3) that protects the screen when your Visor is riding in a pocket or purse or briefcase. It locks on by hooking the two nubs into the holes on the bottom of the Visor, and then snapping onto the top. Because the cover is reversible—meaning it can lock onto the back of the Visor during use—you needn't worry about it getting misplaced.

Using Your Visor for the First Time

Now that you're familiar with the Visor hardware, you're ready to start using it. That means installing the batteries, working your way through the startup screens, and checking out the Graffiti tutorial.

FIGURE 2-3   The cover protects the front of your Visor, and its clever design also allows it to fit on the backside during normal Visor operation

2

Installing the Batteries

Obviously there's nothing terribly complicated about this, but it's important that you install the batteries properly, following the directions outlined in the instruction manual. If you put them in backward, your Visor won't work.

> **NOTE** *Always use alkaline batteries. You can use rechargeable batteries if you want, although they're not recommended. The reason is they tend to lose their charge more suddenly than alkalines, which can result in lost data. Therefore, if you decide to use rechargeable batteries, make sure to keep a closer eye on the battery gauge (see "The Applications Screen" later in this chapter).*

The Welcome Screens

Once the batteries are in and you've turned your Visor back over, you see a "welcome" screen that asks you to remove the stylus and tap anywhere to continue. You're about to undertake a one-time setup procedure that lasts all of about 60 seconds. The two key tasks accomplished here are the calibration of the screen digitizer and the setting of the date and time.

What Is Digitizer Calibration?

Put simply, *digitizer calibration* is the process of teaching a Visor to accurately recognize taps on the screen. As you know, the screen responds to input from the stylus, and this calibration process simply ensures the precision of those responses. In a way, it's like fine-tuning the image on a TV set.

> **NOTE** *Over time, you might discover that your screen taps seem a little "off." For example, you have to tap a bit to the left of an arrow for the screen to register the tap. At this point, it's time to recalibrate the digitizer, which you can do in the Prefs menu. We tell you how in "Digitizer" in the "Setting Visor Preferences" section later in this chapter.*

Setting the Date and Time

The last stage of the welcome process is setting the date and time (and choosing your country, if you live outside the United States). To set the time, you simply tap the box next to the words Set Time, and then tap the up/down arrow keys to select the current time (don't forget to specify A.M. or P.M.). Tapping the box next to Set Date reveals a calendar; again, a few strategic taps is all it takes to select today's date. When you've done so, tap the Today button.

> **NOTE** *If you find yourself in a different time zone and need to change your Visor's clock, you needn't repeat the whole welcome process to do so. The date and time settings can be found in the Prefs menu, which we discuss later in this chapter in "Setting Visor Preferences."*

The Graffiti Tutorial

On the last screen of the welcome wagon, you're given this option: "To learn about entering text on your handheld now, tap Next." Doing so takes you to a brief but helpful tutorial on using Graffiti, the Visor's handwriting-recognition software. If you'd rather jump right into using your Visor and learn Graffiti later, tap Done instead of Next. You can revisit the Graffiti tutorial at any time, just by finding and tapping the Graffiti icon in the main Applications screen.

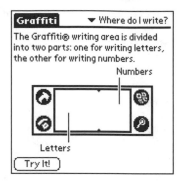

Why Use the Tutorial?

Mastering Graffiti is arguably the most difficult aspect of using a Visor because it requires you to learn and use a special character set. Thus, you should definitely spend some time with the tutorial.

The Pros and Cons of Graffiti

Dave: The coolest thing about the Visor is Graffiti. Graffiti lets you interact with your Visor using a form of handwriting that's virtually 100 percent accurate. That means you don't have to worry about whether it's understanding you or not—you just input words and concentrate on the business at hand. That's why I'll never understand people like Rick who insist on messing with perfection. He's always trying out all kinds of Graffiti alternatives—overlays that change the way you tap on the Graffiti screen, keyboards, completely different recognition systems, even direct cranial implants so he can just think into his Visor (for Rick, of course, the output always looks like this: "ugh . . .ugh . . .bananas . . ."). Give it a rest already! If you don't like Graffiti, go buy another handheld!

Rick: Unlike Dave, I prefer to think for myself and not let others make decisions for me. Hence my interest in Graffiti alternatives and enhancements (which we discuss in Chapter 21). Certainly Graffiti is a pretty good handwriting-recognition system, but it's not perfect. (Dave also thought his Apple Newton was perfect, and now he's using it to scoop out the cat box.) If you find Graffiti unwieldy or just plain don't like it, check out the alternatives in Chapter 21.

How to ... **Improve Your Graffiti Accuracy**

As you'll discover, Graffiti isn't difficult to learn—but writing accurately is a challenge for many users. You draw an *o* and a *g* appears, or your *r* turns out a *b*. One of the most common explanations for Graffiti inaccuracies is writing too small. If you make your strokes large, so they almost touch the top and bottom of the Graffiti area, you'll find that your accuracy increases dramatically.

That said, most users can gain a working knowledge of Graffiti in about 20 minutes. And, after a few days' practice, you should be writing quickly and accurately. We show you the ins and outs of Graffiti in Chapter 4.

Getting to Know the Operating System

We aren't exaggerating when we say that working with a Visor is roughly eight-gazillion times easier than working with traditional computers. Though plenty powerful, Visors are just a lot less complicated. There's no confusing menu system to wade through, no accidentally forgetting to save your document. Here we've highlighted some of the fundamental—but still important—differences between a Visor and a computer:

- When you turn on a computer, you have to wait several minutes for it to boot up. When you turn on a Visor, it's ready to roll instantaneously. Same goes for shutting it off: just press the power button and the screen goes dark. There's no lengthy shutdown procedure.

- On a computer, when you're done working with a program (say, your word processor), you must save your data before exiting that program. On a Visor, this isn't necessary. Data is retained at all times, even if you, say, switch to your to-do list while in the middle of writing a memo. When you return to Memo Pad, you find your document exactly as you left it. This holds true even if you turn the Visor off!

- In that same vein, you don't "exit" a Palm OS program so much as switch to another one. This is a hard concept for seasoned computer users to grasp, as we've all been taught to shut down our software when we're done with it. No exit procedure exists on a Visor, and you never find that word in a drop-down menu. When you're done working in one program, you just tap the Applications button to return to home base or press one of the program buttons.

We strongly encourage experimentation. Whereas wandering too far off the beaten track in Windows can lead to disaster, it's virtually impossible to get "lost" using a Visor. So tap here, explore there, and just have fun checking things out. Because there's no risk of losing data or "running too many programs at once" (impossible in the Palm OS), you should have no fear of fouling anything up. Play!

The Icons

Icons are, of course, little pictures used to represent things. In the case of the Palm OS, they're used largely to represent the installed programs. Thus, on the Applications screen, you see icons labeled Address, Calc, Date Book, and so on—and all you do is tap one to access that particular program.

Say, didn't you just learn that tapping a button in the Graffiti area was the way to load the calculator? And that you are supposed to press a button below the screen to load Date Book? In the Palm OS, there are often multiple ways to accomplish the same task. In this case, you can load certain programs either by tapping their onscreen icons or using their special buttons.

The Menus

As with most computers, drop-down menus are used to access program-specific options and settings. In most Visor and Palm OS programs, tapping the Menu button makes a small menu bar appear at the top of the screen. You navigate this bar using the stylus as you would a mouse, tapping each menu item to make its list of options drop down, and then tapping the option you want to access.

Let's work with menus a bit so you become comfortable with them:

1. If you're not already at the Applications screen (the one with all the program icons), tap the Applications button to get there.

2. Tap the Menu button, and notice the menu bar that appears. This particular menu has two items: App and Options. The App list is already open.

3. Tap the last item on the list: Info. In a few seconds, you see the Info screen, which shows you the programs installed on your Visor and how much of the total available memory is used by them.

4. When you're done looking, tap the Done button to return to the Applications screen. We return to menus later on when we talk about cutting, copying, and pasting text.

The Applications Screen

On a Visor, *home base* is the Applications screen, which displays the icons for all the installed programs. (It also shows you the time and a battery gauge, as the following illustrates.)

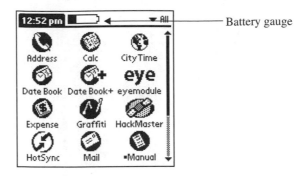

——— Battery gauge

In the upper-right corner of the screen, you'll also notice a small arrow next to the word All. What this means is the Applications screen is currently showing you all of the installed programs. If you tap the arrow, you see a list of categories into which you can group your programs.

Why Use Categories?

The use of categories is entirely optional. They're intended solely to help you keep your applications organized. See, as you install more software, you wind up with more icons. Right out of the box, a Visor has only about a dozen of them—a manageable number. But suppose you install a few games and a mail program and an e-book reader. Now things are getting a little cluttered, icon-wise.

Categories offer you a way to minimize the clutter. As you saw in the drop-down list, the Visor comes with a number of categories already created: Main, System, Games, and so forth. You can use them if you want or create your own.

How to Create and Modify Categories   Look again at the drop-down list in the upper-right corner of the Applications screen, shown previously. Notice the last option: Edit Categories. Tapping this takes you to a screen where you can add, rename, and delete categories. To rename or delete one, first select it by tapping it with the stylus (you'll see it becomes highlighted), and then tap the appropriate button.

To create a new category, tap the New button, then write in the desired name. That's all there is to it!

How to Assign Programs to Categories   Once you tailor the categories to your liking, you must next assign your programs to them. Here's how:

1. In the Applications screen, tap the Menu button, and then select Category.

2. Identify any one program you want to assign (you may have to scroll down the list, which you can do using the onscreen arrows or scroll bar, or the scroll buttons), and then tap the little arrow next to it.

Category	ℹ
HackMaster	▼ Utilities
HotSync	▼ System
Impactor	▼ Unfiled
InkSnap	▼ Unfiled
IR Pong	▼ Unfiled
LauncherIII	▼ Unfiled
Mail	▼ Main
Memo Pad	▼ Main
Messenger	▼ Unfiled
Mirror	▼ Unfiled

(Done)

3. The list of categories appears. Pick one by tapping it.

4. Repeat the procedure for the other programs you want to assign.

5. Tap Done to return to the Applications screen.

Now, when you tap the category arrow in the corner and select one, you see all your reassigned icons have been placed in the respective screens.

One way to change the displayed category is to tap the aforementioned arrow. There's a quicker way, though: if you tap the Applications button repeatedly, the Visor cycles through the categories that have programs assigned to them. Again, the Visor offers us two ways to accomplish the same goal.

Setting Visor Preferences

What would a computer be without a control panel where you can tweak the settings and customize the machine? The Visor has one and it's called *Prefs*. Find the Prefs icon in the Applications screen, tap it, and meet us at the next paragraph.

Divided into eight different sections (all of them accessible by tapping the arrow in the upper-right corner of the screen), Prefs is the place to reset your Visor's digitizer, change the date and time, input any necessary modem settings, and more. In listed order, the following sections give the scoop on each individual "Pref."

Buttons

As we explained earlier, the four physical buttons below the screen are used to quick-launch the four main Visor programs (Date Book, Address Book, To Do List, and Memo Pad). It's possible, however, to reassign these buttons to launch other programs instead. If you find you rarely use, say, Memo Pad, but use Expense all the time, it may make sense to reassign the Memo Pad button accordingly.

After selecting Buttons from the drop-down menu in the Prefs screen, you see an icon that corresponds to each button. (You can customize the Calc button as well.) All you do to change the function of any given button is tap the little arrow next to it, and then select the desired application.

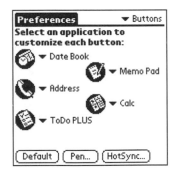

Notice, too, the three options at the bottom of the Buttons screen. Default restores the button assignments to their original settings. Pen enables you to choose what happens when you drag the tip of your stylus from the Graffiti area to the top of the screen. This action can be made to load the built-in Graffiti help screens, invoke the onscreen keyboard, turn on backlighting, or one of several other options. Finally, HotSync enables you to reprogram the HotSync button on your docking cradle or optional modem—something we don't recommend.

Digitizer

Noticing a little drift in your stylus taps? You tap someplace, but it doesn't quite register or it registers in the wrong place? It may be time to reset your screen's digitizer. You should do so the moment you notice a problem; the worse it gets, the harder it may actually be to get to this screen. All you do is select Digitizer from the menu and follow the instructions.

 Digitizer drift does occur over time, but if it becomes a frequent occurrence, it could point to a hardware problem. If your Visor is still under warranty, contact Handspring's customer service department to see if a replacement is warranted.

Formats

Few users need to spend much time in the Formats screen, where you can change the way dates, times and numbers are displayed. You can also specify whether you want the calendar week to start on Sunday (the default) or Monday.

General

Probably the most frequently visited of the Prefs screens, General is the place to do the following:

- Set the date and time.
- Specify the period of inactivity—one, two, or three minutes—before the Visor shuts itself off. If you want to extend your battery life as much as possible, set it to one minute.

■ Set the volume level—low, medium, high, or off—for the system sounds, alarm sounds, and game sounds.

■ Turn Beam Receive on or off. If it's off, you won't be able to receive information beamed to you from another Visor or Palm OS device.

Modem

As you might expect, the Modem screen enables you to set up whatever modem you might be using with your Visor. You probably won't need to fiddle with these settings too much; the documentation included with your modem will notify you if anything requires modification.

```
Preferences              ▼ Modem
 Modem: ▼ Standard
  Speed: ▼ 57,600 bps
Speaker: ▼ Low
Flow Ctl: ▼ Automatic
 String: AT&FX4
         ................................
         ................................
         ................................
         [ TouchTone™ ] Rotary
```

Network

The slightly misnamed Network screen is where you enter the relevant information about your ISP, should you be using a modem to dial into it. A handful of major ISPs are already listed in the Service menu, but you still need to provide your account username and password, plus the phone number for the ISP. The Details button takes you to a screen with some advanced Internet settings, while Connect tells the modem to go ahead and dial in. We run you through a sample modem setup in Chapter 14.

```
Preferences              ▼ Network

▼ Service: Mindspring
User Name: ms564933
 Password: -Assigned-
Connection: ▼ -Current-
    Phone: 327-5940


( Details... )  ( Connect )
```

Owner

In the tragic event that you lose your Visor, you'd probably be most grateful to have it returned. The Owner screen is where you can enter your name and contact information (address, phone number, e-mail address—whatever you want). If you use the Visor's security features (which we discuss in Chapter 12) to lock the device every time you turn it off, the information on the Owner screen is displayed when the unit is turned on again. Thus, if someone happens to find your Visor, they'll know how to return it to you, but won't have access to all your data. Smart!

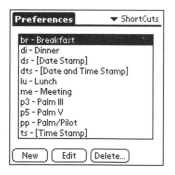

ShortCuts

Finally, we come to *ShortCuts,* a tool designed to expedite the entry of often-used words and phrases. Let's say you're a Starfleet engineer, and you use your Visor to keep track of your repair duties. The phrase "holodeck emitter coils" comes up quite a bit—but do you really have to write it out every time? What if you could just write **hec** instead and have the words magically appear? That's the beauty of ShortCuts.

As you see when you reach the ShortCuts screen, a handful of the little time-savers have already been created. There's one each for your daily meals, one for "meeting," and even a couple of date and time stamps (used to quickly insert the date and time, natch). Let's walk through the process of creating and using a new shortcut:

1. Tap the New button.

2. In the ShortCut Name field, write the abbreviation you want to use for this particular shortcut. As an example, let's use **bm** for Buy milk.

3. Tap the first line in the ShortCut Text field to move your cursor there. Now enter the text you want to appear when you invoke the shortcut (in this case, **Buy milk**).

4. Tap OK. Now, let's invoke the new shortcut. Press the To Do button to launch the To Do List, and then tap New to create a new task.

5. To invoke this or any other shortcut, you must first write the shortcut stroke in the Graffiti area. This lets Graffiti know you're about to enter the abbreviation for a shortcut. The stroke looks like a cursive, lowercase letter *l* (see our Graffiti guide in Chapter 4). After you make the stroke, you see it appear next to your cursor. Now enter the letter *b*, followed by the letter *m*. Presto! The words "Buy milk" magically appear.

An Introduction to Palm Desktop

So far, we've talked mostly about the Visor itself: the hardware, the operating system, the basic setup procedures and considerations. One area is left to cover before you venture into real-world Visor use: the Palm Desktop.

NOTE   *Remember, the Visor is a licensed Palm OS device, which is why the software isn't called "Visor Desktop."*

What Is the Palm Desktop?

Wondrous as a Visor is in its own right, what makes it even more special is its capability to synchronize with your computer. That means all the data entered into your Visor is copied to your PC and vice versa. The software that fields all this data on the computer side is Palm Desktop.

Viewed in a vacuum, Palm Desktop (see Figure 2-4) resembles traditional PIM or contact-management software. It effectively replicates all the core functionality of the Palm OS, providing you with a phone list, appointment calendar, to-do list, and memo pad. If you've never used such software before, you'll no doubt find Palm Desktop an invaluable addition, as it helps keep you organized at home or in the office (whereas a Visor keeps you organized while traveling).

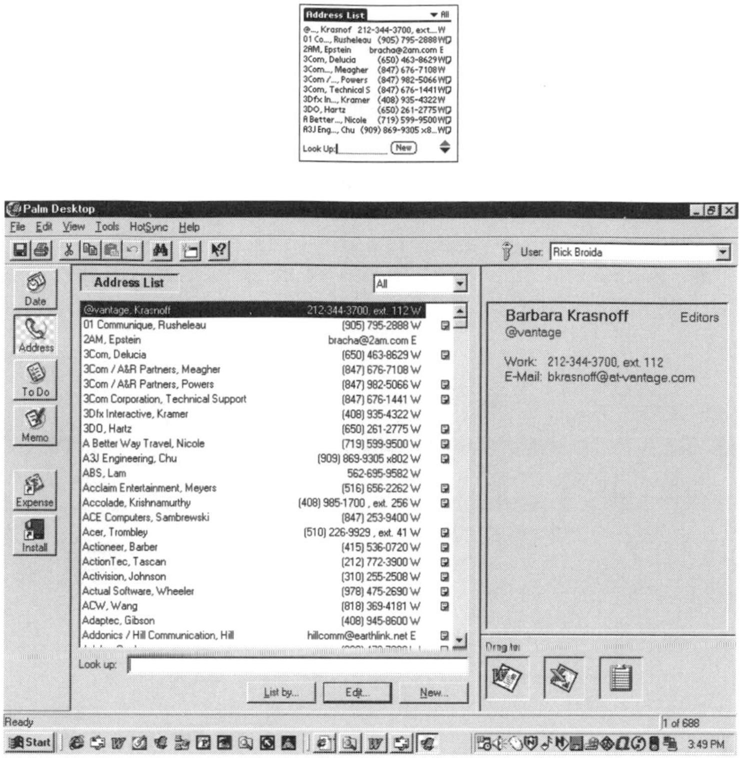

FIGURE 2-4   Palm Desktop duplicates the information that's on your Visor—and vice versa

A Word About Synchronization

What happens when you synchronize your Visor with your computer? In a nutshell, three things:

- Any new entries made on your Visor are added to Palm Desktop.

- Any new entries made in Palm Desktop are added to your Visor.

- Any existing records that have been modified in one place will be modified in the other, the newest changes taking precedence.

Therefore, synchronizing regularly assures that your information is kept current both in your Visor and in Palm Desktop.

NOTE *Already entrenched in another contact manager—namely, Microsoft Office? The Visor comes with special software that enables you to synchronize with Office instead of Palm Desktop. We discuss this in greater detail in the next chapter.*

The Differences Between the Windows and Macintosh Versions

While functionally similar, the Windows and Macintosh versions of Palm Desktop are actually different programs. Palm Desktop for Windows was built from scratch, while the Macintosh version is actually a modified version of Claris Organizer, a popular contact manager. The two versions are fairly similar in terms of features (see Figures 2-5 and 2-6), but the user interface is different on each platform. Therefore, we cover them in separate chapters. If you're a Windows user, read Chapter 5. If you're a Mac user, skip ahead to Chapter 6.

FIGURE·2-5   Palm Desktop for Windows

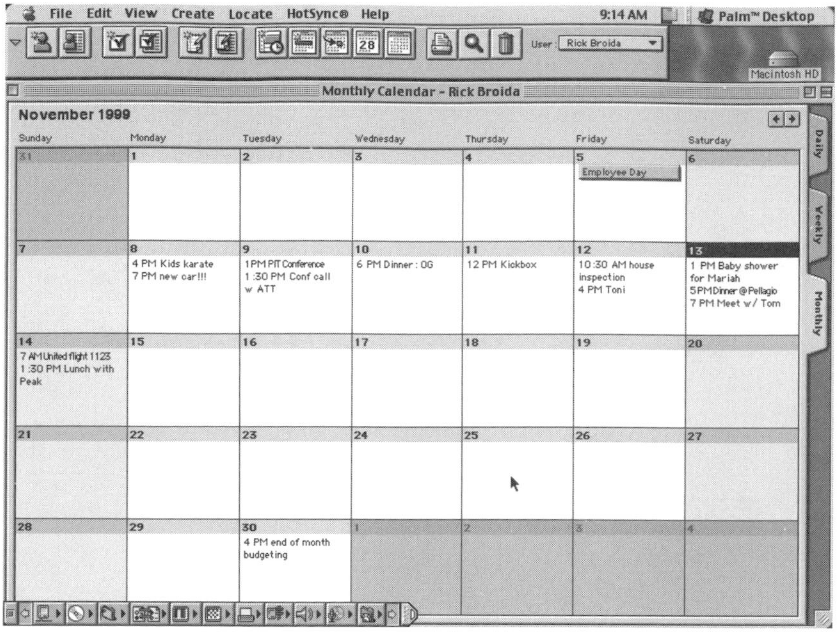

FIGURE 2-6   Palm Desktop for Macintosh

Chapter 3

Getting Set Up with Your PC or Macintosh

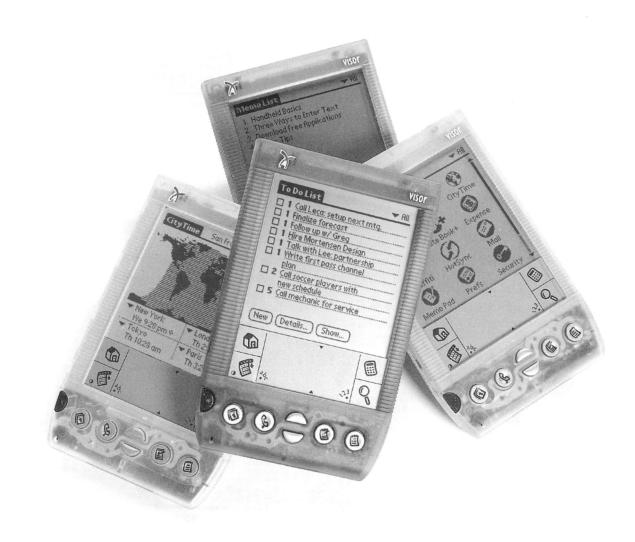

How to...

■ Find and access the instruction manual

■ Install the HotSync cradle

■ Identify USB ports on your computer

■ Obtain the optional serial HotSync cradle

■ Install the Palm Desktop software

■ Set up the HotSync Manager

■ Perform your first HotSync

■ Understand the intricacies of HotSync Manager settings

■ Interpret the HotSync log

■ Keep your data synchronized just the way you like it

One of the coolest things about Palm OS devices like the Visor is that they synchronize so seamlessly with your desktop computer. No more does using a handheld PC mean maintaining two different sets of contacts and appointments. No more does it mean laboriously transcribing tons of important data by hand. The Visor synchronizes with your desktop so elegantly, it's as if they were born to work together.

Now that you've had a chance to explore the Visor itself in Chapter 2, it's time to learn about how the device works with your desktop computer.

Unpacking Your Visor

Inside the Visor box, you'll find the Visor itself, a HotSync cradle, miscellaneous promotional materials, and a CD. What, no instruction manual? To keep down the cost of the Visor, Handspring elected to take the electronic route: the instructions are contained on the software CD and presented in a format that's viewable on your computer (akin to an electronic book). While we tell you everything you need to know about your Visor, we do recommend perusing this documentation.

Accessing the Instruction Manual

Whether you're configuring your Visor for use with a Macintosh or a Windows-based PC, you use the same CD to install the Palm Desktop software and to read the instruction manual. The latter was created using Adobe's ubiquitous PDF (portable document format) standard, which means you need the free Adobe Acrobat Reader to view it. Many Windows computers (and all Macs) already have Acrobat installed; if yours doesn't, you can find it on the CD. Just open the Acroread folder, then double-click the icon that appears.

With Acrobat installed, all you need to do is double-click the UserGuide.pdf icon found in the main directory on the CD. That launches Acrobat and loads the instruction manual, which, while fairly comprehensive about the operation of the Visor itself, doesn't do a great job of explaining the connection of the HotSync cradle—one of the only potentially tricky aspects of Visor setup. Fortunately, we're here to help.

Installing the HotSync Cradle

The sole function of the HotSync cradle (see Figure 3-1) is to transfer information between your desktop computer and your Visor. The standard cradle employs a Universal Serial Bus (USB) interface, which affords plug-and-play simplicity and fast synchronization.

 As discussed in Chapter 1, the Visor Solo does not come with a HotSync cradle.

It's easy to find USB ports on your computer; just look for small, flat, rectangular connectors that don't have pins sticking out of them (unlike most other computer ports).

 If your computer is relatively old, it may not have any USB ports. In that case, you need to buy Handspring's optional serial cradle, which connects to older-style serial ports. It's available directly from the company for $29.95.

While you might think a good first step would be to plug the cradle into one of your computer's USB ports, you should first install the Palm Desktop software—which instructs you to connect the cradle at the appropriate time.

Installing the Desktop Software

Before you can enjoy the benefits of synchronizing your Visor and your desktop PC, you first need to install the Palm Desktop software suite (see Figure 3-2) on your computer. This software is a *personal information manager* (PIM): It duplicates all the core applications from your Visor, essentially giving you big-screen versions of the address book, memo pad, and so on.

FIGURE 3-1   The Visor HotSync cradle

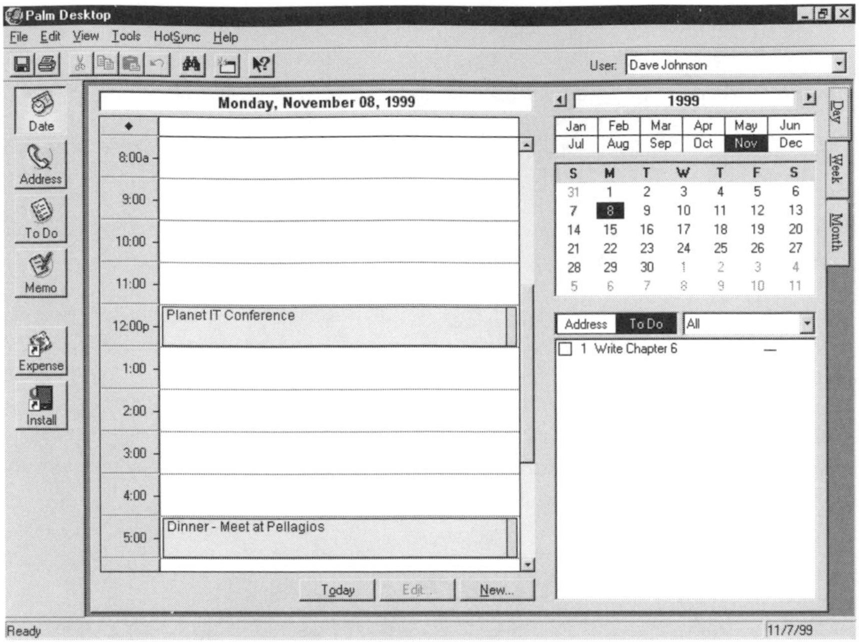

a)

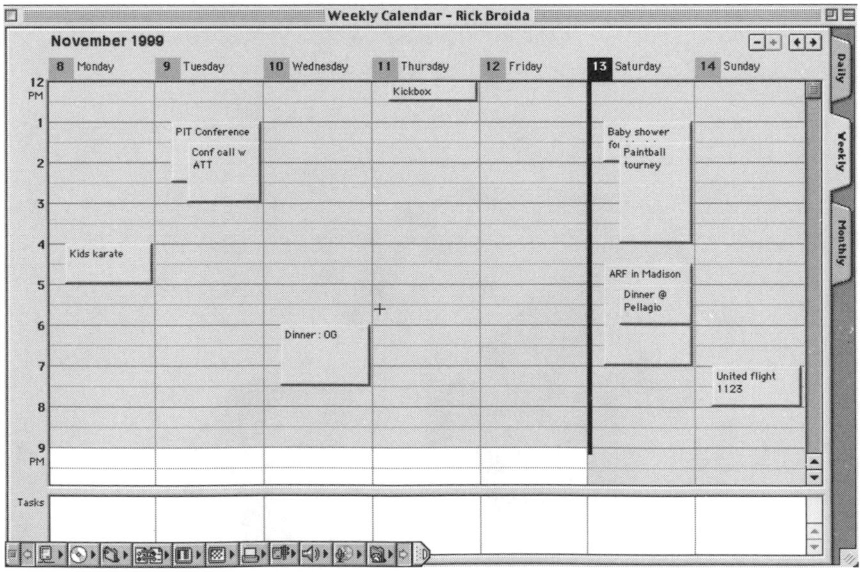

b)

FIGURE 3-2 Palm Desktop for a) Windows and b) Macintosh

While it is necessary to install Palm Desktop before you begin synchronizing with your PC, it's not necessary to use Palm Desktop as your PIM. That is, if you already use another program, like Microsoft Outlook, you can synchronize your Visor to that instead and avoid Palm Desktop entirely.

The CD that accompanies your Visor includes everything you need. Installation is straightforward; simply follow the installation instructions that appear after you insert the CD. (Mac users should double-click the icon for their CD-ROM drives, and then launch the setup program that appears.)

Setting Up Palm Desktop

The Handspring CD-ROM includes an installer that places most of the key Palm Desktop components on your hard disk. Most of the main installation is completely automated, but you do have to make a few decisions along the way:

■ **Outlook or Palm Desktop?**   If you have a copy of Microsoft Outlook installed on your Windows-based PC, the installer detects it and gives you the option of synchronizing your data to it, if you want.

What data are we talking about? Stuff like contacts from the address book, appointments from the calendar, as well as notes and tasks. If you're a regular Outlook user, you should certainly choose to synchronize your Visor with it. If you're not committed to Outlook, you can choose to synchronize with the Palm Desktop instead. The Palm Desktop is a serviceable PIM, though not as comprehensive as Outlook.

NOTE   *The software that links your Visor to Outlook is available only for Windows. While a Mac version of Outlook does exist, currently there's no conduit available for synchronizing it with a Visor. The good news is that the Macintosh version of Palm Desktop is more robust than the Windows version, so you're getting a powerful PIM anyway.*

■ **Configure Mail** The installer offers you a list of e-mail programs with which to synchronize your Visor. We discuss the workings of the Mail applet in Chapter 14; in the meantime, simply choose the e-mail program you currently use on your PC. If it's not listed or you don't plan to use your Visor for e-mail purposes, you can skip this step. (You can always come back to it later.)

■ **Connect the Cradle** During the installation of Palm Desktop, you are instructed to connect the HotSync cradle to one of your computer's USB ports. It doesn't matter which one, but make sure you don't connect the cradle until you reach this step. (Once the software is installed and configured, you can remove and reconnect the cradle at will. That's one of the benefits of USB.)

Your First HotSync

Believe it or not, the hard part is already over. Now it's time to perform your first HotSync. (We recommend having a friend videotape this special event.) Seriously, it's pretty cool to get all your desktop-based data like appointments, contacts, and to-dos to appear on the Visor, and you're probably eager to try it. Here's what you need to do to be certain you're ready:

1. Make sure your HotSync cradle is connected to the PC.

2. Place the Visor in the cradle, making sure it's fully seated.

 3. Make sure the HotSync Manager software is running. You should see the HotSync icon in the System Tray. If you don't see it, start it now. Choose Start | Programs | Palm Desktop | HotSync Manager; if you're on the Mac, it's located in the chooser or the Palm folder.

NOTE *The System Tray is the region at the bottom of the Windows Desktop to the right of the Task Bar. It contains the clock and the icons for special programs, such as the HotSync Manager.*

Ready? Great. Now let's take a closer look at the HotSync Manager software and make sure it's ready to exchange data.

Exploring the HotSync Manager

The *HotSync Manager* software does exactly what it sounds like—it manages the connection between your Visor and your computer, enabling you to synchronize. HotSync Manager contains all the options and configurations needed to keep the two devices talking to each other.

NOTE *It's actually pretty rare that you need to modify HotSync Manager's settings. Most users may never have to fiddle with them at all. In fact, if you prefer to jump right in and perform your first HotSync, you can skip ahead to the section titled "Pressing the HotSync Button."*

To get to the HotSync Manager's options in Windows, you need to access the HotSync menu. To do so, click the HotSync Manager icon in the System Tray, noting the pop-up menu that appears.

TIP *You can click the HotSync Manager icon with either the right or the left mouse button; the result is the same.*

The first thing you encounter in the HotSync menu are three options:

■ Local

■ Modem

■ Network

For now, the only one that must be checked is the first option: Local. This means you can perform a HotSync using the serial or USB port. For information on modem and network HotSyncs, consult the Visor's documentation.

Configuring HotSync Setup

Click the Setup option on the HotSync menu. You should see the Setup dialog box.

This is the place where you get to configure how HotSync Manager behaves. The four tabs on the Setup dialog box are described in the following sections.

General The *General tab* enables you to specify how often the HotSync Manager listens to the serial port (or USB port) for a HotSync request. The General tab has three options:

■ **Always available** This is the default setting when you install the Palm Desktop software. If you keep this option, HotSync Manager constantly waits for a press of the HotSync button on the cradle. That's fast and convenient, and probably the way most people use their Visors.

■ **Available only when the Palm Desktop is running** If you're using a serial HotSync cradle and you often share the serial port with another device, like a modem, this might be a better solution. The HotSync Manager won't lock the serial port or listen for the HotSync request unless Palm Desktop is actually running. But what if you don't use the Palm Desktop? Then keep reading, because option number three is the one for you.

■ **Manual** Just like it sounds, the HotSync Manager doesn't run at all unless you choose it from the Start menu (Start | Programs | Palm Desktop | HotSync Manager). This is the least convenient of all the options, but you might want to choose it if you HotSync only on rare occasions, if the serial port is frequently used by another device, and if you don't use the Palm Desktop at all (so the second option wouldn't work for you).

TIP *If you try to use another serial device like a modem and Windows reports the serial port is in use, click the HotSync Manager icon and choose Exit. Then try your serial device again. You can easily restart HotSync Manager later if necessary.*

NOTE *On the Macintosh, these options are slightly different. Start HotSync Manager and choose HotSync | Options. On the HotSync Controls tab, you can enable or disable HotSyncing, and specify whether the HotSync Manager should start when you turn on the computer.*

Local The Local tab is where you specify the serial port and speed for your HotSync. Most of the time, the installation process automatically determines your serial port, so it's all taken care of for you. This is especially true for the USB cradle. However, if you're using the optional serial cradle, you may need to venture into the settings here in order to choose the correct COM port.

You can almost always leave the speed set to As Fast As Possible. If you need to troubleshoot connection problems, though, this is where you can specify a slower speed.

NOTE *On the Mac, serial port settings are controlled from the Serial Port Settings tab of the HotSync Setup dialog box (choose HotSync | Settings to display it). Because the Mac doesn't have to mess with serial port nonsense, this dialog box is much simpler than the PC version.*

Modem and Network Both these tabs are used to specify settings for more advanced HotSyncing techniques. Consult the Visor's documentation for more information.

After you have seen all the tabs in the Setup dialog box, click OK to save changes or click Cancel to leave the dialog box without changing anything.

Customizing the HotSync Operation

From the HotSync Manager menu, choose Custom.

NOTE   *On the Mac, choose HotSync | Conduit Settings.*

This is arguably the most important dialog box in the HotSync software because it enables you to specify with greater detail exactly what data gets transferred. Before we look at this dialog box, however, we should define a few essential terms the Visor uses to perform data synchronizations. If you make the wrong choice, you can destroy data you need.

Conduit Setting	Effect
Synchronize the files	Suppose you added new files to both the PC and the Visor since the last HotSync. The new data on the Visor is copied to the PC, and the new data on the PC is copied to the Visor. Both devices will have a copy of everything.
Desktop overwrites handheld	This option supposes the desktop data is correct at the expense of anything that may be on the handheld. For instance, if you added new files to both the PC and the handheld, and then perform this kind of synchronization, the new files on the Visor are lost. The desktop data overwrites whatever was on it.
Handheld overwrites desktop	This is exactly the opposite of the previous case. Assuming the handheld data is more correct for some reason (we assume you have your reasons), any files that are different or new on the desktop PC are lost after the synchronization. Both systems will have the latest Visor data.
Do nothing	With this option selected, no changes are made to either device during this HotSync.

With those terms in mind, let's look at the Custom dialog box.

As you can see, the top of the box displays the name of the Visor unit. It's possible to manage more than one Visor from each PC, so you'd select the proper unit from the list menu before continuing. If you have a single Visor, don't worry about this option.

Most of this dialog box is used to display conduits and their actions. *Conduits* are software drivers responsible for transferring a single kind of data between the Visor and the PC. As you can see from the list, a unique conduit exists for each kind of application on the Visor. Palm Desktop includes these conduits:

- **Mail**   E-mail messages are synchronized between your desktop mail application and the Visor.

- **Expense**   Shares expense entries between the Visor and a desktop application such as Excel.

- **Calendar**   Shares data between the Visor and desktop calendars.

- **Contacts**   Shares data between the Visor and desktop address books.

- **Tasks**   Shares data between the Visor and desktop to-do lists

- **Notes**   Shares data between the Visor and desktop memo pads.

- **Install**   Transfers Palm OS applications from your PC's hard disk to the Visor.

- **Install Service Templates**   Manages dial-up instructions for accessing ISPs using your Visor.

- **System**   Transfers other files created by Visor applications between the PC and Visor.

NOTE   *If you install new software, you can end up with more conduits. Many programs come with their own conduits to control the flow of information between your Visor and desktop applications.*

To configure a conduit, either double-click an entry or click once to select it, and then click the Change button. Depending on which conduit you open, you may find you have all four synchronization options or, perhaps, fewer.

When you configure a conduit, whatever selection you make applies only to the very next time you HotSync. After that, it reverts to the default action.

Pressing the HotSync Button

With all that buildup, you might think HotSyncing is going to be difficult or confusing. In reality, it's a piece of cake. Just press the HotSync button on the cradle—that's all there is to it (see Figure 3-3).

CAUTION *Before you HotSync, we highly recommend you check the action assigned to your conduits by right-clicking the HotSync icon and choosing Custom. If you accidentally configured the HotSync Manager to "Handheld overwrites Desktop," on the very first HotSync, for instance, you might want to know that before, not after, you erase your desktop's calendar and address book.*

After you press the HotSync button, here's what should happen:

1. Your Visor turns itself on (if it wasn't on already).

2. You hear three tones indicating the HotSync has begun.

3. A message box appears on the computer's and Visor's screen that informs you of the HotSync status.

4. You hear another set of tones when the HotSync is complete.

5. The Visor displays a message indicating the HotSync is complete.

HotSync button

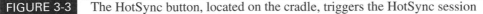

FIGURE 3-3 The HotSync button, located on the cradle, triggers the HotSync session

HotSyncing Without a Cradle

You don't need a cradle to synchronize your Visor—you can also use a HotSync cable (available from Handspring). The cable is handy because it takes up less room in a suitcase or travel bag than a bulky cradle, and thus is a fine choice for notebook-carrying road warriors. The cable doesn't have a button to launch the HotSync session, though, so you need to start the process from the Visor itself. Tap the HotSync icon, and then the HotSync button in the middle of the screen.

Now you can take your Visor out of the cradle and browse information—like the calendar and address book—that were synchronized and transferred from the PC.

Reading the HotSync Log

Did the HotSync go as planned? Did all your data get transferred properly and did files get copied the way you expected? Usually, it's pretty obvious if everything went well, but sometimes it's nice if your computer can tell you what actually happened.

How to ...   HotSync

You'll probably HotSync quite often; most Visor users do so daily. After spending half of this chapter explaining the subtle nuances of the process in gory detail, here's a six-step summary of the process:

1. Plug the cradle into your computer.

2. Place the Visor in the cradle.

3. Make sure HotSync Manager is running (by default, it always is).

4. Verify the conduits are set properly to transfer and synchronize data the way you want (this isn't necessary if you haven't changed any settings and simply want straight synchronization).

5. Press the HotSync button on the cradle.

6. Wait until you hear the "HotSync complete" tones before removing the Visor from the cradle.

Well, you're in luck. During every HotSync, the HotSync Manager makes a record of everything that happens during the session. This log is easy to read and it can answer that nagging question, "Why didn't the calendar update after I added an entry for the Sandra Bullock fan club meeting?" If the HotSync manager noticed something went wrong during a HotSync, it even tells you. Figure 3-4, for instance, shows the result of a HotSync that generated an error. The log reveals what happened.

To see the log at any time, right-click the HotSync icon in the System Tray and choose View Log if you're using Windows. On the Mac, choose HotSync | Log from the menu. The HotSync Log window should then appear.

CAUTION *You can't perform a HotSync when the log is open.*

The log displays a list of the actions that occurred for each of your last ten HotSync sessions. The top of the log is the most recent. You can find other log entries by date and time—just scroll down to see older HotSyncs.

What kind of information does a log reveal? These are the messages you're most likely to see:

- **OK**   This is good news; the conduit's action succeeded with no errors.

- **Sync configured to do nothing**   If something didn't happen, this may be the cause—the conduit was intentionally or mistakenly set to do nothing.

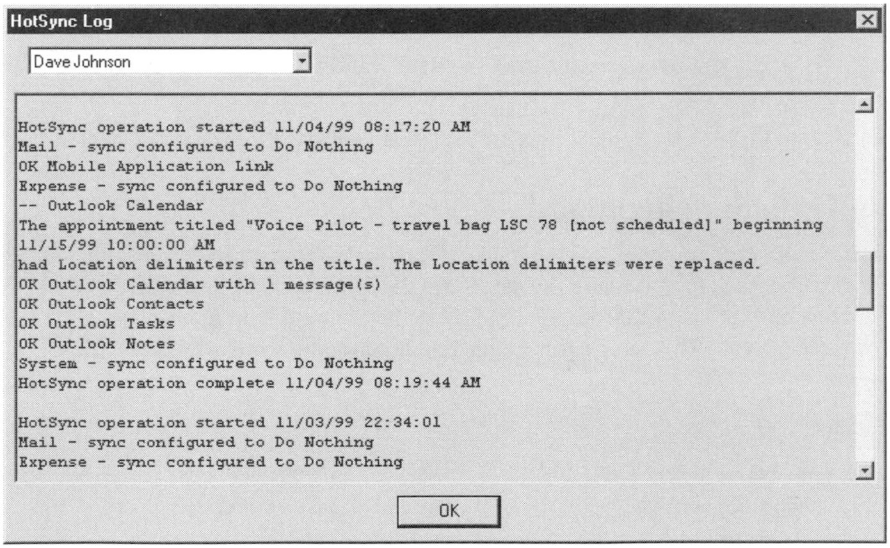

FIGURE 3-4   The HotSync log records the details of the last ten HotSyncs, along with any errors that occurred along the way

- **Truncated** This means a file stored on the PC (such as an e-mail or address-book entry) was so long that not all of it would fit on the Visor. There are limitations to the size of notes and memos, which are discussed in later chapters.

- **Records were modified in both Handheld and PC** You made changes to the same file on both the PC and the Visor. Because the HotSync Manager doesn't know which change is "right," it duplicated both files on both systems. You now have a chance to update the file and delete the one you don't want.

- **Synchronization failed** There can be any number of reasons for this, but it's probably related to a problem with a USB or serial port (depending on the kind of cradle you're using). Very often, restarting your computer and/or resetting your Visor can correct such problems.

NOTE *The HotSync log is also available on the Visor itself, albeit only for the most recent HotSync session. To reach it, tap the HotSync icon, and then tap the Log button.*

HotSync as a Way of Life

After your first HotSync, you may begin to see how convenient it is to have a duplicate of your desktop data on your Visor. But how often should you HotSync? The short answer is as frequently as you like. Some people HotSync every few hours, some daily, and some—those whose data changes much less frequently—once a week or even less. Use this guide as a rule of thumb:

- HotSync before any trip.

- HotSync when you return from a trip to update your PC with new info stored on the Visor.

- HotSync to install new applications on your Visor (this is discussed in Chapter 4).

Keeping Data Synchronized

After your first HotSync, you have a set of data on both your Visor and your desktop. The goal of the HotSync process is to make sure the data stays the same on both systems. So what happens when you change data on one of the computers? This chart should help you understand the subtleties of the HotSync. This table assumes the conduit is set to synchronize the files:

Before the HotSync	After the HotSync
You added an entry to the Visor (or the PC)	That entry is added to the PC (or the Visor)
You deleted an entry from the Visor	The entry is also deleted from the PC
You changed an entry on the Visor	The entry is changed on the PC
You changed the same entry on both the Visor and PC—they're now different	Both versions of the entry are added to both the Visor and PC. You need to modify the file and delete the one you don't want to keep

Did this answer all your questions? If not, this flowchart describes the logic the HotSync Manager uses when synchronizing your Visor and desktop computer:

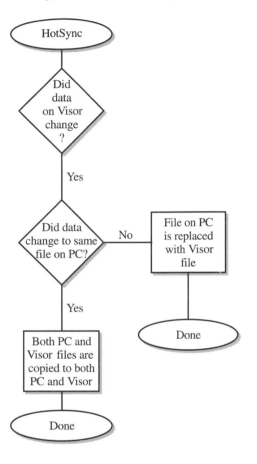

With this in mind, you might not always want to use the Synchronize the Files option for all your conduits. Why not? Any number of reasons. Here are a few situations:

■ You might rely on your Visor to take notes you have no interest in copying to your PC. In other words, you want to keep one set of notes on the PC—which is relevant to what you do at your desk—and another set of notes for when you're on the road. In such a case, Do Nothing is probably the best option for your needs.

■ You might take notes you don't need to keep after a trip is over. In such an instance, you can use Desktop Overwrites Handheld for that conduit. After your trip is over, the handheld notes are erased during the HotSync and replaced by the desktop notes.

NOTE   *Don't forget, you can configure each conduit individually. For example, this means the address book might be set to Synchronize the Files while the calendar is set to Desktop Overwrites Handheld.*

Chapter 4

Getting Information In and Out of Your Visor

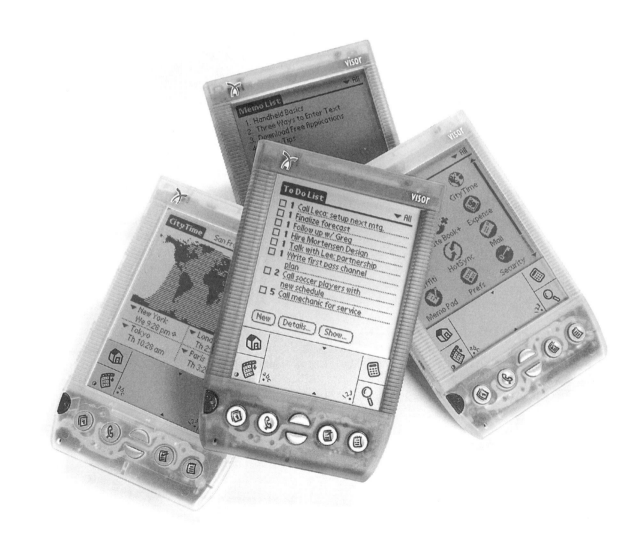

How to...

- Use Graffiti to enter data into your Visor
- Type using the onscreen keyboard
- Enter data using the Palm Desktop
- Use alternate gestures to write in Graffiti more effectively
- Turn abbreviations into long text using shortcuts
- Display Graffiti help
- Receive data from another Palm handheld via the IR port
- Beam items to another Palm OS device
- Beam your business card to another Palm OS device
- Lock your Visor so it can't receive beams
- Install new software on your Visor
- Delete old applications from your Visor

A handheld computer is only as good as the information you store inside it. Or, perhaps more to the point, it's only as good as the methods you have for getting information into it. After all, if you make it too hard to store your appointments on the computer, you won't bother doing it—and then you own an expensive paperweight that has the word "calendar' written on it.

Case in point is a tiny, credit card-sized PDA called the Rex. This device debuted a few years ago to generally favorable reviews. The little guy was so small, it even slipped easily into a wallet, yet it carried contacts and appointments like a champ. The problem? You couldn't update it away from your PC, so a schedule change or new contact couldn't be entered on the fly. For some people that may not be a big deal, but public reaction was underwhelming; the Visor sells well because of the very fact it can be updated on the go, and quite easily to boot.

You already know about some of the ways you have at your disposal for getting data in and out of your Visor. HotSyncing was already discussed in detail in Chapter 3, and you know you can enter data directly in the device using Graffiti, an almost-ordinary style of handwriting. In this chapter, you learn everything you might ever need to know about Graffiti. But we also cover other data entry methods, including the onscreen keyboard and beaming data directly between Visors and other Palm OS devices using the built-in IR port.

The Three Ways to Enter Data

Without a doubt, one of the first things you'll want to do with your new Visor is to enter data—text and numbers—into your various applications. Hey, don't look so surprised. The core applications, like Date Book, Address Book, Memo Pad, and To Do List rely on you to fill them up with interesting things you can later reference.

Certainly, you can use the Visor's capability to HotSync to enter data, but HotSyncing is only part of the story. Unlike some handheld computers, the Visor doesn't include a keyboard. Instead, there are three completely different methods at your disposal for entering information into your Visor:

- Entering text using Graffiti
- Entering text using the onscreen keyboard
- Entering text into the Palm Desktop, and then HotSyncing the data to your Visor

 You can actually connect a real keyboard to your Visor and type the ordinary way. For information on Visor keyboards, see Chapter 24.

If you're on the go, you'll definitely need to use either Graffiti or the keyboard to enter data. If you're at your desk, though, you might find it easier to enter data into the Palm Desktop, and then HotSync, because your desktop computer sports a full-sized keyboard.

Using Graffiti

Graffiti is a specialized handwriting recognition system that enables you to enter text into the Visor almost error-free, each and every time you use it. Unlike other handwriting recognition systems, Graffiti neither interprets your ordinary handwriting nor does it learn or adapt to the way you write. Instead, you need to modify the way you write slightly and make specific kinds of keystrokes that represent the letters, numbers, and punctuation you are trying to write.

$$\Lambda = A$$
$$\daleth = T$$

Don't worry, though, it's not hard to do. You can learn the basics of Graffiti inside of a day—heck, you can probably master most of the characters in an hour or less.

When entering text into your Visor, you can't write directly on the part of the screen that the Visor uses as a display. Instead, you write inside the small rectangle at the bottom of the display—the one that sits between the four silk screened icons.

TIP   *Actually, there is a Hackmaster hack available that enables you to write directly on the Visor screen. Some people find this way of entering text more intuitive because the characters appear directly under where they're writing. See Chapter 18 for more information on this tool.*

4

As you can see in Figure 4-1, the Graffiti area is a rectangle divided in half. The left side is used for entering letters, while the right side is used to enter numbers.

> **TIP** *If you aren't getting the results you expect from Graffiti, make sure you're writing on the correct side of the rectangle. The right side is for numbers, the left side is for letters, and either side works for punctuation. Small arrows on the top and bottom of the Graffiti area draw an invisible line between the text and numeric portions.*

Your Visor came with a Graffiti cheat sheet. Take a look at the Graffiti guide and you see most characters are single-stoke shapes (called *gestures* in Graffiti-ese). The characters must be drawn in the direction indicated on the Graffiti guide: the heavy dot indicates the starting position. To write a character, mimic the Graffiti guide by drawing the shape starting with the dot and—in most cases—finish the character in a single stroke without lifting the stylus.

For more details on writing in Graffiti, see the section called "Getting to Know Graffiti" later in this chapter.

Using the Onscreen Keyboard

Even after you get comfortable writing with Graffiti, no doubt, there'll be times when you need or want to select specific characters without using pen strokes that need to be interpreted by a handwriting recognition engine. After all, remembering how to make some rarely used characters in the middle of taking real-time notes can be hard, and having access to a keyboard can be a real lifesaver.

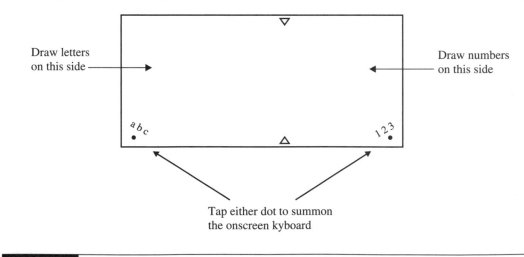

Draw letters on this side

Draw numbers on this side

Tap either dot to summon the onscreen kyboard

FIGURE 4-1 The Graffiti area

To use the onscreen keyboard, just tap. At the bottom of the Graffiti area, you see the letters ABC wrapped around a small dot on the left and the numbers 123 on the right, also curved around a dot (see Figure 4-1). Tap either spot to call up the appropriate keyboard.

NOTE *The keyboard will only appear in situations where it is appropriate. If no application is open into which you can insert text, for instance, you'll simply hear a beep when you tap on the keyboard dots.*

Once the keyboard is open, note that you can switch between letters and numbers by tapping the selector at the bottom of the screen, as shown in Figure 4-2. There is a set of "international" characters to choose from as well.

Remember the following tips about the onscreen keyboard:

- You can't use Graffiti while you have the keyboard open. Drawing on the Graffiti area has no effect.

- Use the SHIFT button on the keyboard in the same way you'd use a real keyboard; tap it to create an uppercase letter.

- The CAP key is actually a CAPS LOCK key; it makes all subsequent letters uppercase until you tap it again.

- If you're typing with the CAPS LOCK on and you want to make a single character lowercase, tap the SHIFT key.

- The Numeric keyboard provides access to special symbols and punctuation.

NOTE *Some users find they prefer the keyboard to Graffiti and use it regularly for data entry. It's a personal choice, of course, but if you just can't get the hang of Graffiti or find you can work faster with the keyboard, by all means use it.*

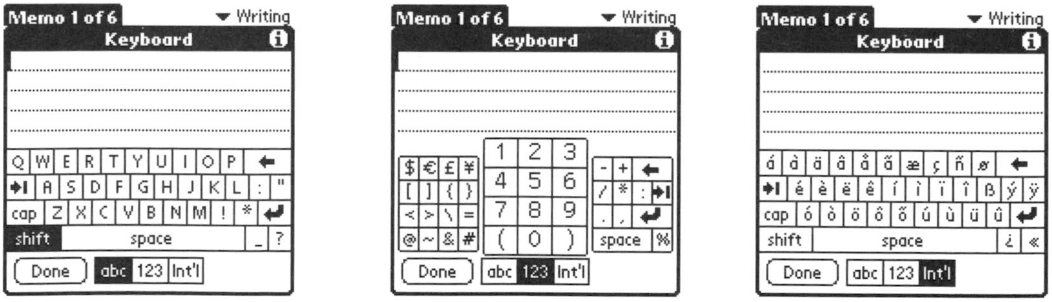

FIGURE 4-2   The selector at the bottom of the screen lets you choose between the onscreen keyboards

Using the Palm Desktop

Those other methods are great when you're on the go, but what about getting data into your Visor when you're comfortably sitting at your desk? There's nothing wrong with entering notes into the Visor with Graffiti even in the office, but long notes can get tiresome. Instead, you can use the keyboard on your desktop PC to type into the Visor much more quickly and efficiently.

How? By using the Palm Desktop or another program with a HotSync conduit. In other words, suppose you need to enter a long note into your Visor. Instead of writing it slowly using Graffiti, just create a note in the Palm Desktop, and then HotSync.

Let's add a note to the Visor's Memo List using the Palm Desktop. Do this:

1. Start the Palm Desktop in Windows by choosing Start | Programs | Palm Desktop | Palm Desktop. On the Mac, you can find it in the Chooser or in the Visor folder. (Windows and Macintosh versions of the Palm Desktop are shown in Chapter 3, Figure 3-2.)

2. In Windows, switch to the Memo Pad view by clicking the Memo button on the left side of the screen. On the Mac, choose View | Note List instead.

3. If you're using Windows, click the memo page and type a note. On the Mac, click the Create Note button in the toolbar at the top of the screen.

Type here to add a memo

4. When you're done typing your note, close the New Note dialog box (on the Mac) or click anywhere in the Memo list (in Windows). The note is automatically saved and the memo's subject line shows as much of the note as would fit on the line in the list.

5. Enter any additional notes, tasks, calendar appointments, or contacts in the address book.

6. When you're done entering data, place the Visor in its HotSync cradle and press the HotSync button. For details on how to HotSync, see Chapter 3.

> NOTE   *If you configured your Visor to synchronize with Microsoft Outlook or another PIM, use that program to copy data to your Visor instead.*

4

Getting to Know Graffiti

Earlier in the chapter, we took a quick look at using Graffiti to enter data into your Visor. Graffiti deserves a lot of attention, though, because it's your principal way of interfacing with your favorite handheld PC. We're willing to bet that more than 90 percent of the time you need to add a note, contact, or to-do, you end up whipping out the Visor stylus and entering your info with good old Graffiti. Knowing Graffiti like the back of your hand is essential to using your Visor effectively.

As we pointed out earlier in this chapter, Graffiti doesn't rely on interpreting whatever chicken-like scrawl you happen to draw into the Visor's Graffiti area. While it might be nice if the Visor could interpret unmodified handwriting, we've all seen what happened to that technology.

Specifically, Apple's Newton MessagePad was a great little PDA that understood free-form handwriting. And, while it did a pretty good job, first-time users faced an uphill battle getting it to understand them; it wasn't until you had a chance to use the Newton for a few hours that it started acting like it comprehended English. To make matters worse, Apple insisted on putting MessagePads in stores with big signs inviting people to saunter over and try them. The result? People would scratch out a sentence in sloppy handwriting and the Newton would convert the result into total gibberish, kind of like what you think Lou Reed might be muttering in a Velvet Underground song. The public never got any confidence that Apple had a workable handwriting recognition engine, and though it actually was pretty darned good, it failed because of public perception.

Palm Computing didn't make the same mistake with the Palm line of handhelds. The Visor's handwriting recognition engine is designed to recognize particular gestures as specific characters, thus reducing the possibility of error. In fact, if you routinely draw the characters according to the template, you'll get 100 percent accuracy. Graffiti doesn't have to understand 50 different ways of making the letter *T*, so it's both fast and accurate.

> NOTE   *Here's a bit of trivia to round out your day. The Palm OS may be known for the Graffiti handwriting recognition language, but it first surfaced for the Apple Newton MessagePad as a third-party alternative to the handwriting recognition built in to that pioneering device.*

General Tips and Tricks for Graffiti

Before we get started with the nuts and bolts of writing with Graffiti, it may help to keep a few things in mind. Despite Graffiti's simplicity, a few tips and tricks can make writing on the Visor a lot easier.

- Draw your characters as large as possible, especially if you're having trouble with Graffiti misinterpreting what you're writing. Use all the Graffiti area, if necessary.

- Don't cross the line between the letter and number portion of the Graffiti area, and make sure you make your gestures on the correct side of the fence to get the characters you want.

- Don't write at a slant. Some handwriting recognition engines can account for characters being drawn at an angle to the baseline, but Graffiti can't. Vertical lines should be perpendicular to the Graffiti area baseline.

- Don't write too fast. Graffiti doesn't care about your speed but, if you go too fast, you won't have sufficient control over the shape of your gestures and you'll make mistakes.

- If you have a hard time making certain gestures consistently, try the character a different way. Specifically, refer to Table 4-1 for a list of primary and secondary gestures for each character. Use the ones that work best for you.

Writing Letters and Numbers

The genius behind Graffiti—if that's not too strong a word—is that almost every letter and number at your disposal has two important characteristics:

- It can be drawn in a single stroke of the stylus.
- It bears a strong resemblance to its normal, plain English counterpart.

The easiest way to learn Graffiti is simply to practice writing the alphabet a few times. Use the Graffiti reference card that came with your Visor or refer to Table 4-1 for a guide to how to draw each character. The advantage to using this book, of course, is we show you a few alternative gestures that may make certain characters easier to draw consistently. Give them a shot.

Letter	Gestures
A	∧
B	ß ß 3
C	C <
D	D D △
E	ε ξ
F	⌐ ⌐
G	G G
H	h ᴎ
I		
J	J ⌡
K	∝
L	L ∠
M	m m
N	N ∝
O	O O
P	p p
Q	ʊ ʊ
R	ℛ ℛ

Letter	Gestures
S	S ʓ
T	⅂ ⟩
U	U ⌴
V	∨ ∨
W	ɯ ɯ
X	X ⤢
Y	ყ ɣ
Z	Z 2
0	O O U
1		∧
2	2 ⟩
3	3
4	L <
5	5 5
6	6 ⤢
7	7 ⌐ ⟩
8	8 8 ⤢
9	9 ε

TABLE 4-1   The Graffiti Numbers and Letters

4

The Hardest Characters

It seems everyone has trouble with some Graffiti character. Even if you can never get your Visor to recognize your letter *B,* that doesn't make you a freak—it just means you should learn an alternative stroke for that letter or put extra care into drawing it carefully and slowly. Even we have trouble with some letters. . . .

Dave: It's unfortunate my last name is *Johnson,* because I can't get Graffiti to take my letter *J* to save my life. Half the time, it's my own fault. As many times as I've made the *J,* I can't remember that it starts at the top and curves down. I always try to start at the bottom and hook up—which gives me a letter *U* every time. But even when I remember how to do it, I end up with a *V* or a new paragraph. Of course, because I'm drawing it right now for this chapter, I can't seem to do it wrong—ten perfect *J*'s out of ten. I think the letter just hates me. And I know I'm not crazy, by the way, despite what my dog keeps telling me.

Rick: If you'd ever seen Dave's chicken-scratch excuse for handwriting, you'd understand why he sometimes has trouble with Graffiti. But, to be fair, a few characters seem tougher to make than others. It's the *V* that drives me up the wall—I always forget to put the little tail on the end of the upstroke. But I know a secret: if you write the letter backwards, it comes out perfectly every time—and you don't need to draw the tail!

There's only one exception to the single stroke rule: the letter *X.* When you make an *X,* you can pick the stylus up off the screen to cross the letter in the traditional way. Of course, there's also a single-stroke alternative you can use as well (see Table 4-1 for the scoop on that).

You might notice that some letters and numbers have identical gestures. The letter *L* and the number 4, for instance, are both made in the same way (see Figure 4-3). How does Graffiti tell the difference? That's an easy one—don't forget the Graffiti area is divided into a number side and a letter side.

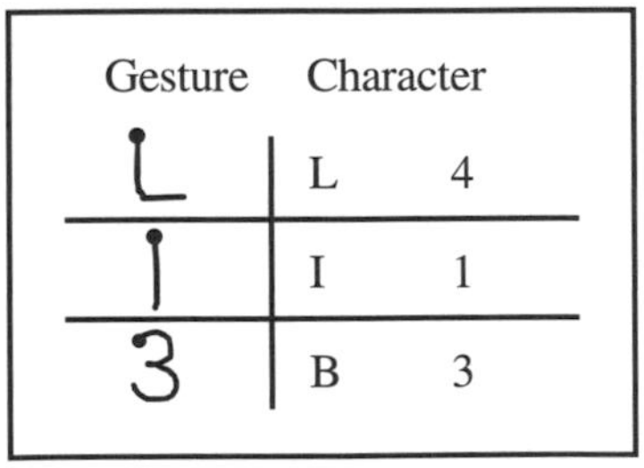

Gesture	Character	
L	L	4
I	I	1
3	B	3

FIGURE 4-3 The *L* and the 4 are made in the same way. So are the *I* and the 1

Capitalizing Letters

If you've reviewed Table 4-1, you no doubt have noticed there's no distinction in the Graffiti gestures for lowercase and uppercase characters. That's a good thing, actually—we don't have to learn over 100 gestures, because uppercase and lowercase letters are drawn the same way. Here's how to tell Graffiti you want to make an uppercase letter:

■ **One capital letter**   To make the next character, you draw an uppercase letter—draw a vertical line from the bottom of the Graffiti area to the top. This only works on the left side of the screen; it won't work in the number area. You see a symbol like this one, which indicates you are now in uppercase mode:

Indicates next letter will be a capital

■ **All capital letters**   To switch to All Caps mode and type in all capital letters, draw the vertical gesture twice. You see this symbol to indicate All Caps mode:

Indicates all caps

■ **Lowercase letters**   If you're already in All Caps mode, you can exit and write in lowercase again by making one more vertical gesture. The All Caps symbol should disappear to show you've changed modes.

TIP   *Uppercase mode doesn't affect numbers, so it doesn't matter which mode you're in when writing numbers. That means you needn't drop out of uppercase mode just to write numbers amid a bunch of capital letters.*

Spaces, Backspaces, and Deleting Text

Words are arguably more useful when you can put a space between them, thus enabling the casual reader to discern where each one begins and ends. In Graffiti, it's easy to insert spaces. So easy, in fact, you might be able to figure it out on your own (but we'll tell you anyway). Just draw a dash that starts on the left and goes to the right, and the cursor skips ahead a space. You can use this gesture to insert spaces between words or perform any other space-making task you might need. And, yes, you can insert multiple spaces just by performing this gesture as many times as needed.

The backspace, not surprisingly, is exactly the opposite. Just draw a gesture from right to left and the cursor backs up, deleting any text it encounters along the way.

> **TIP** *Space and backspace gestures work just fine in both the letter and number sides of the Graffiti area.*

Using the backspace gesture is great if you want to delete one or two characters, but what if you want to delete a whole sentence at once? That backspace swipe can get tiring if you have a lot of text either to kill or replace all at once. Luckily, there's an easy solution: just select the text you want to delete. The next thing you write will replace the selected text. Here's how to do it:

1. On the Visor, find a region of text you want to replace.

2. Tap and hold the stylus down at the start of the text you want to select—then drag the stylus across the text and pick it up when you've selected all the text in question.

Drag the stylus to select text

3. In the Graffiti area, write some new text. The old text will be immediately erased and replaced with the new text. If you simply want to delete the text, use the backspace gesture instead.

Adding Punctuation

To add punctuation to your prose, you need to (surprise, surprise) enter Graffiti's special punctuation mode. All it takes is a tap in the Graffiti area. You'll see a dot appear, which indicates you're now able to enter punctuation. Table 4-2 displays the punctuation gestures you commonly need.

Punctuation	Gestures
Period	•
Comma	/ (draw low)
Question mark	? ⌐
Exclamation point	!
Colon	V
Semicolon	⩘
Open parenthesis	C
Close parenthesis	)
Tab	⌐
Apostrophe	∣ (draw high)
Quotes	N
Slash	/
Backslash	\
At Symbol	∪
Asterisk	∞
Number sign	∪ ∩
Greater than	<
Less than	>
Percent	∪∪ ∞
Equal sign	Z
Plus sign	∝
Dollar sign	S

The Most Common Graffiti Punctuation Gestures

4

> **TIP** *If you enter the punctuation mode by tapping on one side of the Graffiti area, you need to complete the punctuation gesture on the same side. Tapping once on the number side and again on the letter side has no effect, for instance.*

The most common punctuation mark is a period and, because it's simply a dot, you can add a period to the end of a sentence by performing a quick double-tap. Some other symbols are trickier, though, and may take some practice. The comma, parenthesis bracket, and apostrophe are so similar, for instance, that it isn't unusual to get one when trying to gesture another.

> **TIP** *If you have a lot of trouble with specific symbols, you can always use the onscreen keyboard to get the right character, and then return to Graffiti.*

Using Shortcuts

Everyone seems to love shortcuts. In desktop applications like Microsoft Office, many folks eschew the mouse for keyboard shortcuts that speed tasks like text formatting and saving files. The Visor also has the capability to save you time and effort using shortcuts. Even better, Visor shortcuts are user-definable, so you can create your own library of them and not have to be satisfied with whatever came in the box.

So what are shortcuts, exactly? If you have a word or phrase you frequently write over and over, you can assign an abbreviation to it and let Graffiti do the hard work of writing it out in its entirety. To see how easy using shortcuts is, try this using one of the shortcuts that come built into your Visor:

1. Open the Memo Pad and tap the New button to open a new memo page.

2. Draw the shortcut gesture, as shown here. The shortcut gesture tells Graffiti the next thing you write will be an abbreviation that should be expanded in accordance with the shortcut library.

3. Write **br**, which is the shortcut for breakfast. As soon as you finish writing the *r*, the text should expand into the word "breakfast."

That's all there is to it. Hopefully, you can see the value of creating shortcuts that are relevant to what you frequently write.

Storing Your Own Shortcuts

Your Visor comes with a half dozen shortcuts, and you can easily create new ones whenever you want. To create a shortcut, so this:

1. Display Preferences by tapping the Prefs icon.

2. Choose Shortcuts from the list of Preferences in the upper-right corner of the screen.

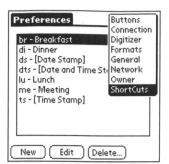

3. Tap the New button to display the ShortCut Entry window.

4. Give your shortcut a name. This is actually the abbreviation you will write to summon to entire shortcut text. If you want to create a shortcut that reads, "Dear Sir," for instance, you might want to use **ds**.

5. Enter the complete shortcut text. Remember, you are limited to a maximum length of 45 characters. If you reach that limit, you simply hear a beep when you try to write additional text.

6. Tap the OK button to save your shortcut.

Once you create a shortcut, you can use it anywhere in your Visor that you can write with Graffiti.

TIP

Don't go overboard with shortcuts right away. Shortcuts become a lot less cool if you have so many of them that you can't remember what the abbreviation is to summon the entire text. Start with two or three and, once you know them like the back of your hand, add a few more.

Another Kind of Shortcut: Menu Commands

If you're a big fan of choosing CTRL-S in Microsoft Word to save your work, then you'll love this. The Visor has its own menu shortcuts that you can access with Graffiti. To do this, though, you need to be prepared by remembering two important items:

- How to draw the Graffiti command stroke
- What the shortcut character is for the menu command you want to invoke

The command stroke is easy. To put your Visor in command mode, draw this gesture:

After you draw the gesture, your Visor displays the word Command and you simply need to write the proper character to invoke the menu item.

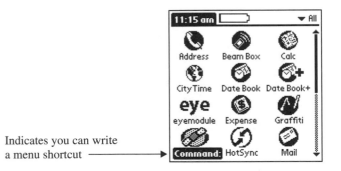

Indicates you can write a menu shortcut ⟶

To learn what the shortcuts are for each menu item, display the menu (tap the Menu button on your Visor and you see something similar to Figure 4-4). You can see that many menu items have a shortcut associated with them.

NOTE *The Command mode only lasts for about two seconds. If you don't write the shortcut character quickly, Command mode is deactivated, and then you need to perform the command stroke again.*

Getting Help with Graffiti

Graffiti help is never far away. You should know about a few resources that can help you master this almost-but-not-quite-normal alphabet.

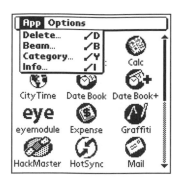

FIGURE 4-4   Many menu items have Graffiti shortcuts associated with them

■ **Play a game**   When you start out with Graffiti, you might want to use one of the core applications that comes with your Visor. Called *Giraffe*, it's a game that lets you get up to speed quickly on the art of shaping Graffiti characters. You need to draw the correct gesture for letters that fall from the top of the screen. Time is limited, so a few rounds of Giraffe can build up your speed and accuracy at drawing letters and numbers. See Chapter 20 for more information about Giraffe.

```
┌──────────────────────────┐
│ Giraffe                   │
│ Score:  5      Crashes Left:  10
│                           │         Write the gesture for the
│    I  ◄───────────────────────────  falling letters to get points
│                           │
│                           │
│                           │
│                           │
│                           │
│ ( End Game )  ( Help! )   │
└──────────────────────────┘
```

■ **Display the Help Screen**   A Graffiti reference is built into the Visor. To display it, start your stylus at the very bottom of the Graffiti area and draw a vertical line that extends all the way up to the top of the Visor screen. You see a multipage display, shown next, that covers every kind of character the Visor can make, including some we don't discuss here in the book. When you're ready to return to writing, tap the Done button.

■ **Use the Guides** Keep a copy of the Graffiti guide that came with your Visor in your Visor carrying case or in your wallet. Tables 4-1 and 4-2 in this chapter are also handy for learning the ropes, though we know you're not likely to carry our book around with you everywhere you go.

Beaming Data Between Palm OS Devices

On *Star Trek,* transporters are used to "beam" people and equipment from one location to another. While we're a long way from being able to beam physical things around, the Visor makes it possible to beam almost any kind of data between handheld PC users. All Palm models (except for first-generation Palm Pilots) have an infrared port. On Palm models from Palm Computing, the IR port is on the front. On your Visor, it's located on the side. If you haven't seen it yet, you can find it now. It's a thin, translucent, red piece of plastic (see Figure 4-5). Using this IR port, you can beam information in a surprising number of ways. You can

■ Use your Visor as a TV or stereo remote control

■ Send data between your Visor and a cell phone or pager

■ Print Visor data on an IR-equipped printer

■ Send data to other Palm device users

■ Play two-player games "head-to-head"

While you can do a lot of things with your Visor's IR port, most commonly you'll just want to exchange mundane business data with other Palm device users. All of the core applications support beaming, so you can beam

■ Address Book entries

■ Appointments and meetings

■ Memos

■ Tasks

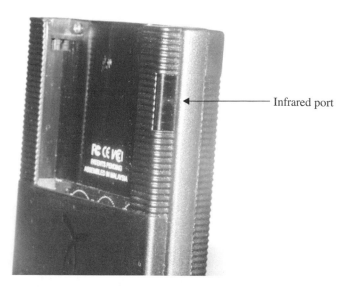

Infrared port

FIGURE 4-5   Almost all Palm devices come equipped with an infrared port in front for sending and receiving information wirelessly

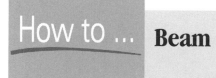 **Beam**

No matter what you're planning to beam—or receive—the process is essentially the same. Actually seeing the process demonstrated is faster than reading about it but, because neither Dave nor Rick is handy to stop by your office today, here's the process in a nutshell:

1. Orient your Visor and the other Palm device so their IR ports face each other and are between about four inches and three feet apart. Any closer than four inches and the devices may have a hard time locking onto each other. Too far away and the signal won't be strong enough to reach.

2. As the sender, you should choose the item you want to beam.

3. Choose the Beam command from the menu.

> **TIP** *If you beam often, you might want to know about the menu shortcut for beaming, which is a command slash gesture followed by the letter* B.
> *Also, you can configure your Visor so that a stroke from the bottom of the Graffiti area to the top of the screen can start a beam. To do that, tap the Prefs icon, and then select the Buttons item in the list at the top right of the screen. Tap the Pen button and choose Beam Data.*

4. A dialog box appears to indicate the beam is in progress. First you see a message that your Visor is searching for the other Palm device. Then that message goes away, and the data is transmitted.

5. After the beam, your Visor goes back to business as usual—you won't get a message indicating the beam was successful. The receiver, on the other hand, gets a dialog box that asks permission to accept the beamed data. As the receiver, you need to tap either Yes or No, depending on whether you want to keep the item. If you tap Yes, the data is integrated into your Visor.

6. After you accept a beamed item into your Visor, it appears in the *Unfiled* category. You can leave it there or assign it to one of your categories.

> **CAUTION** *If you accept a duplicate item—that is, if someone beams you a copy of something you already have—you end up with two copies of the item. The exception is applications, of which you can't have duplicates.*

to other users. In addition, you can beam entire applications to other Palm users. If you download a freeware program from the Internet and you want to share it with friends or coworkers, go ahead: it's a snap to transmit the item wirelessly.

To Accept or Not to Accept

By default, your Visor is set to accept beamed items. There are two reasons why you might want to disable auto-receive for beaming, though:

- Because the IR port is constantly on and searching for transmissions from other Palms, your Visor uses slightly more battery power when it's set to the default auto-receive. Is this a big deal, though? We don't think so. The extra power consumption is rather marginal.

- With all the concerns about viruses and other malicious programs that exist for PCs today, some folks are nervous about leaving their Visor in a state that receives software all the time. Our call: no malicious programs are out there for the Visor or any other Palm device (yet), and you explicitly have to accept a beamed program after reception anyway.

So, while we obviously don't think auto-receiving beamed items is a big deal, here's how to disable that feature if you want to:

1. Open the Visor's references by tapping the Prefs icon.

2. Choose the General category from the list at the top-right of the screen.

3. Change Beam Receive from On to Off.

After changing your preferences to disable beaming, other Palm devices can't send you data unless you reenable beaming from Preferences.

You can receive a beam from someone even if you have disabled beaming in Preferences. When someone starts to beam something to you that you want to receive, draw the shortcut gesture and double-tap to make a period. Then draw the letter I. You'll receive the beam just that one time. But beware: you must receive a beam signal within about five seconds, or you revert to no-beaming mode.

Selecting Items for Beaming

So now that you know the rudiments of beaming, you're no doubt eager to start. While we're usually a pretty down-to-Earth couple of guys, we have to admit a certain coolness factor is involved in beaming things in the middle of a meeting or on the show floor at a trade show. It's definitely better than writing notes by hand or trading easily scrunched business cards.

Beaming Appointments

If you work with other Palm device users, you can make sure everyone is on the same schedule by beaming entries from the Date Book. To do that, select an appointment, and then choose Beam Event from the menu.

Beaming Contacts

If you're like most people, the Address Book is the most well-exercised part of your Visor. And, instead of exchanging paper-based business cards, now you can beam the information between Palms, which can later be HotSynced back to your PC's contact manager. In recognition of just how important the Address Book really is, you have not one, not two, but three options for sending data from this application:

- **Beam the current entry** To send an Address Book entry to another user, find the name you want in the Address List and choose Beam Address from the menu.

- **Beam a whole bunch of entries** You can send any number of contacts to someone else all at once—every name in your Visor, in fact—using Beam Category. To do that, first choose the category you want to beam by picking the category from the list at the top-right corner of the screen. Then choose Beam Category from the menu. To beam all the entries in your entire Address Book, set the category to All.

CAUTION *Be careful before you beam or try to receive a whole category's worth of contacts—make sure it's something you really need to do. This operation could include hundreds of entries, which will take some time and consume a fair bit of memory.*

■ **Beam your own entry**   What's more common than handing your business card to someone? You can configure your own Address Book entry as your personal business card and beam it to other Palms. For details on configuring an entry as your business card, see Chapter 8. Once configured, however, you can send it by opening the Address Book and choosing Beam Business Card from the menu.

TIP *There's a faster way to beam your business card to someone; just hold down the Address Book button for two seconds. That automatically tells the Visor to beam your business card.*

Beaming Memos and Tasks

Memos are handy to pass off to other Palm device users. You can give them notes, action items, short documents, and even meeting minutes in this way. Likewise, if you want to delegate a task to someone else in your office, tell them to "visit my cubicle—and don't forget to bring your Visor." You can beam memos and to do items in two ways:

■ **Beam a Memo or a To Do**   To beam a single item, select it and choose Beam Memo (for a Memo) or Beam Item (for a To Do) from the menu.

■ **Beam a bunch of stuff at once**   Like the Address Book, you can select a category in the Memo List or To Do List, and then choose Beam Category from the menu. To beam all your memos or tasks at once, remember to set the category list to All.

Beaming Applications

Now for the best part. You can use the Visor's beaming prowess to transfer entire applications from your Visor to another. If you meet someone who shows you his cool new Palm game or utility, for instance, you can ask him to send it to you instantly so you can have it, too.

Not all applications are free, so don't use your Visor's beaming capability for piracy. Actually, many commercial programs are "locked" to prevent beaming, but remember not to trade software if it's commercial in nature.

Not all programs can, in fact, be beamed. The core applications that come with your Visor are "locked," making them nonbeamable. Many commercial programs are also locked, and some programs have a resistance to beaming—like Hackmaster Hacks (discussed in Chapter 18). In addition, if you have a program that requires supporting database files, the files won't be beamable. That means you have to go home and install the program the hard way.

Now that we've told you what you can't do, let's talk about what you can do. Beaming an application isn't much different than beaming data from one of the Visor's programs. Do this:

1. Tap the Application button on your Visor to return to applications.

2. From the menu, choose Beam. You see a dialog box with a list of all the applications on your Visor, as in Figure 4-6. Some applications have little locks; these are not beamable.

3. Select an application and tap the Beam button.

TIP *If you beam lots of stuff, get a program called Beam Box. It simplifies the process of beaming programs and makes it possible to beam certain kinds of apps (like Hackmaster Hacks) that the Visor can't do on its own.*

Installing New Software on Your Visor

Did you know that you can install tons of additional programs on your Visor? There are thousands of free and commercial applications out there, just waiting to be installed. They include enhancements to the core applications, utilities, games, and more. In fact, one of the best reasons for choosing a Palm OS device (instead of a competing Windows CE device or some other kind of organizer) is such a wealth of software exists.

But you might wonder: how the heck do I get all this cool stuff onto my Visor?

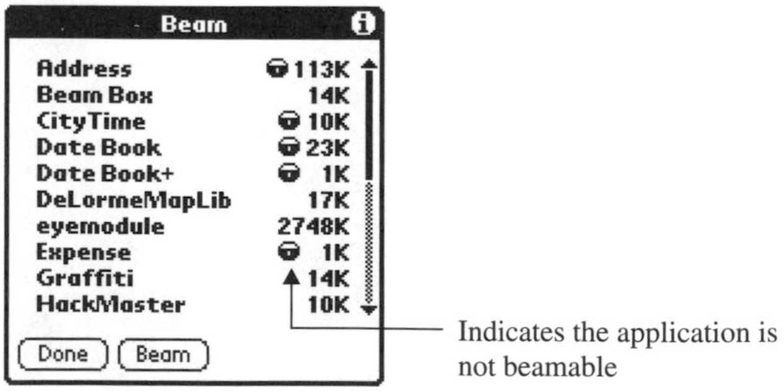

Beam
Address ⊕113K
Beam Box 14K
CityTime ⊕10K
Date Book ⊕23K
Date Book+ ⊕ 1K
DeLormeMapLib 17K
eyemodule 2748K
Expense ⊕ 1K
Graffiti ▲14K
HackMaster 10K
(Done) (Beam)

— Indicates the application is not beamable

FIGURE 4-6 Choose an app from the list to beam it to a friend's Palm OS device

If You Have No Friends

Rick is a lonely guy, and while he loves the ability to beam stuff to other Visors, he's hampered by the fact that he never leaves the house. Thankfully, Dave has turned him on to a hidden feature in the Visor that enables you to, well, beam things to yourself. If you want to experiment with beaming stuff and you don't have a second Palm device handy, you can now do the same thing that Rick does for amusement.

Create the shortcut gesture, and then tap twice to write a period. Now write the letter *T*. When you try to beam, your Visor simulates the process of beaming and "receives" the item all by itself. You're then asked if you want to accept the item, to which you can say Yes or No. When you tire of beaming things to yourself, repeat the shortcut to return to the ordinary beaming mode.

The answer is the Palm Desktop includes a handy *Install Tool* for loading Palm apps. To use it, do this:

1. Start the Palm Desktop by choosing Start | Programs | Palm Desktop | Palm Desktop. On the Mac, select the Palm Desktop from the Chooser or the Palm folder.

2. Click the Install button on the left side of the Palm Desktop screen. The Install Tool appears, as shown in Figure 4-7. If you're using a Mac, choose HotSync | Install from the menu.

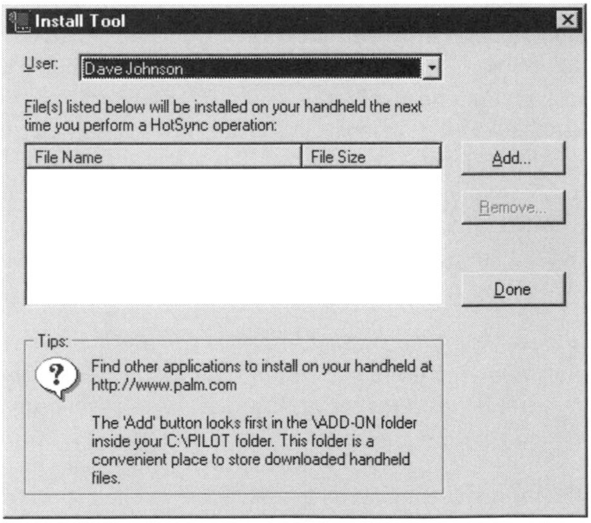

FIGURE 4-7   The Install Tool serves as the conduit for loading new apps on the Visor

3. Click the Add button. You see the Open dialog box for selecting Visor applications.

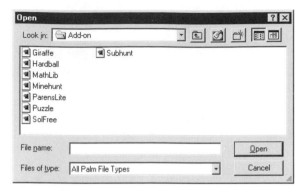

4. Locate the program you want to install and select it. Click the Open button.

TIP *You can select multiple applications at once by holding down the CTRL key as you click programs in the file list.*

5. With your application displayed in the Install Tool dialog box, click Done.

6. The next time you HotSync your Visor, the selected application is installed.

Install Tool Shortcuts in Windows

Not everyone likes to use the Palm Desktop. If you use Microsoft Outlook, for instance, and, hence, don't need to open the Palm Desktop for HotSyncing or entering data, then don't feel compelled to open the Palm Desktop just to install Palm applications. Instead, you can start the Install Tool directly. Choose Start | Programs | Palm Desktop | Install Tool. The Install Tool will start without the Palm Desktop running at all.

And while you can use the Add button to select files for installation, there's a much easier way. On the desktop, open the folder that includes the files you want to install and drag the program icons to the Install Tool dialog box. Drop the icons and they'll appear automatically in the list of files to be installed. Some people who don't use the Palm Desktop, but who are Microsoft Office users, add the Install Tool to the Microsoft office Shortcut bar that appears on the Windows Desktop. That way, the Install Tool is always just one click away.

CAUTION *You may have discovered a folder called Install. If you don't know where it is, look in C:\Program Files\Palm\your username\Install. This folder holds applications waiting for the next HotSync to be installed on the Visor. You can't just drag files to this folder, though, because the Install Tool needs to tell Windows files are waiting to be installed.*

There's another way to install an application quickly: double click it. Double-clicking a PRC file automatically adds it to your Install Tool queue.

Prepping Applications for Installation

As we've said, there's a ton (thousands, actually) of Visor applications available—many free, some for a commercial fee. Throughout this book, we make reference to our favorite applications, and we recommend you try them. Perhaps the single best resource for Visor applications is a Web site called PalmGear H.Q. (www.palmgear.com), shown in Figure 4-8.

Often, downloaded applications aren't immediately ready for installation. If you download an application from the Internet, it usually arrives in the form of a SIT file (if you're a Mac user) or a Zip file (if you use Windows). You need to expand these SIT and Zip files before they can be installed on your Visor. We recommend these tools for managing compressed files:

- **Windows**   Use WinZip 7.0 to uncompress Zip files.
- **Macintosh**   Use Aladdin Stuffit Expander 5.0 to manage SIT files.

Of course, if you already happily expand compressed files with another program, keep up the good work; these are just our favorites.

FIGURE 4-8   PalmGear H.Q. is where we go for Visor software

Once expanded, most Visor files bear the file extension PRC. In a Zip or SIT with lots of little files, you can generally just grab the PRC file and install that. Of course, if in doubt, read whatever documentation accompanied the application.

After the HotSync

Any programs you want to install are stored in the Install Tool's queue until you HotSync. After the HotSync, they're copied to your Visor, as long as the Install conduit is set to Install Handheld Applications (see Chapter 3 for details on configuring conduits).

After the HotSync, remember these two things about your applications:

■ New applications end up in the Unfiled category on your Visor.

■ On your PC, the files are moved to a folder called Backup. It can be found at C:\Program Files\Palm*your Palm's folder*\Backup. This folder is used by the Palm Desktop to reinstall all your applications in case your Visor suffers a total memory failure and you need to reinstall programs from scratch. In a bizarre twist on logic, though, not all versions of the Palm Desktop restore all these apps when you have a total failure. We recommend a program called BackupBuddy to safeguard your Visor configuration; it's covered in detail in Chapter 18. Or, get the Backup Module to create a complete backup of your Visor's data instantly; this device is discussed in Chapter 16.

Removing Applications from the Visor

You won't want every application you install on your Visor on there forever. Some programs you won't like, others will outlive their usefulness. And quite often, you need to eliminate some apps to make room for more because the Visor has limited storage space.

Deleting programs from the Visor is easy. Tap the Applications soft button on your Visor and choose Delete from the menu. You then see a list of all the applications currently stored on the handheld. At the top of the screen, you also see a bar that shows how much memory remains on your Visor.

Delete	ⓘ
Free Memory: 6011K of 8064K	

AmusePark	38K
Astroids	28K
AvantGo	681K
Beam Box	14K
CharonClock	6K
Cuepert	39K
GetRom2	1K

(Done) (Delete...)

To delete an application, select it and tap the Delete button. It's similar to the Beam interface and, in fact, it's so similar, you should be careful you don't accidentally delete an app you're trying to beam to a friend.

CAUTION *When you delete an application, you also delete all the data it has generated. If you have a document reader, for instance, deleting the app also trashes any docs it may contain. To preserve these files, HotSync before deleting anything.*

4

Chapter 5

Working with the Palm Desktop for Windows

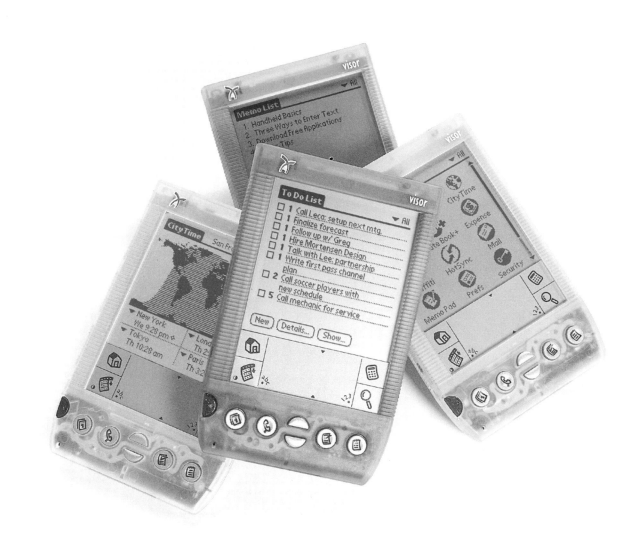

How to...

- Use the Palm Desktop's Date Book
- Use the Palm Desktop's Address Book
- Import contacts from other personal informational managers
- Create mailing lists and labels with the Palm Desktop
- Use address information in other Windows applications
- Use the Palm Desktop's To Do List
- Convert To Dos into Date Book appointments
- Use the Palm Desktop's Memo Pad
- Import text files into the Memo Pad
- Export memos into other Windows applications
- Restore deleted data back to your Visor

The very term Palm Desktop seems slightly oxymoronic—after all, the whole point of Palm OS devices like the Visor is that it's a mobile, handheld device. Why on Earth would you want to put it on your desktop?

Actually, the Palm Desktop software replicates most of the core applications on your Visor, makes it easy to enter data when you're at your desk, and synchronizes perfectly with the apps on your Visor. More important, the Palm Desktop serves as a backup solution for your Visor's data. When you HotSync, all the data on both the PC and Visor are cross-transferred, so you would have to have lightning strike both your Visor and your desktop PC more or less simultaneously to lose all your data permanently.

Of course, not everyone uses the Palm Desktop. To be honest, neither of us uses the Palm Desktop because we prefer more full-featured *personal information managers* (PIMs) like Microsoft Outlook. Rick used the Palm Desktop as his exclusive PC PIM for quite some time, though, and he was reasonably happy with the experience. What can you do with the Palm Desktop? Read on and find out.

Explore with the Palm Desktop

We know what you're thinking . . . why is it called the Palm Desktop and not the Visor Desktop? You're also thinking about losing that basketball game last week, and our advice is to get over it. You're not really that good with a ball anyway.

In any event, the Visor uses the same desktop software as the other Palm OS devices—right down to the copyright notice. That makes it easier to move from one Palm OS device to another because the software all works the same way. So, even though it says Palm Desktop, rest assured it's 100 percent compatible with the Visor and you're not missing out on anything.

CAUTION *If you need to download Palm Desktop software from the Web, we recommend you get it from the Handspring Web site (www.handspring.com), not from Palm Computing. That way, you know it will be 100 percent compatible with your device, including the Springboard module connectivity (which other Palm OS devices don't have).*

The Palm Desktop is easy to use. Start the program by choosing Start | Programs | Palm Desktop | Palm Desktop. You should see something like Figure 5-1.

To switch among any of the four core applications, click the appropriate button on the left side of the screen. If you click the Expense button, Microsoft Excel launches and enables you to display your Visor's Expense data—see Chapter 11 for details on how the Expense program works. You can also click the Install button to add programs to your Visor (though you can also launch that program separately without starting the Palm Desktop first).

NOTE *If you use Outlook as your PIM, your Visor won't synchronize data with the Palm Desktop during HotSyncs—the data is obviously synchronized with Outlook. If that's the case, the Palm Desktop has little to offer you because you can access the Install and HotSync controls without starting this program.*

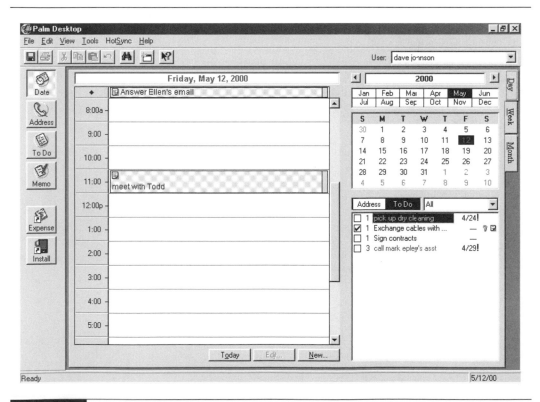

 FIGURE 5-1 The Palm Desktop replicates most of the core applications from your Visor

Configure the Palm Desktop

If you have several Visors or multiple users all connected to the same PC, you need to tell the Palm Desktop which one you want to use. The current user is indicated in a list menu at the top-right corner of the Palm Desktop window, as you can see in Figure 5-1. To select a different user, click the list menu and choose the appropriate name.

Of course, if your Visor is the only one that ever connects to your PC, then only one name will be in the menu. But if you are one of several users, be sure you have the Palm Desktop set to your own name or else you'll be editing someone else's Visor data!

Set HotSync Settings

You can configure your Visor's HotSync settings from the Palm Desktop as well. Choose HotSync | Custom to change the conduit settings (discussed in detail in Chapter 3) and choose HotSync | Setup to change the PC's settings, such as the USB or serial configuration.

Manage Your Schedule with the Date Book

When you start using the Date Book, you really do start from scratch—unlike the Address Book (discussed later in this chapter), the Date Book doesn't let you import previous scheduling information from another program.

The Date Book uses a few unique control elements—but they're quite intuitive and you can master them in no time. After you start the Palm Desktop, you can switch to the Date Book by clicking the Date icon on the right side of the screen or choosing View | Date Book. To change views, click the tabs at the right edge of the screen. You should see three tabs: Day, Week, and Month.

NOTE   *Unfortunately, there is no way to import an existing calendar from another PIM into the Palm Desktop.*

Use the Day View

The Day View looks similar to the Palm Desktop display. Take a look at Figure 5-2 for an overview of the major elements in this display.

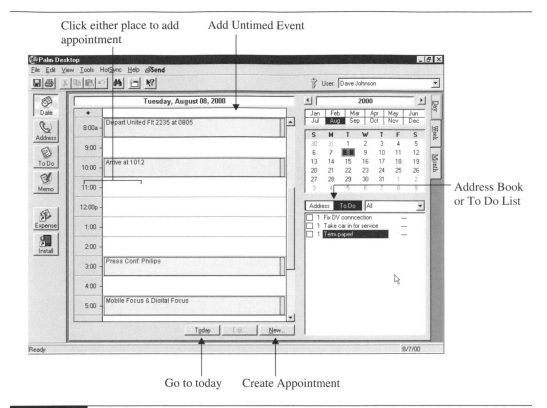

FIGURE 5-2   The Day View combines appointments with either To Dos or Addresses, depending on how you configure it

How to ...   **Add Appointments**

You can add an appointment to the Date Book in several ways:

- Click in the blank next to the time period for which you want to schedule the event. Type the meeting information.
- Click the gray time box to the left of the blank and start typing in the blank.
- Click the New button at the bottom of the screen. The Edit Event dialog box appears, which you can fill in to set the time.

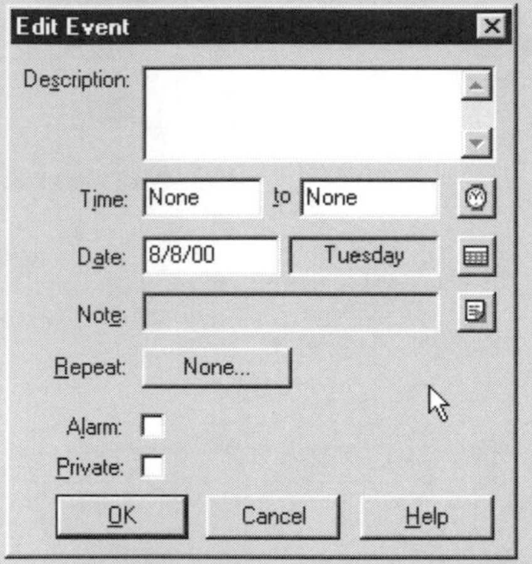

Edit Event	☒
Description:	
Time:	None to None 🕐
Date:	8/8/00 Tuesday 📅
Note:	📄
Repeat:	None...
Alarm: ☐	
Private: ☐	
OK Cancel Help	

TIP   *The easiest way to double-book a time slot is to click the time box. A new blank appears to the right of the existing appointment.*

Under the calendar, you can see the To Do list and Address Book minilists. You can create an appointment from an entry in either of these lists by choosing which list you want, then dragging a name (or a To Do) into a time slot in the Date Book.

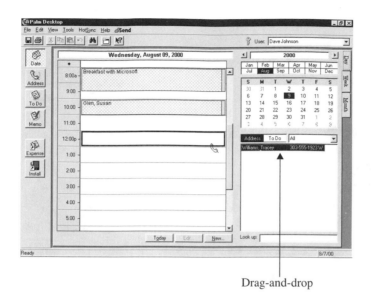

Drag-and-drop

Edit Appointments

Making changes to your appointments is even easier on the Palm Desktop than it is on the Visor. You can actually make lots of changes with the mouse; to change the duration of an event, drag the duration handle up or down. To move the appointment, drag it by its event handle on the right edge. And to see the Edit Event dialog box, which includes alarm and privacy controls, double-click the event handle.

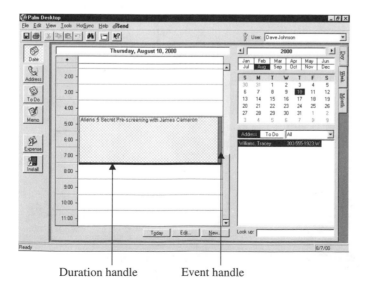

Duration handle   Event handle

TIP *You can move an appointment to another day by dragging it via the event handle to the calendar and dropping it on the desired day.*

Use the Week and Month Views

Both of these views are quite similar to their Visor counterparts. When in the Week View (seen in Figure 5-3), though, the event blocks work a bit differently than you might expect:

- To move an event to a different time, drag it by the event handle.

- To display the Edit Event dialog box and change options like time, repeat settings, or the alarm, double-click the event handle.

- To edit the text of an event, double-click in the block and type.

- To change the duration of the event, drag its duration handle up or down.

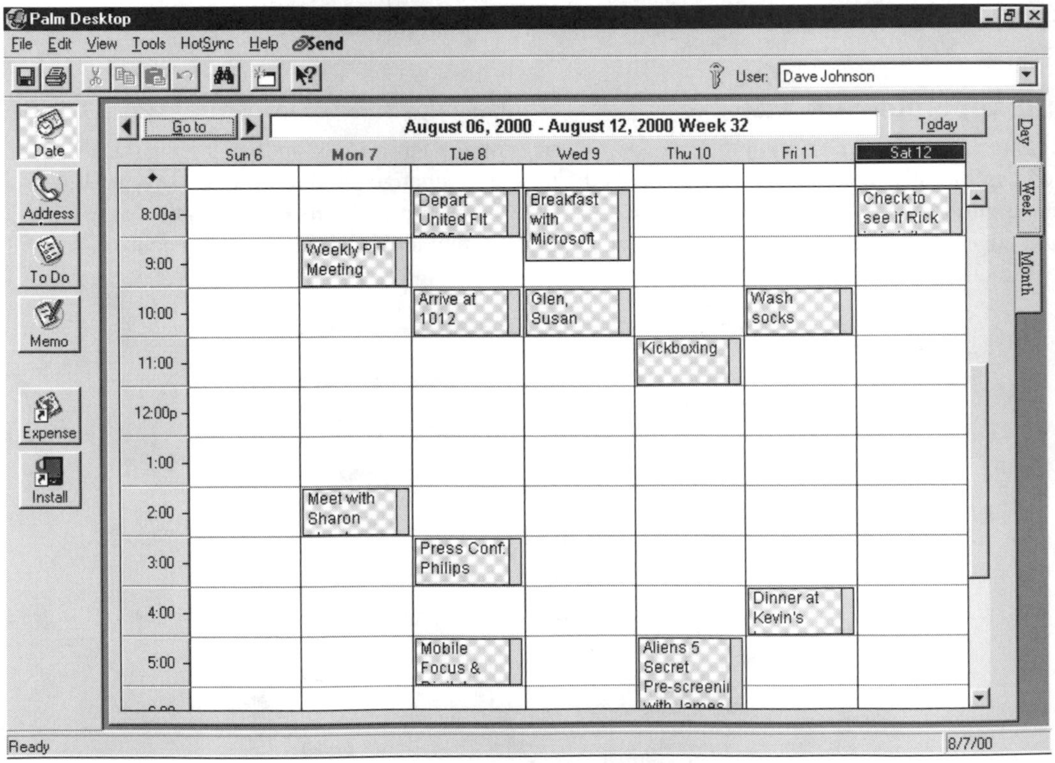

FIGURE 5-3 The Week View enables you to add and edit appointments

Finally, the Month View is a bit more helpful than the one in your Visor. As you can see, the Month View (in Figure 5-4) actually shows you what events are scheduled, not just that you have a mysterious "something" scheduled. You can't edit the events in this view, though. Instead, you can do two things in the Month View:

- ■ To go to the Day View, double-click the appropriate day.
- ■ To add a new event to a specific day, right-click the day and choose New Event from the menu.

NOTE   *The Palm Desktop doesn't include any equivalent to the very cool Date Book+ that's found on your Visor (see Chapter 7 for information on that).*

5

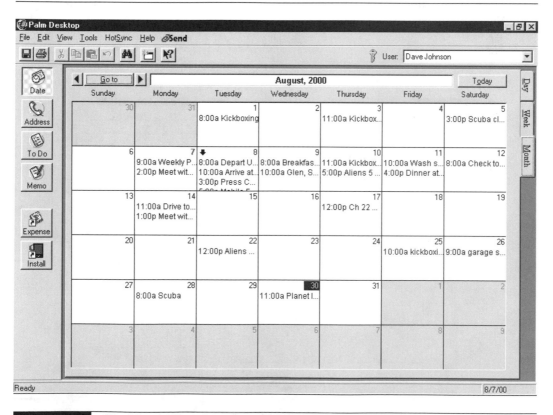

FIGURE 5-4   The Month View doesn't enable any appointment editing

Manage Your Contacts with the Address Book

Using the Address Book in the Palm Desktop is a radically different experience than using it in the Visor. In most respects, it's better because the larger desktop screen, keyboard, and mouse enable you to enter and use the data in a more flexible way. After you start the Palm Desktop, you can switch to the Address Book by clicking the Address icon on the right side of the screen or choosing View | Address Book (see Figure 5-5).

View Address Book Entries

The Address Book interface enables you to see both the Address List and Address View simultaneously. To see a specific record's contents, click it in the list and the information will appear in the shaded area on the right.

Many of the Address List conventions from the Visor have made the transition to the PC intact. Some important features to remember are:

■ The List By button enables you to change the sorting method from Last Name, First Name to Company, Last Name.

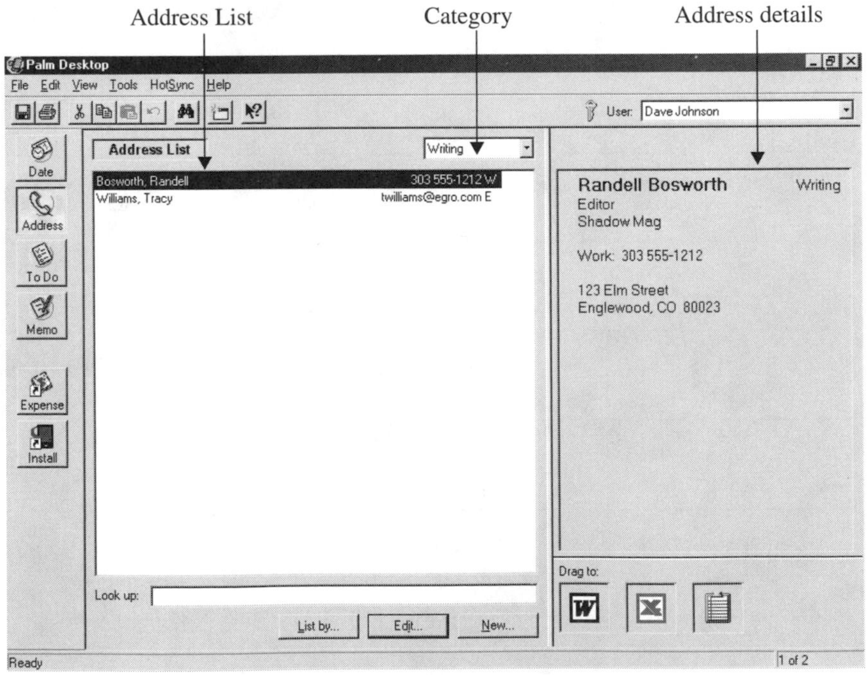

FIGURE 5-5   The Address Book looks sparse, but it is every bit as functional as the Visor equivalent

- You can change categories by choosing a different category from the list menu at the top of the Address List.

- The Look Up field at the bottom of the screen is useful for finding specific entries quickly. If you need to use the Find tool to search for a specific word (like a first name or company name), use the Find button in the toolbar.

> **TIP**   *You can print a detailed address book based on your Visor's contacts just by choosing File | Print. The address book is nicely formatted.*

Create and Edit Entries

Some of the most dramatic differences in the Address Book appear when you create and edit entries. Keep these notes in mind:

- To create a new entry, click the New button at the bottom of the screen or click the New Item button in the toolbar at top.

- The Edit Address dialog box has three tabs for entering all the same information you can enter on the Visor. The dialog box also has a list box for specifying the category and a check box to make the entry private.

- To specify which phone number appears in the Address List, click the Show In List radio button.

- To edit an existing entry, either double-click the entry in the Address List or its equivalent in the Address View on the right.

- You can change the custom fields on the Palm Desktop as well. To do that, choose Tools | Custom Field Labels.

Import Contacts into the Palm Desktop

If you have a history with another contact manager, you could have dozens or hundreds of names and addresses that need to be copied over to the Palm Desktop to be synchronized with the Visor. Thankfully, the Palm Desktop makes it possible to import all of those contacts with a minimum of fuss. All you need is a contact manager capable of saving its data in either a *comma separated* (CSV) or *tab separated* (TSV) format. To import your data from another program, do this:

1. In your old contact manager, find the menu option to export your data in either CSV or TSV format. If the program gives you an option to "remap" your data as it's saved, don't worry about it. We'll map it properly as it's imported into the Palm Desktop. Save the exported data to a file on your hard disk. Make a note of where you save this file, because you need to find it again in about two steps.

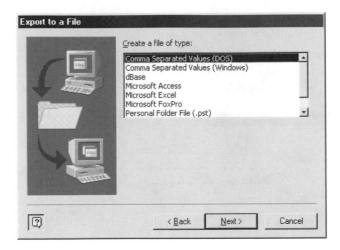

2. In the Palm Desktop, choose File | Import. The Import dialog box should appear.

3. Select the file you just created with the old contact manager. You may have to choose the proper file extension (like CSV or TSV) from the Type of file list box to see the file you created. Choose Open.

4. Now you see a Specify Import Fields dialog box, as in Figure 5-6. This is the hardest part of the process, and the one part that isn't terribly automated. Here's the deal: the data in a typical contact entry includes items like name, phone numbers, and address. But those fields won't be in the same order in any two contact management programs, so you need to help the Palm Desktop put the old data in the right fields as it imports. To map the fields properly, drag each field on the left (which is the Palm Desktop) until it is lined up with the proper field on the right (which represents the old program). Line up last name with last name, for instance, and match phone numbers, e-mail addresses, and any other fields that are important. If you don't want to import a certain field, deselect its check box.

Drag to match imported data

Specify Import Fields

Palm Fields	Data in "test.CSV"	
	Title	OK
☑ First Name	First Name	
	Middle Name	Cancel
☑ Last Name	Last Name	
	Suffix	Reset
☑ Company	Company	
	Department	Help
☑ Title	Job Title	
☑ Address	Business Street	
	Business Street 2	
	Business Street 3	

◀ Scan Records ▶   Record 1

Tip

To change the field order, click a field name on the left and drag it up or down the list to match the data on the right.

If the 'ALL' category is selected before importing records, the category field will be available in the field list. Drag the category field to match the data position on the right.

Only existing categories will be matched. Unmatched categories will be placed in 'Unfiled'.

Source file character set: Windows (ANSI)

FIGURE 5-6   Carefully rearrange the fields in the Specify Import Fields dialog box, so your old data is imported properly into the Palm Desktop

TIP   *You can use the arrows to cycle forward through the database and make sure you've assigned the fields properly.*

5. When you're done lining up the fields, click the OK button.

If you did everything right, you should see your contacts in the Palm Desktop. Any newly imported entries are highlighted. If you messed something up, all is not lost. Just delete all your records, and then try to import your contacts file again.

Use Addresses in Other Applications

Once you create a robust address book in the Palm Desktop, either through importing an old one or creating a new one from scratch, you can use it to simplify your life. Look at the Palm Desktop, for instance, and you should see three icons at the bottom of the screen. By dragging one or more entries to these icons, you can perform a few cool tricks.

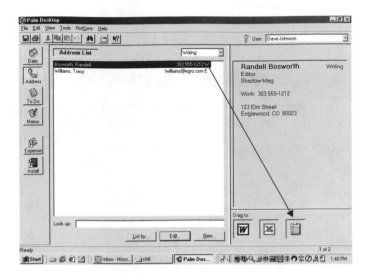

The Clipboard

If you drag records to the clipboard and release the mouse, the obvious happens: the data is copied to the clipboard. You can then choose Edit | Paste in virtually any application and paste the data from those contacts into another document. Once you paste the data into the other application, just delete those parts of the records you don't want.

Microsoft Excel

If you drag some records to the Excel icon and release the mouse, Windows automatically launches Excel and places the selected data into a new spreadsheet. Note, the sheet is automatically organized into a sort of table with the names of each field, spanning row 2 of the sheet. Empty fields are left blank. From here, you can format the data, edit it, or print it.

Microsoft Word

Among the three drag-and-drop icons in the Address Book, the Palm Desktop has the best support for Word. If you drag records to the Word icon, Word launches and creates an elegant table (similar to the one Excel generates) with a header and listing all the field names. It then displays the Address Book Macro dialog box with the option of creating several useful documents:

- **Formatted Address**   This option strips out the mailing address information from each selected record and puts it on a different page of the document.

TIP   *To insert a formatted address into e-mail or other documents, right-click the entry in the Address List and choose Copy from the menu. Then choose Paste in the other document. You can select multiple documents and right-click to get more than one record at a time.*

- **Form Letters**   Choose this option to create a mail merge letter template. Word inserts all the mail merge fields for you and instructs you to complete the body of the letter. When you're done, click the Merge button in the Word toolbar and you get a fully merged version of the letter with all the contact information filled in for each selected contact.

■ **Mailing Labels**   If you use printer-friendly adhesive mailing labels, you can use this option to print selected contacts.

■ **Envelopes**   This option generates a document with selected contacts that is ready for you to feed envelopes through your printer.

■ **Leave Data as Table**   This option simply gives you the nicely formatted table full of contact information that Word generated before displaying the dialog box. You can edit or print the table if you want.

TIP   *To select more than one entry at a time in the Address List to drag to an icon, hold down the CTRL key when you click the records.*

Track Tasks with the To Do List

It's not identical, but you'll have no trouble recognizing the To Do List on the Desktop. All the same elements are there, they just appear in somewhat different places than you'd expect if you're already familiar with the Visor's To Do List. After you start the Palm Desktop, you can switch to the To Do List by clicking the To Do icon on the left side of the screen or choosing View | To Do List (see Figure 5-7).

View Your To Dos

The To Do List's interface is a bit more spacious than the one in your Visor. As a result, the Palm Desktop pulls off a cool trick—it displays both the list itself and the contents of the Details dialog box onscreen simultaneously. Click a To Do and the details on the right automatically update to show you more information about the particular task you've selected.

Here are a few tips to help you navigate around this screen:

■ If you want to modify the display of the To Do List, click the Show button at the bottom of the screen (or choose View | Show from the menu). You see the Show Options dialog box that enables you to hide completed items and show different columns of information in the display.

■ To change the category of tasks displayed onscreen, use the list menu at the top-right of the To Do List names.

■ Just like on the Visor, you can change specific information in a task by clicking the item. To read or change a note, for instance, click the note icon in the To Do List.

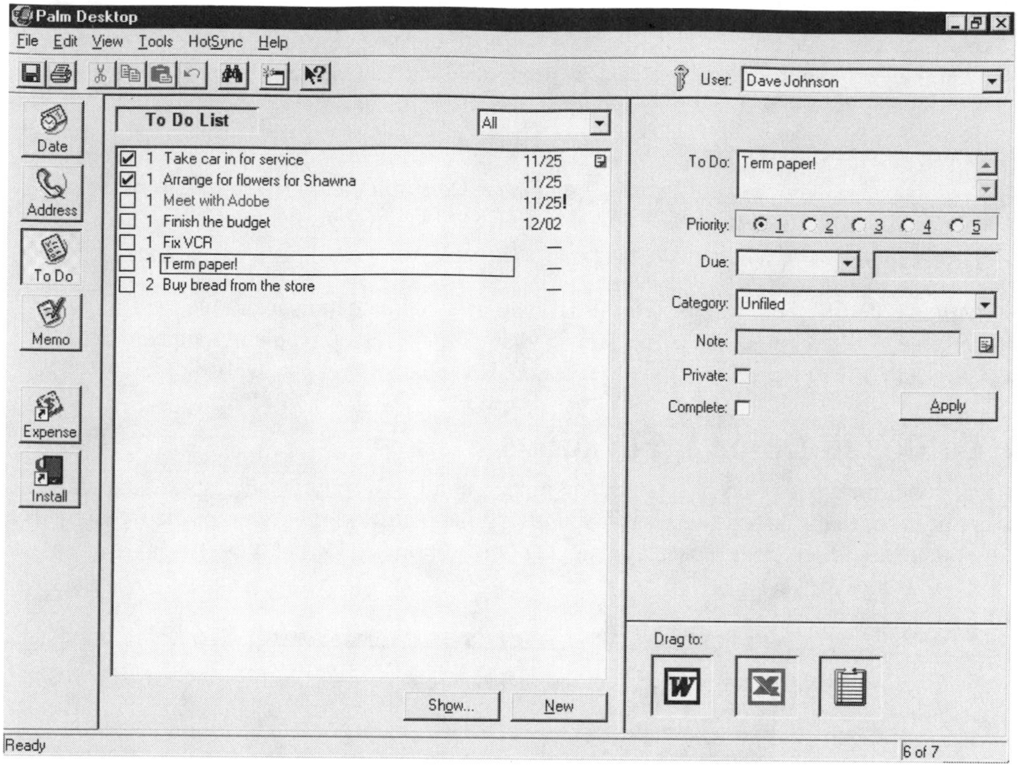

FIGURE 5-7   The To Do List puts the details right on the same screen as the list itself—a clever way to use the extra space afforded by Windows

Turn To Dos into Appointments

Your Visor understands a tight relationship exists between your calendar and your To Do tasks. Switch to the Date Book in the Palm Desktop and you'll find the right side of the screen has a window for displaying either addresses or To Dos. Click the To Do box to show To Dos; click Address to return to the phone number lookup mode. What good is that? Well, you can actually grab a To Do and drag-and-drop it into a calendar appointment. That lets you turn a task into a bona-fide appointment. You can't go the other way, though, and turn an appointment into a task.

Create and Edit To Dos

Just like on the Visor, you needn't use the New button to create a new task. Just start typing, and the Palm Desktop automatically creates a new To Do with the description you're currently entering. You can use the New button, of course, but what's the point?

> **TIP**   *You can create a To Do with a description that's many lines long, but the complete description won't appear in the list on the desktop; you can only see it by scrolling through the To Do name field on the right side of the screen. When you HotSync, though, the complete item appears on the Visor.*

After you enter the To Do name, you'll find you have all the details available for editing on the same screen. When you select a due date, the day of the week conveniently appears to the right of the date. Likewise, the first line of any note is visible onscreen as well.

Use To Dos in Other Applications

Now that you have a list of To Dos assembled in the Palm Desktop, you can import them into other applications. This isn't as weird as it sounds. At the bottom-right corner of the Palm Desktop, you should see three icons. By dragging one or more To Dos to these icons, you can perform a few cool tricks:

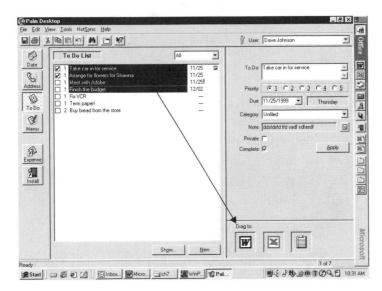

The Clipboard

If you drag To Dos to the clipboard and release the mouse, the data is copied to the clipboard. You can then choose Edit | Paste in virtually any application and paste the data from those contacts into another document. The format of the clipboard data is the same, regardless of whatever Show preferences you have selected: you get the task name, deadline (if any), priority, completion status, note (if any), and category, separated by tabs. Here's an example of three To Dos that have been copied to the clipboard and pasted into Microsoft Word:

```
Call Wayne          11/26/2000  Priority: 1 Completed: Yes    Personal
Finish the budget   12/02/2000  Priority: 1 Completed: No     Business
Buy bread from store            Priority: 2 Completed: No     Personal
```

Once you paste this data into another application, you can delete whatever part of the To Dos you don't want.

Microsoft Excel

If you drag To Dos to the Excel icon and release the mouse, Windows automatically launches Excel and places the selected data into a new spreadsheet. Note, the sheet is automatically organized into a sort of table with the names of each field, spanning row 2 of the sheet. The sheet includes the To Do name, due date, priority, completion status, note, and category. Empty fields are left blank. From here, you can format the data, edit it, or print it.

Microsoft Word

If you were impressed by the clipboard or Excel, the Palm Desktop's support for Word is really going to knock your socks off. If you drag one or more To Dos to the Word icon, Word launches and builds a table (much like the one you saw in Excel) based on the data you supplied. You then get a dialog box like this:

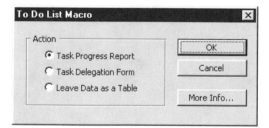

Use it to choose what you want to do with the data. Here are your options:

- **Task Progress Report** This option creates a professional-looking memo that describes the status of all the selected tasks. It prints the task name and note information, followed by completion status and due date. You can e-mail or send this memo to your boss to advise him about your progress, or just print it and use it as a personal reminder of your pending tasks.

- **Task Delegation Form** This option is similar to the progress report, but it's aimed at reminding subordinates about projects you want them to finish. It prints tasks, priority, due date, and note information complete with check marks, so the task can be crossed off when done.

■ **Leave Data as a Table** This option simply gives you the nicely formatted table full of To Do information Word generated before displaying the dialog box. You can edit or print the table if you want.

> **TIP** *To select more than one task at a time to drag to an icon, hold down the CTRL key when you click the items.*

Take Notes with the Memo Pad

The Memo Pad is virtually identical to the Visor's built-in app on the Windows version of the Palm Desktop. And, while the Memo Pad is fully functional, it is perhaps the simplest of the Palm Desktop applications. First, though, you need to get there. Start the Palm Desktop, and then switch to the Memo Pad by clicking the Memo icon on the left side of the screen or choosing View | Memo Pad (see Figure 5-8).

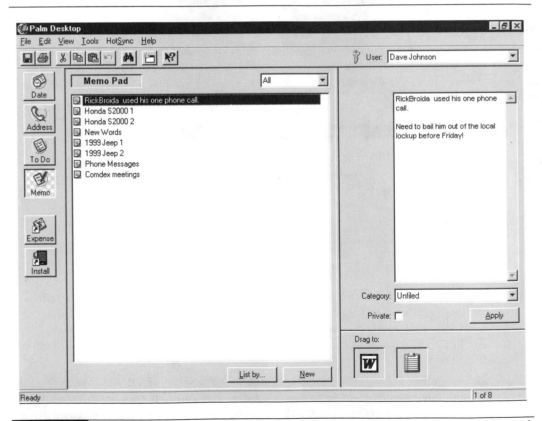

FIGURE 5-8 The Memo Pad works the same as on the Visor—but you can see the memo and the list onscreen at once

View Your Memo Pad

Because the Visor has pretty limited real estate on the small screen, you have to switch between the Memo List and Memo View. But on the Palm Desktop, you can see both at once. To see a memo, click the header on the left, and the memo's contents appear in the window on the right. Double-clicking a memo header has no effect.

Most of the Memo Pad's operation is pretty obvious. The controls aren't identical, though. Here are some things to remember:

- You can't rearrange your memos using the drag-and-drop technique described in Chapter 10.

- The List by button at the bottom of the screen lets you arrange memos alphabetically or in the order they are listed on the Visor.

- Use the Category list at the top of the screen to choose which category is displayed in the Memo List.

Create and Edit Memos

To create a new memo, just start typing (you can also click the New button at the bottom of the screen to do the same thing). The memo contents are entered in the box on the right side of the screen. You can also specify the category using the list box at the bottom-right side of the screen.

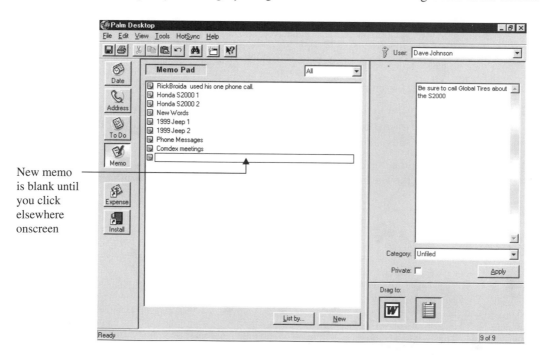

New memo is blank until you click elsewhere onscreen

TIP *Like the New button, the Apply button is superfluous. When you finish entering a memo, the changes are saved automatically when you click somewhere else on the screen. You never need to click the Apply button.*

Import Text Files

You don't have to create memos from scratch. Heck, you don't even have to cut-and-paste to create a memo. The Palm Desktop lets you import text files from elsewhere on the computer. To import a text file, do this:

1. Choose File | Import. The Import dialog box appears.

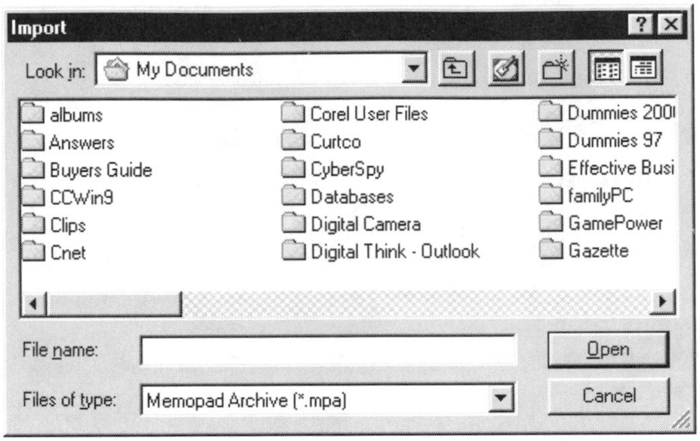

2. Choose Text (*.txt) from the "File of type" list box.

3. Find the file you want to import. It has to be a plain text file in ASCII format—no Word or other specially formatted file types are allowed. Select the file and click the Open button. Then you see the Specify Import Fields dialog box.

4. The text file should be ready to import, with the text lined up with the Memo field. If it isn't, drag the Memo field on the left until it lines up like the one shown next:

Specify Import Fields

Palm Fields

☑ Memo
☐ Private
☐ Category

Data in "ot01.txt"

Flat Screens Save Space, Energy by Da

OK

Cancel

Reset

Help

◀ Scan Records ▶   Record 1

Tip

To change the field order, click a field name on the left and drag it up or down the list to match the data on the right.

If the 'ALL' category is selected before importing records, the category field will be available in the field list. Drag the category field to match the data position on the right.

Only existing categories will be matched. Unmatched categories will be placed in 'Unfiled'.

Source file character set: Windows (ANSI)

5. Click OK.

6. If your text file is too large to fit in a single memo, the Palm Desktop automatically divides it into multiple memos. When it's done, you see this:

Palm Desktop

ⓘ   Updating Memo Pad...

2 Record(s) Imported.

OK

7. Click OK.

After importing the text file, you see it appear in the Memo List. If the memo had to be divided into more than one, then you see it appear with numerical designations, as in Figure 5-9.

 The memo entry in the list stays blank until you are done entering the memo. Don't panic because it looks blank as you type in information.

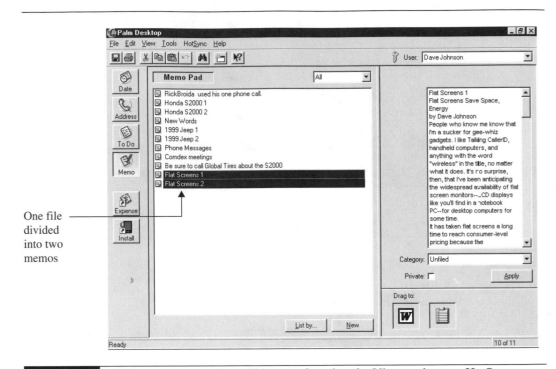

One file divided into two memos

FIGURE 5-9 This imported text file will be transferred to the Visor at the next HotSync. It was divided into multiple memos due to length

Use Memos in Other Applications

Just like the Date Book and To Do List, the Palm Desktop's Memo Pad can be used in other Windows applications. Specifically, you can drag one or more memos to the clipboard or Microsoft Word.

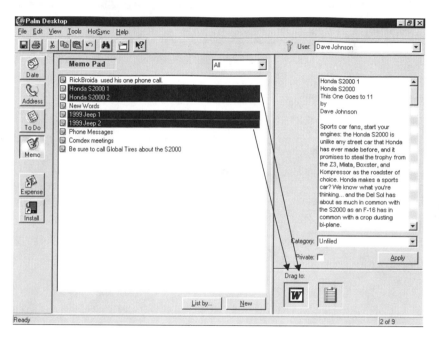

The following sections describe what happens if you drag-and-drop some memos.

The Clipboard

If you drag memos to the clipboard and release the mouse, the data is copied to the clipboard. You can then choose Edit | Paste in virtually any application and paste the memos into another document. When you paste the memos, they are separated by a page break so each memo appears on its own page.

Microsoft Word

Dragging memos to Word is similar to dragging them into the clipboard. The only real difference is each memo is preceded by its category, as you can see here:

If you didn't assign a category to the memo, it simply displays Unfiled.

> **TIP** *If you want to import memos into Word, but don't want or need the category heading, drag them to the clipboard instead—and then create a new Word document and paste the clipboard. That saves you the trouble of deleting the categories.*

Restore Deleted Data to Your Visor

As you use your Visor, you inevitably delete data you no longer need. Thankfully, a safety valve, like the Recycle Bin in Windows, lets you recover data you might have accidentally destroyed or later discovered you still need.

To take advantage of this capability, though, you need to *archive* data from your Visor when you mark it for deletion. Here's what we mean: select any item from your Address Book, Date

Book, To Do List, or Memo Pad, and then choose Record | Delete from the Visor's menu. You see something like this:

Note the option to Save Archive Copy on PC. If you want to be able to restore this data later, make sure that check box is selected before you tap OK.

The deleted data is transferred to your PC at the next HotSync session, where the data is then stored in an archive file on your hard disk. Unless you need to access this deleted data, you probably won't even know it's there. But if you do need to get to the data, the process for retrieving it isn't obvious. Here's what you need to do:

1. Open the Palm Desktop and select the module (such as the Date Book or Address Book) that contains the data you want to restore.

2. Choose File | Open Archive. You should see the Open Archive dialog box for whatever core application you have open.

3. Locate the archive from which you want to get deleted data. Note, a different folder exists for each core app and, inside each folder, is a separate file for each category of data that was on your Visor. You need to remember which category held the data you want—if not, you can always open them all and check the hard way. When you find the category with the data, select it and click the Open button.

4. Back on the Palm Desktop, you see the deleted (actually, the archived) data open in the application window. Select the items you want to restore to your Visor and choose Edit | Copy from the menu (see Figure 5-10). This copies the data to the clipboard.

5. Now you need to switch from the archived data to the current Visor data. Choose File | Open Current from the menu. Select the correct application and select the category where you want this data to go. Then choose Edit | Paste from the menu.

The data is now restored to your current Palm Desktop. When you HotSync, the data is also returned to your Visor.

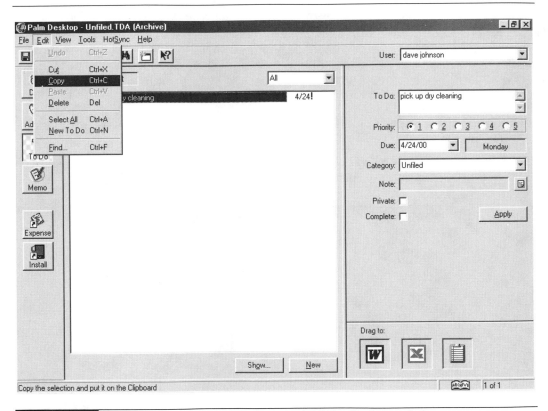

FIGURE 5-10　The archived data appears in a special Palm Desktop window

Palm Desktop or Outlook?

Dave: For my money, Outlook is the only way to go. The core apps may look great on your Visor, but that's because you only have 160 pixels to work with. On the desktop, it becomes apparent the Palm Desktop is a weak, weak, weak information manager. If you have Outlook on your PC already, I highly recommend you use it with your Visor instead of relying on the Palm Desktop. If you've already installed your Visor software and mistakenly specified the Palm Desktop as your information manager, you can reinstall it from the CD and you'll get an opportunity to load the conduits for Outlook.

Rick: Dave is a glutton for punishment. Palm Desktop is actually a capable information manager (especially the Macintosh version, though that's a different chapter . . .), one that's much easier to use than Outlook and a lot less intimidating to the entry-level user. If you need features like integrated e-mail and sophisticated calendaring, by all means use Outlook. But don't let Dave bully you into it. Palm Desktop may not be as comprehensive, but it's still an extremely adept PIM.

5

Chapter 6

Working with Palm Desktop for Macintosh

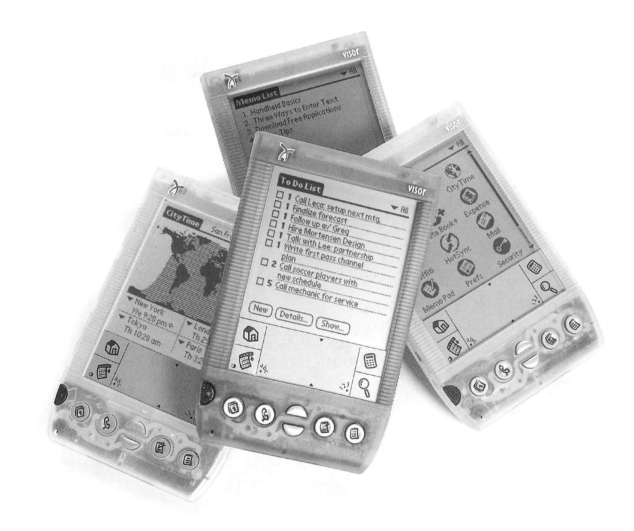

How to...

- ■ Recognize what's different about Palm Desktop for Macintosh
- ■ Create new appointments
- ■ Access the various calendar views
- ■ Set up untimed events
- ■ Create new contacts
- ■ Sort and filter contacts
- ■ Create new tasks
- ■ Sort and edit tasks
- ■ Create new notes (a.k.a. memos)
- ■ Attach notes to various entries
- ■ Sort and filter notes

As discussed in previous chapters, Palm Desktop for Macintosh is quite different than Palm Desktop for Windows. That's because the latter was written from scratch, while the former is based on Claris Organizer, a popular Mac personal information manager (PIM). If you're already familiar with that program, you'll have an easy time adapting to the Visor-oriented version. And even if you're not, you should find it fairly simple to master.

Just as the Visor has four core applications—Address Book, Date Book, Memo Pad, and To Do List—so does Palm Desktop for Macintosh have four corresponding core components. Their names are a bit different—Contact List, Calendar, Note List, and Task List, respectively—but their functionality is the same. Let's take a look at these four tools and learn the basics of how they work.

Date Book (a.k.a. Calendar)

Right off the bat, the Macintosh Date Book is something of a misnomer. The Mac version of the Palm Desktop calls the Date Book the *Calendar*. And that's okay; we're all adults and can adjust pretty well. Well, everyone except Rick, who insists on calling it the Date Book anyway.

To see the Calendar, you need to click the View Calendar button in the Palm Desktop toolbar. Like the Visor's Date Book button, you can click this button repeatedly to cycle among the Day View, Week View, and Month View. Also, note that you can see all the appointments you have scheduled for today by clicking the Instant Palm Desktop icon in the Desktop's menu bar.

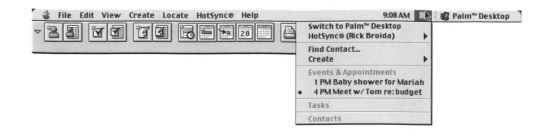

NOTE   *The Mac version of the Date Book has a lot of extra features that aren't directly applicable to the Visor. As a consequence, some HotSync mismatches occur. The Mac enables you to categorize appointments, for instance, but this feature doesn't HotSync because the Visor's Date Book doesn't do likewise.*

6

Use the Daily View

The Daily View (in Figure 6-1) is divided into two parts: the daily calendar and the Task View. You can create a new event in this view in two ways:

- ■ Click-and-drag the mouse to define the start and end time of the appointment. When you release the mouse, you can write in the appointment name.

- ■ Double-click in a time slot to display the Appointment dialog box. You can fill out the event time, alarm, and frequency information here. Click OK to save the appointment.

If you need to add an appointment in the same time slot as an existing event, you can either double-click or click-and-drag in the space between the event and the hour markers, at the left edge of the window.

Note that the Daily View stacks appointments in a cascading style when they overlap in time slots. Appointments look like they're "stacked" on top of one another.

Once you create an appointment, you can change its time slot by clicking-and-dragging it to a new location. If you need to change the duration, you can simply drag the top or bottom higher or lower. Double-click an appointment to open the Appointment dialog box, which sets alarm and timing options.

TIP   *To change the increment of the time slots (say, from 30-minute blocks to 10-minute blocks), choose Edit | Preferences and click the Calendars button. Then you can change the interval to suit your needs.*

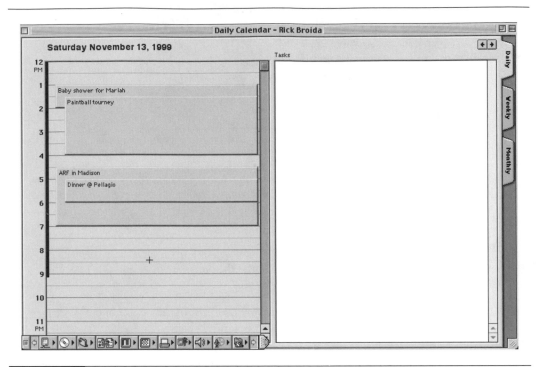

FIGURE 6-1   The Daily View stacks appointments in layers for better readability

Add an Untimed Event

In Palm Desktop for Macintosh, untimed events are actually called *Event Banners*. To add an Event Banner to the current day, double-click above the time slots, but below the date. You then see the Event Banner dialog box. Fill it in and click OK.

Use the Weekly and Monthly Views

The Weekly View (seen in Figure 6-2) works much the same as the Daily View. Adding and editing appointments—both Timed Events and Untimed Events—are done in the same way.

```
Weekly Calendar - Rick Broida
```

November 1999

	8 Monday	9 Tuesday	10 Wednesday	11 Thursday	12 Friday	13 Saturday	14 Sunday
12 PM				Kickbox			
1		PIT Conference				Baby shower for	
2		Conf call w ATT				Paintball tourney	
3							
4	Kids karate						
5						ARF in Madison	
6			Dinner : OG	+		Dinner @ Pellagio	
7							United flight 1123
8							
9 PM							

Tasks

FIGURE 6-2   The Weekly View is perhaps the most useful mode in the Calendar, thanks to its thoughtful design

TIP

If you want to see more or less days in the Weekly View, click the plus and minus buttons on the right edge of the window. Depending on your preferences, you can see as few as one day or as many as seven days onscreen at once.

The Monthly View (in Figure 6-3) has the most surprises. Unlike on the Visor, this Monthly View is fully editable and enables you to see the contents of your appointments (they don't just appear as gray blocks). Here's what you can do with the Monthly view:

■ Double-click an empty space to display this dialog box, then click the item you want to create in the designated day.

What do you want to create?

Task   Appointment   Event Banner

Cancel   OK

```
┌──────────────────────────────── Monthly Calendar - Rick Broida ────────────────────────────────┐
│ November 1999                                                                          ◄ ►  │
│  Sunday      Monday        Tuesday       Wednesday    Thursday     Friday        Saturday  │
│ 31          1             2             3            4            5            6            │
│                                                                   Employee Day             │
│                                                                                            │
│ 7           8             9             10           11           12           13           │
│             4 PM Kids karate  1PM PIT Conference  6 PM Dinner : OG  12 PM Kickbox  10:30 AM house  1 PM Baby shower │
│             7 PM new car!!!   1:30 PM Conf call                                inspection   for Mariah     │
│                               w ATT                                            4 PM Toni    5PM Dinner @ Pellagio │
│                                                                                            7 PM Meet w/ Tom │
│ 14          15            16            17           18           19           20           │
│ 7 AM United flight 1123                                                                    │
│ 1:30 PM Lunch with                                                                         │
│ Peak                                                                                       │
│ 21          22            23            24           25           26           27           │
│                                                                                            │
│ 28          29            30            1            2            3            4            │
│                           4 PM end of month                                                │
│                           budgeting                                                        │
└────────────────────────────────────────────────────────────────────────────────────────────┘
```

FIGURE 6-3   You can add or edit appointments directly from the Calendar's Monthly View

- Click-and-drag an appointment to move it to another time.
- Double-click an appointment to open the Appointment dialog box and edit the event details.
- Double-click the gray date bar across the top of any day to switch to the Daily View.

TIP   *Gray events in the Weekly and Monthly views are Untimed Events.*

Address Book (a.k.a. Contact List)

Like the other applications in Palm Desktop for Macintosh, the Address Book doesn't precisely match the name or even the function of its related Visor core app. On the Mac, the Address Book is called Contact List. Its appearance is quite different as well. To see the Contact List program, you need to click the View Contact List button in the Palm Desktop toolbar.

The Contact List is essentially the only view or module in the program—you needn't learn to switch between multiple views to use all the features in the Address Book. The Contact List is visible in Figure 6-4. As you can see, the Contact List is made of just a few parts:

- A view menu for choosing which memorized view you want to use.
- A set of filters for customizing the view.
- A button to revert to displaying all the contacts.
- A display window in which you can see contacts and their information.

You can create a new contact in the Address Book in two ways:

- Double-click any blank space in the Contact List window.
- Click the Create Contact icon in the Palm Desktop toolbar.

6

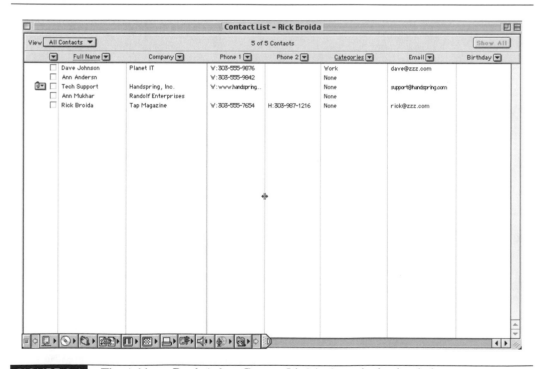

	Full Name	Company	Phone 1	Phone 2	Categories	Email	Birthday
☐	Dave Johnson	Planet IT	W:303-555-9876		Work	dave@zzz.com	
☐	Ann Andersn		W:303-555-9842		None		
☐	Tech Support	Handspring, Inc.	W:www.handspring...		None	support@handspring.com	
☐	Ann Mukhar	Randolf Enterprises			None		
☐	Rick Broida	Tap Magazine	W:303-555-7654	H:303-987-1216	None	rick@zzz.com	

FIGURE 6-4   The Address Book (a.k.a. Contact List) is deceptively simple in appearance

Whichever way you choose to create a new contact entry, filling out the contact information is painless, thanks to an excellent interface. The Contact dialog box is composed of five sections: Name, Phones, Work Address, Home Address, and Other Information. As you complete each section, you can use the TAB key to move from one field to the next. Complete as many or as few of the fields as you need to for each contact.

TIP *The first phone number in the list (not the first one you complete) is the one the Visor uses in Address Book as the main number. Also, to synchronize properly with the Visor, you should enter the contact's e-mail address only in the Other Information field. Don't use one of the phone number fields for e-mail.*

How to ... Work with Third-Party Software on a Mac

As you begin to scour the Web for third-party Palm OS software to use on your Visor, you may notice that many of the files you download are "zipped." That means they've been compressed using the Zip format, which is popular among Windows users but incompatible with the Mac OS. Thus you'll need a third-party decompression utility that supports the Zip format. We recommend Aladdin Systems' Stuffit Deluxe (www.aladdinsys.com), which will let you access zipped files.

Sort and Filter Your Contacts

You can customize the way your contacts are displayed by using the controls at the top of each column. If you want to see only some of the contacts, for instance, you can filter the display to show only certain entries. You can establish filters based on any column. To see contacts in your own area code, for instance, choose Phone 1 and set the filter accordingly. Here's how:

1. Click the menu for the column you want to use as the filter criteria. You should see the filter and sorting menu.

2. If the criteria you want to sort appears in the menu, click it. If not, click Custom Filter. That displays the Custom Filter dialog box.

3. Choose the filter operator that will accomplish what you want to do. If you want to display contacts who have an area code of 303, for instance, choose Starts With in the Filter Contacts Whose Company drop-lown list and enter 303 in the field. If you want to display contacts who work at a company called OmniCorp, then choose Contains and type OmniCorp in the blank field.

4. Click OK to close the dialog box and display the results.

TIP *You can create detailed filters by combining different columns. You can apply a filter to both the Phone 1 and Company columns, for instance. Anything that passes the first filter must then also pass the second filter to appear in the Contact List.*

If you create a filter set you want to use often, you can tell the Contact List to memorize it. To do this, click the View menu and choose Memorize View. Give this view a name, and then you can display it in the future without going thorough the process of setting up one or more filters every time. To exit this memorized view and revert to the normal view, click Show All.

You can also sort your results alphabetically. To sort, decide which column you want to use as the sorting column. Then click the column menu and choose Sort.

To Do List (a.k.a. Task List)

This should come as no particular surprise: The To Do List on the Mac is quite different than the Visor version—after all, they come from two different application heritages. On the plus side, the Mac is powerful and easy to use, so we don't think you'll complain a whole lot about it.

On the Mac, the To Do List is called the *Task List*. To see the Task List, you need to click the View Task List button in the Palm Desktop toolbar. The Task List, which is shown in Figure 6-5, is composed of a few key elements:

- A View control for displaying only specific tasks.

- Filters for sorting and displaying the tasks, found at the top of each column.

- The task entry, which includes the name, priority, date, category, completion status, and note.

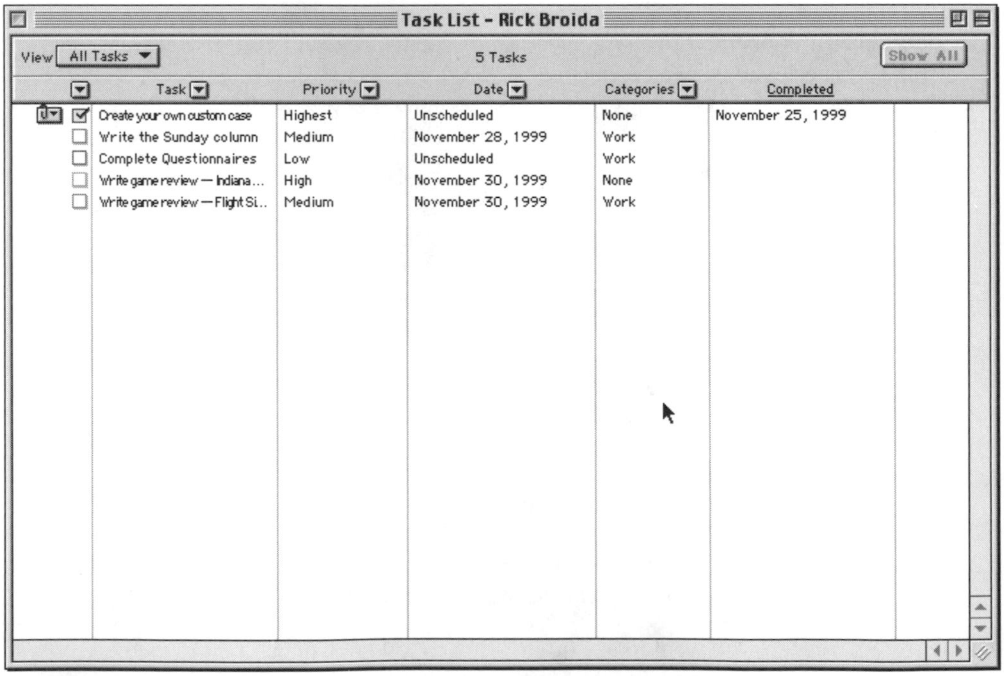

FIGURE 6-5   The Task List displays all the pertinent information about your tasks in one screen

Create and Edit Tasks

You can create a new task in either of two ways:

■ Double-click anywhere in the Task View. The Task dialog box appears, which you can fill in; then click OK when you're done.

■ Click the Create Task icon in the Palm Desktop toolbar.

The Task dialog box has everything you need to complete your task, but it looks somewhat different than the Palm equivalent.

Look for these elements:

■ **Priority** The Mac uses a word-based priority system (Highest to Lowest) instead of numbers (1 to 5). Highest corresponds to 1; Lowest corresponds to 5.

■ **Categories** Two categories are available in the Mac's Palm Desktop, but only the first one is used by the Visor when you HotSync.

■ **Carry Over After Due** Use this item to make sure the task is still visible after its deadline has passed. On the Visor, though, tasks are always carried over anyway, so it ignores this option.

■ **Remind** You can set up Palm Desktop to remind you about upcoming tasks, but the Visor doesn't use this feature.

> **TIP** *If you need to create a task like the one you just made—complete with scheduling and priority information—use the Add Another button on the Task dialog box instead of clicking OK. The current task gets saved and a new task is created in the same mold as the one you just made.*

Repeat a Task

You can create a task that, like Repeating Events in the calendar, occurs over and over on a schedule you determine. To do this, create a new task and click Repeat Task in the Task dialog box. Select the kind of repetition you want from the list menu and you can set the task to repeat indefinitely or until a date you specify.

Task

☑ **Task** Planet IT meeting

Priority Low ☐ **Completed**

☑ **Schedule Task**   ☑ **Repeat Task**

Date November 1, 1999   Every Day

☐ Carry Over After Due   **Until** November 28, 1999

☐ Remind

Categories Work

[?] [Delete...] [Add Another]   [Cancel] [**OK**]

NOTE

All the instances of a repeating task are transferred to your Visor when you HotSync, but they aren't related to each other on the Visor. This means if you later decide to change the series, the change will occur to only one task, not all of them. For this reason, use Repeating Tasks with care.

Sort and Filter Your Tasks

You can customize the way your tasks are displayed by using the controls at the top of each column. If you only want to see some of the tasks, for instance, you can filter the display to only show certain entries. You can establish filters based on any column. To see only those tasks with a priority of Highest, for instance, choose Highest from the Priority column. Here's how:

1. Click the menu for the column you want to use as the filter criteria. You should see the filter and sorting menu.

Task List - Rick Broida

View All Tasks ▼   Show All

☐	Task ▼	Priority	▼	Categories ▼	Completed

	☑	Create your own custom case	Highest	None	November 25, 1999
	☐	Write the Sunday column	Medium	Work	
	☐	Complete Questionnaires	Low	Work	
	☐	Write game review — Indiana...	High	None	
	☐	Planet IT meeting	Low	Work	
	☐	Planet IT meeting	Low	November 2, 1999	Work
	☐	Planet IT meeting	Low	November 3, 1999	Work
	☐	Planet IT meeting	Low	November 4, 1999	Work
	☐	Planet IT meeting	Low	November 5, 1999	Work
	☐	Planet IT meeting	Low	November 6, 1999	Work
	☐	Planet IT meeting	Low	November 7, 1999	Work
	☐	Planet IT meeting	Low	November 8, 1999	Work

Sort
• No Filter
  Custom Filter...

  Highest
  High
  Medium
  Low
  Lowest

2. If the criteria you want to sort appears in the menu, click it. If not, click Custom filter. This displays the Custom Filter dialog box.

3. Choose the filter operator that can accomplish what you want to do. If you want to display tasks that include the word "meeting," for instance, choose Contains and enter **meeting** in the field.

```
═══════════ Custom Filter on Title ═══════════

Filter Tasks whose Title

 Contains          ⬍

 meeting                                        ◀

 ?                           Cancel      OK
```

6

> **TIP**   *You can create detailed filters by combining different columns. You can apply a filter to both the Task and Priority columns, for instance. Anything that passes the first filter must then also pass the second filter to appear in the Task List.*

4. Click OK to close the dialog box and display the results.

If you create a filter set you want to use often, you can tell the Task Book to memorize it. To do this, click the View menu and choose Memorize View. Give this view a name, and then you can display it in the future without going thorough the process of setting up one or more filters every time. To exit this memorized view and revert to the normal view, click Show All.

You can also sort your results alphabetically or numerically. To sort, decide which column you want to use as the sorting column. Then click the column menu and choose Sort.

A Better To Do List

We hear what you're saying (figuratively, of course): the Visor's To Do List application isn't powerful enough. Well, there's a great alternative called ToDo PLUS from Hands High Software (www.handshigh.com). This core-app replacement enables you to attach freehand drawings to your tasks, use templates to customize your entries, add alarms (a major plus), and much more. One of its most interesting features is a comprehensive set of filters that enable you to display your tasks in a variety of useful ways. Give it a try and you may never want to use the built-in task list again.

Memo Pad (a.k.a. Note List)

The Note List is the Mac's unique name for the Memo Pad. And not just the name is different—this module is strikingly different than the Visor's equivalent core application. That's good, though, for the most part—if you use Palm Desktop as your primary information manager, you'll find that Note List is a powerful and flexible tool for creating long or short notes. In addition, the very concept of attaching notes is more open-ended on the Mac, as you see in a few moments. First, though, let's open Palm Desktop and display the Note List to review its major features.

You can see the Note List, which is composed of a few key elements, in Figure 6-6:

- A View control for displaying only specific notes
- Filters for sorting and displaying notes, found at the top of each column
- The Note list, which displays both the title and the first line of the note's contents
- An attachment icon that indicates whether the note is already attached to another item

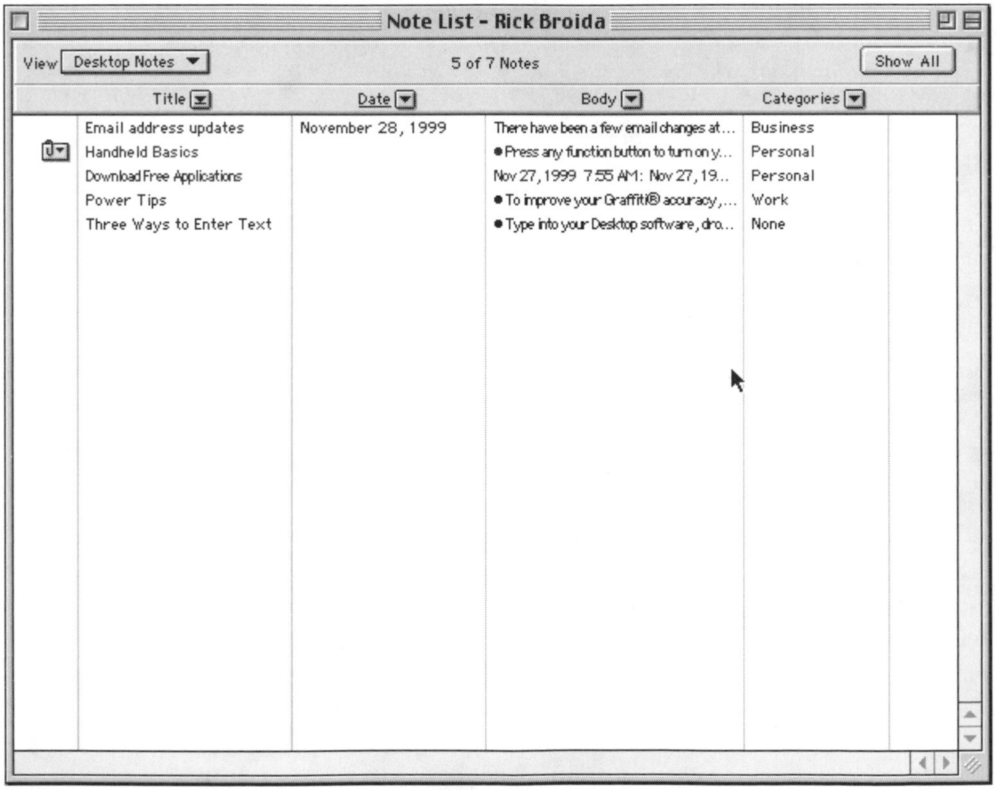

Note List - Rick Broida
View
Desktop Notes
5 of 7 Notes
Show All
Title
Date
Body
Categories
Email address updates
November 28, 1999
There have been a few email changes at...
Business
Handheld Basics
• Press any function button to turn on y...
Personal
Download Free Applications
Nov 27, 1999 7:55 AM: Nov 27, 19...
Personal
Power Tips
• To improve your Graffiti® accuracy,...
Work
Three Ways to Enter Text
• Type into your Desktop software, dra...
None

FIGURE 6-6 The Note List has the same filtering and sorting tools as you've seen in the Contact List and Task List

Creating and Editing Notes

You can use notes on the Mac just like on the Visor—to track phone messages, leave yourself little "sticky" notes, or just about anything else. To create a new note, you can use either one of these techniques:

- ■ Double-click anywhere in the Note View. The Note dialog box appears, which you can fill in and close when you're done (there's no OK button to save the changes).
- ■ Click the Create Note icon in the Palm Desktop toolbar.

To create a note, fill out the Title field, and then enter information in the body of the message. The title becomes the first line of the note on the Visor. In addition, watch for these other differences between the Visor and Mac versions of the note:

6

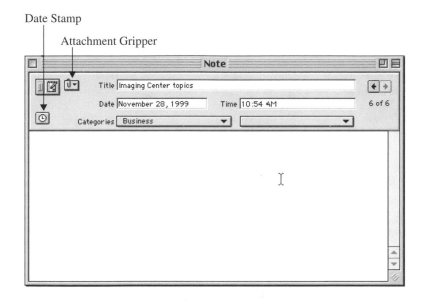

- ■ **Date and Time Fields**   The date and time fields don't get transferred to the Visor because it doesn't remember when you created a note.
- ■ **Date Stamping**   A date-stamp icon on the Note dialog box inserts the current date and time in the body of the note. You can use this to create a log or a journal-like note. This data is stored in the body of the message, so it does get transferred to the Visor during a HotSync.
- ■ **Categories**   Two categories are available in the Mac's Palm Desktop, but only the first one is used by the Visor when you HotSync.

- **Length**   The Mac can accommodate extremely long notes, but only the first 4,096 characters are transferred to the Visor. This is an example of the kind of "truncating" mentioned in Chapter 3.

- **Attachment Gripper**   You can drag the gripper to another item to attach the note—we discuss this in the next section.

Attaching Notes

Attaching notes is a bit different on the Mac than on the PC or Visor. Specifically, you're not limited to notes but, instead, you can attach any kind of item to any other kind of item. You can attach a note to a contact, of course—that even works on the Visor and Palm Desktop for Windows—but you can also attach a contact to a note or a task to a calendar appointment. There's no limit or restriction on how you attach stuff.

> **TIP**   *This may sound odd, but you can actually attach a memo to another memo. This can come in handy if you have related information in different memos and want to connect them to each other.*

This flexibility makes managing your life on the Mac easy, but an important caveat exists: most of those attachments won't get transferred to the Visor properly. Remember these rules about attachments and the Visor:

- The only kind of attachment that will HotSync to your Visor is a note attached to an item created in one of the other three primary apps (Address Book, To Do List, or Date Book). Any other kind of attachment (like a task attached to an appointment) is ignored during the HotSync.

- For the note to attach, you must name it exactly like one of these titles: **Handheld Note: Address Book, Handheld Note: Date Book,** or **Handheld Note: To Do Item,** as seen in Figure 6-7. After you name the note with one of those titles, then you can attach it to another item.

You can attach a note or other item in the Palm Desktop in several ways. Each one has its advantages: use the method that works best for you at any given time.

- **Drag an item onto another item**   If you can see both windows onscreen at once, then the easiest way to attach an item to another one is to grab the first item, drag it onto the second, and then release the mouse (see Figure 6-8).

- **Use the Attach To menu item**   Open the item you want to attach to something else, and then click the paperclip icon. Choose Attach To | Existing Item. You should see the Attach Existing Item dialog box appear at the bottom of the screen. Now open the item you want to attach it to, and drag the item from the Attach Existing Item dialog box onto it. This sounds convoluted, but it makes sense when you can't easily display both items onscreen at once.

Note

Attach To ▸   Existing Item...
Detach...
     New Appointment...
Date   New Task...   6 of 8
     New Contact...
Categories   New Note...
     New Event Banner...
     File...

● To improve your Graffiti®

● In Date Book Day View, press the scroll button on your handheld to move backward and forward one day at a time. To move an event to another day or time, tap Details and change the day or time there.

● In Memo and To Do, you don't have to tap New to create a new record; just start writing. In Date Book, this creates a new UNTIMED event. To create a new TIMED event, just write the time in the Graffiti number area.

● To set up your business card for beaming, go to Address Book and select your own name & address. Tap Menu. Then tap Select Business Card.

● To quickly find an application icon in the Launcher, switch to the All category and use Graffiti to write the first letter of the application's title. The icons with titles starting with that letter spring to view.

Attach Existing Item

To attach this note to another item:
1) Locate the other item.
2) Drag this note onto that item.

| Power Tips |

[?]   [Cancel]

6

Note List – Rick Broida

View [All Notes ▼]   8 of 8 Notes   [Show All]

Title ▼	Date ▼	Body ▼	Categories ▼
Imaging Center topics	November 28, 1999		Business
Email address updates	November 28, 1999	There have been a few email changes at...	Business
Handheld Basics		● Press any function button to turn on y...	Personal
Download Free Applications		Nov 27, 1999 7:55 AM: Nov 27, 19...	Personal
Handheld Note: Address Book		Check the User Guide on the CD-ROM fo...	None
Power Tips		● To improve your Graffiti® accuracy,...	Work
Three Ways to Enter Text		● Type into your Desktop software, dra...	None
Handheld Note: To Do List		Visit our web site at www.handspring.c...	None

FIGURE 6-7   You need to give your memo a specific name if you want to attach it to another item and have it appear on the Visor

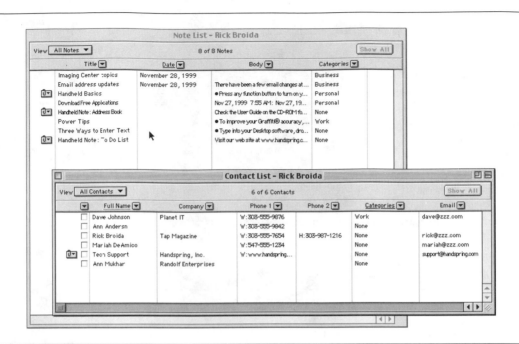

FIGURE 6-8   You can drag-and-drop items between Palm Desktop windows

■ **Drag an item to the toolbar**   If you want to attach an existing item to one you haven't created yet, use this method. Grab the item and drag it to the Palm Desktop toolbar. As you move the item across the toolbar, you see it highlights the Create icons for each kind of item. Drop it on the icon that represents the item you want to create. The new item appears with the old item automatically attached. Or, you can achieve the same result by clicking the item's paperclip icon and choosing Attach To. Then choose the appropriate item, such as New Appointment or New Task.

Sorting and Filtering Your Notes

You can customize the way notes appear onscreen by using the controls at the top of each column. This feature works just like the filtering tools you've probably already seen in the Contact List and Task List. Essentially, it enables you to hide note entries you don't want to see, using a set of easy-to-use filters. Here's how it works:

1. Decide what basis you want to use to filter your notes. Suppose, for instance, you want to see only notes with a specific word in the title. You'd obviously want to use the Title column. Click the menu for the appropriate column. You should see the filter and sorting menu.

2. If the criteria you want to filter appears in the menu, click it (if you were displaying only today's notes, for instance, there's an entry for that in the Date menu). If not, click Custom filter. That displays the Custom Filter dialog box.

3. Choose the filter operator that will accomplish what you want to do. If you want to display memos that include the word "home," for instance, choose Contains and enter **home** in the field.

4. Click OK to close the dialog box and display the results.

> TIP
> *You can create detailed filters by combining different columns. You can apply a filter to both the Title and Date columns, for instance. Anything that passes the first filter must then also pass the second filter to appear in the Memo List.*

If you create a filter set you want to use often, you can tell the Memo List to memorize it. To do this, click the View menu and choose Memorize View. Give this view a name, and then you can display it in the future without going through the process of setting up one or more filters every time. To exit this memorized view and revert to the normal view, click Show All.

The View menu includes another option you may want to use. As we already discussed, attached notes on the Visor look different and can get in the way. That's why the View menu features an option to display only Desktop Notes, which you can see in Figure 6-9. If you choose this option, an entry that conforms to the Visor standard for attachments—that is, it starts with the words Handheld Notes:—won't appear in the list.

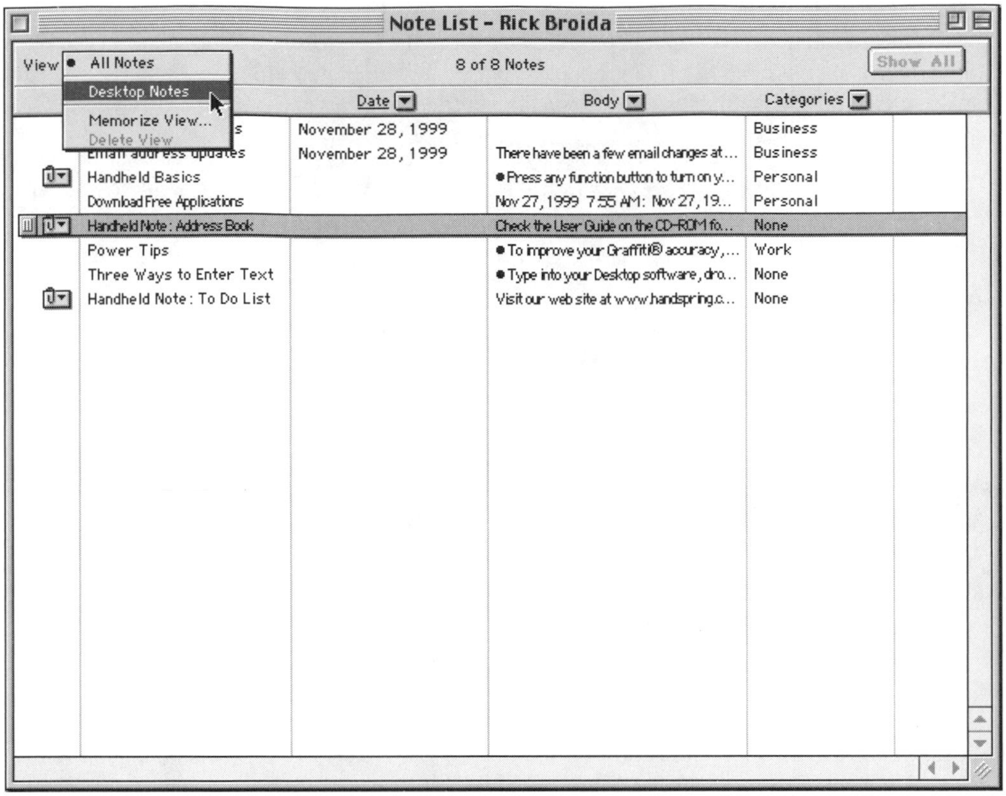

View	● All Notes		8 of 8 Notes	Show All
	Desktop Notes			
	Memorize View...	Date ▼	Body ▼	Categories ▼
	Delete View	November 28, 1999		Business
	s	November 28, 1999	There have been a few email changes at...	Business
	Email address updates			
▼	Handheld Basics		● Press any function button to turn on y...	Personal
	Download Free Applications		Nov 27, 1999 7:55 AM: Nov 27, 19...	Personal
▼	Handheld Note: Address Book		Check the User Guide on the CD-ROM fo...	None
	Power Tips		● To improve your Graffiti® accuracy, ...	Work
	Three Ways to Enter Text		● Type into your Desktop software, dro...	None
▼	Handheld Note: To Do List		Visit our web site at www.handspring.c...	None

FIGURE 6-9   With this menu option you can display all the notes in Palm Desktop or just Desktop Notes

Part II

Get Things Done

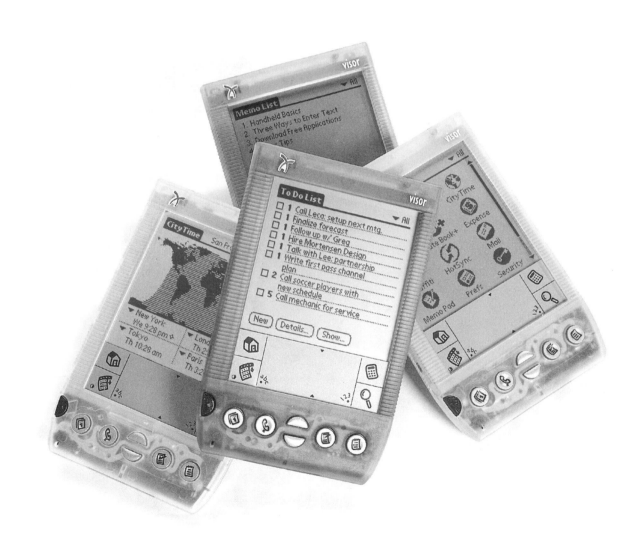

Chapter 7

The Date Book

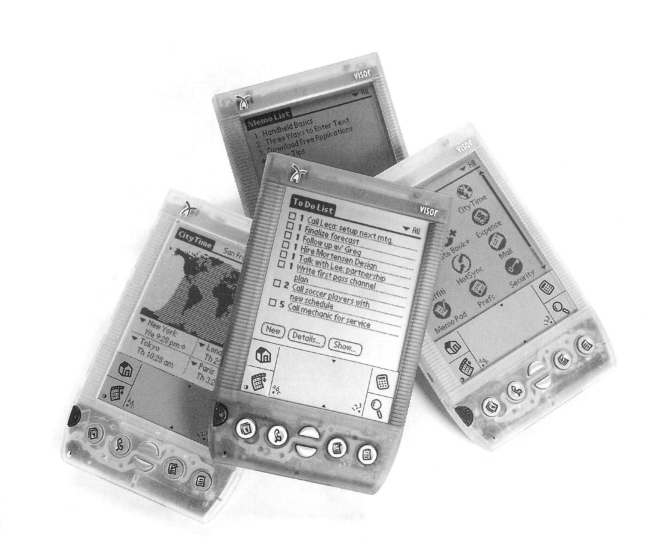

How to...

- Use the Day, Week, and Month Views
- Customize the Date Book's appearance
- Add appointments to the Date Book
- Beam an appointment to someone else
- Create an appointment using the Address Book
- Create repeating events
- Add a Note to an appointment
- Make an appointment private
- Edit appointments in the Date Book
- Delete events in the Date Book
- Set an alarm for an appointment
- Use the Date Book+
- Use floating events
- Add events with templates

Are you busy on Tuesday at 3 P.M.? If you had your Visor handy, you'd probably know the answer to that question. In an informal survey, we found the Date Book is the single most popular core application on the Visor. In a way, many people buy their Visor just for its scheduling prowess.

The Date Book is a modern miracle. That may sound like an overstatement, but consider how useful it is. It can track all your appointments. It can show you your schedule by day, week, or month. It handles recurring appointments and can alarm you about upcoming events. It synchronizes precisely with your desktop calendar. And it all fits in the palm of your hand. It's better, Rick might tell you, than *Star Trek*. Dave might say it's better than discovering a rare Velvet Underground song—but he'd be lying.

Oh, and one more thing—if you already know your way around the Date Book from a previous Palm device, consider skipping straight to the end of the chapter, where we talk about the Date Book+. It's an exclusive Visor application, and it's chock full of tools for helping you get even more organized.

View Your Appointments

When you switch to the Date Book, by default it starts by showing you any appointments you have for today. You can get to the Date Book in two ways:

■   Press the Date Book button on your Visor's case. It has an icon of a calendar page on it.

DateBook

■   Tap the onscreen Date Book icon in the Visor's applications screen.

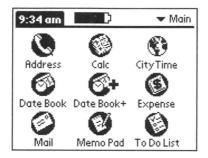

Navigate the Day View

When you start the Date Book, the first thing you see is the Day View, shown in Figure 7-1. You can see it shows the currently selected date in the tab at the top of the screen. This isn't necessarily today's view; it shows the date of whatever day you're looking at. Next to that are seven icons, one for each day of the week.

> **TIP**   *Tap the date tab to see the current time. If you use Menu Hack, which enables you to access menus by tapping the top of the screen (see Chapter 18), this trick won't work.*

In the middle of the screen, you see the current day's calendar. You can enter new events on the blank lines. If you have any appointments already entered, note that long appointments (ones that last for more than 30 minutes) have duration brackets. *Duration brackets* appear to the immediate left of the appointment time and show you what time an appointment is scheduled to end.

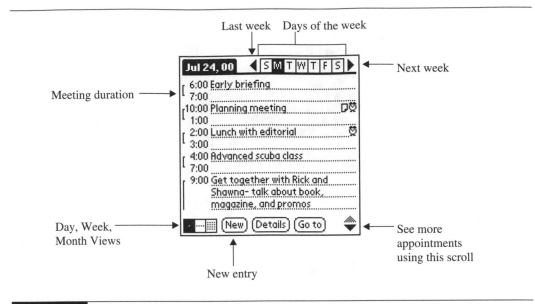

Last week   Days of the week

Next week

Meeting duration

Day, Week,
Month Views

See more
appointments
using this scroll

New entry

FIGURE 7-1   The Day View

Other icons appear near appointments as well. In fact, you should get used to seeing three of them:

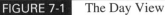

■ **Alarms**   This icon indicates you'll get notified by the Visor alarm sound that the appointment is due to start.

■ **Notes**   If you attach a note to your appointment (perhaps with directions to the location or agenda details, for instance) you see this icon.

■ **Repeating meetings**   If the meeting is configured to happen more than once, this icon appears.

If you tap on any of these icons, you see the Event Details dialog box, which we talk about in detail later in this chapter.

Finally, the bottom of the screen has several important controls. There are icons to change the current view, as well as create a new appointment, view the Event Details dialog box, and go to a specific day.

Changing View Options

You have to love the Visor's ingenuity. (Actually, you really do have to love its ingenuity. A recently passed Federal law now requires it. And who said Congress doesn't ever legislate meaningful reform?)

By default, the Day View does something very clever. If you have 11 lines or less of appointment information (that's as much as the Visor can display onscreen at once), then the Date Book compresses your calendar by not showing blank times of the day.

That way you can have appointments that span from 6 A.M. to 11 P.M. and have them all appear onscreen without needing to scroll at all. However, whenever it can, it includes blank events between existing events for better readability.

What happens if you have such a busy day that all your appointments won't fit onscreen at once, even with the Visor's compression in place? You need to scroll. There's a scroll button at the bottom of the screen for seeing more appointments in the same day. It only appears when needed.

NOTE *Lots of users try using the Scroll button on the case to see more appointments in the same day. Of course, pressing the scroll button simply changes the view to the next day.*

Not everyone likes the Day View compression. If you frequently add events to your schedule during the day, for instance, you might want to have blank lines available for all the hours of the day. If that sounds like you, here's how to turn off compression:

1. Choose Options | Display Options from the menu.

2. Uncheck the Compress Day View option.

Display Options ❶

Day View:
☑ **Show Time Bars**
☐ **Compress Day View**

Month View:
☑ **Show Timed Events**
☑ **Show Untimed Events**
☑ **Show Daily Repeating Evts**

(OK) (Cancel)

3. Tap the OK button.

Now when you use the Day View, you see all the blank lines for your day. On the other hand, using this setting virtually guarantees you'll need to use the scroll button to surf around your daily schedule.

When you configure your Day View, you also have to decide what kind of person you are. Are you:

■ Neat and orderly—and opt for less clutter whenever possible?

■ Impatient—and want everything at your fingertips all the time?

■ Apathetic—and don't want to bother changing the default settings?

You can change the display of the Date Book to accommodate the way you want your Visor to look. If you are the neat and orderly sort, for instance, you might want the Date Book to be a blank screen unless it actually has appointments already scheduled for that day.

Jul 26, 00 ◀ S M T W T F S ▶
6:00 ....
12:00 Conference with Peter ....
1:00 ....

(New) (Details) (Go to)

If that's the case, choose Options | Preferences and set the Start Time and End Time to be the same thing—like 7:00 A.M. After configuring your Visor in this way, you should find that days without appointments are essentially a blank screen with just a single blank line—the time you set in Preferences.

   More of an impatient sort? Then choose Options | Preferences and configure your Start Time and End Time to span the full range of hours you plan to use. If you ever add events to the evening, for instance, set the End Time for 10 P.M. or later. That way, you have a blank line available immediately where you can write a new entry.

If all this sounds extremely pointless to you, just leave the Preferences alone. The default settings cover most of the hours you routinely need.

Get Around the Days of the Week

As you might expect, you can change the view to a different day in several ways. You can figure most of them out on your own, but we bet you can't find 'em all. Here's how you can do it—use the method that's easiest for you:

- Switch to a specific day by tapping the appropriate day icon at the top of the screen (see Figure 7-1).

- To move ahead one week at a time, use the forward button to the right of the week icons, as seen in Figure 7-1. If you are currently on Tuesday, for instance, tapping the arrow takes you one week ahead to the following Tuesday. Obviously, you can go back a week at a time by tapping the Back arrow instead.

- To move forward or back one day at a time, press the scroll button. If you hold it down, you scroll quickly, like holding down a repeating key on a computer keyboard.

- If you want to find a specific day quickly, tap the Go to button and enter the date directly in the Go to Date dialog box. When you use Go to, remember to choose the year and month first, because you go to the selected date as soon as you tap a date.

- To get back to "today" from somewhere else in the calendar, tap Go to, and then tap Today on the Go to Date calendar dialog box.

Navigate the Week View

Now that you're used to the Day View, we'll let you in on a little secret: there's more where that came from. In addition to viewing your appointments by day, you can also see them by week. That's where the three icons at the bottom of the screen come in. Tap the middle one to change the view.

TIP   *The Date Book button on the Visor's case also serves as a view changer. Every time you press the button, the view cycles from Day View to Week View to Month View and back to Day View again.*

This screen uses a grid to display your appointments. The top of the grid is labeled by day and date, while the left side contains time blocks throughout the day. The gray blocks represent scheduled events.

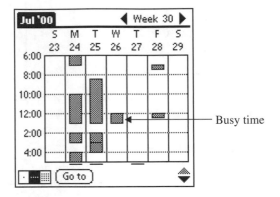

— Busy time

Obviously, this view isn't ideal for determining your daily schedule in detail, but it is handy for getting your week's availability at a glance. Use it to pick a free day or a clear afternoon, for instance, when you're in a meeting and trying to choose a good time to get together with an equally busy person.

Here's an overview of most important elements of this view:

- **Changing weeks**   You can change weeks using either the arrows at the top of the screen or the scroll button. If you need to skip directly to a specific week, use the Go to button. This screen cleverly highlights an entire week at a time; tap anywhere in a given week to go to that time period.
- **See more of the day**   To see more of the day, use the arrow at the bottom of the screen.
- **Go to a day in the Day View**   To go directly to a specific day, tap the day/date label at the top of the grid.
- **Seeing Untimed Events**   A dot under the date represents an Untimed Event. An Untimed Event is something you've associated with the day, but not at a specific time (like Ellen's birthday, for instance).

■ **Reveal appointments**   You can see exactly what a particular gray block is by tapping on it. The appointment details stay on the screen as long as you hold the stylus on the block and for a few seconds afterwards.

■ **Choosing free time**   If you tap a part of the grid in which there is no scheduled appointment, the Visor switches to the Day View in inset mode, so you can add a new appointment at the designated time.

TIP   *We haven't talked about creating or editing appointments yet, but here's a handy tip for moving appointments around on the Week View screen. If you have an appointment you need to move to another time anywhere in the week, tap the event, hold the stylus down, and then drag it to another place on the schedule. As you move the block around, you can see exactly to what time the event is being moved. To abort this process without changing anything, move the block back to its original location without lifting the stylus.*

Navigate the Month View

If you press the Date Book button again or tap the Month View icon on the screen, you are transported to the last of the three views. The Month View is even more compact than the Week View: it displays an entire month at a time in a familiar, month-like grid.

The first thing you might notice about this view is the blocks of busy time are now replaced by little hash marks. You can tap on these marks to see the appointment details because they don't actually represent individual events. Instead, they show you appointments you have scheduled in the morning, afternoon, and evening, as seen in Figure 7-2. If you tap any day in this view, you're automatically taken to the Day View for that day.

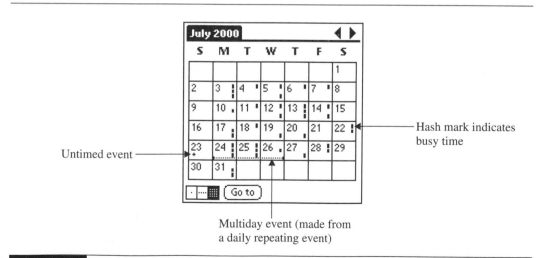

Untimed event

Hash mark indicates busy time

Multiday event (made from a daily repeating event)

FIGURE 7-2   The Month View packs a lot of general information about your schedule into a little space

In addition to appointment marks, two other event indicators are on this screen:

■ **Untimed events**   Small plus signs under the date indicate the presence of an Untimed Event.

■ **Mutliday events**   If you create an event that spans more than a single day, you see a series of dots under the days to connect them into a single event.

NOTE   *By default, both of these special display features are disabled on your Visor. To turn them on, choose Options | Display Options from the Day View screen. Then in the Month View section of the Display Options dialog box, enable Show Untimed Events and Show Daily Repeating Events.*

Create New Appointments

Now that you've mastered the fine art of viewing your schedule from every conceivable angle and perspective, you probably want to know how to add new events to the schedule. As you can probably guess, you can add appointments to your Visor in two ways: via the Palm Desktop—which we talk about in Chapters 5 and 6—and right from the Visor itself. While you can choose a meeting time from the Week View, it's important to know that the only place you can actually enter data about a meeting is from the Day View.

Add Timed Events

Most of the time, your schedule will be full of meetings that take place at a specific time of day, like:

```
Meet with Susan from accounting
3-5 pm in Conference Room A.
```

This is what the Visor refers to as a timed event—but most people just call it an appointment. In any event, you can add an event like this to your Visor in several ways:

■ **Use the New button**   Tap the New button on the Day View. Then, within the Set Time dialog box, select a Start Time and an End Time, and then tap OK. Now enter the meeting information on the blank line provided for you.

■ **Just start writing**   Tap on a blank line that corresponds to the meeting start time and write the details of the meeting on the line.

■ **Pick a time from the Week View**   If you're looking for a free space to place a meeting, the Week View is a good place to look because it gives you the "big picture" of your schedule. When you find a spot you like, tap it and the Day View should open to the desired start time. Then write in your meeting info.

TIP   *If you need to start your meeting at a strange time—like 4:45 P.M., then you should tap the New button and choose the time directly, or find a time close to when you want the meeting to start in the Day View and tap the time itself. The Set Time dialog box will open, and then you can modify it to suit your timing needs.*

A Closer Look at the Set Time Dialog Box

The Set Time dialog box is an important tool for creating appointments. To set a time in this dialog box, tap an hour (in the selector on the left) and a minute (on the right) for the Start Time. Note, you can change you mind as often as you like, but the time must be in increments no smaller than five minutes. You can't set a Start Time of 11:33 A.M., for instance.

When you have set the Start Time, tap the End Time box and configure that time as well. By default, the End Time is initially an hour later than the Start Time—if that's okay, tap OK and be done with it.

You can also use Graffiti to set the time, a real convenience for folks who are faster at writing than tapping. Write the hour and minutes as you normally would: 335 is interpreted as 3:35, for instance. To change between A.M. and P.M., write an *A* or a *P* in the letter side of the Graffiti area.

If you need to back up and start over, use the backspace gesture. When you want to move between the Start Time and End Time box, use the Next Field gesture. Finally, when you're done entering times, use the Return gesture to simulate tapping OK. You'll find yourself back at the Day View, ready to write in your meeting name.

> **TIP** *A fast way to create a new event at a specific time is to write the start time in the Graffiti area. A Set Time dialog box appears, and you can proceed from there. As an example, writing a 4 automatically launches the Set Time dialog box for 4 P.M.*

Add Untimed Events

If we wrote about something called a timed event, you must have assumed we'd get to something called an untimed event, right? *Untimed events* are pretty much what you'd expect—they're events associated with a day, but not with a specific time. Typical untimed events include birthdays and anniversaries, reminders to pick up the dry cleaning, and deadline reminders (though you might also put those kinds of things in the To Do List, described in Chapter 9). To create an untimed event, perform one of these two techniques:

- On the Day View with no time selected (in other words, the cursor isn't waiting in a blank line for you already), start writing. The event appears at the top of the screen as an untimed event.

■ Tap New to display the Set Time dialog box. Instead of setting a Start Time and an End Time, though, tap the No Time button and tap OK.

Make a Date

If you're setting up an appointment with someone in particular, you can have a lot of fun with your Visor. Okay, it's not better than listening to Pink Floyd with the lights out, but it's pretty cool nonetheless. Suppose you need to meet with someone who is already in your Address Book. Just switch to the Day View and tap on a blank line at the time you want to start your meeting. Then choose Options | Phone Lookup. You'll see the Phone Number Lookup dialog box, which displays all the names in your Address Book. Find the name of the person you're meeting with and tap it. Tap Add. What do you get? The person's name and phone number positioned at the start time of the meeting. In fact, there's an even faster solution: you can write only the person's last name, choose Phone Lookup, and the person's name and number will be automatically inserted for you.

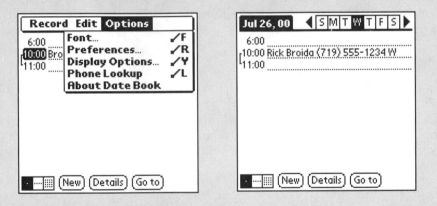

Now it gets even better. Does your associate have a Palm device? If so, make sure the appointment is still selected and choose Record | Beam Event. You've just given your associate a copy of your meeting in her handheld. She now has no excuse to be late.

How to ... **Make Your Appointments Repeat**

Some schedule events just don't go away. Weekly meetings, semiannual employee reviews, and the monthly cat grooming sessions are all examples of events that will dog you till the end of your days and that you might want the Visor to automate somehow. After all, you don't have the time or energy to write exactly the same weekly event into your Visor 52 times to get it entered for a whole year. There's an easier way. To create a recurring event, do this:

1. Select the entry you want to turn into a recurring event and tap the Details button at the bottom of the Day View screen. You can tap this button when you're creating a new event, or you can go back later and edit an existing one. It doesn't matter.

2. You see the Event Details dialog box. The Repeat box should currently be set to None; tap it. The Change Repeat dialog box should now appear.

3. Now you need to tap a repeat interval. Will the event repeat daily, weekly, monthly, or annually? In other words, if the event takes place just once a year, or once every five years, tap Year. If you have a meeting that takes place once a month, or every other month, tap Month. Meetings that occur every week or every five weeks should use the Week button. Finally, if you need to schedule daily, every other day, or every tenth-day meetings, tap Day.

7

Change Repeat	ℹ
None | Day | Week | Month | Year	
Every: __1__ Week(s)	
End on: ▾ No End Date	
Repeat on: S | M | T | W | T | F | S	
Every week on Saturday	
OK Cancel	

4. You now have more options, depending on which interval you chose. A common interval is Week, which would enable you to set up a weekly meeting. Tell the Change Repeat dialog box how often the meeting will occur, such as Every 1 Week or Every 3 Weeks.

5. If you chose a monthly interval, you can also choose whether the meeting will repeat by day (such as the first Monday of every month) or by date (as on the 11th of every month).

6. If the event will repeat more or less forever (or at least as long as you can imagine going to work every day), then leave the End on setting at the default, which is No End Date. If you are creating an event with a clear conclusion, though, tap End on to set the End Date for this repeating event.

7. Your selection is turned into a plain-English description. If you agree the repeat settings are what you want, tap OK.

> **TIP** *If you are attending a multiday event like a trade show, you can show this in your Visor by creating an Untimed Event and set it to repeat daily (Every 1 Day). Don't forget to set an End Date.*

Add a Long Note

Notes are handy for entering information into your appointment that won't fit within the name text. You can use a note to provide driving instructions or agenda information, for instance. Adding a note isn't hard. To create a note, do this:

1. Select the entry to which you want to add a note.

2. Tap the Details button on the Day View screen.

3. Tap the Note button on the Event Details dialog box.

```
          Event Details      ⓘ
    Time:  10:00 am - 11:00 am
    Date:  Wed 7/26/00
   Alarm:  ☐
  Repeat:  None
 Private:  ☐
   ( OK ) ( Cancel ) ( Delete… ) ( Note )
```

4. Enter the note. It can be fairly long but, remember, a definite limit exists. No note can exceed 4,096 characters in length, which, as a rule of thumb, is generally about 700 words. You probably won't get into a problem creating notes that long—if you do, you should be storing them in another format.

5. When your note is complete, tap the Done button.

TIP   *You can add a note with just two strokes of the stylus by writing the Command gesture and the letter A. If you can remember the shortcut, it can save you a lot of taps.*

Make an Appointment Private

You may not want all your appointments to be available to the public. While we generally believe honesty is the best policy, you can flag certain appointments as private—and they will be hidden from everyone except you. If you want to hide an appointment, do this:

1. On the Day View screen, select an appointment.

2. Tap the Details button.

3. On the Event Details dialog box, tap the Private box to add a check mark. Once you select this option, the current record is flagged for privacy. Tap the OK button and you see this dialog box:

Private Records

(i) **You have marked this record Private. Go to the Security application and tap the Hide button to hide all Private records.**

[OK]

4. Tap OK to close the dialog box.

You might notice the event probably isn't hidden yet. To make it go away, you need to enable the Private Records feature in the Security app. For details on how to do this, see Chapter 12. You can hide and show private data whenever you want using this feature.

Edit Your Appointments

Once created, your appointments are always subject to change. Meetings are delayed, canceled, and changed, so it should come as no surprise that you can modify existing meetings on your Visor. To change the name of your appointment, tap the line of text and make any necessary changes. But what if you need to change a meeting time? You can do that in two ways:

■ Select the appointment and tap the Details button. Tap the Time or Date box to change the event's timing and, when you're done, tap OK.

■ In the Week View, tap-and-drag the event to a different location in the week's grid.

Edit Recurring Meetings

Repeating meetings require a little more care. In general, when you change some aspect of a meeting that repeats, the Visor asks you if you want to change just this one meeting or every meeting in the series, as shown by the following dialog box.

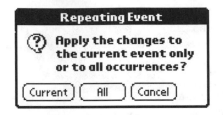

Editing one event in a series of repeating appointments takes care, so that you don't make a drastic change you'll later regret.

If you need to move a specific meeting—like the one in November—to a different time, but all the other meetings continue to be at the traditional time, you want to select Current. The event is actually unlinked from the series, and any changes you subsequently make to the rest of the repeating event do not affect the one you changed. On the other hand, if the meeting is moving to a new day permanently, choose All.

An exception exists to this rule, though: if you change any of the text in the name of the appointment, then the Visor makes the change to the entire series without asking. If you want to change the text of one instance of the event without changing the rest, you need to unlink it from the series. To do that, try this:

1. Change something else about the event, like its time.

2. You will be asked if you want to change the current event or all the events. Choose Current. The event is now unlinked from the series.

3. Change the name of the unlinked event.

4. If you need to, fix whatever you changed in Step 2.

Delete Old Appointments

As time goes on, your Visor (and your desktop computer) will start to accumulate a considerable number of appointments. Often, after an event has passed, you no longer need a record of it. If that's the case, you might want to delete it to save memory. Granted, each appointment takes up a miniscule amount of memory but, eventually, it can add up. Even if you don't care about memory savings, meetings do sometimes get cancelled—and you need a way to delete them. You can get these events off your Visor in a few ways:

- ■ **Erase it**   The easiest way to delete an event is to erase it from the Day View. Tap the stylus at the end of the line and backspace over it to delete all the characters. Or, you can highlight the text by dragging the stylus over the name of the meeting, and then use a single backspace gesture to erase it.

> **CAUTION**   *Watch out! If you use this method to delete a repeating event, the Visor erases all the events in the series without warning.*

- ■ **Use the Delete button**   If you prefer, select the event and tap the Details button. Then tap Delete.

- ■ **Purge a bunch at once**   If you want to delete a bunch of appointments at once, a special tool is designed just for this task. Choose Record | Purge from the Day View. Then choose how much data to delete—you can choose to delete events that are more than a week old or, if you want more of a safety cushion, delete events that are more than a month old.

Work with Alarms

If you need a reminder about upcoming events, you should use the Visor's built-in alarm feature. Any event you enter can be set to beep shortly before the event, giving you enough time to jump in your car, pick up the phone, or start saving for the big day. You can assign an alarm setting to your events as you create the event or at any time afterwards.

> **NOTE**   *Timed events play an audible sound. Untimed events don't play a sound, but simply display a screen advising you the event is pending.*

Set Alarms for Specific Events

To enable the alarm for a particular appointment, do this:

1. On the Day View, select an appointment.
2. Tap Details.
3. On the Event Details dialog box, tap the Alarm check box. You should see a new control appear that lets you set the advance warning for the event.

7

4. Select how much advance warning you want. You can choose no warning (enter a zero) or set a time up to 99 days ahead of time. The default is five minutes.

```
┌─────────────────────────────────┐
│        Event Details      ⓘ      │
│  Time: ⌐12:00 pm - 1:00 pm⌐      │
│  Date: ⌐Wed 7/26/00⌐             │
│ Alarm: ☑  15 ┌Minutes┐ es        │
│              │Hours  │            │
│ Repeat: ⌐Weekly│Days  │          │
│ Private: ☐                       │
│ (OK) (Cancel) (Delete…) (Note)   │
└─────────────────────────────────┘
```

5. Tap OK.

Set Alarms for Everything

By default, the Visor doesn't turn the alarm on for your appointments. Instead, you need to turn the alarm on for every event individually. If you find you like using the alarm, though, you can tell the Visor to turn the alarm on automatically for all your appointments. Then, for any events you don't want to be notified about, it's up to you to turn the alarm off on a case-by-case basis. To enable the default alarm setting, do this:

1. On the Day View, choose Options | Preferences.

2. Tap the check box for the Alarm Preset. Set your alarm preference; configure the alarm time, the kind of alarm sound, and how many times the alarm will sound before giving up.

```
┌─────────────────────────────────┐
│        Preferences        ⓘ      │
│  Start Time:  │ 6:00 am │ ▲▼     │
│  End Time:    │ 6:00 am │ ▲▼     │
│                                  │
│ ☑ Alarm Preset:  5 ▼ Minutes     │
│ Alarm Sound: ┌Alarm ┐            │
│              │Alert │            │
│ Remind Me:   │Bird  │ s          │
│              │Concerto│ tes       │
│ Play Every:  │Phone │ tes         │
│              │Sci-fi│            │
│ (OK) (Cancel)│Wake up│           │
└─────────────────────────────────┘
```

> **TIP** *You can try each of the alarm sounds by selecting them from the list. After you choose a sound, it plays so you can hear what it sounds like.*

3. Tap OK.

Import Alarm Settings

Much of the time, you'll probably get appointments into your Visor via the desktop—you'll HotSync them in from the Palm Desktop or another contact management program. In that case, the rules are different. The Visor keeps whatever alarm settings were assigned on the PC, and doesn't use the preference settings on the Visor. If you want a specific alarm setting, you need to change the alarm setting on the desktop application before HotSyncing or change the alarm on the Visor after you HotSync.

> **TIP** *Some folks would like to have two separate sets of alarms for their appointments: one for the Visor and another for their desktop calendar program. If you have a PC and Microsoft Outlook, try Desktop to Go. This alternative conduit enables you to configure the Visor to use a completely independent set of alarms from Outlook.*

Control Your Alarm

If you use an alarm clock, you must surely know the only thing better than having an alarm to begin with is actually being able to turn it off. Ah, the indescribable ecstasy of blunting the shrieking attack of the alarm first thing in the morning. . . .

The Visor is certainly not that bad. In fact, it's not even particularly loud. If you need to hear it, don't bury it in a backpack or a briefcase. Instead, put it in your pocket or on a tabletop. But what if you are in a quiet meeting room and the last thing you need is your Visor to start chirping in front of the CEO? In that case, you can temporarily silence it. Just open Prefs and choose the General view. You should see an option for Alarm Sound; choose Off from the Alarm Sound list.

Use the Date Book+

For the most part, the Visor's built-in applications work just like those in other Palm devices like the Palm III, Palm V, and WorkPad. But the Visor has an exclusive application that, no doubt, can make your scheduling significantly more efficient. Called the Date Book+, it's a second Date Book application that works exactly like the original Date Book we've been using, but it has a few new views. Worth noting is that any data you enter in the Date Book will appear in the Date Book+, and vice versa. You can't lose data by alternating between applications.

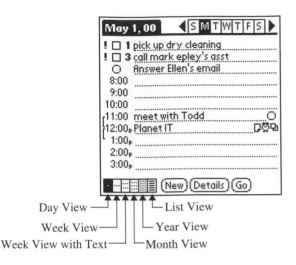

Day View ——⌐   ⌐—— List View
Week View ——⌐   ⌐—— Year View
Week View with Text ——   ⌐—— Month View

To start the program, tap the Date Book+ icon in your Visor's apps.

TIP *Handspring wasn't sure you'd want to use this program all the time, so it didn't assign it to the Date Book button by default. But if you want to use the Date Book+ as your full-time, permanent Date Book, that's easy to do. Just choose Options, Default Date Book from the Date Book+ menu and choose Date Book+. Then tap OK to save your change.*

Navigate the Week View with Text

You're already familiar with some of the Date Book+ views. The Day View and original Week View are the same as before. The new Week View, though, is a much more flexible way of seeing your appointments because the grid displays the actual appointment text, not just busy times. Figure 7-3 shows the highlights of this view.

Navigate the Year View

The Date Book+ also includes a Year View that displays all 12 months at a glance.

Display two weeks
onscreen at once

Tap to see more entries that
won't fit onscreen

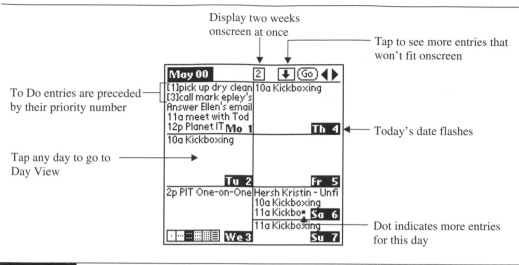

To Do entries are preceded
by their priority number

Today's date flashes

Tap any day to go to
Day View

Dot indicates more entries
for this day

FIGURE 7-3 The Week View in Date Book+

This view is convenient for seeing days that have events associated with them—a great long-term planning tool. Tap a day in the calendar and a sample of the events for the day appears at the top of the screen. To make this view even more useful, set up the display preferences to suit the kind of information you want to see. Tap the Prefs button at the bottom of the Year View and you see the Year Preferences dialog box.

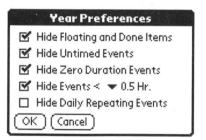

From this box you can choose which kinds of events and appointments appear on the calendar screen. We recommend hiding short, floating, and untimed events, for instance, if you're looking for a day that's available for a long appointment.

Navigate the List View

The List View, shown in Figure 7-4, is a completely original way of looking at your Date Book information that's not found in other Palm devices. Switch to this view and you see all the calendar entries listed in text form.

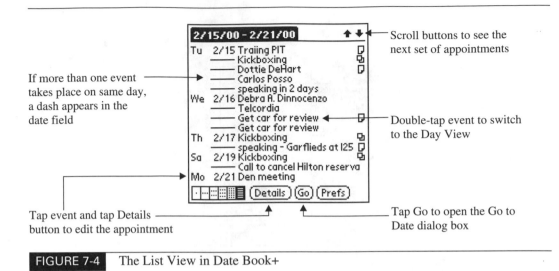

FIGURE 7-4 The List View in Date Book+

Use Integrated To Dos

One of the nicest things about the new To Do+ program is that it elegantly incorporates To Do tasks into the Date Book, so you can see all your daily responsibilities in a single glance. To Dos appear in most views, right along with appointments and untimed events.

NOTE   *You can check a To Do as complete in both the Day View and List View by tapping the To Do box.*

If you can't see To Dos in your Date Book, they haven't been turned on in the preferences. Do this:

1. From the Options menu, choose To Do Preferences. You should see the To Do Preferences dialog box.

2. In the Show Categories section, tap the name of each category you want to appear in the Date Book.

3. Tap Ok to close the dialog box.

TIP   *Use the To Do Preferences to reduce clutter in the Date Book. If you file your To Do tasks according to work and business, for instance, you might want to turn off personal To Dos most of the time.*

Use Floating Events

One limitation of the ordinary Date Book is that appointments and events are rigidly assigned to specific days. What if you want to create an appointment to retrieve some documents from the shipping department, though, and it doesn't absolutely have to be today? If you miss the appointment, it would be nice if the event slid through the calendar with you, appearing each day until you finally manage to complete it.

That's the idea behind floating events. These floaters can be assigned to a specific time of day—like a regular appointment—or left untimed, so they appear as an event attached to a day. When inserted in the Date Book, floating events can be identified by a circle and look like this:

```
┌──────────────────────────────────┐
│ May 1, 00   ◀ S M T W T F S ▶    │
│ ! ☐ 1 pick up dry cleaning        │
│ ! ☐ 3 call mark epley's asst      │
│ ▶○   Answer Ellen's email         │
│  8:00                             │
│  9:00                             │
│ 10:00                             │
│┌11:00  meet with Todd          ○ │
│├12:00▸ Planet IT            ▯☼⊡  │
│└ 1:00▸                            │
│  2:00▸                            │
│  3:00▸                            │
│ ·⠿⠿⠿▤▥ (New)(Details)(Go)        │
└──────────────────────────────────┘
```

No assigned time — (points to ▶○ Answer Ellen's email)

Assigned time — (points to 11:00/12:00)

Note, when given an appointed time, the circle appears on the right side of the screen. If untimed, the circle appears on the left, where the time would otherwise be. The appointment floats until you mark it as complete. To do that, tap the circle—it's actually a check box, but the shape is different to distinguish it from a To Do task.

To create a floating event, do this:

1. Make sure you are in the Day View.

2. Tap the New button at the bottom of the screen.

3. Choose Floating Event from the pop-up menu.

4. Enter the name of the event.

5. If you want to assign this event to a specific time of day, tap the Details button and choose a time in the same way you would assign a time to an ordinary appointment.

Use the Journal

Some people love to take notes about their day, active projects, or shoes they've stolen from the local gym (that one really only applies to Rick). If you want to use your Visor as a daily journal, you'll appreciate that a journal feature is built into Date Book+. To add a journal entry, do this:

1. Switch to the Day View.

2. Tap the New button.

3. Choose Daily Journal from the pop-up menu. The Daily Journal window then appears.

```
┌─────────────────────────────┐
│        Daily Journal        │
│ 9:53 am:                    │
│ ........................... │
│ ........................... │
│ ........................... │
│ ........................... │
│ ........................... │
│ ........................... │
│ ........................... │
│ ........................... │
│ ........................... │
│ ........................... │
│                             │
│ (Done) (Delete...) (Restore...) ↑ │
└─────────────────────────────┘
```

4. Start writing. When you're done, tap the Done button to close the Journal.

Your Journal entries are always time stamped as of the time you opened the Journal window. If you make several entries in one day, each is time stamped in the same document window. Journal entries appear at the top of the Day View and look like Untimed Events—they are preceded with a diamond shape. To open the journal without creating a new time stamp, tap the Note icon on the right side of the screen.

```
┌─────────────────────────────┐
│ Apr 30, 00  ◀ S M T W T F S ▶│
│  ◆  Daily Journal ........ ◻│◄──── Tap here to read
│ 8:00  ....................... │      the journal
│ 9:00  ....................... │
│ 10:00 ....................... │
│┌11:00 Kickboxing ......... ◻│
│└12:00ₚ....................... │
│ 1:00ₚ ....................... │
│ 2:00ₚ ....................... │
│ 3:00ₚ ....................... │
│ 4:00ₚ ....................... │
│ 5:00ₚ ....................... │
│ ■ ⋮ ▦ ▤ ▤  (New)(Details)(Go)│
└─────────────────────────────┘
```

Add Events from a Template

Do you frequently need to create events that look similar to appointments already in your Date Book? Then use a template. Templates are handy for adding recurring appointments or events to which you need to add the same note over and over. When you make a template, all you're really doing is pointing to an existing Date Book entry and saying to your Visor, "Hey! Remember everything about this entry. In the future, I might want to add it elsewhere in the calendar without reentering all the information all over again!"

To make a template, locate an entry you'd like the Visor to memorize. Tap somewhere in the entry (in the Day View) and choose Record | Create Template from the menu.

Everything about that entry—including the entry name, time, recurring data, and note text, will be retained.

To insert a memorized entry into the calendar, tap in the text field for the time you want the event to occur. Then tap the New button and choose Template from the pop-up menu. You need to choose the desired template from the list of templates you added, and the event is added to the Date Book. You can then edit the entry to suit you needs.

Chapter 8 The Address Book

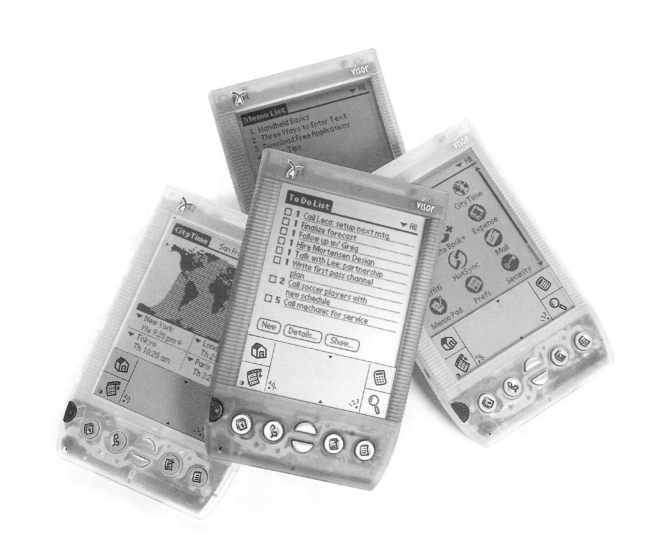

How to...

■ View Address Book entries

■ Customize the Address Book display

■ Search for an entry by name

■ Search for an entry by keyword

■ Create new Address Book entries

■ Display a specific phone number in the Address List

■ Use the custom fields

■ Add a note to an entry

■ Assign a category to an entry

■ Make an entry private

■ Delete Address Book entries

■ Beam your business card

What's the big deal? It's just an address book. Yes, but as one of the four big core applications, you'll use the Address Book a lot. And the Address Book is an elegant program, designed to get the information you need quickly, perhaps more quickly than any other contact manager on the market.

We're sure you will get a lot of mileage from the Address Book. You can store literally thousands of entries and not run out of memory. Despite how many names you add to the list, your Visor never slows down—that's a claim desktop applications simply can't make. In addition, the Address Book isn't a stand-alone application (though it can be if you want). The Address Book synchronizes with desktop applications like the Palm Desktop and Microsoft Outlook. This means you only need to create a contact list once and it'll be maintained on both your PC and your Visor.

View Your Addresses

When you switch to the Address Book, the program displays all the entries in your list onscreen. You can start the Address Book two ways:

■ Press the Address Book button on your Visor (the button has an icon of a telephone).

Address Book

■ Tap the onscreen Address icon in the Visor's applications.

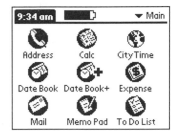

As you can see in Figure 8-1, the Visor lists your contacts alphabetically in a view called the *Address List*. There's room for 11 entries onscreen at one time; the rest appear above or below the screen, depending on where you are within the Address List. Getting around in the Address List is easy. You can simply scroll down to see more names.

As you might expect, you can scroll around in two ways:

■ Tap the scroll arrows at the bottom-right corner of the screen.

■ Press the scroll button on the Visor's front panel.

Each time you scroll, the Visor moves the list by one complete page. This means if you scroll down, the bottom entry on the page becomes the top entry after scrolling.

Another way to get around the Address List is by using the categories. We discuss categories later in the chapter but, for now, know that if your contacts are divided into more than one category, every time you press the Address button, you switch categories. You can cycle through the first page of names in each category just by pressing the Address button repeatedly.

8

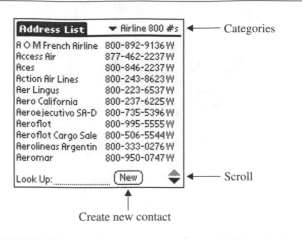

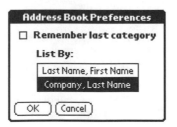

Categories

Scroll

Create new contact

FIGURE 8-1   The Address List is a database of all your contact information

View by Company Name

For most folks, the default Address Book is great. This list displays the entries by name (last, first) and a phone number. If you tend to work with your contacts according to the company they work with, though, you can change the way the Address Book works to accommodate you.

To change the view mode of the Address Book, do this:

1. Display the Address List view.

2. Choose Options | Preferences from the menu.

3. Choose Company, Last Name from the List By list.

4. Tap OK to save your changes.

Notice that after making the change, you can see the company name in the list. If no company is associated with a particular entry, then you only see the individual's name, as you did before. You can switch back to the default view at any time.

Find a Specific Name

If you're looking for a specific entry in the Address List, you can simply scroll down until you find it. If you only have a few dozen contacts, that's not so hard. But what if you're like us and your Address Book is brimming with over a thousand contacts? Scrolling might take a while, especially if the guy you're looking for is named Nigel Walthers or Earnest Zanthers. That's when you use the Look Up function.

To search for a specific name, start writing the person's last name in the Look Up field at the bottom of the screen. The Address Book adjusts the display as you write, so if you enter the letter *U*, it displays all the names that begin with *U*. If you write UN, it narrows the search and shows names that begin with those letters.

Address List	▼ Airline 800 #s
Ukraine Intl Airlines	800-876-0114 W
United Airlines	800-241-6522 W
US Airways	800-428-4322 W
USA Jet Airlines	800-872-5387 W
USAir Shuttle	800-428-4322 W
Vanguard Airlines	800-826-4827 W
Varig	800-468-2744 W
Vasp Brazilian Airlin	800-433-0444 W
Viasa International	800-327-4470 W
Vietnam Airlines	800-565-2742 W
Virgin Atlantic	800-862-8621 W
Look Up: un	(New) ▲▼

  If you are using the List By: Company, Last Name option in the Address List view, it's a little more complicated. If the entry has a company name, you need to search for that entry by company name—you won't find the entry by entering the last name in the Look Up field. If the entry doesn't have a company name, though, you must find it by last name.

As you can probably deduce, two handy ways exist to use the Look Up tool:

■ Keep writing letters until the Visor displays exactly the name you want.

■ Write one or two letters, and then use the scroll button to find the name you need.

  If you try writing a letter, but your Visor just beeps at you, this means no name in the list is spelled with the letter you're trying to add. You've probably misspelled the name.

If you're searching for more than one name, you can use this handy way to clear the Look Up field to write in a new name. Just press the scroll up or scroll down hard button.

Conduct a Detailed Search

You may have noticed the Look Up field only searches by last name. What happens if you want to find someone, but you can only remember that person's first name or the company where he works? Unfortunately, the Look Up field won't do any good.

In this case, use the Find tool. Tap the Find soft button, enter the word you want to search for, and then tap OK. You get a list of every entry in the Visor with that word, as shown in Figure 8-2.

> **TIP** *The current application is searched first, so make sure you're in the Address Book before you start using the Find tool.*

View a Name

Once you locate the name you were looking for, tap it. You'll see the Address View, which displays the contact's name, address, and phone numbers, as shown in Figure 8-3. When you're done with the entry, tap Done to return to the Address Book.

The Address View isn't particularly customizable—some would say the reason is it's quite elegant as is. If you like, though, you can experiment with changing the font for a more readable display. To do that, choose Options | Font from the menu. Three font choices are at your disposal. The smallest font is the most professional looking, though you might appreciate the larger fonts if you have trouble seeing the text onscreen.

Create New Entries

You can add contacts to the Address Book either from the PC or the Visor. We discuss creating new entries on the PC in Chapter 5 and on the Mac in Chapter 6. For now, we show you how to use the Visor to add new entries.

To create a new Address Book entry, tap the New button at the bottom of the screen. From there, start filling in the blanks. Start by writing the last name of the person you're adding. When you're ready to move on to the first name, you need to change fields. You can do this in two ways:

■ Tap the next field with the stylus, and then write in the Graffiti area.

Find

Matches for "Airline"

———— Addresses ————
A O M French Airlin   800-892-9136 W
Air Inter-French Air   800-237-2747 W
Air North Airlines   800-764-0407 W
Airatlantic Airlines   800-223-5552 W
Alaska Airlines   800-426-0333 W
ALM Antillean Airlin   800-327-7197 W
America West Airlin   800-235-9292 W
American Airlines   800-433-7300 W

(Cancel) (Find More)

FIGURE 8-2   The Find tool is a powerful way to locate an entry, even if you don't remember the person's name

FIGURE 8-3   The Address View shows you all the details about the selected person

■ Use the Next Field gesture to move to the next field. This is akin to using keyboard shortcuts on the PC to move around in a form or a database. If you're the kind of person who doesn't like to move your hand from the keyboard to mouse to change fields, then you'll probably use this gesture a lot.

NOTE   *The Next Field gesture takes a little practice because it's so easy to get the letter* U *by mistake. Although the gesture template shows a curve in the first part of the stroke, you'll get best results by going straight down, and then straight up again.*

Even though you only see a single line for text in each field, the Address Book secretly supports multiple lines of text in each field. If you're entering the company name, for instance, you can use two or more lines to enter all the information you need about the company, department, and so on for the individual. To write multiple lines of text in a field, use the Return gesture (a diagonal line from the upper-right to the lower-left corner) to create a new line. You won't see the multiple lines in the Address List view, but you can see them when you select the entry and view the Address View.

TIP   *What if you're Canadian, French, or living in some other non-American location? The Visor defaults to address details like city, state, and ZIP code—which may not be appropriate for your locale. The solution is to tap the Prefs icon in Apps and select Formats from the menu. Then, set the Preset To: menu to whatever country you want.*

When you're done adding information about this new person, tap the Done button.

Use Multiple Phone Numbers

The Address Book gives you a few options when you enter contact information. Specifically, you can set what kinds of phone numbers your Visor has for each contact. Conveniently, this needn't be the same for everyone. For one person, you might list a home phone and a pager, for instance, while another entry might have a work number and an e-mail address. Your Visor keeps track of everything for you.

To control these numbers, tap the phone number list and choose the desired label. Then, write the number or e-mail address in the field next to the label. You can specify up to five entries for each person in your Address Book.

```
┌─────────────────────────────────────┐
│ Address Edit          ▼ Unfiled     │
│ Last name: Broida                   │
│ First name: Rick                    │
│     Title: Editor                   │
│ ┌────────┐ ▼: Tap                   │
│ │Work    │ <: 3035551234            │
│ │Home    │ ≈: 3035555678            │
│ │Fax     │                         │
│ │Other   │ <:                       │
│ │E-mail  │ r:                       │
│ │Main    │                         │
│ │Pager   │                    ▲     │
│ │Mobile  │ (Details...) (Note) ▼    │
│ └────────┘                         │
└─────────────────────────────────────┘
```

If you're on the ball, you might wonder which of those numbers shows up in the Address List view. Remember, the list shows the name and a phone number for each contact—this means you may not have to open an entry just to dial a phone number because it's right there in the list view. The answer, though, is the first phone number you enter into the Edit view is the one that appears in the List view—no matter where it is in the list of phone numbers. If you want the home phone number to appear in the Address List, then enter the number into the Home field (which is typically the second phone number entry on the page).

TIP   *If you decide you want another number to appear in the list, you needn't start over or do anything rash like that. Instead, tap the Details button and select the number label you want from the Show in List menu.*

Use Extra Fields

The Address Book has plenty of preconfigured fields (like name, company, and phone numbers) for most users, but it's flexible enough also to accommodate the special needs of everyone else. You might want to track birthdays, Web pages, spouse names, or other personal information. If so, you're in luck—four custom fields are at the bottom of the Address Edit view, which you can rename as you like.

To label these four bonus fields into something more useful, do this:

1. Choose the Address Book. Any view will do.

2. Choose Options | Rename Custom Fields from the menu.

3. Select the text on the first line (which should say Custom 1) and write a name for the field. Name the other fields—or as many as you need—in the same way.

Rename Custom Fields

Create your own field names
by editing the text on the
lines below:

Shoe Size

Spouse

2nd Email

User 4

(OK) (Cancel)

4. Tap OK when you're done.

Once you create labels for these fields, you can find them at the bottom of the list of contact
info in the Address Edit view.

NOTE   *The custom fields are global. This means you can't have different custom fields for each
entry or even for each category. Once named, the custom fields apply to all entries in
the Address Book. You needn't fill them out for every entry, though.*

Add a Long Note

The four custom fields are good for standardized information you might need to track that isn't
contained in typical information managers (for some unusual reason, Rick uses a custom field to
track the shoe size of everyone in his Address Book). But what if you need to associate a long,
unique note with a contact? You might want to use a note for:

- Directions to a home or office
- Personal information about the person, such as the name of his or her kids and pets
- Information about what the contact's company does
- Notes from a phone call

Luckily, the Address Book includes the capability to attach notes to a contact. To create a
note, do this:

1. Tap the Note button on the Address Edit screen.

2. Enter the note. It can be fairly long but, remember, a limit exists. No note can exceed
4,096 characters in length, which, as a rule of thumb, is generally about 700 words. You
probably won't run into a problem creating notes that long—if you do, you should store
them in another format.

3. When your note is complete, tap the Done button.

8

NOTE *If you're adding a note to a completed address entry, you need to choose an entry, tap Edit, and then tap Note instead.*

When you finish your new entry and view the Address List view, note that a small document icon appears on the right edge of the screen, next to the phone number. You can view (and even edit) the note directly by tapping on that icon.

A note has been added
—to this address entry

TIP *To add a note to an existing entry, tap in the blank spot to the right of the phone number, where the note icon would be if a note were already attached. The note window immediately appears, saving you the trouble of digging down for it in the ordinary way.*

A portion of the note also appears in the Address View. The note should be visible below the contact information, though you won't see the entire text of the note—this view has a maximum number of allowable characters as well.

Assign Categories and Privacy

Your new contact can easily get lost within a sea of names and addresses if you aren't careful. With just a few names to manage, this is no big deal. But what if you have 500 or 1,000 contacts in your Address Book? This is when categories could come in handy.

Choose a Category

As you might remember from Chapter 2, categories are a way of organizing your Visor's data more logically into groups you frequently use. To assign a contact to a specific category, do this:

1. From the Address Edit screen, tap Details. The Address Entry Details dialog box should appear.

2. Tap the Category list and choose the category name you want to assign to this contact.

3. Tap OK to close the dialog box.

Of course, you needn't assign a category if you don't want to do so. By default, new contacts are placed in the Unfiled category.

Make a Name Private

Do you have secrets? This is none of our business (though Rick would like to know your shoe size. Please e-mail this information to him at your earliest convenience), but you may want to keep a few bits of information to yourself. If you want the contents of your Address Book to be secret, then you might want to consider using the privacy feature built into the Visor. You can hide all your contacts or just specific ones—the choice is yours.

If you want to hide a contact, do this:

1. On the Address Book screen, choose a name. You should then see the Address View screen.

2. Tap the screen to enter the Address Edit screen.

3. Tap Details. The Address Entry Details dialog box appears.

4. Tap the Private box to add a check mark. Once you select this option, the current record is flagged for privacy. Tap the OK button and you see this dialog box:

5. Tap OK to close the dialog box.

You might notice the contact probably isn't hidden yet. To make it go away, you need to enable the Private Records feature in the Security app. For details on how to do this, see Chapter 12. You can hide and show private records whenever you want using this feature.

Edit and Delete Addresses

In this fast-paced world, a contact once entered in an address book isn't likely to stay that way for long. You may need to update an address, phone number, or e-mail address, or delete the entry entirely.

To edit an entry, all you do is find the entry in the Address Book and tap it. You'll be taken to the Address View where you can see the existing information. Then tap the screen and the display changes to the Address Edit view, which you can change to suit your needs.

NOTE   *Why is there an Edit button on the Address View screen when you don't actually need to tap it? That's hard to say—but the fact remains it's an unnecessary decoration on the screen, kind of like a digital hood ornament.*

If you have a contact you simply don't need anymore, you can delete it from the Visor to save memory and reduce data clutter. To delete a contact, do this:

1. Choose the entry from the Address Book. You see the Address View.

2. Tap anywhere in the Address View to enter the edit mode.

3. Tap Details. You see the Address Entry Details dialog box.

4. Tap the Delete button.

5. Tap the OK button to eliminate the contact from your Visor.

NOTE   *If you check the box marked Save archive copy on PC, then a copy of this entry is preserved in the Palm Desktop in archive form. In general, you probably don't need to archive your data but, by using the archive tool, you can restore deleted data, as explained in Chapter 5.*

Create and Beam Your Business Card

As we mentioned in Chapter 4, one of the coolest things about taking your Visor to meetings and trade shows is the capability to beam your personal information into other people's Palm OS devices. This is a lot easier and more convenient than exchanging a business card. Heck, a paper business card? That's so . . . '80s! Use your Visor instead.

How to ... **Create an Address Book Entry**

In summary, here is how you can create entries in the Address Book:

1. Press the Address Book button on your Visor to switch to that app.

2. Tap the New button on the bottom of the Address List view.

3. Enter all the information to create an entry for the person in question.

4. Tap the Details button and assign the entry to a category, and then tap OK.

Before you can beam your personal information around, though, you need to create a business card. That's not hard to do. Find your own personal information in the Address Book (or, if you haven't done this yet, create an entry for yourself). After you select your card and you can see your personal information on the Address View screen, choose Record | Select Business Card from the menu.

8

From here on out, you can beam your card to others in either of two ways:

■ Choose Record | Beam Business Card from the Address Book menu.

■ Hold the Address Book hard button down for two seconds.

TIP *Is your Address Book entry really selected as your business card? It's easy to tell. On the Address View, you can see an icon representing a Rolodex page at the top of the screen, to the right of the title. If you don't see that icon, the current record is not the designated business card.*

Business Card Advice

Dave: I like to beam my business card to people at trade shows, especially because I've never figured out a good way to carry paper cards. Do they go in my pocket? My backpack? I never have a card ready when someone wants it. But with the Visor, I just hold down the Address Book button and the card travels through the ether. Cool. On the other hand, I've beamed people my Address Book information without realizing I had personal information stored there that I didn't want other people to have. It pays to double-check your entry before you start beaming stuff you might regret.

Rick: Indeed, remember you're beaming not just your contact information, but also any notes you've added to your listing. I've created a special "personal business card" entry I use for beaming, and a second one I can fill with more of the information I like to keep handy—and private.

Chapter 9

The To Do List

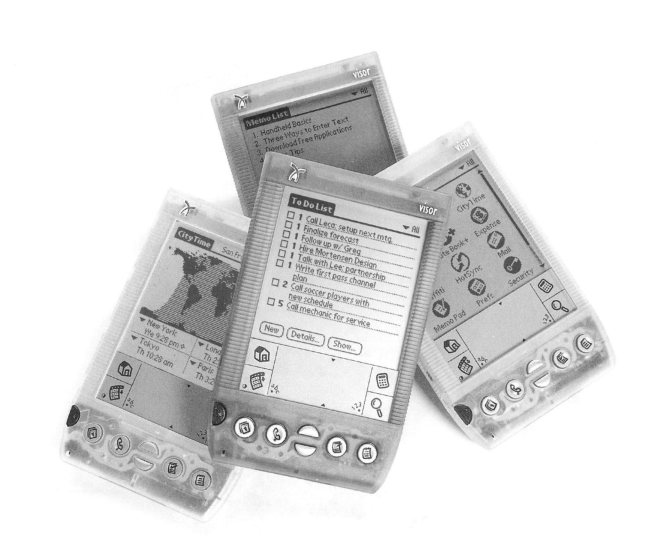

How to...

- View To Do List entries
- Create new To Dos
- Create a To Do based on an Address Book entry
- Prioritize your To Dos
- Add notes to your To Dos
- Edit To Dos from the List view
- Customize the To Do List view
- Beam To Dos to others

The To Do List is admittedly one of the smallest of the core Visor applications, but don't let that fool you. There's a lot of convenience under the hood. What good is this little program? Well, think of it this way: would you be more organized if you actually carried a list of things you need to do—big and small—around with you all the time? Finish a task and cross it off the list for a sense of immediate gratification. Or, think of something you need to do while you're away from the office and add it immediately to your Visor, knowing the entry will be added to your PC's master To Do list as soon as you HotSync. The To Do List is a way to take charge of all the little things that make up your daily agenda.

View the To Do List

When you switch to the To Do List, the program displays all your existing To Do entries. You can start the To Do List in two ways:

- Press the To Do List button on your Visor. It has an icon that shows three lines with check boxes.

To Do List

■ Tap the onscreen To Do List icon in the Visor's applications.

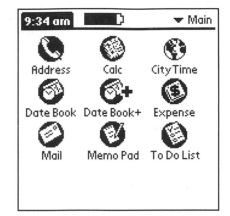

As you can see in Figure 9-1, the Visor lists your To Dos in a fairly straightforward list, which you can use to see what tasks you have coming up or, in some cases, past due (you might want to take care of those). There is room for 11 entries onscreen at one time; the rest appear above or below the screen, depending on where you are within the To Do List. Getting around is easy. You can simply scroll down to see more names. Just like in other Visor applications, you can scroll around in two ways:

■ Tap the scroll arrows at the bottom-right corner of the screen.

■ Press the scroll button on the Visor's front panel.

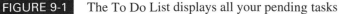

FIGURE 9-1   The To Do List displays all your pending tasks

Each time you scroll, the Visor moves the list by one complete page. This means, if you scroll down, the bottom entry on the page becomes the top entry after scrolling.

Another way to get around is by using the categories. If your tasks are divided into more than one category, every time you press the hard To Do button, you switch categories. You can cycle through the first page of tasks in each category just by pressing this button repeatedly.

Create a To Do

You can add new to-do entries using either the Visor or the Palm Desktop. We cover the Desktop procedure back in Chapters 5 and 6. For now, we cover the process of adding entries to your Visor, which is, as you might expect, quite easy.

You can add a new To Do in two ways. Use whichever one is easier for you:

- **Start writing** From the To Do List, write the description of your task in the Graffiti area. The text appears automatically in a brand new To Do entry.

- **Tap the New button** If you tap the New button, the cursor appears on a blank line, ready for you to write the name of the To Do.

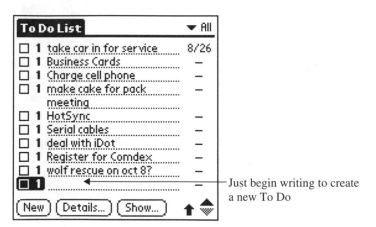

Just begin writing to create a new To Do

TIP *If you want to create a task with a specific priority, tap a To Do entry that has the priority you want, and then tap New. The new To Do takes the priority of the previously selected task, saving you the trouble of choosing a priority later.*

While most tasks can be summarized in just one line of text, no reasonable limit exists for how long you can make a To Do entry. If you need more than one line of text to describe your task, you can use the Enter gesture to get the Visor to display a new blank line in the same To Do. Remember, though, creating multiline To Dos may make reading your tasks in the To Do List hard when you refer to it later (this should be obvious from Figure 9-2). Instead of making

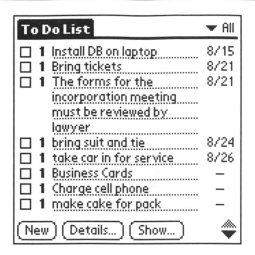

FIGURE 9-2   Multiline tasks can be a real mess

long, multiline tasks, we recommend you add a note to your task instead (explained later in this chapter, in "Add Notes to a Task").

Friends Are a Chore

It's true! Having friends and coworkers can be actual work. Suppose you need to meet with Ed Grimpley from accounting sometime this week to talk about why you've gone through 18 mouse pads in the space of a week. You don't have an appointment in your calendar; you'd rather just pop in sometime when it's convenient. The To Do List is your answer. Create a new To Do and choose Options | Phone Lookup from the menu. Find Ed in the Phone Number Lookup dialog box and tap Add. What you get is Ed's name and phone number in the To Do entry. This is a handy way to remind yourself to call someone without setting up a rigid appointment in the Date Book.

Add Details to the To Do

Once you finish entering the name of the task, tap elsewhere on the screen to save the entry. If you prefer, you can enhance your To Do with additional information, like priority, category, and due date. You certainly don't need to enter any of these special settings, but using them enables you to track your tasks with greater accuracy. Here's what you need to do:

1. Select the task you want to edit by tapping the name of the To Do.

2. Tap the Details button and the To Do Item Details dialog box appears:

```
┌─────────────────────────────────┐
│  To Do Item Details         ⓘ  │
│ ┌─────────────────────────────┐ │
│ │ Priority: 1 2 3 4 5         │ │
│ │ Category: ▼ Unfiled         │ │
│ │ Due Date: ▼ No Date         │ │
│ │   Private: ☐                │ │
│ │                             │ │
│ │ (OK) (Cancel) (Delete...) (Note) │ │
│ └─────────────────────────────┘ │
└─────────────────────────────────┘
```

3. Tap a number to represent the priority of your task. You can select any number from 1 to 5 (obviously, the lower the number, the higher the priority).

4. Choose a category from the Category list.

5. Choose a due date from the Due Date list. You can choose to make a task due today, tomorrow, in a week, or you can choose a date directly from the calendar dialog box.

6. Tap OK to save your changes to the task.

Add Notes to a Task

While you can make a task almost any length, most people find it more convenient (and more readable) to keep the To Do name short, and then to expand on any subtle details with a note. To add a note to a To Do, you need to go back to the Details dialog box. Select your To Do, tap the Details button, and then tap Note.

Remember, the note is limited to 4,096 characters, which is about 700 words. How long is that? Well, you can write about two or three double-spaced pages in Microsoft Word with 700 words, which means you can write quite a bit before running into length issues.

To Do or Appointment?

Okay, we know what you're thinking—if you can assign due dates to the To Do List, why bother with appointments? Or, from the other perspective, why use To Dos if you have the Date Book? Well, that's a good question. We use the To Do List whenever we have tasks that need doing by a certain date—but not at a certain time of day. If a task requires a time slot, we put it in the Date Book. So stuff like, "buy lemons" and "finish Chapter 11" are To Dos. "Meet with Laura for lunch at 11:30" is a Date Book entry. There's also the matter of alarms: your Visor can beep when it's time for an appointment, but not when it's time for a task.

Work with the List View

When you switch to the To Do List, you see all your existing tasks arranged onscreen, usually in order of importance (as determined by the priority number assigned to each To Do). As you can see in Figure 9-3, six elements are associated with each task:

■ **Check box** If you complete a task, you can indicate it's done by tapping the check box. That places a check mark in the task. Depending on how you configured the To Do preferences, the entry either disappears or remains onscreen, but is marked as done.

To Do List			▼ All
☐	1	Install DB on laptop	8/15
☐	1	Bring tickets	8/21
☐	1	bring suit and tie	8/24
☐	1	take car in for service	8/26
☐	1	Business Cards	—
☐	2	charge cell phone	—
☐	3	make cake for pack	—
	4	meeting	
☐	5	HotSync	—
☐	1	Serial cables	—
☐	1	deal with iDot	—

(New) (Details...) (Show...)

FIGURE 9-3 The To Do List enables you to modify each entry without using the Details button

■ **Priority**   Not everything is the most important thing on your task list. If you want to arrange your tasks by importance or urgency, use the priority numbers, from 1 through 5. Tap the number to get a list of all the priority choices.

TIP   *We recommend you use priority numbers for your tasks—they help you sort through the clutter of your various To Dos and determine what's really important from one day to the next.*

■ **To Do description**   You can edit the description of the task by tapping in this field and editing the existing text.

■ **Note icon**   If you have already created a note for the task, you can read the note or edit it by tapping the icon to the right of the To Do name field. If no note already exists, you can add one by selecting the task and choosing Record | Attach Note from the menu.

■ **Due date**   You might have tasks that need to be accomplished by a specific date. If that's the case, use the final column. If a dash is in that slot, it means you haven't yet assigned a due date. Tap it and choose a date. You can also change the due date in the same way.

NOTE   *The To Do List uses the somewhat unusual style of month/date to designate the date.*

■ **Category**   Change the category to which a task is assigned by tapping the category column and choosing the desired category from the list.

NOTE   *As the saying goes, your mileage may vary. Specifically, some of these columns aren't displayed by default—to enable them, tap the Show button and choose the columns you want to appear in the To Do Preferences dialog box.*

How to ...   Create a To Do Entry

We've talked a lot about To Dos, so here's a summary of how to create tasks on your Visor:

1. Press the To Do button on the Visor.
2. Start writing in the Graffiti area—this creates a new To Do.
3. Tap the Details button.
4. If you want to, assign a priority, category, and due date on the Details dialog box. Tap OK to close this dialog box.

Change the View Options

If you're anything like us (and that could be a very, very bad thing, if you know what we mean), you may be perfectly happy with the default look of the To Do List. Out of the box, the To Do List uses a pretty logical scheme for displaying tasks and arranges the information in an uncluttered way. It's easy to modify, though. Tap the Show button and you see the To Do Preferences dialog box. The following sections describe your options.

Sorting Options

The first item you encounter on the Preferences dialog box is a Sort-by list. This determines the way the To Do List shows the tasks onscreen.

- ■ **Priority, Due Date**   This groups all the priority 1 tasks first, then priority 2, and so on. Within each priority group, the earliest deadlines are listed first, and no deadline tasks are listed last. This option works best if you need to work on tasks with the highest priority, and due dates are not particularly important to you.

- ■ **Due Date, Priority**   This selection arranges all the tasks by due date, with the soonest due dates listed first and no due dates listed last. If several tasks have the same due date, they're listed by priority order. This is probably the best display option for most people—it lists your tasks with the ones due soonest at the top of the page, and within each due date you can see the top priorities arranged first. You can compare the difference between Priority, Due Date and Due Date, Priority in Figure 9

- ■ **Category, Priority**   Arranges your tasks by category. The categories are arranged in alphabetical order. If you have more than one task in a given category, they're arranged in priority order within the category. Use this category if it's more important for you to see tasks visually arranged into different categories—like work and personal—than arranging them by due date or category.

Sorted by Due Date, Priority 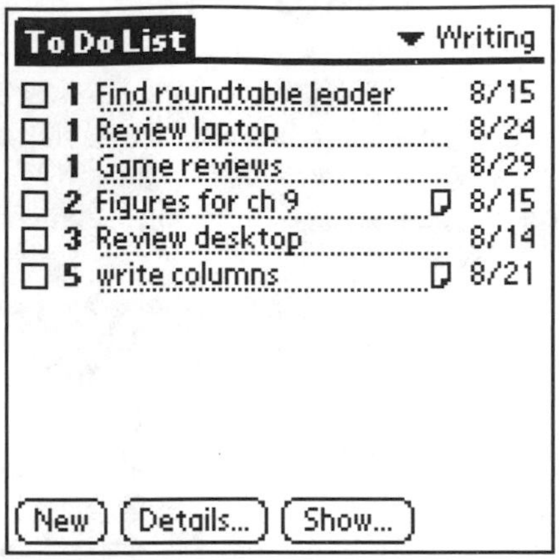   Sorted by Priority, Due Date

FIGURE 9-4   You can see how changing the Sort by option enables you to see your tasks in a different light

- ■ **Category, Due Date**   This selection also arranges your tasks by category, and the categories are arranged in alphabetical order. If you have more than one task in a given category, they're arranged by due date within the category. Soonest deadlines appear first and tasks with no due date are placed last within each category.

Use Filters to Customize the Display

The next section in the To Do Preferences dialog box controls what kind of tasks are displayed onscreen. Actually, that's not true, but we're trying to apply some logic to the way the Palm OS chose to group the items on this screen. Here's what each of these three items does:

- ■ **Show Completed Items**   As you check off tasks you've completed, slowly, but surely, they clutter up your screen unless you do something about them. If you uncheck this option, completed items are hidden. If you need to see items you've completed, simply check Show Completed Items and they reappear.

NOTE   *If you hide completed tasks in this way, they're not deleted. They still take up memory on the Visor and, if you have enough of them, they can eventually slow down your handheld. Later in this chapter, you learn how to delete old To Dos.*

■ **Show Only Due Items**   If you're only concerned about tasks due today, check this item. Any tasks that have a due date after today disappear from the screen and only reappear on the day they're due.

CAUTION   *Be careful with this option because it hides To Dos from the screen that aren't due today, regardless of priority. Getting caught off-guard this way by a major deadline is easy.*

■ **Record Completion Date**   This interesting little feature changes the due date of a completed item to the date it was completed. If you didn't assign a due date to a task, the completion date becomes the due date. In this way, you can track what day you completed each of your tasks.

CAUTION   *This option overwrites the due date with the completion date. You can't get the original due date back, even if you uncheck the task or turn off the Record Completion Date option.*

Modify the Task Columns

As you've probably already seen, you can tweak the data the To Do List shows for each task in the list. That tweaking occurs here, in the last three options of the To Do Preferences dialog box. With all the options disabled, the basic To Do List view looks like this:

9

```
┌──────────────────────────────────┐
│ To Do List          ▼ Writing     │
│ ☐ Find roundtable leader          │
│ ☐ Review laptop                   │
│ ☐ Game reviews                    │
│ ☐ Figures for ch 9              ◻ │
│ ☐ Review desktop                  │
│ ☐ write columns                 ◻ │
│                                   │
│                                   │
│                                   │
│                                   │
│ ( New ) ( Details... ) ( Show... )│
└──────────────────────────────────┘
```

Obviously, the only features on this screen are the check box, the task name, and the note icon, if a note is attached to the To Do. You can expand on this basic display by using one or more of these options. With all the options enabled, the display looks like this:

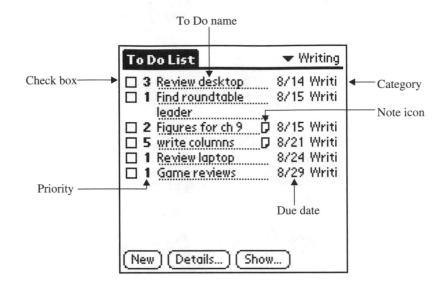

- ■ **Show Due Dates**   The due date format is day/month, which takes some getting used to. If you don't assign a due date to a task, you see a dash instead. On the To Do List, if you tap a due date, you see a list for changing the date.

- ■ **Show Priorities**   This displays the priority to the left of the To Do name. The priority can be adjusted by tapping the number on the To Do List view.

- ■ **Show Categories**   The category of the task appears on the right edge of the To Do List view if you use this option. You can assign a category to an unfilled To Do (or change the category of a previously filed entry) by tapping the category name on the To Do List view.

Delete Old To Dos

For most people, To Dos are not like diamonds—they don't last forever. After you check off a task that says "pick up a loaf of bread," how long do you need a record of having accomplished that goal? That's why your Visor provides a method of removing tasks you no longer want.

Each individual task takes up an embarrassingly small amount of memory, but when you accumulate a few hundred To Dos, they can start to add up. If you have enough of them, your completed To Dos can actually mean the difference between installing and not installing that cool new utility you found on the Internet. The Visor offers you two ways to eliminate tasks:

- **Delete tasks one at a time**   If you need to delete only one To Do, tap in the To Do to select it. Then tap Details and tap the Delete button on the To Do Details dialog box. Tap OK and the To Do will be gone from your Visor.

TIP   *A faster way to delete a selected task is to choose Record | Delete Item from the menu.*

- **Delete a whole bunch of tasks at once**   If you use the To Do List a lot and develop a backlist of dozens, or hundreds, of completed tasks from time to time, axing them one at a time could become a full-time job. Instead, you should purge them. A purge deletes all completed tasks, so be sure you want To Do this—some folks like to keep a record of completed To Dos. To purge your To Do List, choose Record | Purge from the menu. The Purge dialog box appears, asking if you really want to delete your completed To Dos. If your answer is yes, tap OK.

TIP   *If you want to preserve a copy of your completed tasks, check the Save Archive Copy on PC option and then load the archive into the Palm Desktop when you need to refer to the entries.*

9

Share and Hide Your To Dos

Delegation is the key to successful management. At least that's what we've been told. We don't actually work with anyone we can delegate to, but it sounds like solid business advice, nonetheless. You can use your Visor as a solid delegation tool by beaming tasks to other people. Just like in other applications, you can beam a single item or all the items in a specific category. Here's the skinny:

- **Beam a single To Do**   To beam one To Do to someone, choose a task by tapping inside the To Do name. Then choose Record | Beam Item from the menu.

- **Beam a whole bunch of items**   You can beam an entire category's worth of To Dos at once. To do this, switch the current view to show the category you want to beam. You can choose a category from the list at the top-right corner of the screen, or press the hard To Do button several times until the category you want appears. Then choose Record | Beam Category from the menu.

But what if your intent is to hide To Dos, not share them? That's easy, too. You can make one or more of your To Dos private. After that, no one but you can see them. Do this:

1. Select a To Do by tapping in the name field.

2. Tap the Details button. You see the To Do Item Details dialog box.

3. Tap the Private box to add a check mark. Now the entry is marked as private. Tap OK and you see this dialog box:

> **Private Records**
>
> (i) **You have marked this record Private. Go to the Security application and tap the Hide button to hide all Private records.**
>
> [OK]

4. Tap OK to close the dialog box.

The To Do probably isn't hidden yet—you still have one more step to go. To make your To Do disappear, you need to enable the Private Records feature in the Security app. For details on how to do this, see Chapter 12. You can hide and show private data whenever you want using this feature.

A Better To Do List

We hear what you're saying (figuratively, of course . . . Rick hears voices all the time, but he assures me it's just his dog telling him to do things). Anyway, you're claiming the To Do List simply isn't powerful enough. Well, there's a great alternative called ToDo PLUS (from Hands High Software at www.handshigh.com).

ToDo PLUS enables you to include drawings in your tasks, use templates to customize your entries, add alarms, and much more. One of its most interesting features is a comprehensive set of filters that enable you to display your tasks in a variety of useful ways. Give it a try and you may never want to use the built-in To Do List again.

Chapter 10 The Memo Pad

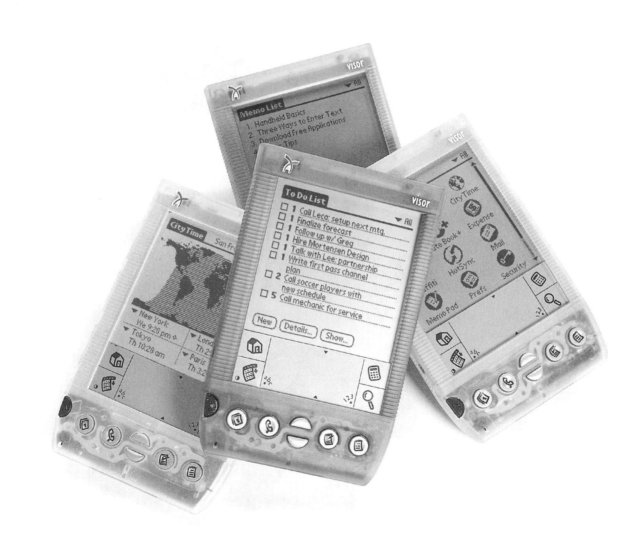

How to...

- View the Memo List
- Create new memos
- Cut, copy, and paste text in a memo
- Assign categories to memos
- Customize the appearance of memos in the Memo List
- Beam memos
- Make memos private
- Delete old memos

Most of your Visor's applications enable you to attach long notes to your entries. A note in the Address Book, for instance, enables you to list directions to a person's house, the names of all his kids, or ten reasons not to visit him for Thanksgiving. But there's also an application designed to do nothing but create long notes. These memos can be memory joggers, information you need to take on a trip, or anything that isn't explicitly connected to an address, an appointment, or a to-do. The Memo Pad is your chance to color outside the lines, in a sense, and leave yourself any kind of message you want.

View the Memo Pad

The Memo Pad has two views—the Memo List (which is, not surprisingly, a list of all the memos you've created) and the Memo View, which shows you the contents of whatever memo you select from the Memo List. When you start the memo Pad, it always starts in the Memo List view. As with all the other core applications, you can start the Memo Pad in two ways:

- Press the Memo Pad button, which is the right-most button on your Visor's case.

Memo Pad

■ Tap the onscreen Memo Pad icon in the Visor's applications.

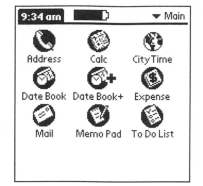

As you can see in Figure 10-1, the Visor displays each of your memos in a list, with the first line of the memo visible as a kind of title that lets you know what's inside. There's room for 11 entries onscreen at one time; the rest appear "above" or "below" the screen, depending on where you are within the Memo List. Getting around is easy—just scroll down to see more memos. As in other Visor applications, you can scroll around in two ways:

■ Tap the scroll arrows on the right edge of the screen

■ Press the scroll button on the Visor's front panel

Each time you scroll, your Visor moves the list by one complete page. This means, if you scroll down, the bottom entry on the page become the top entry after scrolling.

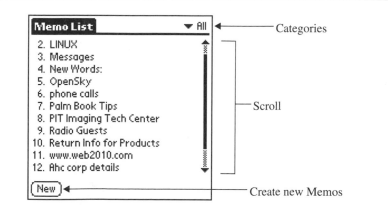

FIGURE 10-1   The Memo List displays all your memos

10

TIP *Another way to get around the Memo List is by using the categories. If your memos are divided into more than one category, every time you press the Memo Pad button, you switch categories. You can cycle through the first page of tasks in each category by pressing this button repeatedly.*

Create New Memos

Sure, a New button is at the bottom of the Memo List—but you don't need to use it. Just start writing, and the Visor switches from the Memo List view to the Memo View. Whatever you write appears in the new, blank memo you're creating. Do you ever need to use the New button? No, not really.

The memo can be as long as you want to make it—all the way up to 4,096 characters, or about 600 words on average. That's pretty long, and should suit your needs most of the time. You can include blank lines and divide your memo into paragraphs—anything you need to make it logical and readable.

TIP *You can't really name your memos in the sense that you can save files on the PC with a specific filename, but the first line of the memo is what appears in the Memo List. To keep things neat and organized, you can write a brief description of the memo on the top line, and then start the memo itself on the next line.*

Use Editing Tools

The familiar cut, copy, and paste tools are available in every Visor app, but nowhere are they more important than in the Memo Pad, where you're likely to be writing more than a sentence or two. Don't forget you needn't create text from scratch all the time; using these edit tools you can move text from other applications and rearrange it to suit your needs.

Suppose, for example, you previously had a Date Book appointment that read:

```
Meeting with Ted
```

Within that appointment, you might have created a note that looked like this:

```
Discuss performance review
Get feedback on budget for 2Q
Agree on approach for marketing plan
```

If you want to have a record of your meeting with Ted, take notes in a Memo. Open the appointment note and select the three lines of text from the note. With the text selected, choose Edit | Copy from the menu (or you can use the Command gesture and write *C*). Then switch to the Memo Pad, create a new memo, and paste the text into the memo using Edit | Paste (or Command-P using the Graffiti shortcut).

After pasting the text into the memo, you can use it as your agenda items—and insert notes as needed, giving you a complete record of the meeting. When you HotSync your Visor, you can paste that data into Word or some other application, and then generate a formal report.

Memo Pad Assistants

Many tools around can enhance the experience of creating long notes in the Memo Pad. Here are a few examples you might want to try:

■ A program called TextPlus suggests common words as you write. Even before a word is complete, TextPlus offers likely options for what you might be writing. This can significantly reduce the time you spend creating text in the Memo Pad.

■ EVEdit does a few things, but one of the most interesting is it enables you to store up to ten items at once in the clipboard, so you can "collect" things to paste into a memo from a variety of apps and drop them all into the memo at once.

■ If you don't like using the menu to access cut, copy, and paste, try FieldEditHack. This program gives you a pop-up list of editing tools when you select words on the Visor screen.

■ ScreenWrite lets you write directly on the Visor's screen. If you feel limited by the small Graffiti drawing area, this utility is for you.

TIP *Don't forget you can choose Edit | Select All and Edit | Copy to transfer the entire contents of a memo into another Visor app, like a Date Book note.*

10

Assign Categories

After you accumulate a few memos, you might find the Memo List view getting a bit crowded. It's hard to find the right memo when you're surfing through dozens of entries. Instead, use the Visor's ever-helpful category filing system. Assign a category in this way:

1. Create a new memo.

2. Tap the Details button. The Memo Details dialog box appears.

3. Choose a category from the Category list.

4. Tap OK to close the Memo Details dialog box.

After your memos are arranged into categories, you can cycle through them easily by pressing the Memo Pad button on the Visor's case.

Add a Phone Number

Sometimes you may want to add information from the Address Book to a memo. Suppose, for instance, you just wrote someone's name in a memo and you'd like their phone number to appear there as well. Ordinarily, you'd have to switch to the Address Book, look up the phone number, copy the information to the clipboard, and then paste it into the memo. That's an awful lot of work.

There's an easier way. Using the Visor's Phone Lookup feature, you can tell the Memo Pad to insert that information automatically. Here's how to do it:

1. In an open memo, write the last name of someone who is already stored in the Address Book.

2. Leave the cursor at the end of the name.

3. Choose Options | Phone Lookup from the Visor's menu.

If only one entry with that name is in the Address Book, it'll be inserted into the memo. If several names exist, then your Visor will switch to the Address Book and wait until you choose the name you want, and then switch back to the Memo Pad.

Arrange Memos in the Memo List

Computer users are, for the most part, fanatical organizers. Windows users spend hours straightening up the Desktop so icons appear in exactly the right place when the computer starts each morning. Mac users drag folders around so everything looks "just so," applying a lot more effort to the digital cleaning process than they ever would to their actual office space.

That said, we're sure you'll be interested in a cool way of organizing your memos in the Memo List. This isn't just pointless busy work, either: if you need to open the same memo over and over, it can help to have it appear at the top of the list whenever you open the Memo List. At the very least, we're sure you want to understand how to take control of the way in which memos appear onscreen.

When you add memos to the Memo List, by default the newest ones always appear at the end of the list. In a sense, then, the default order of Memo List entries is chronological, with oldest entries at the top and newest ones at the bottom.

It's a little more complicated than that, though. You can specify the sort order of memos by choosing Options | Preferences. You get two choices:

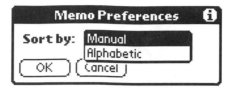

- **Manual**   This is the default mode your Visor uses out of the box. New memos are added to the bottom of the list, but you can actually drag-and-drop memos to different positions in the list. Suppose you have a frequently used memo you want to appear at the top of the screen. Tap and hold the stylus on the entry, and then drag the stylus up to the position you want it to appear. You should see a line move with the stylus, indicating where the memo will land if you release the stylus (see Figure 10-2).

- **Alphabetic**   This option sorts all entries into alphabetical order. If you select this option, the drag-and-drop method of moving memos won't work unless you revert to the manual method.

 If you like, you can organize your memos alphabetically, and then switch back to manual and fine-tune the list layout by dragging-and-dropping specific memos. If you switch to the Alphabetic mode, though, all the manual changes you made to the list will be lost.

10

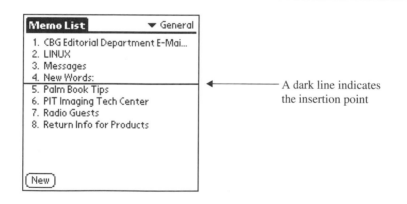

A dark line indicates the insertion point

FIGURE 10-2   You can drag-and-drop memos to put them in a specific order

Blank Lines for Emphasis

Here's a trick you can try if you think the Memo List is too cluttered. If you use the manual ordering method and arrange your memos in a specific order in a near-fanatical way, you might be bothered by the fact that memo number 4 is "touching" memo number 5. Rick, for instance, is adamant about not eating his mashed potatoes if they comes in contact with his peas. Maybe you suffer from the same kind of problem on your Visor.

Try this as a solution: create a new memo with a blank first line. You need to enter at least one character on the second line because the Visor doesn't let you create a completely blank memo. Close the memo and you'll find you've made a new memo with a blank header. Drag this memo between two memos you want separated and voilà—you've found a way to separate memos.

```
┌─────────────────────────────────┐
│ Memo List          ▼ General    │
│  1. CBG Editorial Department E-Mai... │
│  2. LINUX                       │
│  3. Messages                    │
│  4. New Words:                  │
│  5. Palm Book Tips              │
│  6.                             │
│  7. PIT Imaging Tech Center     │
│  8. Radio Guests                │
│  9.                             │
│ 10. Return Info for Products    │
│                                 │
│ ( New )                         │
└─────────────────────────────────┘
```

Work with Your Memos

You have the same 4,096-character limit on writing memos as you have with notes in other parts of the Visor suite of applications. That's plenty of space to write, though, as long as you're not trying to create your autobiography on the Visor (if you are, in fact, trying to create a really long document, see Chapter 17 for details on applications that enable you to do that).

When you have a long document, scrolling around can become an issue—you may need to get to the top, bottom, or middle of a memo quickly. You can move around in a memo in a few ways:

- ■ **Scroll one line at a time**   Tap the scroll arrows at the top or bottom of the screen.
- ■ **Scroll a page at a time**   Tap in the scroll bar or press the scroll button on your Visor's case.
- ■ **Move to the first line of a memo**   Choose Options | Go to Top of Page from the menu.
- ■ **Move to the last line of a memo**   Choose Options | Go to Bottom of Page from the menu.

You might also be interested in changing the memo's font. We prefer the default font because it makes the text small and puts the most memo text on the page at once, but some folks have trouble reading the type. If you want to make the font bigger, you can choose from three fonts. Just choose Options | Font and pick a typeface that makes you happy.

Beam Memos

You can send a memo or a group of memos to another Palm OS device just as easily as beaming any other kind of information. Here's how:

- **Beam one memo**   To beam a memo, you need to tap the memo you want to beam—this displays the memo in the Memo view. Then choose Record | Beam Memo from the menu. That's all there is to it.

- **Beam a bunch of memos**   To beam more than one memo, they all have to be in the same category. Make sure you are in the Memo List view and switch to the category you want to beam. You can do this by choosing the category from the list at the top-right of the screen or by pressing the Memo List button on the Visor case until you see the category you want. Then choose Record | Beam Category from the menu.

Make a Memo Private

If you have private information stored in a memo, you can easily hide specific memos from prying eyes. The procedure is essentially the same as with other Visor applications. Do this:

1. In the Memo List, select a memo by tapping it.

2. Tap the Details button. You see the To Memo Details dialog box.

3. Tap the Private box to add a check mark. Now the entry is marked as private. Tap OK and you see this dialog box:

4. Tap OK to close the dialog box.

The Memo probably isn't hidden yet—you still have one more step to go. To make your Memo disappear, you need to enable the Private Records feature in the Security app. For details on how to do this, see Chapter 12. You can hide and show private data whenever you want using this feature.

10

How to ... Create a Memo in the Memo Pad

Working with the Memo Pad is a snap. In summary, here's what you need to do to create memos:

1. Press the Memo Pad button on your Visor.

2. Start writing in the Graffiti area to create a new memo.

3. Tap the Details button and assign your new memo to a specific category.

4. Tap the Done button to close your new memo.

5. Drag the memo to put it in a specific place in the Memo List.

Delete Memos

No matter how much you like your memos, eventually you may need to delete some. To delete a memo, do this:

1. In the Memo List, tap the memo you want to delete. The Memo view appears.

2. Tap the Details button. You should see the Memo Details dialog box.

3. Tap the Delete button.

4. Tap OK.

The memo is then deleted from your Visor. If desired, you can save a backup of this memo to the Palm Desktop by checking the box that says Save archive copy on PC. You can see how to restore this backup in Chapter 5.

TIP *Here's another way to delete a memo: with the memo already open, choose Record, Delete Memo from the menu.*

Cool Things to Do with the Memo Pad

Do you know what surprises us? Lots of things, actually. Dave is surprised Rick has no appreciation for the fine arts—specifically, bands like Pink Floyd, the Velvet Underground, and especially Kristin Hersh and the Throwing Muses. (Inexplicably, Rick has an entirely different definition of "fine arts.")

More to the point, though, we're surprised at how many people can't seem to come up with good uses for the Memo Pad, and they let it languish while they use the Address Book and Date Book all the time. To help you fully realize the potential of this cool little application, here are some helpful suggestions for how to use the Memo Pad:

- **Create a "Million Dollar Idea" memo**   Create a memo with a header that says **Million Dollar Ideas**. No matter when or where you come up with one of those incredibly amazing ideas that will help you retire before you turn 50, pull out your Visor and jot it down.

- **Create a trade show category**   Got a lot of booths to visit at next month's lawn care trade show? Create a category and put all the memos for that event in the category. As you walk the show floor, you can reference your notes about the show in one easy-to-find set of memos.

- **Store passwords**   This one is dangerous, so make sure you set it to private. But if you have a lot of passwords you routinely need—for your ISP, Web sites, computer logons, and that kind of thing, you can store them all in one place in a memo for passwords. We have to reiterate this is kind of dangerous—if your Visor is stolen, you can give all your passwords away if they're not protected properly. No IT department on Earth will sanction this particular tip, and we won't even admit we wrote it down if questioned in court.

- **Meeting notes**   Take notes during a meeting and beam the memo to others when the meeting is over.

- **Keep a "Phone Messages" memo**   Name a memo Phone Messages and when you check voice mail, jot down the notes in your Visor in this memo. If you're diligent about this, you won't end up with a million yellow stickies all over your desk after each VM-checking session. And names and phone numbers will be in your Visor where you need them, not splayed out all over your desk.

- **Store your new words**   Dave makes up new words in an effort to evolve the English language at a grass-roots level. If you, too, make up new words frequently, store them in a **New Words** memo, so you don't accidentally forget them. Chizzy! (Rick is working on a way to delete that particular memo from Dave's Visor, perhaps by using a large hammer.)

10

Where to Find It

Web Site	Address	What's There
SmartCell Technology	www.smartcell.com	TextPlus
EVSoft	www.evscl.com	EVEdit
Nori Kanazawa's site	www.shin.nu/~kan/	FieldEditHack
Jeremy Radlow's site	www.inkverse.com	ScreenWrite
Hands High Software	www.handshigh.com	Memo PLUS

Chapter 11

The Expense Program

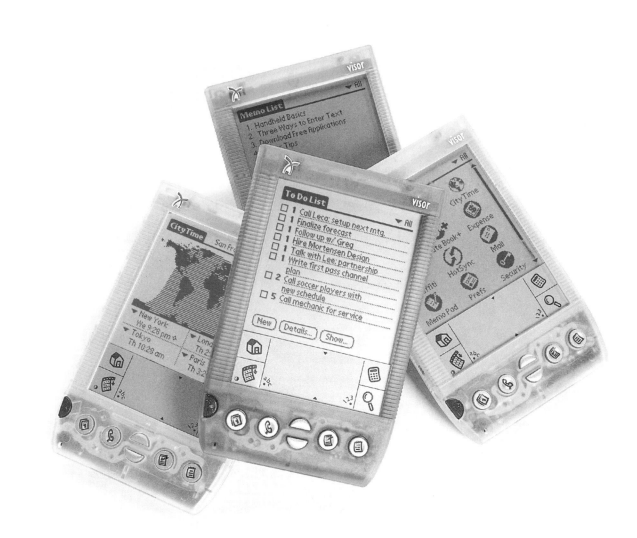

How to...

- Use a Visor to track expenses
- Run the Expense program
- Log new expense items
- Manage expense details
- Use the auto-complete feature
- Use Expense to track mileage
- Select different currencies
- Change the way expenses are displayed
- Make effective use of categories
- Delete expense records
- Synchronize your expenses with Excel
- Change the expense template used by Excel
- Synchronize your expenses on a Macintosh
- Find other expense-management software and solutions

Introduced with version 2.0 of the Palm OS, Expense is an often overlooked but decidedly valuable addition to the Palm software arsenal. With it, you can track and manage all your expenses and mileage, whether for personal reconciliation or reimbursement from your company or clients. While a bit on the rudimentary side, Expense does afford quick and easy item entry and push-button synchronization with Microsoft Excel. Ultimately, it can create detailed and attractive-looking expense reports that are ready to print.

NOTE *What if you're not an Excel user, or you'd prefer to synchronize your expense data with software like Quicken or Microsoft Money? In that case, Expense may not be for you. However, there are third-party alternatives that offer greater compatibility with desktop software. We talk about some of them later in this chapter.*

Getting Started with Expense

Put simply, *Expense* is like an electronic folder for your receipts and a logbook for your mileage. Whenever you buy something, you just add it to your expense list. Whenever you take a business-related road trip, you do the same. On the Visor side, using Expense is a piece of cake. (Using it with Palm Desktop is even easier, but we get to that in "From Expense to Excel," later in the chapter.)

To start Expense, simply tap the Expense icon in the main Applications screen.

Creating New Expense Items

Adding new expense records is a snap. Here's the basic process:

1. Tap New to create a blank expense item. You see a line appear with the date, the words Expense Type, and a blank field next to a dollar sign. Note your cursor appears in that field.

```
┌─────────────────────────────────┐
│ Expense            ▼ Sample     │
│ 11/10 -Expense type-  $ ........ │
│                                 │
│                                 │
│                                 │
│                                 │
│                                 │
│                                 │
│                                 │
│ (New) (Details...) (Show...)    │
└─────────────────────────────────┘
```

2. Write in the amount of the purchase or, if you're recording mileage, the number of miles driven.

3. Now, tap the words Expense Type to see a predefined list of expense categories and choose the one that most closely matches your purchase. If you're recording mileage, select that option and notice the dollar sign changes to the abbreviation mi.

```
┌─────────────────────────────────┐
│ Expense            ▼ Unfiled    │
│ 1/2  │Mileage    ↑│   6.00 ↑    │
│ 1/5  │Other       │  28.64      │
│ 1/6  │Parking     │  10.43      │
│ 1/8  │Postage     │  14.84      │
│ 1/12 │Snack       │  41.58      │
│ 1/13 │Subway      │  33.02      │
│ 1/13 │Supplies    │  22.10      │
│ 1/13 │Taxi        │ 118.91      │
│ 1/13 │Telephone   │  13.16      │
│ 1/20 │Tips        │  18.49      │
│ 1/22 │Tolls       │  35.01 ↓    │
│      │Train       │             │
│ (New) (Details...) (Show...)    │
└─────────────────────────────────┘
```

> **NOTE** *Unlike most lists that appear in Visor applications, the Expense list cannot be modified or expanded. In short, you're stuck with the categories provided. If you can't find one that fits the situation, choose Other.*

4. By default, any new expense is created with the current date. If, however, you're catching up on previous purchases, you can tap right on the date that's shown to bring up the calendar, and then select whatever date is appropriate.

There, wasn't that easy? You've just recorded a new expense. Now let's talk about recording the more specific details of that expense.

TIP *You can save yourself a step when you create a new expense by not tapping the New button first. Instead, just start writing the dollar amount in the numeric portion of the Graffiti area. You see a new expense item is instantly created. This same practice also works in Date Book, Memo Pad, and To Do List.*

Modifying Expense Details

Obviously, any expense report worth its salt needs to have more than just the date, expense type, and amount. As you probably guessed, your next stop after entering these tidbits is the Details button.

NOTE *Before tapping the Details button, make sure you select the expense item you want to modify. You know when an item is selected because the date is highlighted and a cursor appears in the "amount" field.*

The Receipt Details screen (see Figure 11-1) enables you to specify the minutiae of your purchase—from the category to which it belongs to the type of currency used to the city where it took place.

- **Category**   Like most other Visor applications, Expense supports the use of categories. Thus, you can divide your expenditures into "Business" or "Personal," or use any other categories you prefer. We think you might want to modify, or even delete, the two predefined categories—unless you spend a lot of time in New York and Paris. If you need a refresher course in categories, see Chapter 2.

- **Type**   Having second thoughts about the expense type you chose? You can change it right here.

```
        Receipt Details
Category:  ▼ Unfiled
    Type:  ▼ Postage
 Payment:  ▼ Cash
Currency:  ▼ $
  Vendor:  ....................
    City:  ....................
Attendees: Who...
  ( OK ) (Cancel) (Delete) (Note)  ↑
```

FIGURE 11-1   You can record any or all of the crucial details of your expense in the Receipt Details screen

■ **Payment**   Did you pay cash? Pull out the old American Express card? In this list, you choose your method of payment. While Discover and Diner's Club aren't included, you can use the generic "credit card" option for these or other cards.

■ **Currency**   Paying in deutsche Marks? Euro dollars? Take your pick from this list. Five types of currency are displayed and by tapping Edit Currencies you can replace any or all four with monetary symbols from several dozen different countries.

> **TIP** *Don't see the country you need in the currencies list? You can add your own countries by visiting the Custom Currencies screen, which is accessible from the main Expense screen. Just tap Menu | Options | Custom Currencies. The Palm OS enables you to add up to four extra countries.*

```
┌─────────────────────────────┐
│      Custom Currencies      │
│  Create your own custom     │
│  currencies by tapping on   │
│  the country name below:    │
│                             │
│          Country 1          │
│          Country 2          │
│          Country 3          │
│          Country 4          │
│                             │
│  ( OK )  ( Cancel )         │
└─────────────────────────────┘
```

■ **Vendor**   One of the most important fields in the Details screen, Vendor is where you name the restaurant in which you dined or the store where you bought something.

■ **City**   And just where were you when you did all this spending? In this field, you can record the name of the city.

> **NOTE** *The Vendor and City fields are equipped with a handy auto-complete feature that saves you having to write lengthy names more than once. Suppose you buy some supplies at Office Max. In your first expense entry for that store, you have to write out the full name. Next time, however, as you start to enter the name, you see Office Max appear after the first letter or two (depending on how many other "remembered" vendor names start with the letter O). Now you can move right on to the next field or tap OK.*

■ **Attendees**   In creating expense reports, listing who you met or dined with is sometimes important. By tapping the Who button, you see a blank, Memo Pad-like page in which you can write the names of anyone who joined you. Note, too, the Lookup button at the bottom of this screen. Tapping it gives you access to your Visor's address book—handy if you met with folks already in your contact list.

■ **Note**   If you need to jot a few notes about the expense, whether for reimbursement purposes or just as a personal reminder, tap the Note button for access to a blank page. Remember, the note stays attached to that particular expense entry and is not accessible in, say, Memo Pad.

11

NOTE   *The Receipt Details screen changes slightly if you're working with a mileage entry. Specifically, you see no options are available next to Payment or Currency.*

The Show Menu

The third button on the main Expense screen, Show, opens the Show Options dialog box, which enables you to modify a few of the display options for your expense list, as shown in Figure 11-2, and described here:

- **Sort by**   Normally, your expenses are sorted by date, from oldest to newest. If you'd rather have them listed based on the type of expense, select that option from this menu. The expenses will now be shown in alphabetical, categorical order.

- **Distance**   If you live outside the U.S., you'd no doubt prefer to have your mileage listed in kilometers instead of miles. Here's where you can select that option. Mileage entries will now be shown with the abbreviation km.

- **Show currency**   When unchecked, you no longer see dollar signs next to your expenses.

Managing Expenses and Purging Records

Before we dive into the process of turning your expense records into reports, let's talk a bit about effective management of those records. We strongly encourage the use of categories, not just for keeping business and personal expenses separate, but also for keeping track of multiple sets of business expenditures.

For instance, suppose you're a consultant with many clients. You could create a special category for each one of them, keeping his or her expenses separate, instead of lumping them all into a single list. If you record expenses for only one company, you might want to make a category for each month. That could make life easier when the time comes to generate your reports.

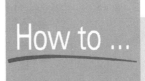 **Track Your Mileage with Expense**

For many business people, keeping accurate mileage records is a must—not just for the sake of reimbursement, but for tax purposes as well. Fortunately, mileage is one of the included expense types in Expense.

1. Create a new entry.

2. Tap the Expense Type field, and then choose Mileage. Notice the amount field changes from a dollar sign to mi.

3. Write in the number of miles you traveled, and then tap Details to record the specifics of your trip.

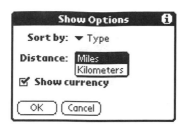

FIGURE 11-2   In the Show Options dialog box, you can modify some basic display and sorting options for your expense list

Deleting Expenses

Whether you file expense reports on a monthly basis or at the conclusion of each business trip, you probably want to eliminate the old records so you can start fresh with the next month or trip. Expense enables you to purge all the records in any selected category (another reason to make frequent use of them). Tap Menu | Record | Purge, and then the category you want to "empty." As with most delete options on the Visor, you're given an "Are you sure?" warning before the category is purged.

To delete an individual expense entry, tap once to highlight it, and then tap the Details button. In the screen that appears, tap the Yes button.

From Expense to Excel

One key difference between Expense and most of the other core Visor programs is that the data you enter isn't replicated—or even accessible—in Palm Desktop. Certainly, the data is transferred to your PC when you HotSync and backed up in a folder on your hard drive. But as for turning those raw numbers into an actual printed expense report, we have good news and bad news.

The good news is it's a one-step procedure. In Palm Desktop for Windows, you simply click the Expense button on the toolbar. The bad news is you must have Microsoft Excel (version 5.0 or later) installed on your computer because the Expense data gets shot directly into an Excel spreadsheet—and can't go anywhere else. (Okay, it's really only bad news if you're not an Excel user.)

Making the Transfer

As you've already discovered, a toolbar located along the left side of the Palm Desktop screen enables you to navigate between Date Book, Memo Pad, and so forth. The fifth button down on that toolbar is labeled Expense—*but don't click it yet*! Not until we explain exactly what's going to happen when you do.

TIP   *Actually, you needn't click the button at all or even venture into Palm Desktop, but it's helpful if you're using Microsoft Outlook or some other personal information manager (PIM). You can launch the expense-report creation procedure by clicking Start | Program Files | Palm Desktop | Expense Report.*

Before commencing, make sure you HotSync, so all your latest Expense data is transferred to your PC. Then, whether you click the Expense button or choose the menu option, two actions occur: Microsoft Excel starts, and then opens a file called *expense.db* (which, for your information, is contained in the C:\Palm\Username\Expense folder on your hard drive). This is the file that's created by Expense and updated with your recorded expense data every time you HotSync.

Expense and the Macintosh

Notice that in our discussion of Expense and Excel, we referenced only Palm Desktop for Windows. Unfortunately, Macintosh users don't have quite the same flexibility in this department. In fact, Expense isn't mentioned anywhere in the help files for Palm Desktop for Macintosh. Inexplicably, the Expense-to-Excel conduit never made it into that version of the software.

Third-party developers to the rescue! Shana Corporation's Informed Expense Creator can convert Expense data into categorized, organized, totaled reports. Even better, the Basic version of the software is free for the download. You can find information on the software and download it from www.shana.com/product/palm/default.html.

NOTE *Depending on the version of Excel you have installed, you may get a warning message about the use of macros and their possible infection by viruses. Because it's impossible for expense.db to become infected, go ahead and click Enable macros. If you don't, you won't be able to access your Expense data.*

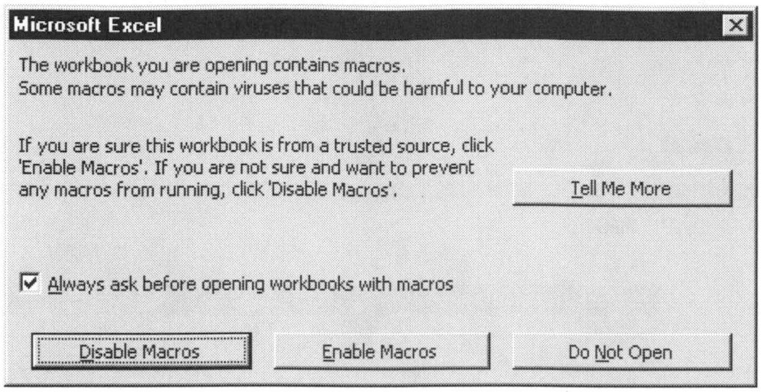

Inside Excel

Once you move past the macro warning (if it appeared at all on your system), you find yourself looking at a dialog box called Expense Report, as shown in Figure 11-3. Here's a rundown of the options available to you and what they mean.

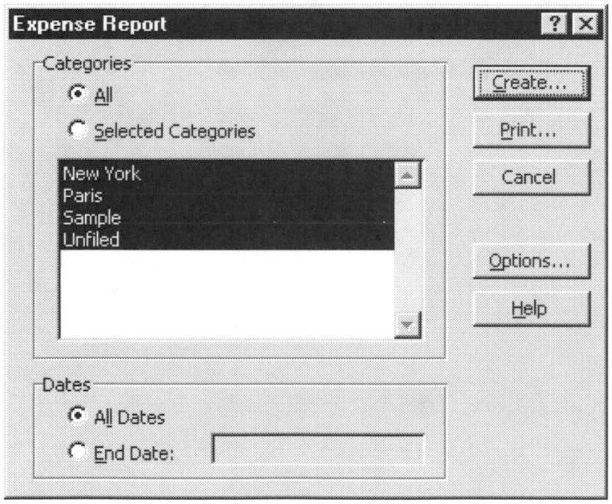

FIGURE 11-3   In the Expense Report dialog box, you can choose a template and specify which expense categories to include

■ **Categories** By default, all your Expense categories are selected for inclusion in the report. However, if you choose the Selected Categories button, you then have the option of including or excluding specific categories. (Hold down the CTRL key while clicking to select more than one.)

■ **Dates** Although you can't specify a range of dates for inclusion in the report, you can choose an end date. Select the End Date option and enter the desired date in this format: MM/DD/YY.

The Options Screen

When you click the Options button, you see a new dialog box in which you can enter the specifics of this particular report:

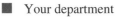
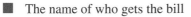

■ Your name

■ Your department

■ Your phone number

■ The name of the project

■ The name of who gets the bill

Below all these fields is a drop-down menu where you can select a template, which determines the type of expense report that will be generated. In addition to a basic expense listing, four report types are available (as represented by the following extremely nondescript names):

■ **SAMPLE1.XLT** A generalized travel-expense reimbursement claim form (see Figure 11-4).

Travel Expense Reimbursement Claim Form

Employee Name: Rick Broida   Client: _____   Office Use Only:

Audited: _____

Date Submitted: 11/11/99   Project: How To Do Everything...   Approved: _____

Processed: _____

Mls/Km Rate
0.29

Date	Country	Currency Amount	Exchange Rate	US Dollar Amount	Expense Type	Note: Description of Expense Claim
1/2/99	United State	6.00	1.00	$6.00	Postage	
1/5/99	United State	28.64	1.00	$28.64	Supplies	
1/6/99	United State	10.43	1.00	$10.43	Postage	
1/8/99	United State	14.84	1.00	$14.84	Supplies	
1/12/99	United State	41.58	1.00	$41.58	Postage	
1/13/99	United State	33.02	1.00	$33.02	Postage	
1/13/99	United State	22.10	1.00	$22.10	Postage	
1/13/99	United State	118.91	1.00	$118.91	Supplies	Biz cards for Bob, postcards for Canada promotion
1/13/99	United State	13.16	1.00	$13.16	Dinner	Boy, was that good Chinese food!
1/20/99	United State	18.49	1.00	$18.49	Postage	

FIGURE 11-4   One of the four sample expense reports Palm Desktop can generate in Excel

- **SAMPLE2.XLT**   A detailed, categorized, ten-days-at-a-glance travel expense report. Depending on how much Expense data you logged, this template can take several minutes to compile.

- **SAMPLE3.XLT**   A variation on SAMPLE2.XLT, this one operates in nine-day stretches and includes fields for indicating who paid for specific expenses: the employee or the company.

- **SAMPLE4.XLT**   A weekly expense report that's rife with details, including foreign-currency exchange rates and boxes for all the people who need to sign off on the report.

As made clear by their filenames, these templates are just samples of what can be done with the raw Expense data. If you're a whiz with Excel, you can no doubt create your own templates and reports.

Local Currency Selection   The last item in the Options box, Local Currency, enables you to choose a country or enter the name of your country's local currency. When you do so, you are then given the option of entering exchange rates before Excel generates the report.

What You Can Do with the Reports

Once Excel has created an expense report, you can either print it as is or make changes and/or additions. One definite perk is any changes made to an expense amount are automatically reflected in the totals for that report. This is also the time to replace any expense types labeled as Other with more accurate descriptions.

> **TIP** *When printing an expense report in Excel, it helps to use the Print Preview function first to make sure your data is properly oriented on the page.*

Alternatives to Expense

Truth be told, Expense is not the most robust expense-management program, especially relative to some of the software created by third-party developers. If your needs extend beyond what Expense has to offer—and for businesspeople who rely heavily on reimbursement reports, they probably do—you should definitely check out one of the many available alternatives.

We've spotlighted some of the major programs but, remember, these are designed for expense-tracking only. Other programs manage billing as well as expenses and enable you to track your bank accounts and stock portfolios. (We talk about those in Chapter 19.) So don't be discouraged if none of these packages fit your particular bill. Chances are good a program out there will fit.

AnyExpense 1.0

One of the newest expense programs to hit the Visor scene, Palm-Top.com's AnyExpense is aimed at professionals who juggle multiple projects simultaneously. It employs different forms for entering client, project, and expense information, and enables you to view expense entries by project, client, day, week, or month.

Expense Sheet	⬛	▼ View	
Date	**Project**	**Amount**	
2.10	Develop-123	13,78	
5.10	meeting-007	2,00	
24.10	Develop-123	7,50	
27.10	manua01-a1	15,00	
31.10	Develop-123	23,55	
3.11	present-1	60,00	
25.11	present-1	128,45	

Expense Entry
Project Entry
Client Entry   250,28

Currently, the only way to transfer AnyExpense data to your PC is via its export-to-Memo Pad option, which generates a memo that is then copied to Palm Desktop when you HotSync. This is a less-than-elegant solution, especially for those who need to print detailed reports, but the company does currently have a specialized Windows conduit in development.

ExpenseDirector 3.1

Iambic Software's ExpenseDirector enables you to track expenses by type, account, payee, client, project, and the currency for the expense. It supports the creation of customized item lists, so your data entry will speed up over time. Particularly noteworthy are the program's filtering and sorting options, which enable you to view records for a single day or a range of days and to sort by any of the aforementioned tracking criteria.

There is one hitch: ExpenseDirector can synchronize data to your Windows PC, but only with Iambic's ExpenseDirector for Windows—a separate program that's equally robust on the PC side. You can buy ExpenseDirector alone for $29.95 or bundled with its Windows counterpart for $59.95.

ExpensePlus

11

One of the most robust and versatile expense managers available, WalletWare's ExpensePlus uses an icon-based interface to simplify the selection of expense types, and automation to fill in dates and amounts for things like hotel stays and car rentals. More important, it can link directly to any existing company expense forms that were created in Excel or FileMaker (including the Mac versions!), so you needn't contend with nonstandard forms. And, if your company's forms aren't based in Excel, WalletWare can design a custom link (for a fee) to other software programs.

ExpenzPro

Zoskware's ExpenzPro works hard to pick up where the built-in Expense application left off. Specifically, ExpenzPro enables you to edit the lists of expense types, accounts, trips, payees, and clients/projects. An included companion program, Reportz, generates expense reports right on your Visor and those are then transferred to your PC using the included ZoskSync conduit. (Alas, Macintosh users are stuck with a save-to-Memo Pad option, similar to the one used by AnyExpense.) The reports are compatible with QuickBooks, Excel, Access, and other programs that support generic data files.

Worth noting is that Zoskware offers a similar product called HourzPro, which manages time and billing, and can integrate with ExpenzPro.

Quicken ExpensAble

The name Quicken is synonymous with finance management. A somewhat lesser-known product, Quicken ExpensAble, began as a PC application and has migrated to the Visor. This software makes it a snap to record reimbursable, nonreimbursable, and personal expenses, and supports split transactions. Also present is the ever-popular AutoFill feature, a Quicken staple that simplifies repetitive data entry.

Naturally, the Visor version of Quicken ExpensAble integrates seamlessly with the computer version, the latter offering report submission via e-mail or the ExpensAble Web site.

Where to Find It

Web Site	Address	What's There
Iambic Software	www.iambic.com	ExpenseDirector 3.1
LandWare	www.landware.com	Quicken ExpensAble
Palm-Top.com	www.palm-top.com	AnyExpense 1.0
Shana Corporation	www.shana.com	Informed Expense Creator, a Macintosh conduit for the Expense program
WalletWare	www.walletware.com	ExpensePlus
Zoskware	www.zoskware.com	ExpenzPro

Chapter 12

The Rest of the Palm OS Team

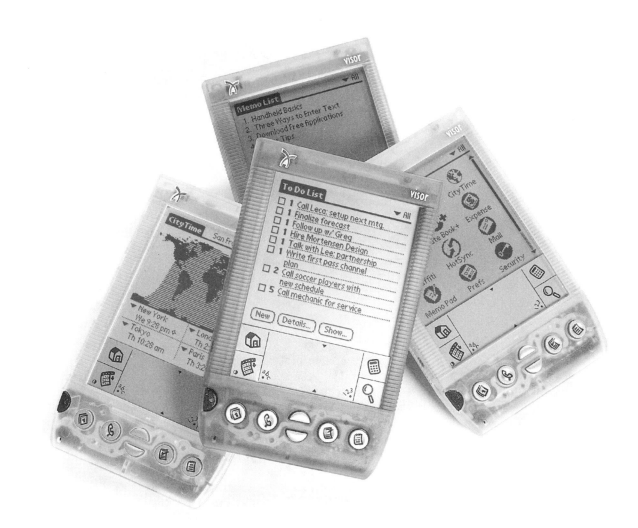

How to...

- Access the Visor's security features
- Set records as private
- Hide or show private records
- Set a security password
- Password-protect your Visor
- Find third-party security measures for your Visor and data
- Help a lost Visor find its way back to you
- Use the Find feature
- Find third-party utilities that extend your search capabilities
- Use the calculator
- Access the calculator's advanced features
- Find third-party calculators
- Use the CityTime world clock application
- Decide whether to use the Mail applet

Now that we've looked at the stars of the Visor's Palm Operating System—Address Book, Date Book, the expense manager, Memo Pad, and To Do List—let's turn our attention to the supporting cast. We're talking about the Security program, which enables you to hide private records and "lock" your Visor; the Find feature, which helps you quickly sift through all your data; the calculator, which, big surprise, calculates; and the potentially mystifying Mail program, used to send and receive e-mail—sort of.

Visor Security

At the risk of sounding like a spy novel, listen up, 007. If your data falls into the wrong hands, it could spell disaster for *M, Q,* and lots of other letters of the alphabet. Fortunately, we've outfitted your Visor with foolproof security measures. Only you will have the access codes. Only you can view Denise Richards' phone number. (Can we have it? Please? Please?)

In all seriousness, it's not unlikely that you'll be storing some sensitive information in your Visor, information that should be kept private. Important passwords, account numbers, meeting locations, contact data—these are among the items you'd be loathe to let a stranger see. Fortunately, the Palm OS offers two effective ways to protect your data: by marking individual records as private and by locking your Visor every time you turn it off.

In both scenarios, you—or anyone who's trying to access your Visor—must supply a password to gain access. The catch-22 is that your Visor and data are totally secure, but you must endure the hassle of entering your password over and over again.

Security 101

To get started with Visor security, find and tap the Security icon. You see the screen shown in Figure 12-1. The first step (although it's the second item on the screen) is choosing a password. Notice the Password box currently says "-Unassigned-"—meaning simply that you haven't entered your password yet. Before you do, read a little further.

What You Should Know About Passwords

The password you choose can be any combination of letters, numbers, symbols, and spaces. You can make it "Spock," or "H4T*Q," or "The quick brown fox." Ideally, it should be something reasonably short, as you'll probably wind up writing it frequently. Don't make it too obvious, like "123," but you could use something as simple as the last four digits of your social-security number or your spouse's initials.

Also, note that capitalization doesn't matter. Even if you make a point to capitalize "Spock" when you enter it as your new password, you can write "spock" to unlock your Visor and it'll work just fine.

CAUTION   *Whatever password you decide on, it's vital that it be something you can easily remember. If you forget it, you could wind up unable to access certain records—or your entire Visor! Thus, if you have even the slightest concern that you might forget your password, write it down on a piece of paper and store it in a safe place. Better safe than sorry.*

Working with Passwords

Okay, let's input a new password on your Visor.

1. Just tap the "-Unassigned-" box, and then use Graffiti or the onscreen keyboard to enter your desired password.

12

Security

Private Records: Show | Hide

Password: -Unassigned-

Password Features:

Forgotten Password...

Turn Off & Lock Device...

FIGURE 12-1   In Security, you select a password for use in hiding private records and locking your Visor

```
┌─────────────────────────────┐
│          Password           │
│ Enter a password:           │
│ spock                       │
│ .......................     │
│                             │
│ If you assign a password, you│
│ must enter it to show private│
│ records.                    │
│                             │
│  ( OK )  ( Cancel )         │
└─────────────────────────────┘
```

Note the warning that's included here: "If you assign a password, you must enter it to show private records." This sounds a little scary, but don't worry—none of your existing records will immediately be affected by your selection of a password. Only when you mark one as private, as we explain later, does your password enter into play.

2. After you tap OK, you are asked to verify the new password by entering it again. And you'll see another warning about what'll happen if your password is forgotten. The moral of the story is, *don't forget your password!*

```
┌─────────────────────────────┐
│          Password           │
│ Verify your new password:   │
│ spock                       │
│ .......................     │
│ If you forget this password │
│ you can tap "Forgotten      │
│ Password...." to delete it, │
│ but any records marked      │
│ Private will be deleted.    │
│                             │
│  ( OK )  ( Cancel )         │
└─────────────────────────────┘
```

3. Tap OK again, and notice the Password box now reads "-Assigned-".

TIP
You can tap this box again at any time to change or delete your password (but you have to supply the original password first).

Now, when you mark records as private, they become hidden from view, and you need to supply your password to "unhide" them. When you use the Turn Off & Lock Device option (see the following section), you need to supply your password the next time you turn on your Visor.

The Forgotten Password Button

Oh, the perils of the forgotten password. For the last time, just don't forget yours, okay? If you do, there's a scary but effective way to reestablish access to those records you marked as private. When you tap the Forgotten Password button, your password will be deleted—and all your marked-as-private records along with it. However, those deleted records will be restored on your Visor the next time you HotSync—provided you set the conduits to Desktop Overwrites Handheld (see "Customizing the HotSync Operation" in Chapter 3 for details).

The Turn Off & Lock Device Button

If you really want to secure what's stored in your Visor, you need to password-protect the entire thing, not just certain records. That's where this button comes in. When you tap it, your Visor switches off and becomes "locked." Translation: When the Visor is turned on again, whether with the power button or one of the application buttons, a screen pops up requiring the password (see Figure 12-2). Without it, there's no getting past that screen.

> **TIP** *While this locking option is undeniably effective, it's a hassle to access. First, you have to find and tap the Security icon, then tap the Turn Off & Lock Device button, and then tap another button labeled Off & Lock. Third-party software to the rescue: Benc Software Productions' LauncherIII, a great utility used to organize your program icons into tabbed windows, also includes a handy "lock" icon. Tap it and your Visor shuts off and locks—one easy step instead of three tedious ones. You can find LauncherIII (which is a free program!) at www.benc.hr.*

You can modify the information that appears on this locked startup screen by going to Prefs | Owner (see Chapter 2 for a refresher). We recommend including your name and phone number, and maybe even a reward offer—all so that anyone who might find your lost Visor will have an easier time returning it (and an incentive to do so). What's a good reward? Considering how much a new Visor would cost you, we're thinking no less than $20.

The Private Records Buttons

Although Private Records is located at the top of the screen, we saved it till last because it relates to the upcoming section on hiding individual records. Simply put, when the Hide option is selected, all records you marked as private will be hidden from view. When you select Show, which you need your password to do, those hidden records are made visible.

12

```
            System Lockout
  This handheld computer is owned
  by:

  Rick Broida
  If found, please call (719)
  555-1234..

  Enter password to access
  this handheld computer:
  |.........................................
  (   OK   )
```

FIGURE 12-2   When you "Turn Off & Lock" your Visor, only the correct password will unlock it

How to ...   Help a Lost Visor Find Its Way Home

The more reliant you become on your Visor—and, trust us, you will become extremely reliant on it—the more devastating it would be to lose it. Fortunately, you can take steps to help ensure its safe return. The easiest is a service called ReturnMe.com, which provides you with an ID tag that you can affix to the back of the Visor. Should someone find the device, all he or she needs to do is call the toll-free number or visit the Web site listed on the tag. ReturnMe.com will pay for pickup and return of the Visor, and even pay a reward to the finder. A mere $9.95 buys you 11 of the specially coded tags (you can use them for other personal items as well), and you pay a service fee only if you wind up using the service.

Hiding Your Records

Having to remember to lock your Visor every time you turn it off, and then having to enter your password every time you turn it on—well, it's a hassle. A more practical means of security might be simply to hide specific records that contain sensitive information. You can do that by marking those records as private.

In the four main applications—Address Book, Date Book, Memo Pad, and To Do List—any record can be marked private, meaning it suddenly becomes invisible and, therefore, inaccessible. Here's how:

1. Select a record (just by tapping on it) in any of the aforementioned programs.

2. Tap the Details button. (In Address Book, you have to tap Edit to get to the screen with the Details button.) You see a window containing some options for that record and a box labeled Private.

Address Entry Details ❶
Show in List: ▼ Work
Category: ▼ PR Contacts
Private: ☑
(OK) (Cancel) (Delete...) (Note)

Event Details ❶
Time: 7:30 pm - 9:30 pm
Date: Tue 11/16/99
Alarm: ☐
Repeat: None
Private: ☐
(OK) (Cancel) (Delete...) (Note)

To Do Item Details ❶
Priority: 1 2 3 4 5
Category: ▾ Unfiled
Due Date: ▾ No Date
Private: ☑
(OK) (Cancel) (Delete...) (Note)

Memo Details ❶
Category: ▾ Unfiled
Private: ☐
(OK) (Cancel) (Delete...)

3. Tap that box, noticing the checkmark that appears. This indicates the record will become private after you tap OK.

4. Tap OK.

Now, if the Private Records option in the Security program is set to Hide, the record you marked as private disappears. Don't freak out—it's still in memory, just not visible. To make it and all other private records visible again, you must return to Security and tap Show. As a reminder, you need to supply your password at that time.

Passwords on the Desktop

Security isn't limited to the Visor itself. It also extends to Palm Desktop, working in much the same ways. Thus, you can hide certain records, or password-protect the entire program. The same password you selected for your Visor is automatically used in Desktop.

> NOTE
> *Unfortunately, this is another area in which Mac users get the short shrift. Palm Desktop for Macintosh doesn't include any security features whatsoever. While you can still keep your data protected on your Visor, anyone who has access to your computer has access to your info (unless you've installed some third-party security software). For what it's worth, we intend to write a long and scathing letter to Palm, Inc., expressing our disappointment over this particular shortcoming.*

12

Hidden Records

Whenever you HotSync, any records marked as private on your Visor become hidden in Palm Desktop—and vice versa. To change whether private records are visible or not, click the View menu, and then select either Hide Private Records or Show Private Records. As on the Visor, when you select the latter, you must then enter your password.

Security

Private Records: | Show | Hide |
Password: | -Assigned- |

On the Visor, when you elect to show private records, there's no way to know which of them are still *marked* as private. In Palm Desktop, however, a little yellow key appears next to those entries, making it a lot easier to spot and/or modify them.

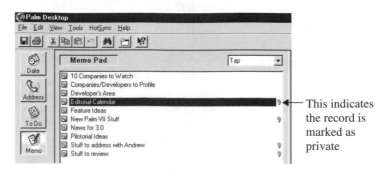

This indicates the record is marked as private

Password-Protecting Palm Desktop

Just as you can lock your Visor, so can you lock Palm Desktop. When you do, and then exit the program, your password will be required the next time it's started—by you or anyone else. Here's how to activate this setting:

1. Make sure Palm Desktop is running, and then click Tools | Options.

2. In the tabbed dialog box that appears, click the Security tab as shown in Figure 12-3.

3. Click the box that says "Require password to access the Palm Desktop data."

4. Click OK, and then exit Palm Desktop.

This security setting applies only to your data. If multiple users are sharing Palm Desktop on a single PC, they need to implement password protection for their own user profiles.

Other Security Options

While the Visor's built-in security features are fairly comprehensive, there's always room for improvement. Hence, the availability of numerous third-party security programs, which generally offer greater versatility and/or convenience. We spotlight some of the more intriguing solutions in the following section.

Matrix

Based on the excellent sci-fi movie of the same name, this clever little program turns your Visor screen into a stream of mysterious code (and a digital clock, if you want). It also has a security feature that uses a button combination instead of a password. That is, you press the four application

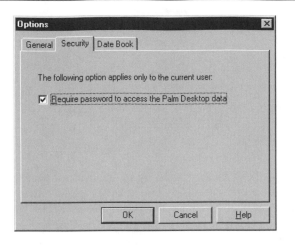

FIGURE 12-3   To restrict access to Palm Desktop, check the box in the Security options window

buttons in a predetermined sequence to unlock your Visor. Dave, who secretly wishes people would call him "Neo," thinks this freeware gem is mighty cool.

Mobile Account Manager

Your Visor can be a handy place to store account numbers, PIN numbers, passwords, and other secret codes, but stuffing them all into a memo isn't the most practical solution. Mobile Generation Software's Mobile Account Manager is designed expressly to organize and protect your important numbers and passwords. You need to remember only one password (which can be different from the one used by Palm Security) to access all this neatly categorized information.

12

```
┌─────────────────────────────────┐
│ ▐Edit Account▌        ▼ Unfiled │
│  ▼ System: Etrade│             ↑ │
│  ▼ ID:     xZ1234             ↑ │
│  ▼ Serial#: jsmith            ↑ │
│  ▼ URL:    www.etrade.com     ↑ │
│  ▼ Phone#: 800-222-3333       ↑ │
│  ▼ Owner:  Jason Smith        ↑ │
│  Password is case sensitive   ↑ │
│                                 │
│  ┌──────┐┌──────┐              │
│  │ Done ││Delete│ □ Private  🔒 │
│  └──────┘└──────┘              │
└─────────────────────────────────┘
```

OnlyMe

Like Security on steroids, OnlyMe locks your Visor automatically whenever it's turned off. Your password is entered by tapping on a special six-button keypad, or by pressing the Visors buttons in a particular sequence, or by entering certain letters or numbers in the Graffiti area. You can even create a password that's based on sliding your stylus over a special keypad. Best of all, OnlyMe lets you set a lock delay, so your Visor won't lock until after a designated period of time has elapsed.

```
┌─────────────────────────────────┐
│ ▐OnlyMe▌                     ❶ │
│                                 │
│ □ Enable OnlyMe                │
│ ┌─────────────────────────────┐ │
│ │        Set password         │ │
│ └─────────────────────────────┘ │
│ ☑ Auto-Hide Private Records    │
│ ☑ Lock Delay: 4 ┌────────┐ tes │
│                 │Seconds │     │
│ Uses: 5         │Minutes │     │
│ Goofs: 1 - 2:41 │Hours   │     │
│                 └────────┘     │
│ ┌─────────────────────────────┐ │
│ │    Set Owner Information...  │ │
│ └─────────────────────────────┘ │
│ Version 1.9                     │
└─────────────────────────────────┘
```

Sign-On

Passwords can be guessed or discovered, but it's a lot harder to duplicate your signature. Communication Intelligence Corp.'s Sign-On automatically locks your Visor when it's turned off, and then requires you to sign your name—right on the Visor's screen—to unlock it again. This is a great choice for those concerned about forgetting their password.

```
┌─────────────────────────────────┐
│ ▐Sign-On Verification▌          │
│      Please sign in the box      │
│   ┌─────────────────────────┐   │
│   │                         │   │
│   │     John Smith          │   │
│   │                         │   │
│   └─────────────────────────┘   │
│   Press Accept when ready.       │
│  ┌──────┐ ┌──────┐ ┌──────┐    │
│  │Accept│ │ Clear│ │Cancel│    │
│  └──────┘ └──────┘ └──────┘    │
└─────────────────────────────────┘
```

The Find Feature

The more you use your Visor, the more data you're likely to wind up storing. And the more data you have, the harder it can be to find what you're looking for expediently. Some examples:

■ A couple days ago, you set up a meeting a few weeks hence, and now you want to check the details of that meeting. Must you page through your calendar a day at a time to find the entry?

■ You have dozens of memos and you need to find the ones containing "Denise Richards." Must you open each memo individually?

■ You have 1,500 names in your address list, and want to quickly find the record for that guy named Apu whose last name and company you can't remember. How can you locate him?

Using the Palm OS's built-in Find feature, you could unearth all this information in a snap. True to its name, Find sifts through your databases to ferret out exactly what you're looking for, be it a name, a number, a word, a phrase, or even just a few letters.

As we showed you in Chapter 2, Find can be found in the lower-right corner of the Graffiti area, represented by a little magnifying-glass icon. Using it couldn't be simpler: Tap it (at any time, no matter what program you're running), and then write in what you want to search for (see Figure 12-4). Capitalization doesn't matter. Even if you're looking for a proper name like "Caroline," you needn't capitalize the first letter.

TIP   *If you use your stylus to select a word or chunk of text (done much the same way you select text using a mouse) prior to tapping the Find button, that text automatically appears in the Find box.*

The search process should take no more than a few seconds, depending on how many records you have on your Visor and the complexity of your search criteria.

12

FIGURE 12-4   Looking for a specific word? Just write it in the Find box and the Visor can find it for you

How It Works

When you execute a search, the Palm OS looks through all stored records (except those marked as private) for whatever text you specified, starting with whatever program you were in when you tapped the Find icon. It looks not only in the main databases—those used by Address Book, Date Book, and so forth—but also in the databases associated with any third-party software you may have installed.

Keep in mind that Find searches only the beginnings of words. Thus, if you look up "book," it will find "bookcase," but not "handbook." There are third-party programs that can perform much more thorough searches—we talk about some of them a little later.

You can make your data a bit more "Find friendly" by using special modifiers. For instance, you might use the letters AP to preface any memo that has to do with Accounts Payable. Then, when you do a search for AP, you quickly unearth all the relevant records.

Running a Search

After you've written the desired search text in the Find box and tapped OK, the Visor gets to work. Items appear in a categorized list as they're found; if you see what you're looking for, you can halt the search immediately by tapping the Stop button. Then, simply tap on the item to bring up the corresponding record in the corresponding program.

If the Visor finds more instances of the word than can fit on the screen at once, it stops the search until you tap the Find More button. This essentially tells it to look up another screen's worth of records. There's no way to backtrack (that is, to return to the previous screen), so make sure you need to keep searching before tapping Find More. (You can always run the search again if need be, but that's a hassle.)

Third-Party Search Programs

Many users find that Find isn't nearly as robust as it could be. If you want to maximize the search potential of your Visor, one of the following third-party programs might be in order. They're a little on the advanced side, meaning they require the program HackMaster (which we talk about in Chapter 18). That doesn't mean you should shy away from them, just that they might prove a little more complicated to install and operate.

FindHack

Possibly the Rolls Royce of search programs, Florent Pillet's FindHack enables you to specify whether to search all the installed applications, just the main applications, or only the current application. It also remembers the last six searches you ran, enables you to preconfigure up to four "permanent" searches, and supports the use of wildcards. Best of all, it's faster than Find.

PopUpFind

One problem with Find is that it forces you to leave the application you're currently working in (when you tap on the "found" record). Bozidar Benc's PopUpFind puts the data into a pop-up window, thus enabling you to stay in your current program. It has viewers for the four main applications and can transfer you to any of those programs with the tap of a button.

The Calculator

What's an electronic organizer without a calculator? Not much, so let's take a peek at the Visor's. The Calc program, activated by tapping the icon in the upper-right corner of the Graffiti area, has two modes: basic and advanced. The former (see Figure 12-5) is a simple four-function calculator that operates just like you'd expect. In fact, it's so self-explanatory, we won't insult your intelligence by explaining how to use it.

There are, however, a couple features of basic Calc we feel obligated to point out. First, you can use the standard Visor Copy option to paste the result of any calculation into another program. Second, you can review your last few calculations by tapping Menu | Options | Recent Calculations.

Advanced Mode

The basic calculator is fine for figuring out the tip on your dinner bill, but it's decidedly limited beyond such rudimentary tasks. Handspring decided to take advantage of the Visor's computational power by outfitting the calculator with an "advanced" mode, which is, in fact, so advanced you can probably toss any fancy HP or Texas Instruments calculator you may have purchased previously.

12

FIGURE 12-5   In its main four-function mode, the Visor calculator functions like every other calculator you've ever used

Activating the advanced mode is really complicated and time-consuming, as evidenced by this three-step tutorial:

1. Tap the calculator icon.

2. Tap Menu | Options | Change Mode.

3. Tap Advanced, and then OK.

Whew! Glad that's over with. As you can see in Figure 12-6, the look of the calculator changes quite dramatically. It has a lot more buttons, and three pop-up menus for selecting the various modes and options. Suffice it to say, we don't have room (or the mathematical knowledge) to teach you how to use all these advanced functions, as they could fill a separate book. However, we can give you a general overview of the calculator's most important features:

- ◼ A comprehensive set of mathematical functions, including exponents, roots, logarithms, and trigonometry.

- ◼ Finance tools such as loan, percentage rate, and amortization.

- ◼ Statistical functions ranging from mean to sum to standard deviation.

- ◼ Conversion modes for weight, length, area, volume, and temperature.

Third-Party Calculators

Whether you're a student, realtor, banker, or NASA engineer, there's no debating the value of a good business and/or programmable calculator (one that's more task-specific than the built-in calculator). Your Visor has ample processing power to fill this role, and the proof is in the numerous third-party calculators currently available. Let's take a look at two of the best and brightest.

FIGURE 12-6   In advanced mode, the Visor's calculator goes from four-function wimp to super-powered number cruncher

FCPlus Professional

Aimed at financial, real estate, and retail professionals, Infinity Softworks' FCPlus Professional is one of the most sophisticated calculators around. It offers more than 400 built-in business, math, finance, and statistics functions, and includes memory worksheets for keeping track of various computations. If you need this kind of power, you'll love the program.

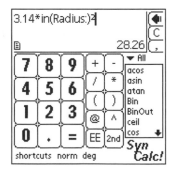

SynCalc

A fully algebraic calculator, Synergy Solutions' SynCalc offers a unique plug-in architecture that allows new functionality to be added. As it stands, SynCalc is already plenty powerful, with algebraic parsing of expressions, a full suite of trigonometric and logarithmic functions, and support for up to 100 macros that simplify the execution of complex calculations.

CityTime

Quick—want to know the time in Prague? Or Port Moresby? Or Phoenix? Just tap the icon for CityTime, a world clock that shows you the hour of day (or night) in four cities simultaneously. This is a handy little applet if you have friends, family, and/or colleagues spread out around the country or across the globe (see Figure 12-7).

12

CityTime tells you what the clock says in four locations around the world

Setting Your Home City

Before you do anything else, you should let CityTime know what city represents home for you. Tap Menu | Options | Select Home City and then choose your city from the list. If it's not there, you can add it yourself by tapping Menu | Options | Edit Cities and then the New button. A few of the options you need to specify:

- **+/- GMT**   This represents the hours ahead or behind Greenwich Mean Time for your city. And what exactly *is* Greenwich Mean Time? Nope, it has nothing to do with little villages in New York City; it's the time in London.

- **DST**   This enables you to select the start and end dates for daylight saving time. If this isn't relevant for your city, set it to Manual.

- **Location**   Here you set the exact location of your city using either a map or latitude/longitude coordinates.

Setting Display Times

As shown in Figure 12-7, the bulk of the CityTime screen is occupied by a global map. The shaded area represents night. You can tap anywhere on the map to see the name and time of that location.

In the bottom portion of the screen are four cities, each shown with its respective time. To change any of the cities displayed, tap the little arrow, and then select the desired city from the pop-up list.

Sunrise and Sunset Information

CityTime can give you sunrise and sunset information for any city in its database. Tap Menu | Utilities | Sun Rise/Set, and then select the desired city. You can also choose a different date, if you prefer, and select one of four definitions of sunrise and sunset (which vary relating to how close the sun is to the horizon). The Civil option tends to be the most practical, as it shows the times when some light is visible at the start and end of the day.

The Mail Program

The last member of the Visor's supporting cast of characters—er, programs—is Mail. We teach you to use it in Chapter 14, but a brief bit of explanation is in order now. Specifically, Mail enables you to read, compose, and send e-mail, but not in the traditional sense. That is, Mail is not capable of connecting to your Internet service provider via a Visor modem and conducting e-mail transactions. Rather, it merely synchronizes with your desktop e-mail program, such as Eudora or Outlook Express, absorbing copies of messages you've received and transferring outgoing messages you've written.

In practical terms, this means your Visor serves as a kind of portable e-mail viewer. Here's an example: In the morning, before heading off to work, you HotSync with your PC. All the e-mail messages you received the night before are transferred to your Visor. Throughout the day, you read through those messages, and reply to those that require it. You can even compose new messages if the need arises. Later, when you return home and HotSync once again, all the outgoing messages are transferred to your desktop e-mail program, and then sent.

12

NOTE   *If you own a Visor modem, you can HotSync from the road, but even this doesn't allow for real-time e-mail transactions.*

How to Decide if You Should Use Mail

Although the Mail program itself is easy to use and relatively capable (it supports signatures, blind carbon copies, delivery confirmation, filters, and more), its inability to work directly with ISPs is a definite shortcoming. Thus, you have to decide if it's the e-mail program for you. As we discuss in Chapter 14, several third-party packages can transact mail in real-time.

Where to Find It

Web Site	Address	What's There
Communications Intelligence Corp.	www.cic.com	Sign-On
PalmGear H.Q.	www.palmgear.com	Matrix (and lots of other Palm software)
Mobile Generation Software	www.mobilegeneration.com	Mobile Account Manager
Tranzoa, Co.	www.tranzoa.com	OnlyMe
Florent Pillet	perso.wanadoo.fr/fpillet/	FindHack
Benc Software Products	www.benc.hr	LauncherIII and PopUpFind
Infinity Softworks	www.infinitysw.com	FCPlus Professional
Synergy Solutions	www.synsolutions.com	SynCalc
ReturnMe.com	www.returnme.com	The ReturnMe service

Chapter 13 Going on a Trip

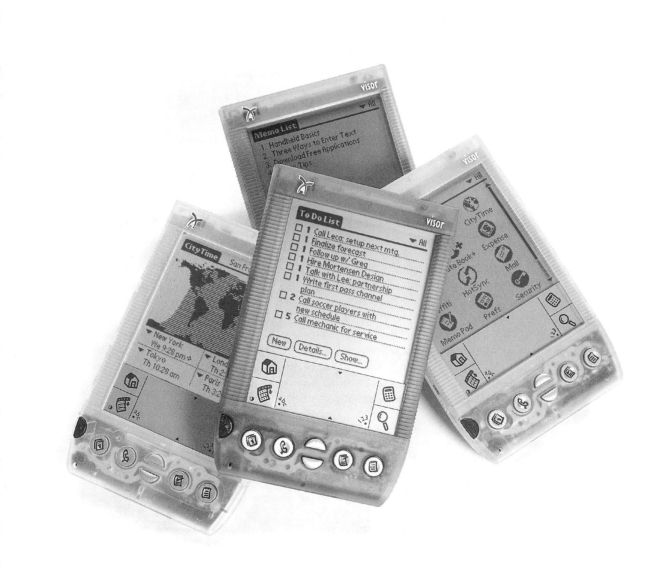

How to...

- Organize your Visor's categories and data for travel
- Pack smartly so you're prepared for trouble
- Make sure your Visor doesn't run out of power during the trip
- Prepare for HotSync opportunities away from home
- Enhance the core apps for life on the road
- View your coworkers' Date Book entries on your own Visor
- Load your Visor with essential travel phone numbers
- Use the Visor as an alarm clock
- Use the Visor as a subway map
- Communicate in a foreign language with your Visor
- Navigate your way around town and country with a Visor
- Use your Visor as a compass
- Get star charts on your Visor
- Read books on your Visor

Some people find the Visor so useful that—imagine this—they put it in their pockets and take it on trips away from the home and office! Daring, we know. And it turns out the Visor is even designed for these kinds of "away missions." Its internal battery means you needn't plug it in, and because it synchronizes with your desktop PC, you can bring important information with you wherever you go. The Visor even has a built-in clock in case you forget your watch. What could be better?

Seriously, we know you already carry your Visor around town—exactly how dumb do you think we are? (Don't answer that.) But if you plan to take it on an extended trip, you might want to read this chapter. We have all kinds of suggestions for how to prepare your Visor for a grueling business trip and what kind of software you might need to make the trip a little smoother. And how about a camping trip? Your Visor might not be the first accessory that springs to mind when you consider roughing it in the Rocky Mountains, but your trusty little handheld has a lot to offer in the wilderness, too.

Prepare Your Visor for the Road

When we go on a business trip, it's usually absolute pandemonium—running around at the last minute, throwing power cords and HotSync cables in the travel bag—it's a wonder we ever make it to the airport in time. Because of our experiences with forgetting data, bringing dead batteries, and not being able to connect to the Internet in strange cites, we offer the following checklist to you for bringing your Visor on trips.

How to ...
How to Keep Your Visor Powered on the Road

A dead Visor is no good to anyone, least of all to you. Take note of the following to keep working when you're away:

- If they're not at least half full, change your Visor's batteries before you go.

- If you're going to be away for a week or more, bring a spare set of batteries with you—it's better to be safe than sorry.

- Use a battery tester on any spare batteries you cart along before each trip to make sure they're not dead.

Remember to bring along any necessary batteries for Springboard peripherals you take as well.

Set Up Your Data

Make sure your Visor is ready for the details of your upcoming trip. Specifically, consider the kinds of data you need to create while you're on the road and prepare your Visor ahead of time. Here's how you can make sure you're ready:

- In the To Do List, create a trip checklist and enter everything you need to do before you go and everything you need to bring with you. If you have a comprehensive checklist, you're less likely to forget something important before you go.

13

```
┌─────────────────────────────────┐
│ To Do List            ▼ Travel  │
│ ☐ 1 Bring tickets               │
│ ☐ 1 Install DB on laptop        │
│ ☐ 1 Charge cell phone           │
│ ☐ 1 Visor batteries             │
│ ☐ 1 Modem                       │
│ ☐ 1 HotSync                     │
│ ☐ 1 Serial cables               │
│ ☐ 1 bring suit and tie          │
│                                 │
│ ( New ) ( Details... ) ( Show...) │
└─────────────────────────────────┘
```

TIP *Often, you'll need to go through the same steps every time you prepare for a trip, and you probably don't want to build a To Do list from scratch each time. One solution is to create a comprehensive list of travel tasks and leave it in the Memo Pad. You can copy the entire memo and paste it into a new memo before a trip, and then erase individual lines as you complete them. The master list is still safely stored in a different memo entry.*

■ Create a new category in which you can store data related to your trip. If you're going to Chicago for a convention, for instance, create a category on the Address Book, To Do List, and Memo Pad called Chicago. (If you want to call it something else, that's okay, too.) The point is that by using a special category on the road, you can find data related to your trip more quickly—both during the trip and after you return home. When you get back, you can recategorize the data any way you like.

■ Create a new expense category. While you might be able to get by with lobbing all your To Dos or contacts in the same Unfiled category, don't try that with expenses. After all, how are you going to distinguish among a dozen cab receipts? We don't want to see you up late at night with a calendar and your Visor, trying to figure out what city you were in when you paid $14 for a cab ride, especially if you don't fill in the details for each entry. A much easier way is simply to create a category for your upcoming trip and put all your expenses in there.

■ Enter your itinerary in the Date Book. If you're flying, enter each flight's number, departure, and arrival time in your Visor so it's available when you need it. An easy way to do that is to enter the flight number in the Date Book at the scheduled departure time and note the arrival time there as well. That way you can check your Visor in-flight to see how much longer you have to grit your teeth and eat peanuts.

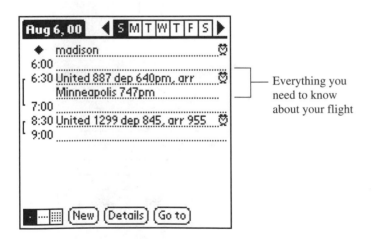

Everything you need to know about your flight

TIP *You can block out the dates of your trip on the Visor using an Untimed Event. The trip appears at the top of the Date Book and still enables you to schedule actual appointments during those days.*

Have a Backup Plan

Call us Luddites, but we don't like to rely 100 percent on a fragile piece of electronic gizmotry. What if you drop your Visor in the airport and it shatters on the nice marble floor? You'd better have a Plan B.

Dave: For me, the most important document to have access to on a trip is my flight itinerary. I always buy e-tickets—so I have no written record of my flight—and then I enter the flight information in my Visor. But to be on the safe side, I also print a copy of my flight info and stick it in the back of my bag somewhere. That way, if my batteries die before I finish my trip or my Visor falls out of a five-story window, I can always refer to the piece of paper and get myself home.

Rick: In the event that your Visor doesn't shatter on the floor, but simply loses all its data, arm yourself with the Handspring Backup Module or a handy piece of backup software like Penguin Backup. The backup module is the easiest solution, but if you haven't gotten one of those yet, try the software alternative. It copies every bit of data in your Visor to a bootable floppy disk. If a full restoration becomes necessary, just find any PC and plug a HotSync cradle or cable into a serial port. Boot from the floppy disk and, in a few minutes, your Visor should be in the pink again.

Get the Hardware Ready

When you leave on a trip, you want to make sure your Visor is fully prepared to go the distance. There's nothing like being a thousand miles from home and remembering you forgot to bring some data from your desktop PC or discovering you forgot an important cable.

To save yourself from calamity, remember these tips:

- Always bring a paperclip or a thin pin you can use to reset your Visor. Nothing's worse than having your Visor crash when you're away from home and discovering you have nothing small enough to fit in the reset hole.

- Perform a HotSync right before you leave. This way, you can be sure to have the latest info on your Visor. And just in case something unfortunate were to happen to your trusty handheld while you're away, you'll also have a current backup.

- Do you plan to do a lot of typing? If so, pack a keyboard. The GoType keyboard from LandWare, for instance, can make entering a lot of data easier than fiddling with Graffiti. See Chapter 24 for more details on keyboards.

Road Tips

We've done our share of traveling and we've amassed a few handy tips for making the best use of our Visor on the road. Not all these suggestions will appeal to you, but you're sure to find a few ideas to make your next trip a little more enjoyable.

■ If you're planning to stay at your destination for more than just a few hours, you should reset the time on your Visor. Otherwise, all your appointments will alarm at the wrong time and you'll show up late everywhere you need to be. To change the time, tap the Prefs app and choose the General page from the list menu. Tap the Set Time box and change it as necessary. Remember to change the time when you leave for your next time zone; in fact, you might want to set reminders in the Date Book so you remember to change the time.

```
┌─────────────────────────────────────┐
│ ▌Preferences▐        ▼ General       │
│          Set Time: ⌐9:53 am¬         │
│          Set Date: ⌐12/5/99¬         │
│     Auto-off after: ▼ 2 minutes      │
│     Stay on in Cradle: ☑             │
│  ┌─────────────Set Time───────────┐  │
│  │                                 │  │
│  │   9 : 5 3   ▲   AM PM           │  │
│  │             ▼                   │  │
│  │  ( OK )  ( Cancel )             │  │
│  └─────────────────────────────────┘  │
└─────────────────────────────────────┘
```

■ Your Visor may set off the metal detector at the airport. To save yourself time, go ahead and pop it into one of those little trays, along with all your change, right at the outset when you go through a metal detector.

■ The Visor is considered a "portable electronic device" and you shouldn't use it at the beginning or end of a flight. You probably already knew that—but your Visor can get you in trouble anyway if you're not careful. Specifically, don't enable any alarms for the start or end of the flight or it will come to life and start beeping during the forbidden times. If you use a program like BigClock to tell you when the flight is almost over, don't set it to Decrement (countdown) mode, as seen in Figure 13-1.

■ You may need to print something stored on your Visor while you're on your trip. The easiest solution is to get a product like PalmPrint if you have access to an IR-capable printer. If that's the case, just aim your Visor and print. If that's not feasible, then as a last resort, you should install a fax program like HandFax. Equipped with a modem, you can fax to your hotel's front desk, and then pick up the printout.

Software to Bring Along

Don't rely on the software that comes with your Visor to get you through your extended trips away from home. Most of the software we discuss in this next section is available from www.palmgear.com. Experiment and see what applications are really useful.

Decrementing can make an
alarm go off at a bad time

FIGURE 13-1   Alarms can cause your Visor to wake up at inopportune moments—like when
you're supposed to have all electronic items turned off on an airplane

CAUTION   *Don't install a new application as you're walking out the door to go to the airport.
Some applications might cause your Visor to misbehave. Others can change the way
your Visor functions or make it hard to access data you've already created. You don't
need to discover those kinds of things on an airplane bound for Topeka. Bottom line:
install and experiment with new software well in advance of a trip.*

Address and Date Book Enhancements

Sure, you love the Address Book and the Date Book. But by enhancing these core applications,
you might find you can significantly improve the way you work when you're away from home.

Synchronize with the Web

Believe it or not, you can synchronize your Visor's Date Book and Address Book with
Web-based information managers. Why would you want to do that? Well, when you're on the
road, you may want to access your schedule and contacts from a PC that isn't yours—and if you
can get to any Web-enabled PC, you can log on to a Web-based calendar and address book. Here
are some cool reasons to try this:

- You can send e-mail from a Web-based e-mail system using contact information culled
  from your Visor.

- You can add calendar appointments on the PC and synchronize it to the Visor later.

- If something happens to your Visor on a trip, you can still access all your data from a PC
  that's connected to the Internet.

13

The Web site Yahoo.com offers the best synchronization support on the Internet. By installing a small utility on your home or office-based PC, you can sync the Visor's Date Book, Address Book, and To Do List with equivalent applications on the Yahoo! site. Because Yahoo! also offers free e-mail, you can use the Visor Address Book to send messages without reentering any data. You can see Yahoo!'s Web site in Figure 13-2.

To get started with Web synchronization, do this:

1. In a Web browser, visit www.yahoo.com. If you don't already have an account there, create one with whatever user name you want to use.

2. Look for a link that includes the word TrueSync and click it. If you can't find it, click the Help link instead, and find the TrueSync link there. Download the software and install it. The Component Install screen wants you to select devices and services with which you'll be synchronizing. You should check TrueSync Plus, Yahoo!, and 3Com Palm (as usual, don't worry that you're using a Visor). If you also want Yahoo! to sync with your desktop PIM like Outlook, choose that item as well.

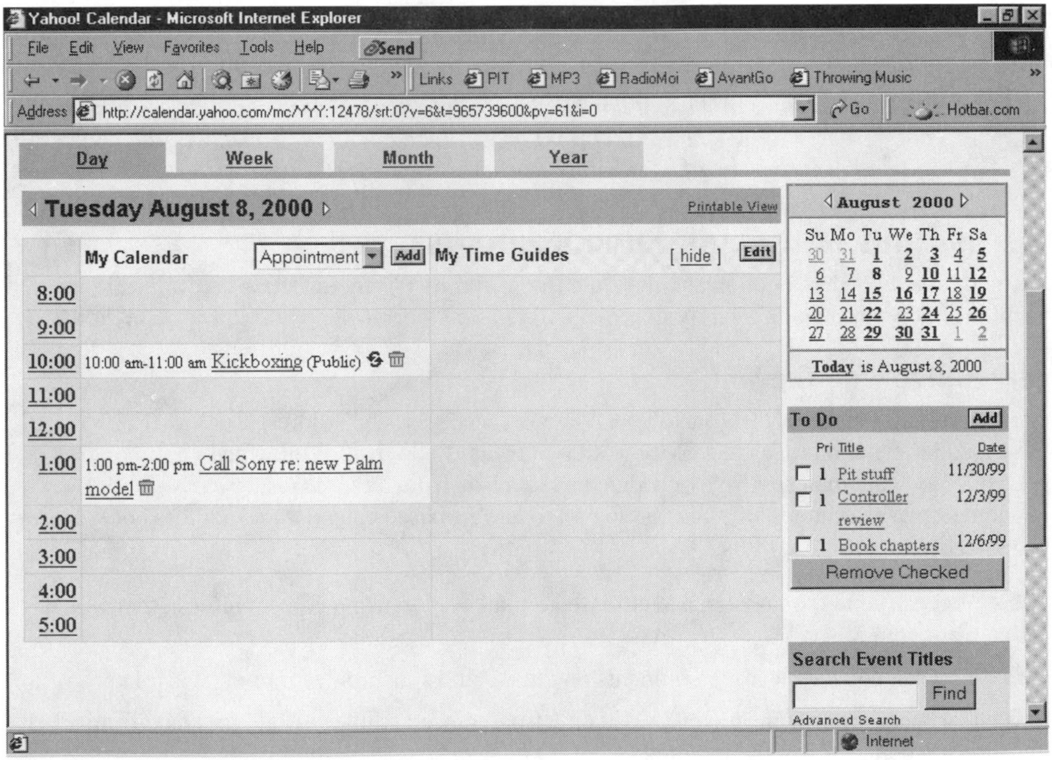

FIGURE 13-2 Yahoo! offers excellent support for synchronizing with a Visor

Click here for synchronization software

3. After the TrueSync software is installed, it will attempt to perform the first sync. You need to put the Visor in its cradle and follow the instructions onscreen.

4. If you've created new Address Book categories, TrueSync will ask you if you want to duplicate those categories as well. Or, you can simply direct Yahoo! to put entries from one of the unmapped categories into an existing one.

5. Finally, TrueSync will synchronize your Visor with Yahoo!. The first time you do this, it may take a while because you have a lot of entries to be transferred to the Internet.

TIP *Can't see entries on your Visor that were created in Yahoo!? That's because, by default, Yahoo! marks all its records private (sigh...don't ask us why). You have to display private records on the Visor to see them.*

Share Your Appointments

You're meeting with coworkers at a trade show to review the newest, most innovative pencil sharpeners. If your associates are as busy as you plan to be, how can you reconcile your schedules to meet for lunch? Or, if you're a little more business-minded, how can you find out where everyone is during the day and schedule meetings everyone can attend?

One solution is to use WeSync. This Web-based calendaring and contact tool enables you to sync your Visor data with a Web-based information manager and share it with coworkers. The best part is WeSync takes the form of a new Date Book-style app on your Visor that can display multiple schedules side-by-side. This means you can visually evaluate free and busy times on two schedules on the same screen.

13

To try out WeSync, visit www.wesync.com and install the WeSync application, shown in Figure 13-3. After you and at least one other person are using the app, you can share your calendar in this way:

1. Start by creating a private community. Visit the WeSync Web site and log in with the user name you selected. Then click Create a New Community.

2. Give the community a name and description, and then enter your user name as the Member/Administrator Name. Then click Create Community. After that, you should find yourself in the My Communities tab.

3. Click Manage Community, and then click Invite New Members (you can see the link below). Enter the e-mail and user name of the person you want to invite, and then click Invite.

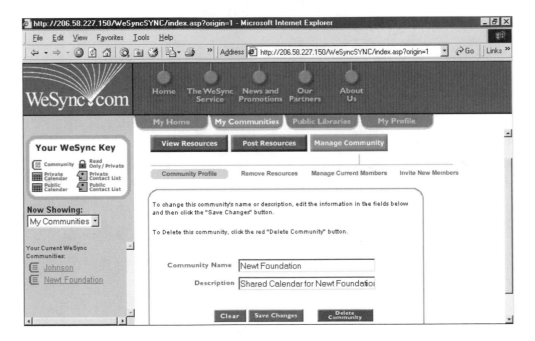

4. Now it's time to share your calendar with this private community. Start the WeSync Desktop Viewer and choose Edit | Calendar Manager from the menu. You should see the WeSync Calendar Manager dialog box.

5. Select your calendar (it should currently be configured as Local). Click the Published button, and then click Close.

6. HotSync your Visor. Your calendar is now transferred to the Web calendar, ready to be shared with others.

After this setup process, any time you change your calendar, the data is updated on the WeSync Web site at the next HotSync, and then updated on all the shared Palm devices. Of course, if you're invited to join a community as in Step 3, you need to accept the invitation before you can see a shared calendar. To join, click the Your Invitations link on the Web site and place a check mark next to the community you've been invited to join.

13

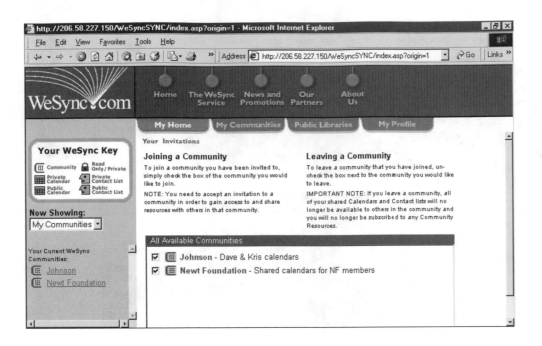

To see calendars side by side on your Visor, start the wsCalendar app and choose +Cal | Calendars from the menu. Check all the calendar entries you want to see onscreen at once and click OK.

Get Rental Car Phone Numbers

The Visor can hold lots of phone numbers—so why not take advantage of that? There are several databases of phone numbers to services like rental car companies, airlines, and hotels. If you travel frequently, you probably want to try one of them:

Application	Data Included
WeSync.com	The WeSync Contact Manager has hundreds of phone numbers to airlines, hotels, and rental car companies. When you implement this feature, these entries are automatically added to the Visor's Date Book in categories.
Travel Telephone Numbers	A smaller list (about 100) of the most popular hotels, car rentals, and airlines.
Palm Rent-a-Car	List of rental car companies and their 800 numbers.
Palm Airlines	List of about 190 airlines and their 800 numbers.

 These apps are all available from www.palmgear.com.

Itinerary Tracker

While you can certainly store your itinerary information in the Date Book, using a specialized program is more efficient for many people. Try Gulliver, which enables you to store all your key travel information in one place. That includes hotel and car rental reservations, flight schedules, your frequent flyer numbers, as well as worldwide airline names and airport cities.

TravelTracker is a similar program that maintains a list of your flight information, hotel reservations, car rental reservations, dinner reservations, and transport details (like limos and car services). We particularly like its capability to reset the system clock to stay in tune with local time.

```
Comdex                11/14 - 11/18
Sun, Nov 14, 1999
✈ 8:00 am  AA 1123  -
  9:00 am  Colorado S ->
🛄 Hilton (check-in)
Thu, Nov 18, 1999
🛄 Hilton (check-out)



( Done )  ( New... )  ( Trip Details )
```

The Ultimate Alarm Clock

You can set alarms with the Visor, but the somewhat anemic alarm system built into the Date Book isn't terribly useful in many applications. Instead, you should download a copy of BigClock (see Figure 13-4). This free application displays the time, has a timer, and has four independent alarms. It also lets you easily change time zones.

13

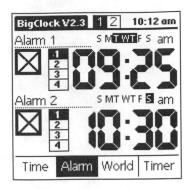

| FIGURE 13-4 | BigClock has multiple alarms and time zones—the perfect companion for life on the road |

BigClock's alarm is good enough to serve as your morning alarm clock, either on its own or as a safety back-up to a hotel wake up call. To use BigClock's alarm function, follow these steps:

1. Start BigClock and tap the Alarm tab at the bottom of the screen. You have four different alarms available. We'll set Alarm 1.

2. Highlight the Alarm 1 title at the top if the screen and rename it **Wake Up**.

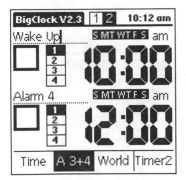

3. Set the time you want to wake. Tap the top-half of a number to increase its value, tap the bottom-half to decrease it. Do this for both minutes and hours.

4. Make sure the am/pm indicator is set to **am** for your morning alarm. Tap it to switch between the two.

5. Tap the day or days you want to alarm. If the day is highlighted in black, it's selected.

6. To enable the alarm, tap the large check box to the left. The alarm will now trigger at the designated time.

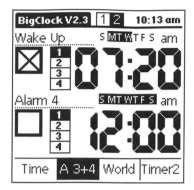

You should test your alarm before trusting it to get you out of bed the next morning. Specifically, you should be sure you haven't disabled system sounds in the Visor's Prefs app. If you did, you'll never hear the alarm. Also, you want to be sure you've remembered to set it up for the right day of the week and the right half of the day.

Get a Snooze

You can set BigClock's alarm to snooze—that is, realarm after a few minutes if you want to nab a few extra minutes of sleep. To enable the snooze feature, choose Options | Alarm from the menu and tap the appropriate alarm number at the top of the screen. Then tap the Snooze check box. You can set how long the snooze will last (a common length is about ten minutes, if you're setting a wake-up) and how many times the snooze will go off before turning off completely. When the alarm goes off, tap anywhere on the Visor screen and the snooze resets the alarm to go off again a few minutes later.

CAUTION
The snooze only works if you tap the screen. Because the alarm only sounds several times, and then shuts off, BigClock runs the danger of letting you fall asleep without actually tapping the screen to activate the next snooze cycle. To avoid oversleeping, you should modify the alarm sound so it chimes for a long time. To do that, choose Sounds | Sound 1 (or whatever sound you want the alarm to play) from the menu, and then set the repeat value to a large number—like 100. That should be enough time for you to rouse from sleep and tap the Visor.

Use Time Zones

BigClock is also handy if you don't want to reset the Visor to local time wherever you are, yet you still want the alarm to work properly. That's why BigClock comes with four World Time settings. Tap the World tab and you can see them. To set alternate time zones for this tab, choose Options | World from the menu, and then choose how many hours to offset from your home time zone.

13

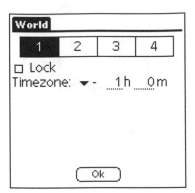

TIP
*Be sure to set whether the time zone is ahead or behind the home zone using the +
and – symbols.*

Once you set some other world time zones, you can enter the Alarm options dialog box and
set the time base for your alarm. From the list menu, choose which time zone to use to make the
alarm go off.

Find Your Way Around

Many tools are around for finding your way around in a strange place. In fact, you can actually
connect your Visor to a GPS navigation system (see "Wilderness Survival Tools" later in this
chapter)! Most people need more mundane assistance, though, so we've collected a few interesting
applications for you here.

Get Metro and Subway Routes

Do subway routes leave you scratching your head? Those maps they put in the train stops are not
exactly intuitive, and finding the best route from one end of Paris to the other can be a nerve-
wracking experience. That's why you should install Metro, a free utility that calculates the best
route between any two stations in over 100 cities. The application comes with database files for
cities like New York, London, Paris, Chicago, and Hong Kong, and you only need to install the
files for cities you are visiting.

There are many other travel guides specific to certain cities. Try some of these:

Region	Service	Program Name
San Francisco	CalTran schedule	CalTran
Montreal	Map of the subway system	Montreal Subway Map
Moscow	Metro guide to city of Moscow, includes maps	TealInfo Moscow Metro Guide
New York	Enter a Manhattan address, and program provides nearest cross street	X-Man
Paris	Metro paths between monuments, museums, and stations	Paris
Southern California	MetroLink schedule	MetroLink

> NOTE   *These apps are all available from www.palmgear.com.*

Language Translators

In the past, traveling abroad often resulted in serious communication difficulties. Do you know how to ask for the bathroom in French? If not, try one of these applications

- **SmallTalk**   This program is a real-time, two-way translator. Hold the Visor up to the person with whom you want to communicate. SmallTalk presents you with complete sentences organized into situation-based categories, such as Basics, Lodging, Emergency, Food, and Entertainment. Select a phrase in English and it's translated into the target language, as you can see in Figure 13-5. The person you are communicating with can then select a response from a menu, which is translated back into English. SmallTalk supports French, Italian, Spanish, German, and Japanese.

- **TourMate**   Available in several versions (including English-Spanish, English-Italian, English-French, and English-German), this program is easy to use. Just choose a common greeting, expression, or question in English and read the phonetically spelled foreign language equivalent expression to the person with whom you're trying to communicate.

- **Translate**   This application enables you to enter a word and instantly translate it among 18 languages. The translator works in both directions, so you can go from English to Italian or Italian to English, for instance.

Unit Conversions

If you're an American in Europe, you have to contend with an alien set of measurements—not only is the currency different, but even the length, weight, and volume of common items are unusual. Heck, unless you're a scientist or an engineer, you may not know if 40 degrees Celsius

13

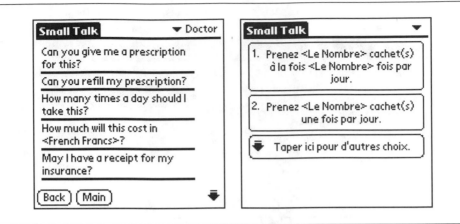

FIGURE 13-5   Choose a phrase from a list, divided by topic (left), and your associate can choose a response (right) that is translated back into English for you

is hot or cold. Try Conversions (see Figure 13-6), a calculator utility that lets you instantly make conversions of the following kinds of measurements:

- Currency
- Temperature
- Length

- Area
- Volume

FIGURE 13-6   Conversions makes it easy for an American to get by in a metric world

Wilderness Survival Tools

It's not surprising to walk into a fancy hotel and see a dozen executives standing around in fancy suits, checking their schedules via their Palm handhelds. But how often do you go camping in the middle of the woods and see people bring a handheld organizer? Not that often, we're willing to bet. And that's too bad because the Visor is actually a handy survival tool. It does almost everything—except open cans of beans or start campfires.

Navigate with Your Visor

Have you ever gotten lost in a strange town or on some deserted stretch of highway? Have you wished you hadn't seen *The Blair Witch Project* because it reminds you of exactly how bad you are at navigating in the wilderness? If so, you might benefit from a GPS navigation system. Combined with a GPS system, your Visor is perfectly capable of telling you exactly where to go.

To turn your Visor into a GPS receiver, you need the Navicom HandyGPS. This is comprised of an Earthmate GPS receiver (built into a Springboard module) and mapping software.

Use Your Visor as a Compass

While we're pretty sure you know a Visor won't open a can of beans, we suspect you wouldn't believe it could be a compass, either. But you'd be wrong. Using Sun Compass, you can get an immediate onscreen indication of north any time, anywhere (during daylight hours).

What Is GPS?

GPS stands for *Global Positioning System* and it's comprised of 24 satellites flying around the earth in semisynchronous orbit (each trip around the Earth takes 12 hours). These satellites transmit extremely precise timing signals toward the Earth.

On the ground, an inexpensive GPS receiver simply listens for these timing signals. At any given moment, the time broadcast from each satellite in the GPS system's field of view will be slightly different because the satellites are at different distances from the receiver. Consequently, it takes longer for some signals to reach the receiver from the satellite. Because the orbit of each GPS satellite is known very, very precisely, the GPS receiver can process the different timing signals and determine its own position through simple triangulation.

The bottom line is that, through this process, a GPS receiver can narrow its position to an accuracy of about 100 feet—not bad for a system that works anywhere on Earth.

For GPS to do its magic, though, you must be able to see enough satellites. You need to see no less than three satellites for accurate position data, which isn't a problem in clearings. In a skyscraper-infested metropolitan area or in a forest with lots of tree cover, though, GPS can have trouble working. Even obstacles like trees can block the GPS signal.

13

Want GPS? Try This

Try SoftGPS (available for download from www.palmgear.com) if you want to get extremely precise navigational data about your current position without resorting to satellite receivers and serial cables. Actually, SoftGPS is just for fun—it doesn't really tell you where you are in any meaningful way—but if you're a GPS navigation fan, download this program and try it. We can't say any more than that without spoiling the joke.

Unfortunately, Sun Compass comes with virtually no documentation, which may make it confusing for new users. To use Sun Compass, all you need to do is input a few pieces of information:

- **Tz** This is the time zone you are currently in. Time zones are calculated from –12 to 0, and then on up to +12. Your time zone value is simply the number of hours away from Greenwich, England, home of *Greenwich Mean Time* (GMT), that you are located. GMT is a time zone of 0. New York would be –5, and California is –8. You can find a complete list of time zones in Windows by opening the Date/Time Properties dialog box (in the Control panel) and looking in the Time Zone tab.

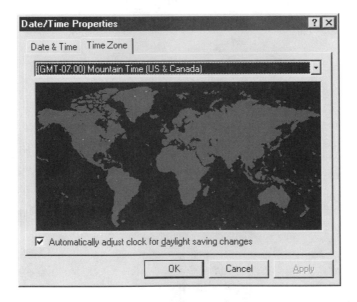

- **La** Enter your latitude. Latitude is measured from 0 degrees (the equator) to 90N and 90S.

- **Lo** Enter your longitude. Longitude is commonly measured from 0 (at the longitude line that cuts through Greenwich, England) to 180E and 180W.

TIP *Looking for your latitude and longitude? Visit www.astro.ch/atlas/atlquest-eng.shtml. This site lets you enter the name of your city and immediately see its lat/long.*

■ **DST**   *DST* stands for *daylight saving time,* and it needs to be set either on or off, depending on the time of year. Daylight saving time is on between the first Sunday in April and the last Sunday in October.

TIP *A few locations in the U.S. don't observe daylight saving time at all. These include Arizona, Hawaii, and parts of Indiana.*

One you enter these values, point the front of your Visor at the sun (keep the Visor level with the ground) and the compass indicates which way is north. That's all there is to it!

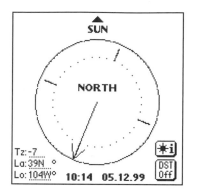

Find Stars

You can also use Sun Compass to find the North Star. Choose Misc | Polarstar from the menu and you see a dark screen with the Big and Little Dipper constellations. By aligning them with what you see in the sky, you can find the North Star and, thus, get a northerly orientation even at night.

That's great, but you can also use your Visor for some real star gazing. Here are a few programs you can try the next time you find yourself far away from city lights with your Visor:

■ **Star Pilot**   This program lets you specify your location, and then see the planets, the moon, and 500 stars in a compact star map. You can identify objects by clicking them and search for celestial objects by name.

■ **Planetarium**   This program calculates the position of the sun, the moon, the planets, and over 1,500 of the brightest stars and deep-sky objects in the sky. You can enter any location and any time period—you needn't use the present system clock. In addition to using this program for stargazing, it can also be used as a compass when the sun or moon is visible (much like Sun Compass).

■ **Pocket StarChart**   This program is distinctive in how pretty it actually is. Pocket StarChart enables you to plot the planets, the sun, the moon, over 1,500 stars up to Magnitude 5, as well as deep-sky objects, such as galaxies and star clusters, for any date and location.

13

NOTE   *These apps are all available from www.palmgear.com.*

Read Late at Night

When all your tent buddies are trying to sleep, and you're the only one wondering if that odd sound was an approaching bear, you can relax in your sleeping bag and read a good book—with your Visor. The Visor's efficient backlighting makes it easy to read both in total darkness and in bright sunlight. What you need is a document reader. While you can see Chapter 22 for details on electronic books and document readers, we thought it was worth pointing out right now that there's nothing like curling up with a good e-book on a camping trip. You can store lots of reading on one Visor, so you can travel light and still have lots to read on those quiet, lonely nights.

Where to Find It

Web Site	Address	What's There
DSI International	www.dsi-usa.com	Compact, folding HotSync cradles
RGPS	www.rgps.com	StayOffHack
IBiz	www.ibizcorp.com	KeySync keyboard
BigClock site	www.gacel.de/palmpilot.htm	BigClock
SmartCode Software	www.smartcodesoft.com	HandFax
Stevens Creek Software	www.stevenscreek.com	PalmPrint
Yahoo!	www.yahoo.com	Web-based information management that HotSyncs to Palm devices
WeSync.com	www.wesync.com	Web-based information management that HotSyncs to Palm devices; side-by-side calendaring
Landware	www.landware.com	Gulliver
SilverWare	www.silverware.com	TravelTracker
Concept Kitchen	www.conceptkitchen.com	Small Talk
Navicom	www.navicom.co.kr	HandyGPS

Part III

Beyond the Box

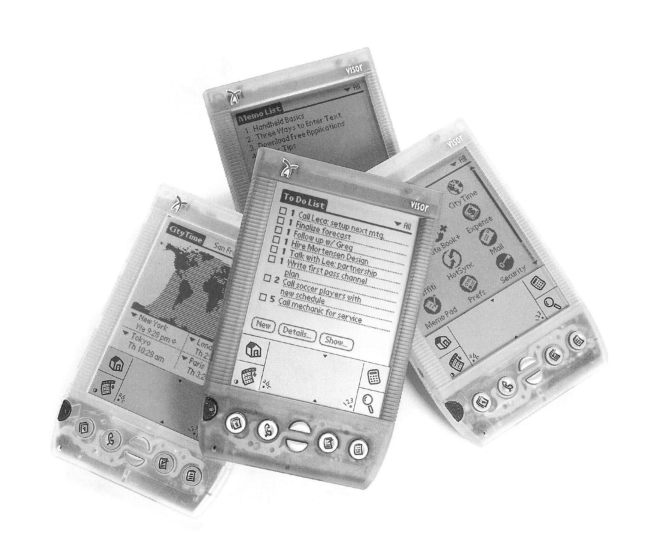

Chapter 14

Modems and More: Using Your Visor to Communicate

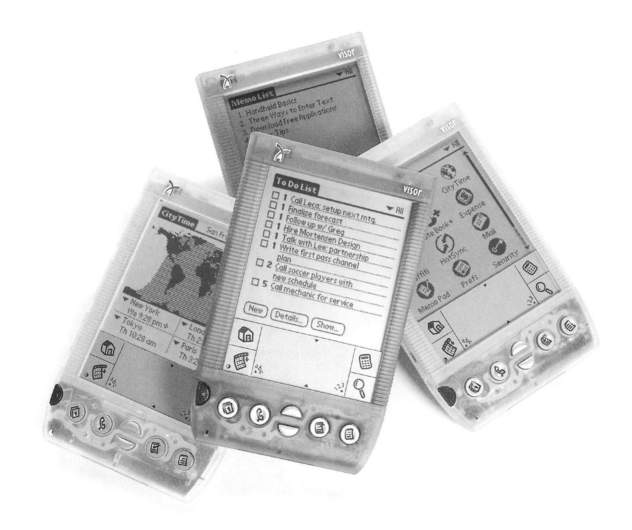

How to...

- Choose a modem for your Visor
- Configure a Visor's modem preferences
- Dial in to your ISP
- Distinguish between Palm Mail and desktop e-mail
- Link the Mail applet to your desktop e-mail program
- Create new messages on your Visor
- Synchronize desktop mail with Palm Mail
- Find and work with third-party e-mail programs
- Use your Visor for instant messaging
- Surf the Web with a Visor
- Read Web pages offline with AvantGo
- Use a Visor to send messages to other people's pagers
- Send and receive faxes with your Visor
- Be prepared while traveling

One thing you may not know about Dave is that he insists on lugging one of the world's heaviest notebook PCs whenever he goes on a trip. Why? Mostly so he can check his e-mail and surf the Web. The funny part is, the notebook's modem never works right, resulting in Dave tearing out what little hair he has. So, in exchange for schlepping nine pounds of bulky, expensive gear, he rarely gets to check his e-mail at all.

Rick, who is far more enlightened, carries his Visor Deluxe and Visor Modem, which weigh less than six ounces combined and still fit in a pocket. With this diminutive combo, he can send and receive e-mail, browse the Web, and even send faxes. Sure, the screen is small, and composing e-mail messages with Graffiti can be a chore. But for pure convenience, nothing beats a modem-equipped Visor.

In this chapter, we discuss the various Visor modems available now and look at those known to be coming soon. We also delve into the software side of Visor communications, from e-mail to faxing to Web browsing. By the time you're done with this chapter, you'll be able to turn your Visor into a full-blown communication station.

Choosing a Modem

At press time, two modems are available for the Visor, both of them requiring landline connections. The term *landline* means the modems plug into a traditional phone jack, just like the modem that's inside your computer. By the time you read this, there should also be at least one wireless modem available for the Visor—a Springboard module that would facilitate wireless access to e-mail and the Web.

Landline, Ho!

Back in the bad old days of computing, installing a modem in your PC could mean hours of grappling with confusing COM-port and IRQ settings. Fortunately, installing a modem in your Visor is about as difficult as reading this sentence. You slide a module into the Springboard slot, and you're done.

Yes, it really is that easy. In fact, the only potentially tricky part about using a Visor modem is finding a phone jack. The two landline modems we discuss in this section rely on ordinary telephone lines (see Figure 14-1), just like the dial-up modems used by most computers.

One nice advantage Visors have over other Palm devices is the location of their modems. That is, because a modem plugs into the Springboard slot, the HotSync port remains untouched—meaning you can drop the Visor into a GoType or Stowaway keyboard (see Chapter 24) and type while you're online. Thus, you could write a lengthy e-mail message, and then send it immediately without having to juggle any hardware.

A Visor modem can be used to dial into your Internet service provider (ISP), a fax machine, or America Online (the latter two options require special software, which we discuss later in this chapter). Before we delve into these connections, let's investigate the two landline modems currently available for the Visor.

FIGURE 14-1   Like most computer modems, Visor modems require a phone jack to make a connection

14

The Handspring Modem

Powered by its own pair of AAA batteries, the Handspring Modem (as shown in Figure 14-2) weighs about two ounces and gets you online at speeds of up to 33.6 Kbps (slower than most computer modems, which clock in at 56 Kbps, but plenty fast for a handheld computer).

Ironically, the Handspring Modem doesn't come with any third-party software, so right out of the box it can't do much. Thus, you'll want to investigate some of the fax, e-mail, and Web programs we discuss later in this chapter.

The Card Access Thincom Portable Modem

A much more compact and elegant solution is the Thincom Portable Modem from Card Access (as shown in Figure 14-3). While it shares the Handspring Modem's 33.6 Kbps speed, it requires no batteries of its own (instead drawing trace amounts of power from the Visor's batteries) and therefore fits flush inside the Springboard slot. That means your Visor can still fit inside a case, even with the modem installed.

What's more, the Thincom comes with communications software installed right on the module. Included are a fully functional Web browser, a trial version of a powerful e-mail program, and a "terminal" program for connecting to corporate computer systems. The module even sports illustrated instruction guides and a setup wizard that walks you through the necessary configuration steps.

FIGURE 14-2   The Handspring Modem doesn't fit flush inside the Visor, but that's because it houses its own pair of batteries

Unsurprisingly, we think this is the better landline modem of the two, especially given that it costs $10 less than Handspring's.

Coming Soon

By the time you read this, a third landline modem should be available: the SpringPort Modem 56 GlobalAccess, which is physically similar to Handspring's modem, but offers 56 Kbps connection speeds—making it the fastest Visor modem yet. Better still, it promises to connect with a variety of mobile phones, thereby enabling wireless Internet connectivity.

FIGURE 14-3   The aptly named Thincom modem is thin indeed, especially compared with Handspring's modem

How Important Is Modem Speed?

If you find it discouraging that most Visor modems top out at 33.6 Kbps, relax. That's actually plenty quick for the majority of handheld computing tasks, which are largely text-based (graphics are the reason we seek faster connections on our desktop computers). Consider e-mail messages: even if the modem were half as fast, it would still take mere seconds to send and receive them. As for Web browsing, it's much the same story: much of the data being downloaded from the Web is text, so 33.6 Kbps is a more-than-adequate speed. And most fax machines send and receive documents no faster than 14.4 Kbps, so there's no deficit there either.

Configuring Your Landline Modem to Work with Your Visor

Setting up a landline modem to work with a Visor is about eight million times easier than setting one up in Windows. That's largely because there are no COM ports or IRQ settings to grapple with (and no rebooting each time you make the slightest change). That said, you may need to tweak a few settings before you can dial out into the world.

All modem configuration takes place in the Visor's Prefs screens, accessible by tapping the eponymous icon in the Applications screen (see Chapter 2 for more details). Then, tap the little arrow in the upper-right corner of the screen. You see a list of options, including one called Modem, as shown in Figure 14-4.

In this area of Prefs, you choose your modem type, add any configuration "strings" that may be necessary, and modify basic settings. Let's walk through basic modem setup.

The Modem Screen The modem-configuration screen is called, simply enough, Modem. Here you find a handful of settings you'll probably never need to adjust. Still, here's a quick overview of the options:

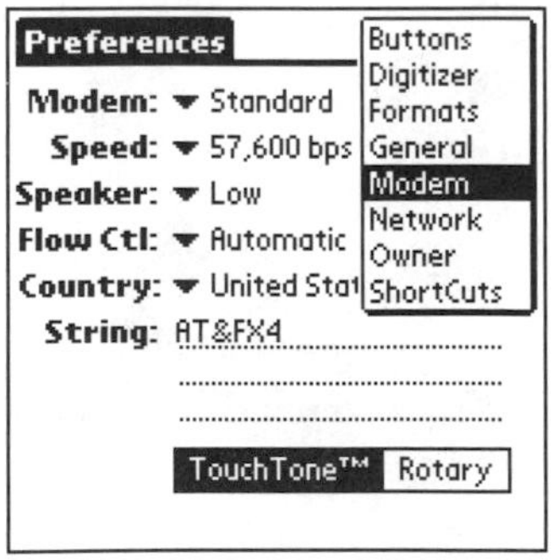

FIGURE 14-4 In the Prefs screen, this menu gives you access to modem settings

- **Modem** Despite the fact that you may be using one of a couple different modems, there's only one option here: Standard. Thus, 'nuff said.

- **Speed** Always choose 57,600 bps, even though your modem isn't capable of that speed. Like all modems, it will "negotiate" with the ISP or fax machine to achieve its maximum possible speed.

- **Speaker** Lets you adjust the volume of the modem's speaker. If you don't want to hear any of the beeping or grinding normally associated with establishing a landline connection, you can set it to Off.

- **Flow Ctl** You'll want to leave this set to Automatic 99 times out of 100.

- **String** For a Visor (or a computer, for that matter) to communicate with a modem, it must first give that modem its initialization codes or *string*. For most modern modems, the string is AT&FX4. You'll want to leave this alone 99 times out of 100 (unless otherwise instructed by any documentation that comes with any given modem).

- **TouchTone/Rotary** On the off chance that you're dialing out on a rotary system, you need to tap the Rotary button.

Setting Up Your ISP

Now that your modem is set and ready to dial, you need to tell it where to call and what to say when the modem at the other end answers. In other words, you're going to configure your Visor to connect to your ISP (assuming you're using one—if you're dialing in to America Online, these settings don't matter). This takes place in Prefs as well, this time in the Network screen (see Figure 14-5).

14

FIGURE 14-5 Take a look at the Network screen, where you configure the proper settings for dialing in to your ISP

It's important for you to supply exactly the right information in these four fields, so let's take a close look at how to work with each one.

■ **Service** When you tap the Service arrow, you see a pop-up list containing several national ISPs. If yours is listed, tap it. If not, don't fret—you can easily add it. Just tap-and-drag your stylus to highlight the name in the Service field, and then draw a Graffiti backstroke to erase it. Now, write in the name of your ISP. In our examples, we added a national ISP called MindSpring.

Preferences	▼ Network
AT&T WorldNet	....
Compuserve	
Earthlink	....
Mindspring	
Minstrel	
◄ Netcom	m
PSINet	
Unix	
UUNet	
Windows RAS	

(Details...) (Connect)

■ **User Name** In this field, you enter the user name (also known as user ID or login ID) that you chose or were assigned for your Internet account. If you don't know or can't find this information, call your ISP. It might simply be your e-mail address (such as rickb@worldnet.att.net) or it could be an alphanumeric code (as with our MindSpring account). Feel free to experiment—if you don't enter exactly the right information, you get an error message when you try to connect. If this happens, return to this screen and try another variation.

■ **Password** By default, this box says "-Prompt-", meaning if you don't supply your password now, you'll be asked for it every time you connect to your ISP. If you're concerned about your Visor getting lost or stolen and someone logging on as you, don't enter your password. If that's not a concern, tap the box, and then write in your account password. It'll be stored permanently, so you won't have to enter it each time you connect.

■ **Phone** Tap this box to enter the phone number for your ISP. If it's a long-distance number, be sure to include a 1 and the area code. Note, too, that by checking the various boxes in this screen, you can include a dial prefix (useful if you're connecting from, say, an office where you need to dial a 9 to get an outside line), disable call waiting (so incoming calls don't disconnect you), and even use a calling card.

```
┌─────────────────────────────────┐
│        Phone Setup      ⓘ        │
│ Phone #: 327-5940 ............... │
│ ............................... │
│ ☐ Dial prefix:   9, ........... │
│ ☐ Disable call waiting: 1170, . │
│ ☐ Use calling card:            │
│     .......................... │
│   ┌──────┐  ┌────────┐          │
│   │  OK  │  │ Cancel │          │
│   └──────┘  └────────┘          │
└─────────────────────────────────┘
```

■ **Details**   When you tap the Details button, you're taken to a screen with some advanced settings. Few users will have to fiddle with these, the exception being if your ISP does not automatically generate an IP address when you connect. If it doesn't, uncheck the IP Address box, and then write in the address (call your ISP if you don't have it).

Connecting to Your ISP   Once you fill in the necessary account information, simply plug in your modem (which, in turn, should be plugged into a phone jack) and tap the Connect button. In a few seconds, you hear it dialing (unless you've turned the speaker off), followed by the familiar sounds of a modem connection. If all goes well, you find yourself back at the Network screen (where you see the Connect button now says Disconnect—evidence you've signed on successfully). Now you can tap the Applications button and load your Web browser or e-mail program.

NOTE   *In some e-mail and Web programs, a connection option is built right in, so you needn't go into Prefs every time you want to dial your ISP. Same goes for disconnecting, although, for some reason, fewer programs include this feature. In many cases, you must return to the Network screen and tap Disconnect.*

What About Wireless?

Wireless modems, which are no doubt the wave of the future, rely on existing cellular and radio technologies to transmit and receive data through the ether. At press time, several companies had announced plans to introduce wireless modems and services for the Visor. We highly recommend checking out GoAmerica (www.goamerica.net), Novatel Wireless (www.novatelwireless.com), and OmniSky (www.omnisky.com), all of which should have wireless solutions available by the time you read this.

Why are we so keen on wireless? We've used wireless modems with other Palm devices, and found them incomparably convenient. There are no phone jacks to seek out, no wires tethering you to a wall. While landline modems tend to be faster, wireless is where it's at.

14

E-Mail and Instant Messaging

It's a little-known fact that Pilot creator Jeff Hawkins originally envisioned the device as a pocket e-mail appliance, not an electronic organizer. Various logistical issues forced that idea onto the back burner when the Pilot was first launched, but it wasn't long after that Palm Computing introduced a modem and mail program.

That program—named, fittingly enough, Mail—makes it possible for you to import copies of messages received on your PC, view those messages (and reply to them, if desired), and create new messages that are then sent *via* your PC.

Notice the presence of your PC in most of those equations. Mail works via synchronization; it cannot connect directly to your ISP, which is the way most of us think about sending and receiving e-mail. Nor can it access America Online. That's where third-party software comes in. In this section, we show you how to work with Mail and introduce you to some other nifty e-mail programs. We also talk about instant messaging, which has become extremely popular on desktop PCs and is slowly making its way to handheld devices.

An Introduction to the Mail Program

It's hard to remember life before e-mail, isn't it? Imagine, actually having to pick up the *phone* every time you wanted to communicate with someone. Now we just fire off e-mail messages. And with Mail, a core component of the Palm OS, we needn't wait till we're sitting at our PC to conduct e-mail business.

What Mail does, in a nutshell, is link to the e-mail program on your desktop computer. Just as Memo Pad, Address Book, and the other apps synchronize with Palm Desktop, Mail synchronizes with Outlook Express, Eudora Pro, or one of various other e-mail programs. The end result is that Mail becomes a portable extension of that program, enabling you to view, delete, and reply to messages and write new ones.

Mail is not a standalone e-mail client. That is, it works only when it's linked to desktop software. You'd think that if you purchased a modem for your Visor, you could use Mail to dial in to your ISP and transact messages. In reality, Mail has no use for a Visor modem whatsoever.

This is not to say that Mail is an underpowered or valueless piece of software—quite the opposite. It comes in very handy when you're on the road and suddenly think of a message you need to send. Presto: you can compose it on the spot, knowing it'll be sent the next time you HotSync. Additionally, if you take the train to work every morning, you can HotSync before you leave and read all your e-mail from the night before.

Mail also sports some reasonably advanced features, such as blind carbon copies, signatures, and delivery confirmation. And, because it's a core Palm OS program, the interface is streamlined and familiar. Let's get you up and running with this great little e-mail manager.

Setting Up the Mail Program

Although Mail comes preinstalled on all Visors, you must set it up for use with your desktop e-mail program. It's possible you did this already while installing the Palm Desktop software, which gives you a choice of configuring your e-mail settings then and there or skipping it till later. In either case, you can access the Mail Setup program in Windows by clicking Start | Programs | Palm Desktop | Mail Setup.

NOTE   *Sorry to be the bearer of bad tidings again, Mac users, but at present there's no way to synchronize the Mail applet with any Macintosh e-mail programs. Fortunately, there are third-party solutions, most notably Actual Software's MultiMail Conduit Pack. We talk more about it later in this chapter.*

The only real step involved in this setup procedure is choosing which e-mail program you use, as shown here:

Which Desktop E-Mail Programs Does Mail Support?

The bad news is Mail doesn't work with every e-mail manager on the planet. The good news is it works with the most popular ones, as listed below:

- Lotus cc:Mail, versions 2.5, 6.0, and 7.0
- Microsoft Exchange 4.0 or later
- Microsoft Outlook (all versions)
- Microsoft Outlook Express (all versions)
- Microsoft Windows Messaging 4.0
- Qualcomm Eudora 3.03 or later

For the sake of continuity, most of our explanations center around Outlook Express, one of the most popular e-mail programs. Some slight differences may exist if you're using an enterprise-based program like Lotus cc:Mail. Consult your office IT manager if you need assistance.

14

Mail and HotSync Manager

After you run Mail Setup, you want to check your HotSync Manager settings to make sure they're properly configured. To open HotSync Manager, click the HotSync icon in your Windows System Tray and choose Custom. (You can also access it from within Palm Desktop by choosing HotSync | Custom.) You see a dialog box listing the installed conduits (which handle the actual synchronization for each program) and the setting (that is, "action") for each one.

If the action for the Mail conduit reads "synchronize the files," then you're all set. (But don't HotSync yet! We still have to configure the settings on the Visor side.) If, for some reason, it still reads Do Nothing, then click the conduit to highlight it, and then click the Change button. In the resulting dialog box, choose Synchronize the files, and then check the box that says Set As Default.

TIP *If you ever decide to stop using Mail, you can simply return to this setup screen and select Do Nothing. Regardless of how you've configured your Visor, this single HotSync Manager setting overrides all others.*

Configuring Mail Settings on the Visor

Synchronizing your desktop mail with the Mail applet is not an all-or-nothing proposition. For instance, you can elect to pull only unread messages into your Visor or create filters so only messages tagged as "high priority" will be synchronized. The settings for such options are found in Mail's HotSync Options screen, which is accessible by choosing Menu | Options.

Figure 14-6 shows the HotSync Options screen. Let's take a look at the four choices therein.

All

This option forces all messages to be synchronized between your Visor and your desktop e-mail program. Take caution when selecting this option; if you have more than a couple dozen messages in your PC's inbox, your HotSyncs may take quite a bit longer (several minutes instead of a few seconds), and you'll eat up that much more of your Visor's available memory.

FIGURE 14-6   The HotSync Options screen contains important settings for use with Palm Mail

Send Only

This one-way solution sends any messages you've composed on your Visor, but doesn't retrieve messages from your desktop mailbox. Use this if you don't want to view your inbound mail on your Visor.

Filter

The most complex of the e-mail options, Filter lets you choose to ignore or retrieve messages that meet certain criteria. Suppose, for instance, you want to retrieve only the e-mail that comes from your coworkers. Or, you want to ignore messages that originate from a specific address. Filter makes such options possible, all in the interest of giving you greater control over the mail that's retrieved from your desktop mailbox. Let's examine the workings of this choice, which is shown in Figure 14-7.

14

FIGURE 14-7   Mail's Filter option lets you decide which e-mail messages do or don't get transferred during a HotSync

CAUTION   *If you intend to use filters, plan on experimenting a bit to get them set up right. There's always the concern that you might accidentally miss an important message if, say, the sender misspells the subject name or sends the e-mail using a different-than-expected account.*

- **Retrieve All High Priority**   When you check this box, it overrides any other filter settings you may have specified. Any e-mail marked as high priority by the sender will be received on your Visor.

- **Ignore Messages Containing**   With this option selected, you're essentially telling HotSync Manager not to retrieve e-mails that meet the criteria laid out in the To, From, and/or Subj fields below.

- **Retrieve Only Messages Containing**   With this option selected, you're essentially telling HotSync Manager to retrieve only the e-mails that meet the criteria laid out in the To, From, and/or Subj fields. This generally downloads much less e-mail than the Ignore Messages option, as you're requesting a specific subset of messages.

- **To, From, Subj**   These three fields are used to specify *filter strings*—the exact information the filter should look for in excluding or accepting messages. Thus, if you want to ignore all messages from *rick@broida.com*, you'd enter that e-mail address in the From: field. If you use multiple e-mail accounts on your desktop PC, but only want to receive messages sent to a specific account, you'd enter that e-mail address in the To: field. In the following screenshot, we configured our Visor to receive e-mails only from *denise.richards@babe.com*. All others will be ignored.

```
┌─────────────────────────────────┐
│  HotSync Options        ⓘ        │
│ Settings for: ▼ Local HotSync    │
│ ┌───┬───────────┬──────┬──────┐  │
│ │All│ Send only │Filter│Unread│  │
│ └───┴───────────┴──────┴──────┘  │
│ ☐ Retrieve All High Priority     │
│ ▼ Retrieve Only Msgs Containing  │
│ To:  .........................   │
│ From: denise.richards@babe.com│  │
│ Subj: ........................   │
│ ( OK ) ( Cancel ) ( Truncate...) │
└─────────────────────────────────┘
```

TIP   *You can specify multiple e-mail addresses in the To: and From: fields, just by separating them with a comma. And, if you run out of room in either field, tap the field name to access a larger data-entry screen (and the Lookup function, should you want to pull e-mail addresses from your contact list).*

Unread

Rather than transferring all the e-mail from your inbox to your Visor, this option transfers only those messages marked as unread. This is an excellent choice if you tend to retain mail after reading it, as it won't download your entire inbox.

Truncate

If you find HotSyncs are taking too long because you often receive lengthy e-mails or you're concerned about messages eating up too much of your Visor's memory, you can instruct Mail to truncate (that is, trim) messages that exceed a certain size. By default, Mail truncates messages longer than 4,000 characters, but you can change the value by tapping the Truncate button in the HotSync Options screen.

> NOTE   *This has nothing to do with file attachments, which Mail never downloads. If an e-mail in your Inbox has an attachment, it is simply ignored during HotSync.*

The Relationship Between Visor and Desktop

It's important to understand that Mail and your desktop e-mail program are not just mimicking each other; they're actually linked together. Thus, when you delete a message on your Visor, it gets deleted on your desktop the next time you HotSync. When you mark a message as read on your desktop, it subsequently gets marked as read on your Visor.

Key Consideration #1

In whatever e-mail program you use on your PC, it's not uncommon to have a variety of different mailboxes set up. You might have one marked "personal," another for "work," and so on. This helps you keep inbound messages better organized, rather than lumping them all into a single folder.

However, regardless of how you've configured Mail's options or filters, the only place it will retrieve messages from is your main inbox. Hey, we never said the program was perfect.

Key Consideration #2

When you compose or reply to a message, the resulting outbound e-mail is sent via Outlook Express (or whatever desktop program you use). Unfortunately, you don't have any control over which desktop e-mail account is used—it's automatically sent via your default account. This might pose a problem if you use multiple accounts, and need to send messages using one that's not the default. Hey, we never said the program was perfect.

Mail's Mailboxes

Like all e-mail programs, Mail uses mailboxes to keep messages organized. Thus, it has the standard inbox and outbox, plus folders for draft, deleted, and filed items (see Figure 14-8). Alas, you can't edit the names of the mailboxes or create new ones, but you can still meet most of your basic organizational needs. Here's a guide to the ins and outs of the inbox, outbox, et al.

Inbox

When you first load the Mail applet, the inbox is the first thing you see. If you haven't set up and synchronized your desktop e-mail program yet, your inbox will look rather empty. If you have, however, you'll see a list of messages, like what's shown in Figure 14-8.

14

FIGURE 14-8   Tap the arrow in the upper-right corner of the screen to access Mail's message folders

The first column shows the name (or e-mail address) of the sender; the second, an abbreviation of the subject heading; and the third, the date the message was received. If you tap the Show button at the bottom of the screen, you can change the method by which these messages are sorted: date, sender, or subject. You can also uncheck the Show Date box, which then eliminates the third column from the message list (making the other two a bit bigger).

Tap any message to open it. A check mark next to any message in the list denotes it has been read. At the top of the screen, you see a numerical description of how many messages are in the list and how many of those remain unread.

Outbox

When you tap Send after composing a new message or reply, the message is directed to the outbox. There it stays until the next time you HotSync, after which it's transferred to your desktop e-mail program and sent. You can tap any message in the list to view, edit, or delete it.

The Show button affords the same options here as in the inbox (and is, in fact, the same in all the folders).

Deleted

As noted earlier, when you delete a message on your Visor, it gets deleted in your desktop e-mail program as well. But that doesn't happen until your next HotSync and, in the meantime, all deleted messages are stored in the Deleted folder. You can undelete a message from this folder by tapping it, and then tapping the Undelete button at the bottom of the screen.

Tap here to retrieve
a deleted message

Filed

Want to keep a message for later reference, but don't want to clutter your inbox? Just file it in the Filed folder. When you have any e-mail message open, simply choose Menu | Message | File. You're then asked if you want to keep the e-mail in the inbox as well—tap Yes or No (or Cancel if you changed your mind about the whole thing). The Filed folder has no connection with your desktop e-mail program, so messages stored there are not synchronized. (They are, however, backed up on your computer's hard drive, along with other Visor data.)

Draft

Suppose you're composing a love letter (make that e-mail) to Denise Richards. You've written the first draft, but don't want to send it right away in case it sounds too corny. You can file it away in the Draft folder, where it'll stay until you're ready to edit it.

You can direct an e-mail to this folder in two ways. First, you can choose Menu | Message | Save Draft. Second, if you tap Cancel while working on a new e-mail, you're given the option of saving it to the Draft folder, instead of deleting it. To continue work on a message filed in Draft, tap it once, and then tap the Edit button. (You can also tap the Delete button to delete it.)

As with the Filed folder, the contents of Draft are not synchronized with your PC—despite the fact that your desktop e-mail program may have a similar folder (as does Outlook Express).

Composing New Messages

Okay, so you've configured Mail to your liking, and now you're ready to start writing messages. You can go about this in two ways: Tap the New button, or choose Menu | Message | New. You can't simply start writing in the Graffiti area, as you can with most of the other core Visor apps.

14

The New Message screen consists of four fields, all of which should be quite familiar to anyone who's worked with e-mail on a PC:

```
┌─────────────────────────────────┐
│ New Message                     │
│  To: rickbroida@magicaldesk.com │
│  CC:                            │
│ Subj: The Palm Mail applet      │
│ Body: When I'm done composing this │
│       message, I'll have to wait till I │
│       HotSync before I'll be able to │
│       send it.                  │
│                                 │
│                                 │
│                                 │
│                                 │
│ (Send) (Cancel) (Details...)    │
└─────────────────────────────────┘
```

- ■ **To**   Enter the address of the recipient here. You can send the same message to multiple recipients simply by writing more e-mail addresses, separating them with a comma. Tap the To: field button for access to a larger address-entry screen (and the Lookup function, should you want to pull e-mail addresses from your contact list).

- ■ **CC**   Want this message to reach additional recipients? Enter their e-mail addresses here in the "carbon copy" field. Tap the CC: field button for access to a larger address-entry screen (and the Lookup function, if you want to pull e-mail addresses from your contact list).

- ■ **Subj**   Enter the subject of the message here. Tap the Subj: field button for access to a larger data-entry screen.

- ■ **Body**   Enter the full message here. Tap the Body: field button for access to a larger data-entry screen.

The buttons at the bottom of the New Message screen should be equally self-explanatory. But let's take a peek at them anyway.

Send

When you tap it, your message is placed in the Mail outbox. The next time you HotSync, all messages in the outbox are transferred to your PC and sent via your desktop e-mail program.

Cancel

This is actually a two-function button. When you tap it, the Visor asks if you want to save the message in the Draft folder. If so, tap Yes; if not, tap No. The latter action erases the message and returns you to the inbox screen. The former action files the message in the Draft folder, a kind of holding tank for messages that aren't ready to be sent.

Details

You can apply a few additional sending options to outgoing messages, all of them accessible by tapping the Details button, which brings up the Message Details dialog box:

> **Message Details** ℹ️
> **Priority:** ▼ Normal
> **BCC:** ☑
> **Signature:** ☑
> **Confirm Read:** ☐
> **Confirm Delivery:** ☐
> (OK) (Cancel)

All five of these features work only if your desktop e-mail program supports them.

- ■ **Priority** Want the recipient(s) to know this message is of high priority? Or low? Or just normal? Tap here to select one.

- ■ **BCC** Checking this box adds a Blind Carbon Copy field to your message, which you see when you return to the New Message screen. This is a way to secretly send copies of the message to additional recipients, without the other recipients being able to see their e-mail addresses.

- ■ **Signature** When this box is checked, your "signature" (as specified in the Mail Preferences screen) is appended to the end of the message. Although it won't be visible when you return to the New Message screen, it will be added.

- ■ **Confirm Read** Kind of like an RSVP, this option requests an e-mail reply that your message was read by the recipient(s).

- ■ **Confirm Delivery** This option requests e-mail notification that your message was delivered to the intended recipient(s).

The latter three options are "sticky," meaning if you select them for one message, they stay selected for all future messages (unless you subsequently deselect them again).

14

Viewing Messages

Regardless of which mailbox or folder you have open, viewing a message is as simple as tapping it. However, the options associated with that message vary a bit depending on the folder that contains it. In the inbox and Filed folders, for instance, you can tap Reply or Delete. In the outbox and Draft folders, your options are Edit and Delete. And, in the Deleted folder, you can choose Edit if the message was originally composed on your Visor, and Undelete if it's one that was in your inbox.

Header Information

When you open any e-mail message, regardless of its folder location, you see a pair of icons in the upper-right corner of the screen. These control how much of the message's header is displayed. If you'd like to see more information, such as the sender's reply-to address, the date and time the message was sent, and the e-mail addresses of all recipients (if others beside yourself were included), tap the right icon. Tap the left icon to "shorten" the display again.

```
┌─────────────────────────┐  ┌─────────────────────────┐
│ Inbox Message 4 of 7  ▤▤│  │ Inbox Message 4 of 7  ▤▤│
│ From: Amy Nemechek    ▲ │  │    To: palm@arpartners.com ▲│
│  Subj: Palm CEO named: Carl│ │ From: anemechek@arpartners.com│
│        Yankowski        │  │        (Amy Nemechek)   │
│                         │  │  Subj: Palm CEO named: Carl│
│ Dear all,               │  │        Yankowski        │
│ 3Com announced this morning it has│ │ Date: 12/2/99 12:30 pm │
│ named Carl Yankowski to the new│  │                         │
│ post of CEO of the Palm Computing│ │ Dear all,               │
│ division. Alan Kessler will continue in│ │ 3Com announced this morning it has│
│ his role as president. The press│ │ named Carl Yankowski to the new│
│ release follows.        ▼│  │ post of CEO of the Palm Computing ▼│
│ (Done) (Reply) (Delete) ◄▶│  │ (Done) (Reply) (Delete) ◄▶│
└─────────────────────────┘  └─────────────────────────┘
```

Replying to and Forwarding Messages

Hey, wait a second. You've seen the Reply button, which is used to answer e-mails. But what if you want to forward a message to someone else? Where's the Forward button?

Surprise—there isn't one; at least, not where you'd expect it. Although most people would agree that replying and forwarding are two very different animals, Mail inexplicably buries the Forward option in the Reply Options window. Let's take a look at that window, as shown in Figure 14-9.

```
┌─────────────────────────┐
│ Inbox Message 4 of 7  ▤▤│
│    To: palm@arpartners.com ▲│
│ From: anemechek@arpartners.com│
│        (Amy Nemechek)   │
│  Subj: Palm CEO named: Carl│
│═══════Reply Options═══════│
│ Reply to: Sender All Forward│
│                         │
│ ☑ Include original text │
│ ☑ Comment original text │
│ (  OK  ) (Cancel)       │
└─────────────────────────┘
```

| FIGURE 14-9 | When you reply to a message, Mail enables you to specify who gets the reply and whether to include the original message |

■ **Reply to**   Who should this reply go to? The person who sent it? Everyone else who received it? Maybe you simply want to forward the message to someone else. Choose the desired option by tapping Sender, All, or Forward, respectively.

■ **Include original text**   It's a common courtesy to include a copy of the original message when replying or forwarding. By checking this box, Mail does exactly that, as you see in the body of the new message that appears.

■ **Comment original text**   Of course, it can be difficult to distinguish the old text from the new, which is why it's a good idea to "comment" the original message. Translation: the old text is marked and indented using ">" symbols. Mail even adds a descriptor ("So-and-so wrote on 12/2/99 at 12:30 p.m:") before the commented text, as the following illustrates:

```
New Message
Body: this is the new message; below
is the old.

Amy Nemechek wrote on
12/2/99 12:30 pm:

>Dear all,
>3Com announced this
>morning it has named Carl
>Yankowski to the new post
>of CEO of the Palm

(Send) (Cancel) (Details...)
```

Mail's Other Options

While perusing the Mail menus, you may have noticed a few choices other than HotSync Options (which we covered in great detail a few pages back). Let's check 'em out, and then you can go back to playing Giraffe.

■ **Purge Deleted**   Accessed by choosing Menu | Message | Purge Deleted, this option empties the contents of the Deleted folder. Said messages are still deleted from your desktop e-mail program the next time you HotSync. So, why bother with this option? There's no particularly compelling reason, except that if you have a lot of lengthy messages stored in the Deleted folder, they're probably eating up some of your precious RAM.

■ **Font**   As with all the core Palm OS programs, Mail lets you choose one of three fonts for viewing data. The procedure here is the same as elsewhere: choose Menu | Options | Font, and then tap the font you want.

■ **Preferences**   Remember a few pages ago, when we told you about the Details screen for new messages? That bit about appending your "signature"? Here in the Preferences screen, you get to create that signature. It can be anything you want, from a standard closing ("Very truly yours," and so forth) to your opinion about which is the best *Star Trek* series (it's *Voyager*, as everyone knows).

14

For some reason, Dave likes to include obscure song lyrics in his signature.

Third-Party E-Mail Programs

Many people are surprised to learn that just because you buy a modem for your Visor it doesn't mean you have direct access to your ISP. Mail, as you now know, connects only to your desktop e-mail program. And the Handspring Modem doesn't come with any additional e-mail software (the Card Access Thincom does, but it's a ten-day trial version).

With third-party e-mail programs (and Web browsers, as discussed later in this chapter), you can dial into virtually any ISP (and America Online!) to send and receive e-mail, just as you would from your desktop PC. Indeed, these programs effectively take the PC out of the equation, turning your Visor into a standalone e-mail machine.

You will, of course, need a modem and you need to have your Visor configured to dial into your ISP. In addition, each program requires you to supply some ISP account information, such as your user name and password, the names of the POP3 and SMTP servers, and possibly a few other technical tidbits. It may be necessary to contact your ISP if you don't know where to find this information.

Accessing America Online

At last count, America Online (AOL) had something like 70 billion subscribers. Okay, we may be off by a few billion, but there's no debating the popularity of the service. And while you can't yet access AOL proper from your Visor, you can send and receive e-mail using your AOL account.

Two programs make this possible. The first, AOL Mail, is supplied by America Online itself. It's a free application, making it the obvious one to try first. The second is Power Media's PocketFlash, which should prove of interest to AOL power users. Both titles dial directly into one of AOL's nationwide access numbers, superceding any settings you may have specified in the Visor's Network preferences. Let's take a look at the inner workings of both titles.

AOL Mail

It's free, it's easy to use, and it offers most of the e-mail functionality of the software that runs on your computer. As shown in Figure 14-10, AOL Mail is divided into three main sections, all of which should be immediately familiar to seasoned AOL users.

FIGURE 14-10   AOL Mail looks and works a lot like its desktop counterpart

The software includes a complete database of AOL access numbers and enables you to set up multiple dial-up locations (helpful if you travel a lot). You can also choose one of the "Anywhere" access numbers, which are toll free but incur $6/hour surcharges. You need to sacrifice a fairly hefty chunk of RAM to load the software onto your Visor; it takes about 400K and needs additional space to store messages. You're also limited to one master account (complete with any screen names you may have added), though you can sign on as a guest if you need to access another account.

AOL Mail enables you to work online or offline, depending on your preference. If you're on the road and connecting with one of those costly Anywhere numbers, you'll appreciate the Auto AOL feature, which logs on, transacts mail, and logs right off again. There's even a Filing Cabinet that functions much like the desktop version.

Unlike the Palm OS Mail program, AOL Mail doesn't make you jump through hoops (that is, tap half a dozen times) to access your Address List. Rather, when you tap the To: field when composing an e-mail message, you're instantly presented with your list of contacts—and their e-mail addresses. Convenient!

A few additional notes about AOL Mail:

- It doesn't support Status or Unsend features.

- It doesn't support attachments and truncates messages larger than 16K.

- It won't work with wireless modems.

- It requires a direct dial-up connection to AOL, and therefore is incompatible with "Bring Your Own Access" service plans.

PocketFlash

Why use Power Media's PocketFlash when AOL Mail is free? While the latter should indeed accommodate most users, PocketFlash does have a few points in its favor. For instance, it allows you to dial directly into AOL or connect via a third-party ISP (important for those who use

AOL's "Bring Your Own Access" service plan). Plus, it supports the use of signatures; message sizes up to 32K (and you get to choose the maximum size); text file attachments; AOL's Unsend feature; and, perhaps best of all, multiple master accounts. PocketFlash also requires roughly half as much Visor memory as AOL Mail: 156K versus 383K.

Accessing Internet Service Providers

If you're not an AOL user, chances are good you connect to the Internet via MindSpring, Earthlink, Prodigy, or some other national or local service provider. Thus, you want to access your e-mail directly from these services, which you can do using a modem and any of the following tools.

What's important in a Visor e-mail program? That depends on how heavily you rely on e-mail and what features you need most. For instance, if you have more than one account, you want a program that supports multiple accounts. If you tend to get deluged with e-mail, look for message-filtering capabilities. In short, the features you value in your desktop e-mail program are probably available in many of the Visor programs as well. So make your list and check it twice.

MultiMail Professional

A program we'd classify as "e-mail for power users," Actual Software's MultiMail Professional pushes the boundaries of the Palm's capabilities. Of particular interest is its support for plug-ins—little programs that let you receive and view specific kinds of file attachments. Thus, others can send you text files, spreadsheets, e-books, even Palm OS programs, all of which you have access to right on your Visor. The following are some of MultiMail's main benefits:

■ Support for up to eight POP3 and IMAP4 accounts—more than any other Palm OS e-mail program. MultiMail is also the only program to support the emerging IMAP4 standard, which is currently in use by many corporations.

■ Support for messages of up to 256K in size and file attachments of up to 60K.

■ Enables you to sort messages by date, subject, sender, or size, by tapping the appropriate column. You can even arrange the columns to your liking by dragging and dropping them.

■ Enables you to preview e-mail messages before downloading them.

NOTE   *Shortly before press time, Actual Software was acquired by Palm, Inc. While MultiMail will continue to exist, it may be selling under the Palm name by the time you read this.*

MultiMail Conduit Pack   Whereas the Palm Mail program can synchronize with a wide variety of desktop e-mail programs, few of the third-party alternatives can do the same. Enter the MultiMail Conduit Pack, which adds this capability to MultiMail. The Windows version supports Microsoft Outlook, Outlook Express, Lotus Domino, Groupwise, Eudora, and IMAP4 servers. The Macintosh version supports Outlook Express, Claris, Eudora Pro, and Eudora Lite.

How to ... **Synchronize Macintosh Mail**

14

Hallelujah, Macintosh users! Whereas Palm Mail can't synchronize with your e-mail program, the MultiMail Conduit Pack can. Of course, you have to use MultiMail Professional as well, but at least a solution exists.

One-Touch Mail

JP Systems' One-Touch Mail is one of our favorite e-mail programs. That's because it's powerful, yet easy to use, and offers many conveniences not found elsewhere. For instance, it includes handy "canned" messages for creating quick and easy messages or replies. All it takes is a couple taps to write things like "need more info" or "will call later." And you can customize the canned-message list, adding your own messages or removing those you don't need.

Some of the program's other amenities:

- Lets you send or receive Address Book, Date Book, Memo Pad, or To Do List entries.
- Seamless integration with your contact list and the capability to select multiple addresses simultaneously. (Other programs make you choose them one at a time, hopping back and forth between the list and your message.)
- Supports multiple and configurable e-mail folders, and filters that can automatically direct inbound mail to those folders.
- Supports up to six POP3 accounts.
- Built-in access to the Visor's Network preferences screen.
- Enables you to sort messages by date, subject, sender, or size by tapping the appropriate column.

ProxiMail

ProxiMail is something of an anomaly among third-party e-mail products. For one thing, it's free. For another, it's not actively supported by ProxiNet, the company that produced it. Don't ask us why—it's as though the company decided to shift its efforts elsewhere (most likely to ProxiWeb, the free Web browser covered later in this chapter). At press time, there was no documentation or help available on the company's Web site, nor even a description of the program's capabilities. Thus, you're pretty much on your own if you decide to try ProxiMail. We recommend only experienced computer users get involved with it.

That said, ProxiMail does something fairly clever: it enables the Palm Mail applet to work directly with your ISP, rather than just with your desktop e-mail program. It's quite easy to configure and it enables you to manage up to five "profiles" (that is, accounts). However, it's not perfect. For instance, you have to hop back and forth between Mail and ProxiMail to compose, send, retrieve, and view messages. And, when you're ready to disconnect from your ISP, you have to take a trip to Network preferences. Still, ProxiMail works as advertised. If you like Mail and want to use it for your Internet accounts, the program is worth investigating.

Instant Messaging

Chances are good you use some kind of *instant messaging* (IM) software on your PC. If so, you've probably come to recognize the value of having quick online chats with your friends and colleagues. Well, who's to say you shouldn't enjoy the same convenience on your Visor? You can, thanks to Yahoo! Messenger—an IM program for Palm OS devices that works much like the Windows and Macintosh versions.

Working with Yahoo! Messenger

Whether you're already a user of one of the desktop versions of this program or new to Yahoo! Messenger, all you have to do is download and install the Palm OS version (which you can do at http://messenger.yahoo.com). If it finds an existing "friend list" on your desktop system, it automatically imports it into the Palm version.

When you tap Yahoo! Messenger's Connect button, your Visor dials in to your ISP as configured in Network preferences. Then, you see a list of any "friends" who are also logged on to Yahoo! Messenger. Double-tap any name to send a message to that person. Location doesn't matter—you can chat Visor to PC, Macintosh to Visor, and even Visor to Visor.

One Fundamental Difference

Like its desktop counterparts, Yahoo! Messenger for the Palm OS enables you to add and remove friends from your list, change your availability status, and so on. However, the way it handles chat sessions is a bit different. Whereas on a computer each party's messages appear in the same window, on the Visor you're switched back and forth between two windows—one for viewing inbound messages, one for creating the replies. This is not terribly convenient, to say the least.

More important, instant messaging on a Visor is of limited value, given the speed of entering data with a stylus. Whether you use Graffiti or the onscreen keyboard, chats seem woefully slow. If you think you want to do a lot of instant messaging on your Visor, consider using a keyboard like LandWare's GoType! or Think Outside's Stowaway.

Turn Your Visor into a Web Browser

We know what you're thinking: The screen is too small. It isn't in color. It's too slow. Well, it turns out the Visor is a pretty handy device for accessing the Internet. It's a pocket-sized Web machine you can use anywhere there's a phone jack. While the screen's diminutive size and lack of color certainly make for a less-than-ideal browsing experience, it works well in a pinch.

To get started, you need a modem, an ISP, and browser software for the Visor. Modems and ISP configurations are discussed earlier in this chapter; here's the skinny on browsers.

Choose a Web Browser

The Visor doesn't come with any built-in Web browsing software. But don't despair: you can easily add your own. Several browsers are available for the Palm OS:

- AvantGo (www.avantgo.com)
- pdQbrowser (www.pdqsuite.com)
- ProxiWeb (www.proxinet.com)

Once you have a browser installed and a modem plugged in, you're ready to start surfing. Be aware that surfing with your Visor is radically different than surfing with your PC. Remember these limitations as you start exploring the Web:

- **Graphics are much more limited**   It doesn't take a rocket scientist to deduce this one, but a Visor gives you neither color nor a lot of screen estate. As a result, graphics appear in 16 shades of gray. You might want to disable graphics entirely in your browser because that speeds things up significantly.

- **Some pages are too darned wide**   A lot of Web pages are built with a specific width in mind, usually 640 pixels or so. This mean you may encounter Web pages that require you to scroll not just down, but also from side-to-side.

- **Don't download**   The Palm OS doesn't support downloading files from the Internet, which makes some degree of sense. After all, you can't run Windows or Mac applications on the Visor, and most data files wouldn't work on it either.

NOTE   *An exception exists to the "can't download" rule—a few browsers (like ProxiWeb) do let you download and install Palm OS apps directly from the Internet without HotSyncing to a PC first. Read about it in the ProxiWeb section later in this chapter.*

Surf with ProxiWeb

ProxiWeb has a different design philosophy than other browsers. In fact, the reason it has the word "proxi" in the name is because it relies on a proxy server to streamline the Web pages before they reach your Visor.

In other words, when you request a Web page using ProxiWeb, the data is actually passed through a proxy server hosted by the company that makes ProxiWeb. The Web page is stripped and streamlined; what is sent to you is optimized for display on the Visor screen. The result is that pages look better and often display faster than with other browsers.

What's more, ProxiWeb is a freebie—you can download it directly from the company's Web site (www.proxinet.com) in exchange for a bit of personal information. Not a bad deal for one of the best Palm OS Web browsers around.

Starting ProxiWeb

When you first start ProxiWeb, you see the designated home page with a few tools displayed across the bottom of the screen.

This is what those tools do:

- ■ **Navigation arrows**   Use these arrows to move forward and backward through cached pages you visited in this surfing session.

- ■ **Open URL**   Use the folder icon to open a bookmarked Web page or to write in a new address to visit.

- ■ **Home**   Tap this icon to go back to the home page.

- ■ **Reload**   Just like in a desktop browser, this icon refreshes the current page from the Internet.

14

■ **Stored pages** This is a list of all the pages currently cached on the Visor. If you want to make sure a specific page is saved permanently so you can see it without accessing the Internet, tap the padlock to close the lock and save the page. Open locks indicate pages ProxiWeb can delete as needed to save space.

■ **Bookmarks** This is a dedicated view of your bookmarks, similar to the Open URL button.

■ **Information** Tap this icon to see the URL of the current Web page.

To open a Web page in ProxiWeb, tap the Open URL icon. You see the Enter a URL to Load Page dialog box. Now you have two options:

■ To open a bookmarked page, tap the Bookmarks list menu and choose a page from the list. If you're not already connected to the Internet, the Visor asks permission to connect, and then it loads the page.

■ If you want to enter a new URL, write the Web address in the field provided. If you tap the Shortcuts list menu, you can tap common URL elements like .com and .net without having to write them out. Tap the OK button. If you're not already connected to the Internet, the Visor asks permission to connect, and then it loads the page.

Using ProxiWeb to View Web Pages

Once you're actually on a Web page, ProxiWeb behaves like a normal Web browser—except it has been optimized for the Visor's small size. The most obvious change is ProxiWeb shrinks graphics to fit on the screen. If you tap a graphic, you see a menu that enables you to display the image at full size. If the image is also a link, you have the option to go to the linked page.

Tap the full-size option to see the entire graphic more clearly. Why would you want to do that? Well, many graphics are too hard to see clearly at the Lilliputian Visor-friendly size. More important, some graphics are *image maps*—that is, they contain several links, and you need to tap on the correct area of the image to go to the correct page. The image-map capability of the image is suppressed when the image is shrunk, so to use an image map, you need to view the image at full size.

If you decide you want to add the current Web page to your list of bookmarks, choose Go | Add Bookmark from the menu. Once added, you can access this page from either the Open URL or the Bookmarks icon at the bottom of the screen.

Installing Palm Apps from the Internet

One of the best reasons to use ProxiWeb is its capability to install files on the Visor. This means you can install Palm OS programs and data files without HotSyncing. Even better, it's okay if the program is enclosed in a Zip file, as they often are—ProxiWeb understands the Zip file format and can see inside to the compressed programs stored within. Here's what you need to do to install a Palm OS app from ProxiWeb:

1. Visit a Web site that has a file you want to download.

2. Surf directly to the program description and download link. Tap the link to download the file. If you're at PalmGear, for instance, you should tap the icon that represents the Zip-compressed file.

3. If the file is compressed in Zip format, the Visor next displays the contents of the Zip file in a list. Tap the file you want to install (it will probably end in .pdb or .prc). Other files, like Adobe Acrobat and .txt files are intended for the desktop—ignore them. The selected file is downloaded to your Visor.

```
 ▪whatsnew.txt (64 bytes)
 ▪readme.txt (887 bytes)
 ▪gp2.prc (39241 bytes)




 ←➡▣⌂⇄$B❶
```

4. After the file has downloaded, you see the Save File screen, which asks if you want to save the file to the Visor. Tap the Yes button.

5. After accepting the application, you are returned to the Zip file list screen. If you want to install more files (many Palm OS programs require two or more files to run properly), install them next. If not, tap the Back arrow to return to your browser window or switch to the new application you just installed.

> **TIP** *You can tap .txt files (that is, text files) and read their contents in the browser window if you like.*

14

Customizing ProxiWeb

You can customize ProxiWeb by choosing Settings | ProxiWeb from the menu. This Preferences screen is where you can specify a custom home page. To change the home page, enter on the bottom line marked Home whatever Web site you want to begin with. Be sure to erase the text on that field, which should say Home:, to indicate the ProxiWeb default screen.

```
┌─────────────────────────────────┐
│      Preferences·          ❶     │
│ History Size 15                  │
│ Cache Size (in K) 200            │
│ Scrolling Rate (Pixels) 120      │
│  □ Map Phone/ToDo as Prev/Next   │
│ Proxy Server: dog.proxinet.com   │
│ Proxy Port: 8000                 │
│ Fallback Server: cat.proxinet.com│
│ Fallback Port: 8000              │
│ Home: www.cnn.com                │
│ ( Save ) ( Cancel )              │
└─────────────────────────────────┘
```

Surf with the pdQbrowser

Qualcomm's pdQbrowser is a bit different from ProxiWeb in that it employs two distinct views. The program starts in the Bookmarks view and lists all the pages you've saved. When you tap on a bookmarked page, you're taken to the pdQbrowser view, which displays the contents of the selected Web page.

Using the Bookmarks View

From the Bookmarks view, you can inspect, edit, add, and delete bookmarked Web pages. To add a new bookmark, tap the New button at the bottom of the screen, which opens the Create Bookmark dialog box. Note that all you must do for most Web pages is to enter the middle part of the URL. If you're entering a .net address, though, you have to delete some of the boilerplate provided for you.

```
┌─────────────────────────────┐
│ Bookmarks          ▼ All     │
│ Palmgear              ❶ ◄──── Information
│    Create Bookmark           │      icon
│ Name: ...................... │
│       ...................... │
│ URL: http://www.│com         │
│       ...................... │
│       ...................... │
│       ...................... │
│ Category: ▼ Unfiled          │
│ ( OK ) ( Cancel )            │
└─────────────────────────────┘
```

For existing bookmarks, tap the Information icon at the right side of the screen to edit the URL or the Web site name, or to delete it entirely. To display a Web page, tap on the site's title.

If you want to go to a Web site that isn't already stored as a bookmark, the procedure is a bit different than in other browsers. Choose Options | Visit Location from the menu and write the URL of the site you want to visit.

Using pdQbrowser to View Web Pages

The pdQbrowser view interface is quite simple. The program doesn't support graphics, so all your browsing takes place in text-only mode. You have two buttons available in this view:

- **Details**   This button displays the URL of the current Web site. From this screen, you can also choose to refresh the page (recall it from the Web) or to save the location as a bookmark.
- **Bookmarks**   Return to the Bookmarks view.

Channel Surf with AvantGo

The last Web browsing option, AvantGo, is by no means the least useful or least important. We simply saved it for last because it's the most unusual of the Web tools. In fact, you don't even need to have a Visor modem to use it.

AvantGo is a Web-based service that has a Palm OS-based component. You can choose from among hundreds of Web sites—called *channels* in AvantGo parlance—that are transferred to your Visor during the HotSync session. After a HotSync, you can browse the information stored in these channels on your Palm without needing to connect to the Internet. In a sense, it's offline browsing taken to the logical extreme: you select the sites you want, they are copied to the Visor, and you read them while you're away from your desk.

Best of all, most of the channels are formatted for the Visor's screen, unlike ordinary Web pages that you visit with an ordinary Palm OS browser. You can even create your own AvantGo channels or turn any existing Web page into a channel. Neat stuff—and the software, service, and channels are all free!

14

Set Up AvantGo

To get up and running with AvantGo, visit the AvantGo Web site (www.avantgo.com) and follow the instructions therein. You go through the process of downloading and installing the necessary software, and then setting up an AvantGo account and choosing your desired channels.

Make sure to keep track of the user name and password you choose when creating your account—you need them in the future to add or remove channels. The AvantGo Web site (which looks like the one in Figure 14-11) administrates the content that appears on your Visor—that is, channel selection occurs right at the site. Adding or removing a channel is as simple as clicking Edit in the My Account box, and then following the onscreen instructions.

So, just what kinds of channels will you find on AvantGo? You name it, they have it—everything from news, sports, and weather to stock reports, maps, and movie listings. Some of the channels come from high-profile sources, like *Rolling Stone,* the *Wall Street Journal,* and the *New York Times.* And, because it's a simple matter to convert existing Web pages into AvantGo channels, you'll also find plenty of user-created content. Some of it lacks the nice formatting of "premium" channels, but the information is still there.

NOTE   *While it's easy to go a little channel-crazy with all this great stuff, remember that the more channels you add, the more memory is consumed on your Visor—and the longer your HotSyncs take. Indeed, it often takes a couple minutes to HotSync when you have more than a few channels installed. Of course, if you don't mind waiting and have RAM to burn, feel free to get crazy with those channels.*

Our Favorite AvantGo Channels

We admit it: We're AvantGo junkies. So much great information, so nicely formatted, so free. What channels make our hearts go pitter-pat? Thought you'd never ask.

Rick: Hollywood.com is a channel I find truly indispensable. I simply write in my ZIP code and it finds movie listings for all the local theaters. As long as I HotSync at least once per day, I'm guaranteed to have all the latest show times with me at all times. I'm also a big fan of Space.com, which delivers a daily dose of space and science news.

Dave: Without a doubt, my favorite AvantGo channels are news sources. I read the *New York Times* Front Page every day, along with Doctor Science's Question of the Day. And, if I have time, I read the *Onion*—now there's top-notch news reporting, delivered right to my Visor.

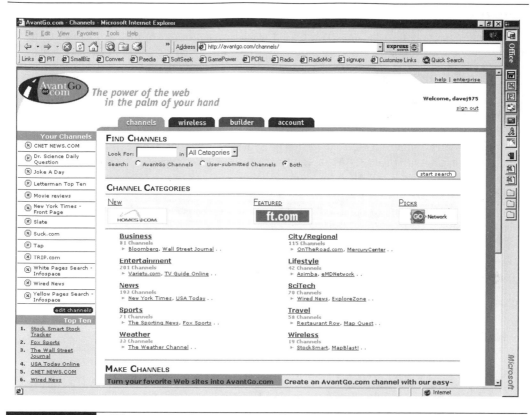

FIGURE 14-11   When you log in to your AvantGo account, you see a page where you can browse available channels and edit your personal list

Use Your Visor as a Fax Machine

So you've jotted down some meeting notes in Memo Pad and now you need to fire them off to company H.Q. Well, you could HotSync your Visor, copy the memo to your word processor, print the page, and then walk over to the fax machine. Or, thanks to a powerful piece of software from a company that virtually invented computer-based faxing, you could clip on a modem and send the memo right from your Visor.

14

Mobile WinFax

Mobile WinFax is a notable piece of software—not just because it brings robust faxing capabilities to Visors, but because it comes from computer-industry giant Symantec Corp. It's also notable for being such a well-designed product. Mobile WinFax allows you to send and receive faxes via your Visor, whether or not you have a modem for it. If you don't, you can still create new faxes, and then use your computer's modem for the actual transmissions. Thus, a Visor modem isn't mandatory equipment and therein lies much of the software's charm.

The package is comprised of two components: a Visor application and a Windows utility (the latter essentially a small, specialized version of Symantec's famous WinFax Pro). The Visor software requires about 250K of RAM for a full install—less if you decide you don't want the fax viewer or don't plan to use a Visor modem. At minimum, you need 150K, plus space for storing any received faxes.

Mobile WinFax is an appreciably simple program to use, especially on the Visor side. The main screen displays three options, all represented by large, attractive icons (see Figure 14-12). Here you can create a new fax, display any faxes in memory, or send and receive faxes. When creating a new fax, you have the option of simply writing out a text message, or attaching one or more items from Memo Pad.

You can also attach documents residing on your PC, though you must first import them into the Windows component of Mobile WinFax, and then HotSync them to your Visor. The software supports Word, Excel, text, and bitmap files, but keep the size of any documents you convert for handheld faxing in mind. A mere half-page Word document turned into a 38K file.

FIGURE 14-12   The main Mobile WinFax screen is a model of simplicity and elegance

Need to annotate an outgoing fax with some additional instructions or your signature? Mobile WinFax lets you do that, too. You can send your faxes to one or more recipients, entering the names and numbers manually or drawing them from Address Book.

```
┌─────────────────────────────────┐
│ Fax Message Recipients          │
│  ┌Address┐Cover┐Attach┐Options┐ │
│       To: Rick Broida           │
│   Number: 719-282-3822          │
│  Company: Tap                   │
│                                 │
│  Subject: Test Fax              │
│                                 │
│           📞  📥  ✖            │
│  Recipient List:                │
│                                 │
│                                 │
│  ( Done ) ( Cancel )            │
└─────────────────────────────────┘
```

Mobile WinFax comes with six different cover pages and even enables you to import any custom covers you created in WinFax Pro. When the time comes to send, you can do so via a modem (if one's connected to your Visor) or a HotSync, in which case the outgoing fax is transferred to the Windows component, and then sent via your PC's modem.

When you tap Display Faxes, you're taken to a tabbed screen with an outbox, a send log, and a receive log. You can view the details of any fax listed (date created, destination, number of pages, and so on), or resend a fax with a single tap. You can also view the fax as a graphic, though the Visor's low-resolution screen makes this a fairly pointless endeavor.

It also minimizes the effectiveness of receiving faxes on your Visor. Doing so is as simple as tapping an icon, but it's virtually impossible to get a good look at received pages. Using the software's image viewer, you have to zoom way in to be able to decipher any text, and navigating around a zoomed-in page is difficult at best. Ideally, you'll HotSync received faxes to your desktop, and then view or print them with the Windows applet.

Unlike most Palm OS software, Mobile WinFax is available in stores like CompUSA and Best Buy. You can also purchase it directly from Symantec's Web site and download it to your PC.

Use Your Visor as a Pager

One of the most intriguing Springboard modules we've seen is the InfoMitt Pager from Global Access (see Figure 14-13). It allows your Visor to receive not only alphanumeric pager messages, but also news, stock, and weather reports, and other custom information. Perhaps most compelling of all is the price: just $49.95, not much more than a standard pager. (There are, of course, service charges as well, but they're only about $13 per month.)

Alas, the InfoMitt wasn't available for testing at press time, but it's no doubt shipping by now. If you're on the go a lot and would rather not carry a separate pager, you should definitely look into this solution.

14

FIGURE 14-13 The InfoMitt turns your Visor into a one-way pager

Use Your Visor to Contact Pagers

If you have a modem for your Visor, you can use Mark/Space Softworks' PageNOW! Software (see Figure 14-14) to contact friends and colleagues who have pagers. This software package enables you to compose text messages on your Visor, and then send them via a Visor modem. This is of limited value, to be sure, but if you often need to send detailed messages to people who are reachable only by pager, PageNOW! is worth a look.

FIGURE 14-14 The PageNOW! software enables you to compose text messages for transmission to alphanumeric pagers—you supply the modem

Travel Tips for Modem Users

Those Boy Scouts were onto a good thing when they came up with the slogan "Be Prepared." That's good advice for any traveler—even those who aren't trying to send e-mail from their Visor. And for those who are, we've prepared this list of handy modem-related tips to help ensure dial-up success.

■ Remember to pack a spare set of batteries, both for your modem (if applicable) and your Visor. The more you're online, the faster you burn through batteries.

■ Before connecting your modem to a hotel or office phone, check with the front desk (or an IT person) to make sure it's safe. If it's a digital phone system, you could wind up with a fried modem—or worse. You can eliminate all doubt by carrying a gizmo like IBM's Modem Saver, which plugs into any jack and lets you know if the line presents any danger.

■ Before you head out, look up (and write down) your ISP's access number for your destination. Better yet, carry its complete list of numbers on your Visor. You may be able to find such a list already formatted for Visor viewing from software sites like Handango and PalmGear H.Q.

■ Landline modem users should always pack an RJ-11 phone cord. You never know if one will be available where you're going.

Where to Find It

Web Site	Address	What's There
Handspring	www.handspring.com	Handspring Modem
Card Access, Inc.	www.cardaccess-inc.com	Thincom Portable Modem
Xircom	www.xircom.com	SpringPort Modem 56 GlobalAccess
Power Media	www.powermedia.com	PocketFlash
America Online	Keyword: Anywhere	AOL Mail
Actual Software	www.actualsoft.com	MultiMail Professional and MultiMail Conduit Pack
JP Systems	www.jpsystems.com	One-Touch Mail
ProxiNet	www.proxinet.com	ProxiMail and ProxiWeb
Yahoo! Messenger	http://messenger.yahoo.com	Yahoo! Messenger for the Palm
AvantGo	www.avantgo.com	AvantGo
Qualcomm	www.pdqsuite.com	pdQbrowser
Symantec	www.mobilewinfax.com	Mobile WinFax
Global Access	www.infomitt.com	InfoMitt
Mark/Space Softworks	www.markspace.com	PageNow!

14

Chapter 15

Enhance Your Visor with Modules

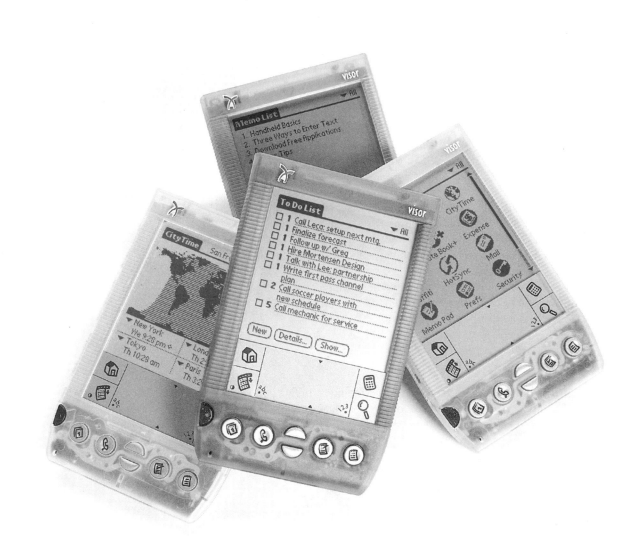

How to...

- Install Springboard modules
- Find new modules
- Take pictures with the eyemodule
- Transfer eyemodule pictures to the PC
- Control your home theater with the OmniRemote
- Program the OmniRemote
- Listen to MP3 music with MiniJam
- Play golf on your Visor
- Access e-books and reference materials
- Find modules that are coming soon

If you're like us, you didn't buy your Visor just because it looks cool. No, you got it because of that great little innovation Handspring added: the Springboard slot. In case you've forgotten, this technology enables you to add all sorts of interesting accessories to your Visor, including an MP3 music player, a radio, a GPS navigation system, a pager, a telephone, a remote control for your television . . . the list goes on and on.

Actually, the Springboard slot is a lot like the cartridge socket on the back of the Nintendo Game Boy. But, while the latter limits you to playing games, Springboard gives your Visor almost unlimited potential. We rounded up the modules that were shipping when we hunkered down in our cabin to write this chapter, and here's the scoop on modules that should be available by the time you read this. (In fact, we recommend you buy the next edition of this book about a year from now, as we'll have updated this chapter with even more exciting modules.)

Buckle in, folks, because this chapter covers the heart and soul of the Visor: its upgrade slot and all the cool things you can do with it.

Find New Visor Modules

Sigh. Your Visor doesn't come with any modules. In fact, all Handspring gives you is a plastic insert to keep unwanted gunk out of the slot. So, how do you find out what modules are available? Your first stop should be the Handspring Web site (www.handspring.com), which is chock full of information about upcoming modules, as well as those that are already shipping. You can even buy them online.

Use Your Modules

Plug and play. That's the beauty of Springboard technology. You simply plug a module into the Springboard slot, and you're ready to start using the device. It doesn't matter if your Visor is on or off at the time (if it's off, the insertion of a module turns it on). And there's rarely any software to be installed because the necessary programs are usually embedded within the module itself (one exception is the eyemodule camera, which comes with a Windows companion program).

TIP *Virtually every module you insert into your Visor adds a program or two to the Applications screen. You can easily spot the ones that are stored on the currently inserted module by the small dot that appears in front of the program name.*

Let's say you just purchased the Handspring 8MB Flash Module for extra memory. Here's how to insert it in your Visor:

1. If the protective plastic insert is currently in the Springboard module slot, pull it out and store it in a safe place so you can use it later if necessary.

2. Hold the module so its label is facing up.

3. Notice the module is grooved so it can slide into your Visor only one way. If you try to insert it upside down, it won't go in any further than about half an inch.

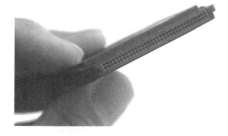

15

4. Slide the module into the Springboard slot all the way until it will go no further. In most cases, you should find the Visor turns itself on automatically when it senses the module and automatically switches to the module's software.

And that's all there is to it! If your module came with any additional software, install it on your desktop computer now.

In the pages to come, we unveil some of the coolest and most practical modules currently available. If you're looking for information on memory and backup modules, skip ahead to Chapter 16, which is devoted exclusively to those two technologies.

NOTE   *When you consider buying any Springboard module, keep its dimensions in mind. The Handspring Modem, for instance, protrudes from the top and back of the Springboard slot. Thus, while it's installed, your Visor won't fit in most cases. You can't do much about this, but if you plan to keep a module like, say, the MiniJam inserted all the time, you may want to choose a case that's more accommodating.*

Take Pictures with the eyemodule

For our money, the eyemodule (as seen in Figure 15-1) is one of the most interesting Springboard modules. It turns your Visor into a handheld digital camera that takes both color and grayscale images, and enables you to transfer those images to your computer for printing, e-mailing, editing, and so on.

The eyemodule is not a professional-caliber camera, as its maximum resolution is a mere 320 × 240 pixels. Most mainstream digital cameras offer upwards of five times the resolution. But the eyemodule is fine for fooling around or taking snaps intended for use on Web pages (where lower resolutions are desirable). In fact, it makes a great "spy cam," as it barely protrudes from your Visor (only its tiny lens suggests its true identity).

FIGURE 15-1 The eyemodule is a tiny digital camera attachment for the Visor

When you insert the eyemodule into your Visor, you should see a display similar to Figure 15-2. This is the Capture view, used for—natch—capturing images. You can take a picture in the Capture view in two ways:

- Press the Scroll up button on your Visor
- Press the small button on the front of the eyemodule, just to the right of the lens

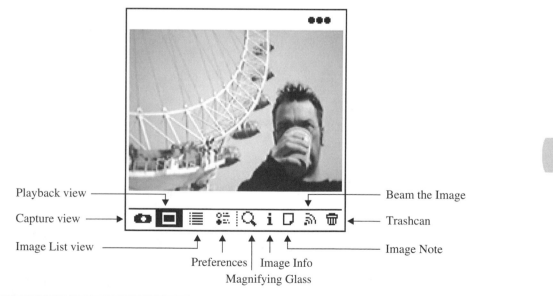

15

FIGURE 15-2 The Visor's display acts as a viewfinder for your eyemodule

Regardless of which method you use, after you press the shutter release, your Visor asks if you want to save the image. You can agree to save it by pressing the Scroll up button on your Visor or tapping the corresponding symbol on the Visor screen. If you don't want to keep the picture (they won't all be Ansel Adams quality), press or tap the Scroll down button. After you complete either action, you're back to Capture view, where you can immediately take more pictures.

View Pictures Stored on Your Visor

Once you have stored pictures on your Visor, you can review them at your leisure. To do that, you need to switch to the Playback view. Tap the icon that looks like a little TV screen, and you'll then see the most recent photo you snapped. In this mode, you can page through all the pictures stored on your Visor by pressing the Scroll up and Scroll down buttons. You can also tap the Magnifying Glass icon to enlarge the picture. Tap it again to return to normal size.

TIP

It's often easier to use the List view to select your images, particularly if you have a lot of them stored on your Visor. Switch to the List view, and then tap any file name in the list. You immediately are taken to the Playback view, with that picture displayed onscreen.

Edit and Delete Your Images

As you may have discovered in List view, your pictures aren't named so much as tagged with a date and a time stamp. Fortunately, you can rename pictures so they're more easily identifiable, and you can even add custom notes to them.

Image List		▼ All
Train tracks	Color	187K
6/20/00 6:51:14 PM	Color	187K
6/20/00 6:51:31 PM	Color	187K
6/20/00 6:51:55 PM	Color	187K
The pond	Color	187K
6/20/00 6:52:28 PM	Color	187K
6/20/00 6:52:46 PM	Color	187K
6/20/00 6:53:05 PM	Color	187K
6/20/00 6:53:16 PM	Color	187K
My cat	Color	187K
6/21/00 1:06:09 PM	Color	187K

To change the name of one of your images, find it in the Playback view, and then tap the Image Info button (easy to find because it looks like a little *i*). By default, new images are labeled according to the date and time they were taken. You can easily overwrite this "name" with whatever moniker you want to give the image.

To add a note to a picture, either tap the New button in the Image Info dialog box or tap the Note button that appears in the Playback view. You can also use the Image Info dialog box to categorize your images and even mark them as private.

If you want to delete a picture, locate it in the Playback view, and then tap the Trashcan icon at the bottom right of the screen. A Delete Image dialog box appears, where you need to tap OK to verify you really want to delete it. If you change your mind, tap Cancel.

Change eyemodule Preferences

By default, your eyemodule images are captured in color, at 320 × 240 pixels, with a beep confirming a picture has been taken. If you don't like these presets or you want to file new images in a specific category automatically, check out the eyemodule preferences.

You can do so by tapping the Preferences button at the bottom of any view. These are the things you can do

■ **Capture format**   Here, you can select from three different formats to save your images: 160 × 120 black and white, 320 × 240 black and white, and 320 × 240 color. As

15

suggested by the memory sizes that appear next to each setting (9K, 37K, and 187K, respectively), snaps taken at higher resolutions (and in color) consume more RAM.

- **Capture sound**   By default, your Visor beeps when you press the capture button. If you want, you can disable this by choosing "No Sound."

- **Capture category**   By default, new images are Unfiled. If you prefer, you can automatically make new images go into any category you specify.

- **Confirm save image**   When you press the shutter release on your Visor, you are automatically asked if you really want to save the picture (as noted earlier in the chapter). If you prefer, you can skip this confirmation. Simply remove the check mark from Confirm Save Image.

Display Pictures on the PC

We're sure you're impressed with the fact that you can take pictures with your Visor and display them on the screen. But we know what you're thinking: shouldn't there be more to life than this? After all, it's great to have pictures on the Visor, but they'd be even better on my desktop PC where I can print them or insert them into e-mail messages and Web pages.

Fret not, because you can do all those things. To use your Visor images on your PC, however, you need to install the software that comes on the CD. And here's the tricky part: when you insert the CD in your PC, the conduit is automatically installed, but the image-editing software, called MediaCenter, is not. You have to do that separately.

NOTE   *At press time, the Macintosh versions of the conduit and imaging software (the latter called FireViewer) were not included on the CD, but could be downloaded free from the eyemodule Web site.*

To install MediaCenter, insert the CD in your computer's CD-ROM drive, and then double-click the My Computer icon on your desktop. Next, double-click your computer's CD-ROM drive icon and find the folder called Media Center. Finally, install the software by double-clicking the file called mediacenter.exe.

TIP   *You don't have to install MediaCenter to transfer images from the Visor to the PC. All you need is the conduit. MediaCenter is just a program that helps you view and catalog your images, and it's entirely optional.*

Once you have installed the desktop software on your PC, you can insert your Visor in the cradle and perform an ordinary HotSync. All the images on your Visor are then automatically copied to your PC, in a folder called C:\eyemodule*your-visor-name*, where obviously *your-visor-name* is whatever your Visor's username happens to be. Your images are stored in this folder, in separate subfolders that correspond to however your images are categorized. For instance, if you have a category called Business, you should see a subfolder with that same name. From here, working with your images is a piece of cake, as they wind up on your PC in the ubiquitous JPEG format. Thus, you can open them in any application, be it a Web browser or Adobe PhotoShop, that can view JPEG files.

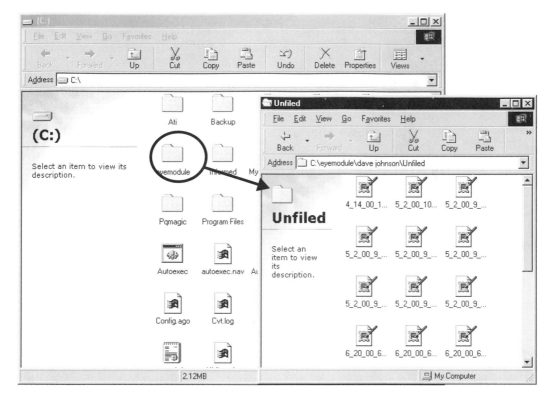

If you prefer, however, you can use the MediaCenter application to view your images as well. Start MediaCenter, and you should see something like what appears in Figure 15-3. Click the Organizer button to see a list of files and folders on your hard disk, as in Figure 15-4. Navigate your way to the eyemodule folder, and then you see all your images appear as thumbnails in the right side of the screen. To view the image at full size, double click any image. If you want to copy this image to the desktop, simply drag it out of the MediaCenter window using the mouse. You can drag-and-drop images to other applications, such as paint or display programs, using the same method.

15

TIP

If you delete images from your hard disk, those deletions are not synchronized with your Visor. In other words, the next time you HotSync, the images are copied from the Visor right back to your desktop again. The only way to eliminate images completely is to delete them from your Visor.

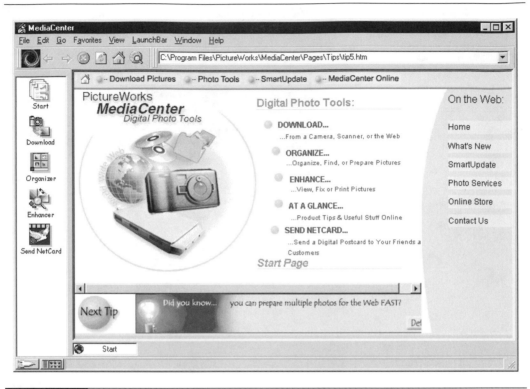

FIGURE 15-3 MediaCenter is an image catalog and viewer that comes with the eyemodule

Control Your Stereo with OmniRemote

One module we had a lot of fun with is Pacific Neo-Tek's OmniRemote, pictured in Figure 15-5. This module is a more practical version of the OmniRemote software that has been available for the Palm OS for some time. With it, your Visor effectively becomes a universal remote, capable of controlling everything from your TV to your DVD player to your entire stereo system.

The problem with the software-only solution, which uses a Palm device's built-in infrared port, is those ports have limited range—about five feet, and who wants to sit five feet from the TV? That issue has been remedied with the OmniRemote module, which includes not only the software, but also a turbocharged infrared port.

After you insert the OmniRemote module into your Visor, you'll find two new icons in the Applications screen: the remote software and the user's manual.

NOTE *The user's manual, which is accessed by tapping the Manual icon in the Applications screen, is the only documentation included with the OmniRemote module.*

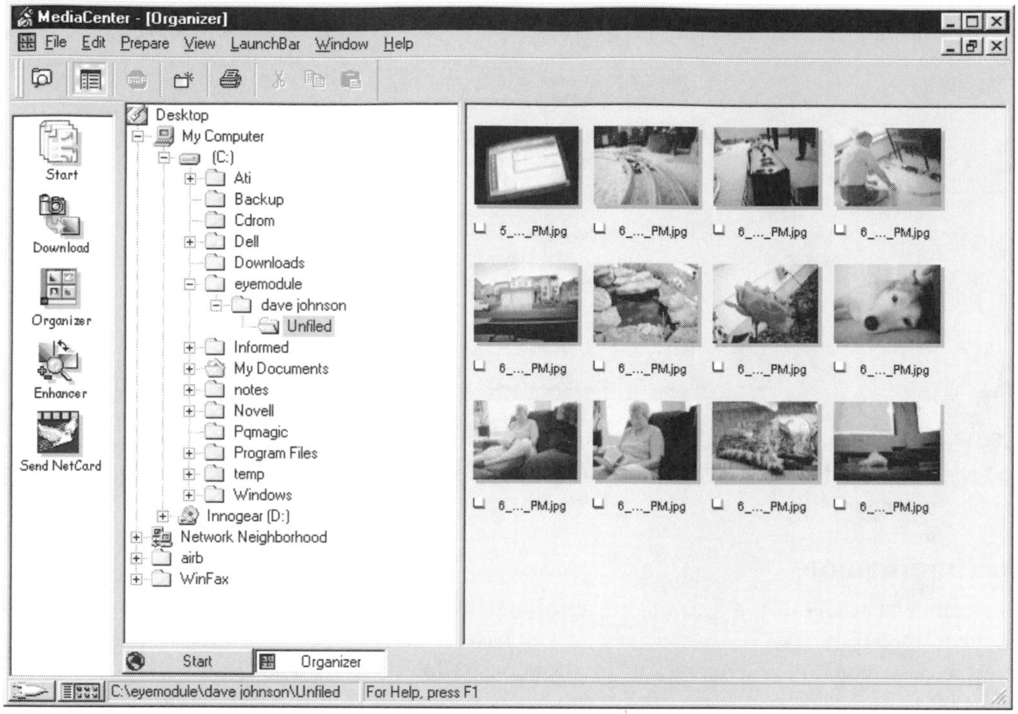

MediaCenter - [Organizer]

File Edit Prepare View LaunchBar Window Help

Desktop
My Computer
(C:)
Ati
Backup
Cdrom
Dell
Downloads
eyemodule
dave johnson
Unfiled
Informed
My Documents
notes
Novell
Pqmagic
Program Files
temp
Windows
Innogear (D:)
Network Neighborhood
airb
WinFax

Start
Download
Organizer
Enhancer
Send NetCard

5_..._PM.jpg   6_..._PM.jpg   6_..._PM.jpg   6_..._PM.jpg

6_..._PM.jpg   6_..._PM.jpg   6_..._PM.jpg   6_..._PM.jpg

6_..._PM.jpg   6_..._PM.jpg   6_..._PM.jpg   6_..._PM.jpg

Start   Organizer

C:\eyemodule\dave johnson\Unfiled   For Help, press F1

FIGURE 15-4   You can view, copy, print, edit, and organize your eyemodule images using MediaCenter

15

FIGURE 15-5   The OmniRemote module turns your Visor into a programmable universal remote control

Start the software by tapping the Remote button. You see a screen that looks something like this:

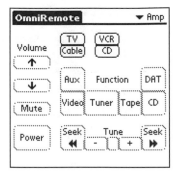

As you can see, the screen is already set up with a variety of buttons. You can completely customize the look of your remote control screens by adding, deleting, and renaming buttons to your heart's content.

Tour OmniRemote

OmniRemote is, at its heart, a learning universal remote control that enables you to control any device that has a remote of its own. That is, if you have something that is controlled with an infrared remote, you can probably train OmniRemote to do it instead. The OmniRemote is most similar to Philips's Pronto remote control, which costs about $400 in specialty audio-visual shops. Like the Pronto, OmniRemote has the capability to support an almost-unlimited number of devices on different screens that you can design to look any way you like. In addition, the OmniRemote can, like the Pronto, be trained to perform several things with one tap of a button, much like a computer macro.

You'll generally want to put different devices on different pages. To do that, you can simply use familiar Palm OS categories to represent different devices. One category might be called Television, and it would have all the controls to operate your TV. Another category might be called CD, with controls on that page to operate your CD player.

There's certainly nothing wrong with combining multiple devices onto a single page if you want to do it that way—it's all up to you. The default OmniRemote configuration places different components on different pages. To change devices, simply select a different category from the list menu at the top-right corner of the screen.

Another thing you should know about OmniRemote is it won't control any of the devices in your home right out of the box. Surprised? Don't be: all universal remote controls work this way. Before you can get started using the module, you need to teach each button on the screen how to control the appropriate feature in your home theater. It's not hard to do, but it might take you a while, depending upon how elaborate your home theater is.

Train Existing Buttons

We found the standard OmniRemote configuration already includes many of the buttons we need to operate our home theater. Thus, if you want to get started using the module without painstakingly building new screens from scratch, you can do what we did and simply train the buttons already provided. Here's how to train a button:

1. Select the category that represents the device you want to teach OmniRemote about— say, TV.

2. Find the actual remote that controls the TV and place it on a tabletop next to the Visor.

3. Select Modes | Training from the menu and double-tap the onscreen button you want to train.

4. Orient the remote control so it is a few inches away from your Visor and point it directly at the IR port on the left side of the Visor case.

5. Press the button on the remote control that corresponds to the button you want to train, as seen in Figure 15-6. If it is an On/Off style button, you can press and release it. If it is a button with multiple positions—like fast-forward or volume control—hold it down for several seconds.

15

FIGURE 15-6   You need to train OmniRemote with your existing remote controls—but once you're done, your Visor is the only remote you need

If the training went well, you should see the button you were trying to train change from a dotted outline to a solid outline. If the training didn't work for some reason (the room might be too bright, for instance) your Visor will beep at you. Try it again.

You can train only one button or do a whole bunch at once. Once you enter Training mode, you stay in that mode until you specifically switch back to Normal mode. To switch back to Normal mode—and, hence, have the capability to test your newly trained buttons—just choose Modes | Normal from the menu.

Once you're in Normal mode, you can actually try out your new remote control. Simply point the front of your Visor at your TV (or whatever device you've trained OmniRemote for) and tap the appropriate button. If all went well, you should now be able to control your device with your Visor.

TIP   *You can always retrain a button later, just by choosing Buttons | Edit from the menu. Then, tap the button you want to retrain, followed by the Retrain button that appears in the Edit Button box.*

Create Custom Remotes

As we mentioned earlier, you needn't settle for the default button layout. In fact, you can create entire new device categories from scratch. To create a new category, tap the arrow in the top-right corner of the screen, and then select Edit Categories. Tap the New button in the box that appears.

```
        Edit Categories...        ⓘ
   ┌──────────────────────────────┐
   │ Amp                          │
   │ Cable                        │
   │ CD                           │
   │ Tivo                         │
   │ TV                           │
   │ Unfiled                      │
   │ VCR                          │
   │                              │
   │                              │
   │                              │
   └──────────────────────────────┘
   ( OK ) ( New ) ( Rename ) ( Delete )
```

It's just as easy to add buttons to an existing remote screen. If your television has a feature that isn't represented on the default TV remote, for instance, just choose Buttons | Create from the menu. Then simply place your stylus on the screen and "draw" a new button (you can see the button appear beneath your stylus as you move it). Drag your stylus until the button is the size and shape you want. After you create the button, the Edit Button dialog box appears, from which you can give your button a name.

> **TIP** *To delete a button you don't want, simply choose Buttons | Delete from the menu, and then tap the button you want to eliminate. There's no warning—the button simply goes away, so make sure you tap the right one.*

Train OmniRemote to Perform Automated Functions

When we talk about macros, we're not referring to obscure features in Microsoft Excel. Rather, macros enable your remote to perform multiple functions with the tap of a single button. Suppose, for instance, you had a button marked Watch Movie. Tap that one button, and your FM receiver, DVD player, and television automatically turn on, switch to the appropriate video input mode, and enter Dolby surround sound.

To create a macro, you should first have all the buttons that will be part of the macro completely trained. If you want to turn on your television and switch to a specific channel, for instance, then the power button and the numbers that select television channels should all be trained. Then, do this:

1. Add a button to the screen by choosing Buttons | Create from the menu.

2. Name the button and tap the Macro check box in the Edit Button dialog box.

15

```
┌─────────────────────────────────┐
│        Edit button          ⓘ   │
│  Name: (Hidden)    ☐ Normal     │
│  Sci-fi channel    ☐ Label      │
│  ........           ☐ Category   │
│  (Icon)  ☐          ☑ Macro      │
│                     ☐ X-10       │
│   ( Retrain )    (Edit Macro)    │
│   ( Recreate )   (    OK    )    │
└─────────────────────────────────┘
```

3. Tap the OK button and the Edit Button dialog box disappears.

4. Now tap each button in sequence that you want to activate during the macro. If you want to turn on the TV, and then immediately mute the sound, tap Power, and then tap Mute. If you need to insert a delay between button presses to give your device time to deal with the inputs, then choose Modes | Macro Pause from the menu.

5. When you are done creating your macro, choose Modes | End Macro from the menu.

Once you finish your macro, you can tap the button to test it.

Train OmniRemote to Work Without You

How often have you wanted to record a live concert from the radio to your cassette deck, but couldn't because you weren't home at the right time? With OmniRemote, you can record shows and command other home theater features even when you're not around. OmniRemote has a timer feature that enables you to perform tasks with your Visor, even when you're away. You can set OmniRemote to perform individual button presses or entire macros at specific times of day. To do this, choose Options | Timers from the menu and simply fill out the Schedule timed macros dialog box.

```
┌─────────────────────────────────┐
│    Schedule timed macros     ⓘ  │
│  ( Time )  ┊4:55 pm - 6:05 pm┊   │
│  ( Date )  ┊6/22/00┊             │
│  ( Start ) ┊-None-┊              │
│  (  End  ) ┊-None-┊              │
│  (Repeat)  ┊Weekday┊             │
│  (◄ Prev)  (  OK  )  (Next ►)    │
└─────────────────────────────────┘
```

The dialog box is fairly self-explanatory: the date and time indicate when you want the scheduled event to occur. You can set up two macros—one at the start time and another at the end time. That way you can, for instance, start recording at 5:00 P.M. and stop recording at 5:30.

Worth Another Visor?

Dave: I could really grow to love the OmniRemote, but here's the problem: I can't keep my Visor on the end table in the living room all the time, on the off chance I might want to watch TV. And I'm certainly not going to run down to my basement office just to get the darned thing every time I want to relax in front of the television. So what's the point? Am I supposed to buy a second Visor and leave it by my home theater? That sounds like a pretty decadent waste of money.

Rick: That's exactly what you should do. You spent nearly $400 on a Philips Pronto, but you could have paid half as much for a Visor Solo ($149) and an OmniRemote module ($59). While I agree it sounds a little crazy, I think anyone seeking a powerful, programmable universal remote for a home theater system should seriously consider the combo.

> **NOTE** *Be careful with the way you leave your Visor before a scheduled event. Make sure it has a clear line of site to the device it's going to control, and also make sure OmniRemote was the last program running before the Visor was turned off. If you had a different program running when the Visor was turned off, OmniRemote won't trigger at the appointed time.*

> **TIP** *Want to use your bedroom TV as an alarm clock? Just program a macro that turns the TV on at the appropriate time, and then leave your Visor pointed at the TV before you go to bed.*

Listen to Music with the MiniJam

No doubt you've heard of the digital music revolution: MP3 music files have roughly the same audio quality as CDs, yet take up a fraction of the space, making them ideal to store on your computer's hard disk. Entire Web sites exist to sell and trade these MP3s, and many people have literally gigabytes of music on their home PCs.

What can you do with these MP3 files? Aside from listening to music on your PC while you work, portable music players enable you to carry your music on-the-go while you are cycling, jogging, or riding the bus. MP3 players (first popularized by Diamond Multimedia and their Rio player), with the right memory cards, can hold hours and hours of music, and they have advantages over both portable cassette players and portable CD players:

- Unlike cassette players, all the music is instantly, randomly accessible
- Unlike CD players, they have no moving parts and don't skip

Thanks to the InnoGear MiniJam (see Figure 15-7), you can turn your Visor into an MP3 player. The MiniJam slips into the Springboard slot and has a memory slot in its own back for storing music. There's also a set of player controls (similar to what you'd find on a CD player) on the top of the MiniJam unit.

FIGURE 15-7   The MiniJam turns your Visor into a portable music player

You can control your MiniJam either from the MiniJam itself (convenient when you're moving around, as the controls are on the top of the Visor) or using the onscreen buttons. Music is stored on tiny multimedia memory cards that ship in capacities as large as 64MB (capable of storing over an hour of music). To insert the card, press it all the way into the MiniJam until it snaps into place (see Figure 15-8).

CAUTION   *Memory cards are delicate. Store them where they can't get bent or scratched, and be careful not to handle the card by the metallic contacts.*

FIGURE 15-8   The Visor doesn't have enough memory to hold music, so the MiniJam relies on tiny SanDisk memory cards

How to ...   **Find Music Online**

Where can you get MP3s online? Glad you asked. A number of Web sites offer music in this increasingly popular format. Many songs are free, while others, which are protected by copyright, are available for a small charge. Here are some of our favorite Web sites for digital music online:

- mp3.com
- emusic.com
- listen.com
- tunes.com
- ubl.com
- rollingstone.com
- rock.com
- getmusic.com

Play Golf

As the saying goes: when it rains, it pours. At least, that's what we think the expression is. It was something Dave's mom always mumbled whenever the washing machine and the refrigerator broke at the same time. Anyway, what we're trying to say is there's not just one golf module available for the Visor, but two. One is a game, the other a golf scorecard package. If you're as much of a golf fiend as Rick's dad, then you're going to be glad you bought a Visor right about now.

Tiger Woods PGA Tour Golf

One of the most ambitious games ever created for the Palm OS, Tiger Woods PGA Tour Golf features everybody's favorite duffer and three renowned 18-hole courses on which to play. The game is available on a Springboard module—great news given that the software-only version takes up roughly 500K of memory.

Anyone familiar with computer golf games should have no trouble figuring out the mechanics of Tiger Woods. The game relies on the same swing meter used in most golf games for the PC: tap once to start your backswing, again to downswing, a third time to try to hit the ball straight. The more backswing you apply, the less precise the drive will be. If you let the meter go past the top of the curve (the 12 o'clock point), the swing will be out of control. As with the real thing, practice makes perfect. Happy golfing!

15

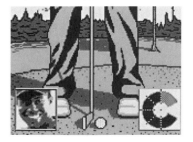

IntelliGolf

Like Tiger Woods, IntelliGolf began life as a software-only product. But this robust golf-scorecard package has migrated to a module, thereby saving you having to install it in main memory. (That's really the only advantage to the module, which costs the same as the software version.)

Whether you're a serious golfer or a weekend duffer, you're sure to find IntelliGolf a welcome asset to your game. Here's a look at some of the program's main features:

- Automated golf scoring
- Performance statistics and graphs
- Shot tracking by club and distance
- Drive, approach, chip, and putt tracking
- Course, hole, and round notes capabilities
- 24 popular wagering games (such as Skins)
- Unlimited custom wagering for sidegames

Although it's not included with the module, there's a Windows companion program available for download from the IntelliGolf Web site. Among its capabilities:

- Historical round tracking
- Handicap calculator
- Scorecard printing
- Game-improving statistics in 250 categories

Reading and Reference

A Springboard module can hold a lot of data—especially if that data is mostly text. Take the *Star Trek* BookPak, which contains seven complete *Star Trek* novels. If you wanted to load those books directly onto your Visor, you'd have to sacrifice many megabytes of RAM. But with the BookPak, you just pop in the module when you're in the mood for a little sci-fi.

Let's take a closer look at that e-book collection, along with three other modules packed with reference material.

Covey Reference Library

Life-management guru Stephen Covey is best known for a little book called *The 7 Habits of Highly Effective People*, which is one of three titles appearing on this module from Franklin Covey. The others are *First Things First* and *Principle-Centered Leadership,* also by Stephen Covey.

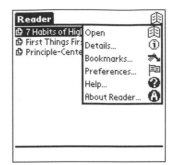

In Chapter 22, we teach you everything you need to know about e-books such as this one. Suffice it to say, the module includes the complete text of each book, and you read them just by scrolling from one page to the next.

The software component of the Covey Reference Library is a program called Reader, which pops up when you first insert the module (and is also accessible from the Applications screen). With it you can open and read the various books, copy a paragraph (for pasting into a memo or other Visor document), add annotations and bookmarks to specific passages, and search for a word or phrase.

Lonely Planet CitySync

Taking a trip to Chicago? Or Los Angeles, New York, or San Francisco? Rather than schlepping a hefty guidebook to help you find the best restaurants, shopping, and tourist attractions, just pop Concept Kitchen's Lonely Planet CitySync into your Visor. Based on the Lonely Planet travel guides, CitySync packs data on the four aforementioned cities into a single module. With a few

15

stylus taps, you can find information on activities, sights to see, public transportation, dining, shopping, nightlife, lodging, and more.

Physician's Desk Reference

Whether you're a healthcare professional or just someone who needs a lot of medication, you're sure to find the *Physician's Desk Reference* of interest. The module includes the full text of the print version, which shows up-to-date prescription drug information. You can search by brand or generic name, and compare drugs within classes such as antihistamines, antidepressants, and others.

The PDR contains information on hundreds of drugs and divides each one into such key topics as Indications and Usage, Contraindications, Warnings, Adverse Reactions, Dosage and Administration, and How Supplied. (We assume healthcare people know what all of this means.) The text also includes the manufacturer and generic name for every prescription drug.

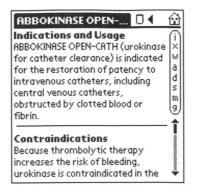

As if all that weren't enough, the module sports the PDR for Ophthalmology as well.

Star Trek BookPak

As noted earlier, the *Star Trek* BookPak contains seven full-length *Star Trek* novels, including the *Q Continuum* and *Dominion War* series. The books come from Peanutpress.com, resellers of commercial fiction and nonfiction in Palm OS format (see Chapter 22), and the module includes the Peanut Reader software that enables you to read, search, bookmark, and annotate the books. It also gives you a choice of two fonts—one large, one small.

> **Chapter One**
>
> RO LAREN LOOKED UP at the yellowing clouds, which rested uneasily upon the jagged teeth of the olive-hued mountains in the distance. She didn't see the beauty of the twilit sky or the flowering land with harvesting season upon it; all she saw were the vapor trails of shuttlecraft and small transports streaking away from the planet Galion. The former Starfleet officer knew that most of those
>
> pg 8

The BookPak costs about $45—about as much as you'd pay for the individual books in paperback form—but you can't beat the convenience. Nor can you beat the irony of this *Star Trek*-like technology, which puts a library of books in the palm of your hand.

15

Upcoming Modules

These are just the first batch of modules you can get for your Visor; many more should be available by now. Here's a quick overview of modules that were "coming soon" at press time.

The CUE Radio

If you were intrigued by the idea of an MP3 music player for your Visor, you might like this even more. The CUE Radio promises not only to let you tune in your favorite FM stations, but also to deliver timely news, weather, and traffic reports. (The latter is a subscription-based service expected to cost $60 per year. The news and weather reports will be broadcast free of charge.)

The CUE Radio can even double as a one-way pager, with coverage available virtually everywhere in the U.S. As with actual pagers, various service plans are available. To find out more about this nifty-sounding module, visit the CUE Web site.

The Minstrel S Wireless Modem

Just minutes before we wrapped up work on this book, Novatel Wireless announced an exciting Springboard product: the Minstrel S, a wireless modem capable of connecting to the Internet for e-mail and Web browsing (see Figure 15-9). We've used the company's Minstrel V with our

| FIGURE 15-9 | The Minstrel S is a wireless modem that plugs into the Visor's Springboard socket |

Palm V handhelds and found it to be an excellent accessory. If the Visor version is half as good, you'll seriously want to consider buying it.

NOTE

Novatel Wireless makes the actual modem, but chances are good you'll buy it from one of the companies that provide the wireless service that goes with it. Thus, check out GoAmerica (www.goamerica.net) and OmniSky (www.omnisky.com), two of the service providers we know for certain will carry the Minstrel.

As if wireless communications weren't enough, the Minstrel will also be available with extra RAM for your Visor. The Minstrel S2 will have 2MB of RAM, the Minstrel S4, 4MB. If you're feeling the memory crunch, this could be an excellent way to kill two birds with one module.

15

Pocket Webster

Students, teachers, writers, this one's for you. LandWare's Pocket *Webster* features 40,000 words and definitions from the *Merriam-Webster Dictionary.* It also includes pronunciations, variant spellings, common abbreviations, a word-of-the-day feature (great for building your vocabulary), and even a guide to using punctuation.

```
Merriam-Webster
dic·tio·nary            h.
\-sh&"nerE\ n, pl      dice
-nar·ies : reference   dicker
book of words with     dictate
information about their dictator
meanings               diction
                       dictionary
                       dictum
                       did
                       didactic
                       die
                       die
Find: dictionary
```

The SixPak

Remember the old commercials for the Ginsu knife? "It dices! It slices! It makes julienne fries!" (We don't know what julienne fries are, but we bought the damn knife anyway.) InnoGear's SixPak promises a similar level of amazing versatility, so here's our Ginsu-esque description: "It's a 56 Kbps modem! It's a voice recorder! It's a vibrating and flashing alarm! But wait, there's more: it gives your Visor an extra 8MB of memory, and has a cell-phone connector for wireless Internet access!"

Indeed, though it sounds a bit too good to be true, the SixPak packs quite a lot of functionality into a single module—one that fits flush inside the Springboard slot. When you consider the hassle of swapping modem, memory, and voice recorder modules, the SixPak sounds like a can't-miss proposition.

Pagers

In addition to the aforementioned CUE Radio, which can receive pager messages, there are a couple of dedicated pager modules in the works for the Visor. The first is the InfoMitt Access, which, at press time, had one foot out the door and should be available by now. The module works with the SkyTel paging service to deliver not only alphanumeric messages, but also news, stock prices, sports, weather, and other information. See Chapter 14 for additional details.

A more robust offering comes from Glenayre in the form of the @ctiveLink, which promises all the features of the InfoMitt, plus two-way messaging (meaning you can send messages as well as receive them). It, too, should be available by the time you read this.

Voice Recorders

You know that tiny hole in the lower-left corner of the Visor case? Beneath it lies a microphone that can be used with—among other things—voice recorder modules. Two such modules were in the works as we went to press: the digital5 Total Recall and Shinei my-Vox. The latter sports a headphone jack and can record up to eight minutes of audio. It also enables you to use a recorded snippet as a voice alarm (for example, "Time to go pick up the kids from kickboxing!").

Shinei is a Singapore-based company, and therefore will probably find a U.S. distributor for the my-Vox. Thus, while you should check the company's Web site for information, you may wind up purchasing the module from a different company—possibly under a different name. For instance, Shinei also made the i-Vox, a voice recorder for the Palm series of handhelds—but it was sold in the U.S. by LandWare under the name GoVox.

The Total Recall promises CD-like recording and playback controls, and can function even when it's not plugged into the Visor. Voice notes can be scanned, edited, and filed into categories. You can find out more about the module by visiting the company's Web site.

GPS Modules

Finally, we come to Global Positioning System, or GPS, modules, which use an orbiting array of satellites to give you precise information (such as latitude, longitude, altitude, speed, and so forth) about your location. Along with graphical mapping software from companies like MarcoSoft (www.marcosoft.com), you'll be able to find your way from place to place using real-time positional data. This could come in handy for anything from hiking in the mountains to traveling in a strange city.

A pair of GPS modules are available for the Visor—the GeoDiscovery Geode and Navicom HandyGPS. You can find out more about both by visiting the companies' Web sites.

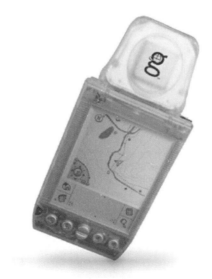

NOTE   *Navicom is a Korean company, and therefore will probably find a U.S. distributor for the HandyGPS. Thus, while you should check the company's Web site for information, you may wind up purchasing the module from a different company—possibly under a different name.*

Where to Find It

Web Site	Address	What's There
Handspring	www.handspring.com	Tiger Woods PGA Tour Golf and other modules
InnoGear	www.innogear.com	MiniJam, SixPak
Pacific NeoTek	www.pacific-neotek.com	OmniRemote
Karrier Communications	www.intelligolf.com	IntelliGolf
Eyemodule	www.eyemodule.com	Eyemodule
Franklin Covey	www.franklincovey.com	Covey Reference Library
PalmGear H.Q.	www.palmgear.com	Star Trek BookPak
Franklin Electronic Publishers	www.franklin.com	Physician's Desk Reference
Concept Kitchen	www.conceptkitchen.com	Lonely Planet CitySync
CUE	www.cue.net	CUE Radio
LandWare	www.landware.com	Pocket Webster
Global Access	www.infomitt.com	InfoMitt Access
Glenayre	www.glenayre.com	@ctiveLink
Digital5	www.digital5.com	Total Recall
Shinei	www.shinei.com	my-Vox
GeoDiscovery	www.geodiscovery.com	Geode
Navicom	www.navicom.co.kr	HandyGPS

Chapter 16

Expand Your Visor with Memory and Backup Modules

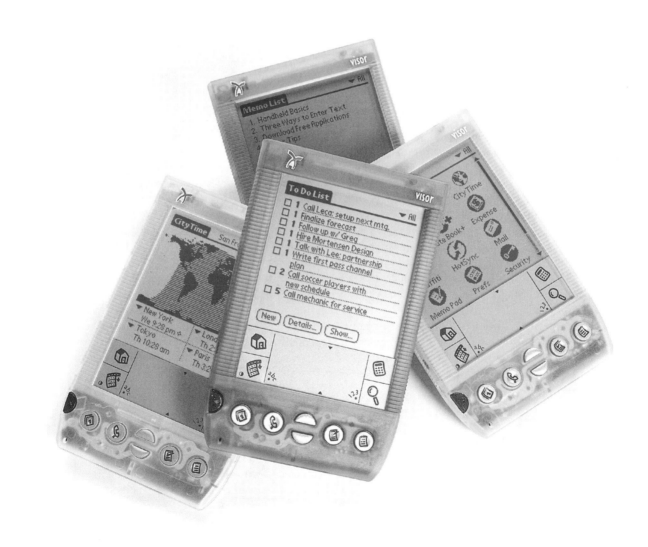

How to...

- Distinguish between internal and external memory
- Install additional memory in your Visor
- Move applications from the Visor to external memory modules
- Use the File Mover application
- Share applications and data among several Visors
- Rename your memory module
- Format your memory module
- Care for your memory module
- Use the InnoPak memory module as a vibrating alarm
- Secure your data on a backup module
- Restore your data from a backup module

So, you're out of memory. Don't say we didn't warn you: we always recommend you get a nice, fat 8MB handheld right off the bat, especially if you envision adding software to play games, read books, or do mobile office work. Heck, we know of at least one reference book that consumes over 5MB of memory. Yes, you read that right: 5MB. That won't even fit on an ordinary 2MB machine and it takes up most of the space you have on a Visor Deluxe. Our Visors don't have any books quite that large on them, but software like SmartDoc, QuickSheet, a handful of games to play when we get bored, along with a whole bunch of data files have sopped up virtually every kilobyte of memory on our handhelds. We hope that gives you some idea of how much space you might eventually need on your Visor.

Thankfully, whether you have a 2MB Visor or an 8MB Visor, you can add more memory at any time using the Springboard slot. Memory upgrades are available in a variety of sizes, from a conservative 2MB to a hefty 8MB—potentially giving you as much as 16MB of memory in your Visor. And when it comes to backing up all the data on your Visor, backup modules make it ridiculously simple to ensure that all your data and applications are preserved in the event of a power failure or catastrophic problem with your handheld. Read on, and see how to use these really cool gadgets.

Add Memory to Your Visor

Adding memory to your Visor is a snap. Because memory modules simply slide into the Springboard slot, you can add and remove additional memory as often as you like. In fact, you can own multiple memory modules and insert only the one you want—with specific applications on it— at any time. The only thing you can't do (and we hope this is obvious) is insert two memory modules at once.

Understand Your Visor's Memory

Perhaps the most unusual thing about working with memory modules for the Visor is, when you add memory, it isn't all available in a single big pool as if you had added memory to your PC or Macintosh. Instead of thinking of a memory module like RAM, which you would insert in your computer, you might, instead, want to think of it as an additional hard drive for your computer. Here's why: *if you start with 64MB of memory in your computer and add another 64MB, your computer will report that you have 128MB of memory available in which to run applications.* But now consider hard disks. If you have a 6GB hard drive in your computer, and then add another 6GB hard drive, you'll see two different icons on your PC. One icon represents the first hard drive, and the other icon represents the second hard drive. You can't store a really big application partially on one hard drive, and partially on the other.

Your Visor memory module works the same way. If you have an 8MB Visor and insert the 8MB Flash memory module, they are two completely different memory resources, which, when combined, give you 16MB of memory. You can copy applications between them and run any application that is in either location, but you cannot install a really big application or data file partially on the built-in memory, and partially on the memory module.

Another thing to remember about your Visor is its memory acts like both RAM and a hard disk at the same time. The memory holds the application like a hard disk would and also serves as memory space for the program to run when you select it. This means if you have an application on a memory module, the application will only run if the memory module is inserted in the Visor.

Once you understand these aspects of using your Visor memory, you're all set.

Install Your Memory Module

Memory modules are perhaps the simplest peripherals you can buy that slip into your Visor's Springboard slot. They require no special software installation and are ready to use pretty much instantly. If the 8MB Flash Module is the first Visor module you've ever had, you'll find it's extremely easy to install.

File Mover

Once you insert the memory module, you should see a new icon appear in your list of applications. Called the File Mover, this application is essential to using your memory module properly. Now let's take a look at how to use the File Mover to manage your applications.

Use the File Mover

As we mentioned, whenever you have a memory module installed in your Visor, you have two different pools of memory with which to work. You may have some applications stored in your Visor's internal, built-in memory, and other applications may be found in your memory module. If you find you have an application you use infrequently, you might want to move it to a memory module to free more memory space in your Visor itself. On the other hand, you might have a program in the memory module that you'd rather have in your Visor's internal memory. Putting it on the Visor itself makes that application available all the time, even if the module is not currently installed. Where you put your applications is largely a matter of personal choice. It's all up to you.

16

But how do you move the stuff around? Using the File Mover application, of course.

So now you have your memory module installed and have an additional 8MB of memory with which to work. That's great. Let's take a look around the File Mover application. Find it in your application list and tap it to start the program. You should see something like this:

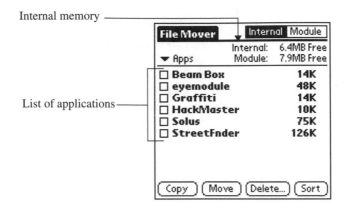

Internal memory

List of applications

File Mover displays all the applications and data in the currently selected memory region and enables you to copy or move those items from the Visor to the memory module and back again. This is also a great place to go for a quick peek at how much memory you have available on either the Visor or your memory module.

Move or Copy Data from the Visor to the Module

Let's say you have a large application on your Visor you want to move to the memory module. This frees a lot of space on the Visor for other data. Here's how to do it:

1. If you haven't already started File Mover, do it now by tapping the File Mover icon in your applications list.

2. Make sure you're looking at the applications on your Visor's internal memory. The list menu should currently say Apps and the word Internal should be highlighted at the top-right corner of the screen.

3. Find an application you don't want to use all the time. In our example, we have an application called StreetFinder, which is a mapping program. We won't use it all the time, so we might as well move it to the memory module. Tap the check box to the left of the application name.

File Mover   Internal | Module

Internal: 6.4MB Free
▼ Apps   Module: 7.9MB Free

☐ **Beam Box**   **14K**
☐ **eyemodule**   **48K**
☐ **Graffiti**   **14K**
☐ **HackMaster**   **10K**
☐ **Solus**   **75K**
☑ **StreetFnder**   **126K**

(Copy) (Move) (Delete...) (Sort)

4. Tap the Move button at the bottom of the screen. You should see the Copy dialog box asking if you want to move a file from the handheld to the module.

Copy

(?) **Move 1 file(s) from the handheld to the Module?**

(OK) (Cancel)

5. Tap OK, and then you should see the Move Files dialog box as the application is copied over to the module. When that dialog box goes away, the application is no longer on the Visor, but is, instead, on the module.

Move Files

Moving
StreetFnder
from the handheld to the
memory module.

WARNING: Do not remove the module while moving files!
(Cancel)

As long as the module stays in your Visor, you can run that program just like any other program on your handheld.

16

Now tap the Applications button on your Visor to switch to the applications list. Scroll down until you find the program you just moved over to your memory module. Notice it has a bullet in front of it. This indicates the application is not in the internal memory, but is instead stored on the module.

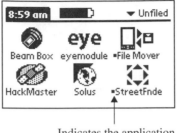

Indicates the application is stored on the module

Tap the icon and the program should run fine.

Now, let's try something different. If you are currently running an application stored on the memory module, switch to an internal application. Then grasp your memory module and gently remove it from the Visor. You should see any applications that were stored on the module (identified with the bullet in front of the name) disappear. Reinsert the memory module, and those applications stored on the module will reappear in your applications list.

CAUTION *Don't remove the memory module if you're running a program stored on the memory module. Some programs behave better than others, but often you'll find that removing the module can cause your Visor to crash, requiring a soft reset. (For details on how to do that, see Chapter 25.)*

You now know how to move an application from the Visor's internal memory to a memory module. Believe it or not, you also know how to copy an application. What's the difference between copying and moving? Just like when you copy or move icons on your computer's desktop, it all comes down to whether you leave a copy of the original behind. If you move an application from the Visor to a memory module, the application is moved without leaving any trace of it behind. On the other hand, if you tap the copy button, you simply place a copy of the data on the memory module, leaving the original intact on the Visor itself. Why would you want to do this? Two main reasons are

■ You can use the memory module as a way to back up important applications and data. By making a copy of it on the memory module, you can be sure that even if something disastrous happens to your Visor, the data will remain on the memory module intact. On the other hand, a much more efficient way of backing up your Visor is with a backup module. We discuss this in more detail later in this chapter.

■ If you have more than one Visor, you can make the same application or data available to both handhelds easily by copying an application to a memory module.

TIP *Your memory module is not married to a single Visor. You can take that memory module and insert it in a different Visor, giving that other handheld the capability to use any applications or data you have stored on it.*

Move or Copy Data from the Memory Module to the Visor

Suppose you have placed some applications on your Visor's memory module and now you want to copy or move them back to the Visor itself. The basic principle remains the same; you simply need to select the application you want to copy or move, and then tap the appropriate button.

But before you do that, make sure you are looking at the applications stored in the memory module. To do this, look for the Internal/Module toggle at the top-right corner of the File Mover application screen. Tap the word Module, and the display should change to show you only those applications and data stored on the memory module.

Change the File Mover View

Most of the time, you will probably want to move specific programs from one place to another. File Mover gives you more flexibility, however. Not only can you move programs, you can also move data. To do that, you need to change the File Mover view, so you can see the data. Tap the list arrow and select Data. In the data view, you can see all the databases and other kinds of data files stored on your Visor or on the module, depending on which memory pool you are currently

16

viewing. You move data from one location to another in exactly the same way as you move applications: tap the check box to select the data, and then tap Copy or Move.

Moving data is not always as useful as moving applications. You should have a specific reason for wanting to move data. If you have an Eyemodule camera for your Visor, for instance, you might want to move the Eyemodule database from one Visor to another, or from the Visor to a memory module. You can do this to save internal memory or to let another Visor owner see the pictures she has taken with your Eyemodule.

TIP

If you select All from the list menu, you get to see both applications and data on the same screen. Know that some applications don't have check boxes and cannot be moved. These are the built-in applications that come with your Visor. You cannot move the Date Book, for instance, to a memory module, but you can move the Date Book's database.

Maintain Your Memory Module

You should now be able to see that managing applications using the Visor's memory module is so easy even Rick can do it. But the File Mover application can do more than just move applications around. It can also be used to help you care for your memory module. If you have several memory modules, for instance, you might want to distinguish among them by naming your modules. To name your memory module, choose Options | Edit Module Label from the menu. You should see the Edit Module Label dialog box. Simply select the default name—usually just Module—and write in any name you want. You can have one module that is simply filled with games and name it accordingly, while another module can be filled with e-books or spreadsheet data. It's up to you how you manage your memory modules.

How to ... Take Care of the Module

Unlike other kinds of portable media, Visor memory modules are fairly rugged devices. Your memory module is thick enough so you can't easily snap it in half or damage it by dropping it from a short height. But be careful! Two rows of pins are in the Springboard slot inside your Visor that insert into tiny holes on the memory module. When the module is not inserted in the Visor, store it somewhere so dirt, dust, or other kinds of gunk can't get into those holes. Also, don't leave it in extreme heat (like on the windshield of your car), step on it, or do anything else silly that may cost you your data.

You can also use the File Mover application to delete all the applications stored on your memory module quickly and at once. This is a dangerous operation, so use it with care. To erase all the contents of a memory module—quickly and permanently—choose Options | Format Memory Module from the menu. You see the Format Memory Module dialog box that warns you are about to lose all the data on the memory module. Tap the Format button to continue.

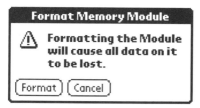

CAUTION *If you format your memory module, you'll lose all the data and applications that may be stored on it. Be sure to check the contents of the memory module using the File Mover application before you attempt to format your module.*

Use Other Memory Modules

While Handspring sells an 8MB memory module for your Visor, it isn't the only one available. InnoGear, for instance, offers several modules called InnoPaks. By the time you read this, at least three InnoPak modules should be available. At the moment, however, the InnoPak/2V is the first and only one of this family of modules we could test while writing this book. The InnoPak modules combine two different features into one package. The InnoPak/2B, for instance, is a 2MB memory module with enhanced beaming features. The InnoPak/2M is a 2MB memory module with an integrated modem. Finally, the InnoPak/2V is a 2MB memory module with a vibrator, which can silently alert you to alarms instead of chiming out loud.

16

You set up the InnoPak/2V in exactly the same way as the 8MB memory module discussed earlier in the chapter. After you insert the InnoPak/2V into your Visor, you should see three new icons appear in the applications list. You were already familiar with the File Mover application, which works exactly the same way. Scroll down, however, and you can see two new icons. They are

- IP Conf
- IP Test

These icons control the vibrator portion of the InnoPack/2V. Tap IP Conf to see the InnoPak/2V dialog box. Here, you can select the alarm mode for your Visor. If you want audible alarms, tap the Audio button, and then tap OK. If, you prefer to have your Visor silently alert you to alarms, tap Vibrating, and then tap OK.

To test your InnoPak/2V, tap IP Test. You can see the InnoPak/2V screen, with three buttons: On, Off, and Pulse. Tap On or Pulse to get a sense of what your Visor will feel like when an alarm goes off. To turn off the vibration, tap the Off button.

Back Up Your Visor

Earlier in the chapter, we mentioned you can back up certain applications and data from the Visor to your memory module. Memory modules don't have any automated backup tools, however. This makes them a relatively inefficient tool for ensuring your data is safe and secure. Instead, we recommend you get the Handspring Backup Module for your Visor.

The Handspring Backup Module is a great little product because it takes all the guesswork and frustration out of backing up and restoring your Visor's data. As long-time Palm OS device users, we have yearned for a device like this for our Palm III or Palm V. The old way of backing up Palm data was to use a program like Penguin Backup or BackupBuddy. Those programs are fine, but they aren't as easy to use as we would like. Now, with the Visor, you simply need to insert your backup module and tap a single button to make sure you get a perfect, 100 percent accurate copy of everything on your Visor. Restoring your data afterwards is just as easy.

Copy Data to the Backup Module

To back up the data from your Visor to the backup module, follow these steps:

1. If the protective dust cover is currently in the Springboard module slot, pull it out and store it in a safe place so you can reinsert it later if necessary.

2. Grasp the bottom of your Visor in your left hand and take the backup module in your right hand, so the module's label is facing down.

3. Slide the memory module into the Springboard slot all the way until it won't go any further. The top of the module should be flush with the top of the Visor, and the Visor should turn itself on automatically when it senses the memory module.

As soon as the backup module is fully inserted in the Visor, the backup program should appear.

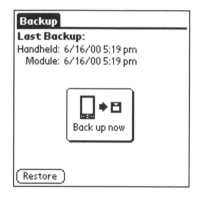

If you've used the backup module before, the Backup application will display some text indicating the last time a backup was performed. Know that the backup module has perhaps the simplest interface ever created in the history of computing. Only two buttons are on the screen: one starts the backup process and the other restores your data from the backup module to your Visor.

To back up the data from your Visor, tap the button labeled Back Up Now. You immediately see the Backup dialog box, which shows the status of the backup process. A fuel gauge indicates the progress of the backup as the module does its thing. If you need to stop the backup for some reason, tap the Cancel button.

16

That's all there is to it. You can now safely remove the backup module and store it in your office or in your travel bag. We recommend you keep it wherever you commonly take your Visor, so you can restore your data in an emergency.

CAUTION *Don't routinely store your backup module in the Visor itself. If your Visor is ever lost or stolen, you wouldn't want to lose your primary backup along with it. On the other hand, it's probably a good idea to keep it in your principal travel bag. Some people even have two different backup modules. They take one on the road and have another one at home, where it can't get lost.*

Restore Data from the Backup Module

Of course, the whole reason to back up your data is in case you someday need to restore it in an emergency. The Handspring Backup Module makes that a snap. To restore your data, insert the module into the Springboard slot. The backup program immediately appears. Tap the restore button in the lower-left corner of the screen. You should see the Restore Data dialog box. This dialog box is designed to ensure you really want to restore your data. Remember, if you tap OK, you will lose any data currently on your Visor because it will be replaced by whatever is on the backup module. If you're sure you want to do this, tap OK.

TIP *If you have more than one Visor, or more than one backup module in your office, it's certainly not out of the question that you could accidentally overwrite important data by using the wrong module. Always label your backup module so you know which Visor it belongs to. As a last resort, your backup module should warn you if it senses it was used on a different Visor, as in this example:*

Where to Find It

Web Site	Address	What's There
Handspring	www.handspring.com	Backup and memory modules
InnoGear	www.innogear.com	InnoPak modules

Chapter 17   The Portable Office

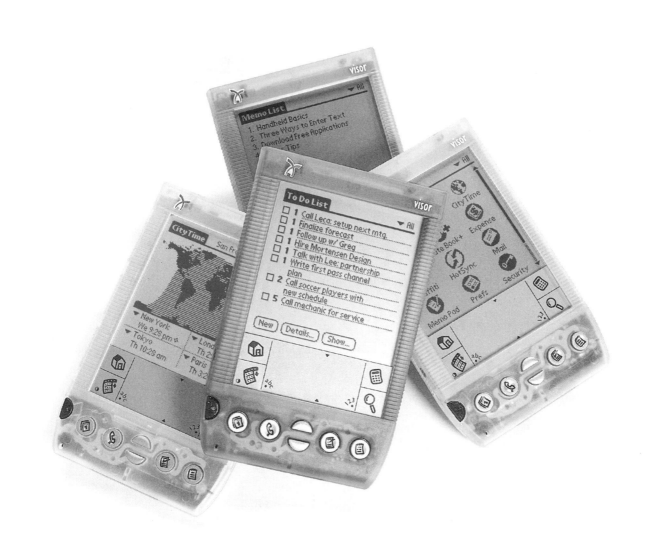

How to...

- Use your Visor as a complete business application computer
- Read Word and Excel documents on your Visor
- Distinguish between Visor Doc and Word .doc files
- Create and edit text documents on the Visor
- Import Visor documents into Microsoft Word
- Create spreadsheets on your Visor
- Generate graphs and charts on the Visor
- Exchange spreadsheets between your Visor and Microsoft Excel
- Create custom databases on your Visor
- Print to wireless printers

The core applications that come with your Visor are fine for most people—they offer all the basic functionality that you need to stay on top of contact information and schedules while on the go. But, as you've already seen in this book, your Visor can do so much more. In fact, it's possible to use your Visor as a full-fledged alternative PC, capable of running applications as varied as a word processor, spreadsheet, and database program.

Why on Earth would you want to do that? Well, which would you rather carry around—a Visor that fits in your pocket or a seven-pound laptop? Which is easier to store in a hotel room? Which is more easily stolen? Which lasts longer on a set of batteries? We think you get the idea. Obviously, using a suite of "office" applications on your Visor isn't for everyone and won't work all the time. But if you're intrigued by the thought of leaving your PC at home and traveling just with a Visor, then read on. This chapter is all about creating the perfect portable Visor office.

Building the Perfect Beast

No, we weren't really big fans of that Don Henley solo album either. But that does describe your Visor if you want to outfit it to be a mobile office, complete with office applications.

The name of the game when it comes to creating a Visor office is convenience and compatibility. What good is it, for instance, to generate documents on your Visor if they're not readable by the word processor on your PC? And why bother trying to do office-style work on your Visor if you can't do it easily, efficiently, and in all the apps and formats you're used to on your desktop? With that in mind, here's a list of products you should have if you plan to do serious work on your Visor:

- **Your Visor**   Have plenty of memory. Working with Word documents, databases, and spreadsheets soaks up memory, so you should invest in a model with plenty of memory (like the Visor Deluxe) or add an 8MB Springboard module when you're ready to get serious. A 2MB Visor probably won't cut it if you plan to install spreadsheets and databases.

- **A Keyboard**   As much as we love Graffiti, the fact remains that you'll hate writing long documents or entering data in a spreadsheet with the stylus alone. Invest in a Visor keyboard. We prefer the Stowaway because it folds down to such a compact size, but any compatible keyboard can work. See Chapter 24 for more details.

- **Document Reader**   If you mainly need to read documents (like Word files and spreadsheets) on your Visor, then you can get by with just a document reader like Documents to Go. This program enables you to copy files from Word and Excel to your Visor and to read them at your leisure.

- **Document Editor**   If you want to create or edit documents from Microsoft Word on your Visor, then a simple document reader won't be enough—instead, you should try a document editor like SmartDoc. While not exactly a full-featured word processor, SmartDoc breaks through the file size limit imposed by the memo pad and makes documents that can be shared with Word.

- **Spreadsheet**   A few options are available for working with spreadsheets on your Visor. Despite the Visor's small size, programs like Quicksheet and TinySheet prove it's possible to work with cells of data in a handheld.

- **Database**   Yes, even database applications are available for the Visor. HanDBase and JFile are the leading database programs for managing data.

- **Enhanced Core Apps**   While you're at it, you can enhance your Memo Pad and To Do List with more powerful alternatives. We recommend programs like PalmJournal, Memo PLUS, and ToDo PLUS.

Work with Documents

Often, all you want to do is refer to documents you created on your desktop while you're away from your desk. This means you'd like to open a Microsoft Word, Microsoft Excel, or perhaps a Corel WordPerfect file right on the Visor. That's not as easy as it sounds, though, because no conduit is built into the Palm OS to grab documents from the desktop and display them on the Visor. That's why you need some alternate options.

Understanding the Doc Format

All Doc files are not created alike. Specifically, when Visor users talk about Doc files—text documents in the Doc format—they're not gabbing about Microsoft Word's .doc format but, instead, about a text format popularized by a program called AportisDoc, generally considered the de facto standard among Visor text readers today. While any Doc file can be read by almost any Doc reader/editor for the Visor (and vice versa), the Doc format is totally incompatible with the version used by Microsoft Word. On the plus side, you can convert .doc to Doc and back again—see "Get Documents Off Your Visor," later in this chapter. Some common document readers for the Visor (designed to read the Visor's Doc format) include AportisDoc, TealDoc, and QED.

17

Read Documents with Documents To Go

Perhaps the most effective tool for displaying Office-style documents on your Visor is Documents To Go. If all you want to do is read documents on your Visor, this program may be the best bet for you. Documents To Go has both Visor and desktop components for shuffling documents to the Visor. To add a document to your Visor, start the Documents To Go app on your desktop and click the Add Item button. Choose the document you want to add to your Visor from the Add Items dialog box, and then click Add. You should see the document appear in the file list on the Documents To Go main window.

> **TIP** *You can add documents to Documents To Go by dragging files from the desktop directly into this window.*

Note, Documents To Go identifies several important pieces of information. Most of it is self-explanatory, but you might be confused by the Status column. Here's a list of what this entry might be telling you:

- **Never Synchronized** You've added the document to the Documents To Go dialog box, but it hasn't been transferred to the Visor yet. Perform a HotSync to get it there.

- **Current**   This file has been HotSynced and resides on your Visor.

- **Modified**   This means you previously HotSynced the document, but you changed the desktop version of the file since then. The next time you HotSync, the file will be updated on the Visor so you have the newest version.

- **Missing**   The desktop version if the document is missing, so Document To Go can't HotSync it.

- **No Space**   Your Visor didn't have enough room to copy the document.

- **Busy**   The document is in use by another application or has been password protected, so it can't be HotSynced.

The View column can also be perplexing. You have two options: Full and None (Full is the default). What's the difference? Well, the Full view mode actually copies the document to your Visor the way you'd expect. But if your Visor memory is limited or you're trying to keep HotSync sessions short because you're dialing in to do a Remote Hotsync, then you might want to set the document to None. This establishes the link to the document within the desktop version of the software, but the document is not actually transferred to the Visor until you go back and change the View to Full.

 To change the View mode of a document or to assign a document to a specific category, double-click it in the Document To Go window. The Item Info dialog box appears, which enables you to make these changes.

On your Visor, Documents To Go actually creates a trio of icons (you need only one): the Documents To Go program, plus separate icons for WordView and SheetView. In reality, you can tap any of three icons to see documents.

Use these navigational aids for getting around Documents To Go:

- To move up or down in a Word document, you can use the scroll bars or tap in the top- or bottom-half of the document itself to move in the desired direction.

> To accommodate your needs, it turns out that telephone companies, Internet Service Providers, and network hardware vendors are all lining up to bring you high-speed broadband access like DSL and cable modem service.
>
> Sizing Up Broadband
> While fast Internet access sounds promising, there's a roadblock: your broadband options are severely limited by geography. Few cities -- if
>
> [Done] [Find]

■ In the SheetView, the arrows in the bottom-right corner of the screen enable you to navigate around.

■ To see more cells at once in the SheetView, choose Sheet | Full Screen View to eliminate the Navigation icons. To navigate in this view, drag the stylus in the direction you want the sheet top to move. To exit the full screen mode, choose Sheet | Normal View.

TIP *The Find menu item can help you locate a specific word in a document, but the Visor's global Find button does the same thing. In other words, the Visor's Find tool can actually search inside Doc files.*

Create Documents with SmartDoc

Viewing existing documents is all well and good, but what happens if you want to create a new document from scratch? Or if you want to edit a Word document you decided to bring along on your Visor? If that sounds like you, a simple document viewer isn't going to do the trick. Instead, you need a document editor.

Use the SheetView Column and Row Menus

If you tap the column headers in the SheetView, you can work with a few options. Here's what they do:

■ **Freeze** This prevents the selected column from scrolling, so you can view it side-by-side with a column that's far away.

■ **Fit** This changes the width of the column to match the widest data in the column.

■ **Min** This reduces the column to the width of a single character.

■ **Widen** This adds two character's worth of width every time you select this option.

■ **Shrink** This narrows the column by two characters every time you select it.

■ **Home** This returns the cursor to row 1 of the column.

The row headers offer Shrink and Home options.

We recommend a document editor/viewer called SmartDoc. The application is easy to use; it looks similar to the Memo Pad because has two views: a list view and a document view.

SmartDoc begins in List view and you choose your document to work with here. You can see it in Figure 17-1.

If you tap the Action icon on the left edge of the screen, you can choose an action to perform on your document. Those include:

- ■ **Open As Copy**   This leaves the original file intact, but creates a copy with which you can work.

- ■ **Info**   Displays the Info dialog box, similar to the Details dialog box in the core apps. Use this to set options like privacy, category, and find preferences.

- ■ **Change Category**   Select a category for the document.

- ■ **Append memo**   This enables you to import the entire text of a memo from the Memo Pad to the end of the selected document.

- ■ **Compression**   This enables you to compress or uncompress the selected document.

- ■ **Duplicate**   Like the action Open As Copy, this creates a file duplicate, but the duplicate isn't automatically opened.

- ■ **Print, Beam, and Delete**   These last options are self-explanatory, though we should point out that you need a copy of Stevens Creek Software's PalmPrint to print the document.

TIP   *The last document you edited is easy to find—its Action icon is darkened.*

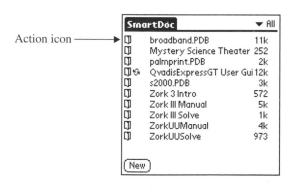

Action icon ⟶

SmartDoc	▼ All
broadband.PDB	11k
Mystery Science Theater	252
palmprint.PDB	2k
QvadisExpressGT User Gui	12k
s2000.PDB	3k
Zork 3 Intro	572
Zork III Manual	5k
Zork III Solve	1k
ZorkUUManual	4k
ZorkUUSolve	973

New

17

FIGURE 17-1   SmartDoc is a great way to create, edit, and read document files on your Visor

Editing Documents

To create a new, blank document, tap the New button or start writing in the Graffiti area. To open an existing document, simply tap it.

Once you're in the Document view, note the Editable icon at the top, just to the right of the Doc tab. If the icon has a line through it, you can't edit the document. Tap it to enter Edit mode. Now you can insert, cut, copy, and delete text as necessary.

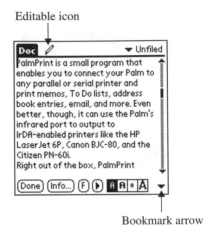

Editable icon

Bookmark arrow

TIP

Unless you're actively editing a document, leave the Edit mode turned off. That way, you won't accidentally change the contents of a file you're simply reading.

SmartDoc works a bit differently than most apps you're probably used to on the Visor. Specifically, SmartDoc won't name a file after the first line of its contents. If you create a new document, enter some text, and choose Doc | Close, you'll find the file is named untitled 1. To name the file, you need to choose Doc | Rename from the menu and enter a name in the Info dialog box.

Adding Bookmarks

Unlike the Memo Pad, there's no limit on how long a Doc file can be. As a result, some can be quite lengthy—you could publish a book to the Visor if you wanted. With that kind of flexibility, you might want to add bookmarks throughout the document to give your readers some navigational help. You can easily add bookmarks to your document. Just do this:

1. Display the document in the Document view. Be sure you are in Edit mode.

2. Scroll to a part of the document you want to bookmark and select some text.

3. Choose Navigate | Add Bookmark from the menu. You see the Add Bookmark dialog box.

4. If desired, change the name of the bookmark. By default, the bookmark is named after the selected text. Tap Add.

Don't simply put the cursor where you want the bookmark to be set; actually select text. If you select no text, SmartDoc puts the bookmark at the top line of text visible onscreen.

To switch to a particular bookmarked part of a document, tap the bookmark arrow at the bottom-right corner of the Document view. Choose a bookmark from the list.

Bookmarks work in any Doc reader, so other Visor or Palm OS device users can make use of them. If you transfer the document to your PC and edit it in Word, though, you should be aware that the plain-text file you end up with in Word will be stripped of any bookmark data.

Get Documents Off Your Visor

Once your document is finished, you probably want to get it off your Visor and make it available to others. You have two choices:

- Beam the document to other Palm device users
- Upload it to your PC, where you can open it in Microsoft Word

Beaming Documents

Beaming your documents is easy. To beam a document to another Palm device, all you need to do is tap the document's Action icon, and then choose Beam. Or, if the Document view is open, choose Doc | Beam from the menu.

17

Making the Screen Bigger

If you feel constrained by the anemic width of the Visor screen, you're not alone. You can squeeze more characters on the Visor screen, though—you just need an app called Screen40×25. Granted, it doesn't have a particularly catchy name, but it works. It's a Hack (so you need HackMaster—see Chapter 18), but after installing it, you can display text in AportisDoc and SmartDoc in a tiny font that squeezes a few extra characters onto the screen. Screen40×25 isn't for everyone—the font is a fixed width, all-cap style, which is hard to read. But if you want to make use of every millimeter of space on the screen, try it.

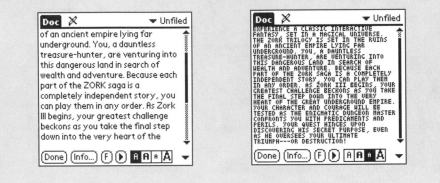

Either way, before you do this, you should get the document ready for general distribution. To do that, choose Doc | Prepare for Distribution from the menu. What does this do, you wonder? Glad you asked. It simply performs a few housecleaning operations that make your document presentable to others. Specifically, it does these things:

- Moves the cursor to the top of the document
- Sets the category to Unfiled
- Turns off Privacy (if it was set)
- Makes the document searchable (sets the Global Find setting to the default)
- Compresses the document to allow it to beam faster
- Sets the document to back up to the PC on the next HotSync

NOTE   *You can beam documents to other users, but for them to read the file, they'll need some kind of Doc reader on their Visor.*

Moving Documents to the PC

Getting your document to the PC is also pretty easy—but making it usable from that point on is a little trickier. For starters, though, let's get it from the Visor to the desktop.

When you make changes to a document, it is flagged in SmartDoc for automatic backup on the PC. You can also manually set a file for backup to the PC; to do that, choose any one of these methods:

- On the List view, tap the Backup region of the screen to display the Backup icon.

Backup icon →

SmartDoc	▼ All
broadband.PDB	11k
Mystery Science Theater	254
palmprint.PDB	2k
QvadisExpressGT User Gui	12k
s2000.PDB	3k
Zork 3 Intro	572
Zork III Manual	5k
Zork III Solve	1k
ZorkUUManual	4k
ZorkUUSolve	973

(New)

- From the Document view, choose Doc | Prepare for Distribution and make sure the Backup on HotSync option is checked.
- From the Document view, tap the Info button and select the Backup on HotSync option.

Info	ⓘ
broadband.PDB	

Category: ▼ Unfiled
20591 bytes
Compressed
☐ **Private**
☑ **Backup on HotSync**
Global Find: Prefs Always Never

(OK) (Cancel) (Delete...) ↑

After your document is ready for its trip back to the PC, your work still isn't done. Before you commence the HotSync, you need to make sure the conduit is properly configured. On the PC, click the HotSync Manager icon in the System Tray and choose Custom. At the bottom of the list, you should see an entry called System. Set it to Handheld Overwrites Desktop (by default, this is usually set to Do Nothing). Close the HotSync Manager and perform the HotSync.

After the HotSync is over, documents set for backup will be copied to the PC. You can find them in the backup folder for your user name. On most PCs, this means you should look in a folder with a path similar to this:

```
C:\Program Files\Palm\username\Backup
```

Open this folder and look for the file, which should have the file extension PDB—and Microsoft Word won't open it. Now what? Now you need one more piece of the puzzle—a program that can translate the Palm PDB file format into a text file Word can understand.

The solution to this problem is a program called PalmDocs. PalmDocs installs a macro in Microsoft Word that acts as an indirect conduit to your Visor. Here's how to use it:

1. Install PalmDocs. The program affects only Microsoft Word by adding a macro to its default template. After installing PalmDocs, close Word (if it was previously open) and reopen it. You should see a new menu called PalmDocs.

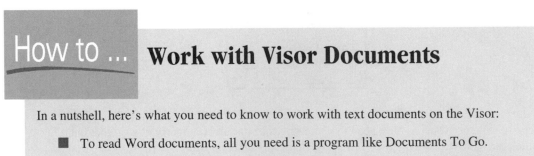

2. Choose PalmDocs | Open PDB File. By default, the program displays the Open dialog box in the Add-on folder. Navigate to the Backup folder and find your document. Click Open.

3. The document opens in Word. Now you can edit, save, print, or e-mail the file, just as if you had created it in Word from the beginning.

How to ... Work with Visor Documents

In a nutshell, here's what you need to know to work with text documents on the Visor:

- ■ To read Word documents, all you need is a program like Documents To Go.
- ■ To create or edit long documents on your Visor, you need an editor like SmartDoc.
- ■ When you transfer completed SmartDoc documents to the PC, they end up in the Backup folder.
- ■ To get those Visor documents into a usable format on your PC, use PalmDocs to import them into Word.

Track Data with Spreadsheets and Databases

Like milk and cereal, or guitars and rock 'n' roll, nothing goes with word processing quite like spreadsheets and databases. In fact, spreadsheets are often reported as the most popular PC-based application in the history of computers. So it makes sense that you might want to dabble with these other office applications on your Visor. You're in luck—like the wealth of document readers and editors on the Visor, you can also choose from several spreadsheet and database apps.

Manage Your Spreadsheets

Obviously, the biggest constraint with viewing and editing spreadsheets on your Visor is the lack of screen real estate (Rick calls this "screen estate"—who knew he was so clever?). This can be a limitation, but the Visor is still a worthy vehicle for working with spreadsheets, especially if you stick to small spreadsheets that don't have dozens upon dozens of columns and rows.

We've already seen a way to view spreadsheet data using Documents To Go, but if you're looking for a spreadsheet app that lets you change data, then you might want to try an application like Quicksheet. Quicksheet is a powerful little spreadsheet with support for multiple sheets in each workbook, 48 mathematical functions, an integrated charting module, and a conduit that links back to Excel on your PC.

Getting Spreadsheets onto Your Visor

After you install QuickSheet, open your desktop copy of Microsoft Excel and you'll find there's a new menu. This is what you will use to send files to your Visor and to open files that have been synchronized with it. To send a spreadsheet to the Visor, do this:

1. Open Excel, and then open the spreadsheet you want to copy to the Visor.

2. Choose Quicksheet | Save As from the menu bar. You see the Save Quicksheet Workbook dialog box.

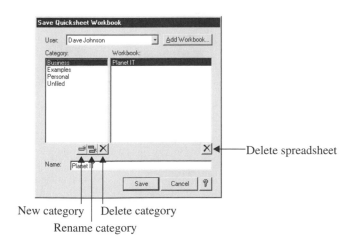

New category | Delete category
Rename category

Delete spreadsheet

3. Assign the new spreadsheet to a category by clicking the appropriate category on the left. If you want to create a new category, use the New Category button first.

4. Type a name for this spreadsheet. This is the name it uses on the Visor.

5. Click the Save button.

The spreadsheet is now ready to be transferred to the Visor. Use HotSync to make the transfer.

TIP *Quicksheet decides whether to transfer a spreadsheet, depending on the conduit settings. To check Quicksheet's conduit, click the HotSync Manager in the System Tray, choose Custom, and look for the conduit entry called Quicksheet.*

Be careful you don't import too massive of a spreadsheet into the Visor. Multisheet workbooks with thousands of cells are not only hard to manage, they also take up a lot of memory. It's easy to choose a huge spreadsheet accidentally—make sure what seems like a small sheet isn't really a huge one, with most of its columns set to Hidden mode in Excel (see Figure 17-2). After you HotSync, the spreadsheet appears on the Visor.

NOTE *If you use a Mac, the HotSync conduits aren't currently available for your system. A beta is available, though—-visit Quicksheet's Web site for details on how to get it.*

A Brief Tour of Quicksheet

Once you install one or two spreadsheets in Quicksheet, take a look around. The List view looks like this:

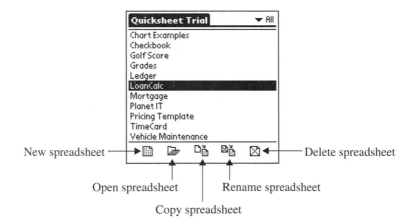

Columns between *E* and *J* are hidden

Microsoft Excel - Planet IT ed sked v39

File Edit View Insert Format Tools Data Quicksheet Window Help

J22 = =WORKDAY(K22,K$1,Holidays)

	C	D	E	J	K	M	S
2	Plane	PlanetIT TC 1-15					
3	Site & Version	Item/Description	Filename	Site Editor done	Copy desk done	Posted	
13	TC2	Best of the Web (original)	TC2BWeb1116-01 thru 03	11/08/99	11/15/99	11/16/99	
14	TC2	Required Reading (hoover)	TC2Book1116	11/08/99	11/15/99	11/16/99	
15	TC2	Home page promo e-mail		11/10/99	11/12/99	11/15/99	
16	TC2	Tech story (hoover)	TC2Tech1123-01, 02	11/15/99	11/22/99	11/23/99	
17	TC2	Prod story (original)	TC2Prod1123	11/15/99	11/22/99	11/23/99	
18	TC2	Ask the Expert (original)	TC2Expt1123-01 thru 03	11/15/99	11/22/99	11/23/99	
19	TC2	Best of the Web (original)	TC2BWeb1123-01 thru 03	11/15/99	11/22/99	11/23/99	
20	TC2	Required Reading (hoover)	TC2Book1123	11/15/99	11/22/99	11/23/99	
21	TC2	Prod story (hoover)	TC2Prod1130-01, 02	11/17/99	11/29/99	11/30/99	
22	TC2	Opinion (original)	TC2Opin1130	11/17/99	11/29/99	11/30/99	
23	TC2	Ask the Expert (original)	TC2Expt1130-01 thru 03	11/17/99	11/29/99	11/30/99	
24	TC2	Best of the Web (original)	TC2BWeb1130-01 thru 03	11/17/99	11/29/99	11/30/99	
25	TC2	Required Reading (hoover)	TC2Book1130	11/17/99	11/29/99	11/30/99	
26	TC2	Home page promo e-mail		11/17/99	11/19/99	11/22/99	
27	TC2	Home page promo e-mail		11/23/99	11/30/99	12/01/99	
28	TC2	Tech story (original)	TC2Tech1207	11/29/99	12/06/99	12/07/99	
29	TC2	Prod story (hoover)	TC2Prod1207-01, 02	11/29/99	12/06/99	12/07/99	
30	TC2	Ask the Expert (original)	TC2Expt1207-01 thru 03	11/29/99	12/06/99	12/07/99	
31	TC2	Best of the Web (original)	TC2BWeb1207-01 thru 03	11/29/99	12/06/99	12/07/99	
32	TC2	Required Reading (hoover)	TC2Book1207	11/29/99	12/06/99	12/07/99	
33	TC2	Home page promo e-mail		12/01/99	12/03/99	12/06/99	

Ed Sked / Newsltr Sked / RTable Sked / Look Up /

Ready   Calculate   NUM

FIGURE 17-2 Hidden columns or rows can disguise the fact that your spreadsheet will take up an enormous amount of space on the Visor

 TIP *The program actually comes with a few samples you can try. They're found in the Examples category.*

You can open a specific spreadsheet in two ways:

■ Double-tap the entry in the list. This is fairly unique among Visor apps; we aren't aware of too many that use double-tapping.

■ Tap the entry, and then tap the Open icon at the bottom of the screen.

17

Once a spreadsheet is open, you should see a display not entirely unlike the one in Documents To Go or any other spreadsheet program. Remember these few key items:

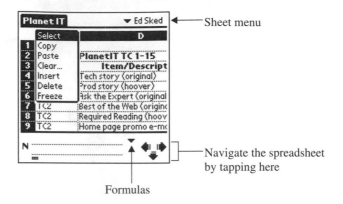

Tap the column and row headers to perform tasks like copying, pasting, and inserting new elements. The Freeze option isolates the selected row or column on screen, so you can move another row or column onto the screen and see them side by side.

To make columns bigger or smaller, tap the space between columns and drag the columns to the left or right.

Navigate around the spreadsheet by tapping the arrow at the bottom right. To see another sheet in a multisheet workbook, tap the Sheet menu at the top right. This is where you'd ordinarily find the categories menu in most apps.

Access the library of mathematical formulas by tapping the list arrow to the right of the cell field at the bottom of the screen.

Loading Visor Spreadsheets into Excel

Thanks to the Quicksheet conduit, spreadsheets are automatically synchronized whenever you perform a HotSync, as long as the HotSync Manager is set properly. To load a spreadsheet that was updated on your Visor, do this:

1. Open Excel and choose Quicksheet | Open from the menu bar.

2. Choose the sheet from the Open Quicksheet Workbook dialog box.

3. When you finish with the spreadsheet, you can save it and prepare the file for transfer back to the Visor by choosing Quicksheet | Save.

TIP   *If you're not crazy about Quicksheet, alternatives to this popular program are available. Instead, try TinySheet or MiniCalc, both available at www.palmgear.com.*

Charts and Graphs on the Visor

Who says you can't do it all with your Visor? If you have data in a spreadsheet that lends itself to visual inspection—in the form of a chart or graph, for instance—you can create it with the right software. Perhaps the easiest way to chart spreadsheet data is with Quickchart, a companion product to Quicksheet. If you have both programs installed on your Visor, all you have to do is open a spreadsheet in Quicksheet and tap an empty cell. Then choose Chart(range) from the list of functions. Select a range of cells for your chart, and tap in another cell or use the Enter gesture. Your chart is created.

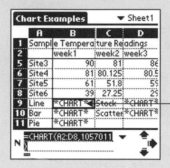

Double-tap to see the chart

To see and modify the chart, double-tap the cell that now says *CHART*. Quickchart will launch, where you can modify the chart and see it in all its grayscale glory.

Create a Database with HanDBase

If you use your Visor to record data on a regular basis, the Memo Pad probably just isn't cutting it for you. Instead, you probably wish you had some sort of database application like Microsoft Access available on your Visor for entering lots of data in a structured manner.

Fear not, because database applications do, in fact, exist for the Visor. One of the best is a program called HanDBase. While HanDBase doesn't synchronize with desktop database apps like Access, it enables you to create standalone databases on your Visor quickly and easily.

> **TIP** *If you want to integrate and synchronize your HanDBase files with Microsoft Access on the desktop, get a copy of HanDJet. This program easily solves the integration program of getting the two programs to talk to each other.*

Assuming you've installed HanDBase, here's how to create a simple database in five minutes or less.

Let's assume we're going to create a database that tracks only two pieces of information: your clients' names and the kind of pet they own (dog or cat). This sounds simple, and it is—but it'll show you how to generate custom database for your Visor.

17

1. Start HanDBase. You see the Choose Database screen, which lets you open, beam, and delete database files, among other things.

2. Tap the New button. You now see the New Database screen.

3. Name your database at the top of the screen. Write Pet Survey.

4. Now it's time to set up some data fields. In the Edit Fields box, tap Field 1. You're taken to the Edit Field dialog box. Enter a name for the field, which we can call Client.

5. In the Field Type list menu, choose Text. We'll be writing the client's name, so text is the appropriate style for this field. After you choose it, new options appear on the screen.

```
┌──────────────────────────────────┐
│ Edit Field 1                     │
│ Field Name Client..............  │
│ Field Type:        ▼ Text        │
│ ☑ Visible      ☑ Export/Print    │
│ Pixels Shown     58.........     │
│ Max Characters   40.........     │
│                                  │
│                                  │
│ ( Edit Popups ) ☐ Popups Append  │
│ ( OK )( Cancel )                 │
└──────────────────────────────────┘
```

6. In this case, we don't have to change any of the defaults, like the maximum number of characters the user can enter for the field. Tap OK.

7. Tap Field 2 to return to the Edit Field dialog box for the next field. This field should be named Pet.

8. Because only two choices are available—dog and cat—we want to let the user choose those from a pop-up menu instead of writing "dog" or "cat" in Graffiti over and over. Choose Pop-Up from the Field Type menu.

9. We can't set up the pop-up menu quite yet. Tap OK.

10. Tap OK to create the database.

The database is almost complete—you could actually start entering data at this point. We haven't created the pop-up list for the pets field yet, though, so finish the database by completing these steps:

1. Choose Prefs | DB Properties from the menu. You see the Edit Database dialog box you've already worked with to set up the fields.

2. Tap the Pet entry in the Edit Fields box.

3. Tap the Edit Popups button at the bottom of the Edit Field dialog box. Tap the New button and write **Dog**, and then tap the OK button. Tap New again and write **Cat**. Tap OK twice to exit the Popups dialog box.

17

4. Close the Edit Database dialog box by tapping OK.

Now you're ready to enter data:

1. Tap the New button and the cursor is waiting for you in the Client field.

2. Write a name, and then tap the Pet field on the left. You should see the pop-up menu, from which you can choose an animal type.

3. Tap OK to close this record.

After you enter several records, you can use the database in several ways:

■ Beam the database to another HanDBase user. While you can beam the database file to anyone, the receiver must have HanDBase to read and use the data.

■ Copy the records to the Memo Pad. To do this, open the database and choose Actions | Export Records. The data is then copied to a new Memo Pad entry in the Unfiled category.

■ Print the database. To print your records (by choosing Actions | Print Records) you need to have PalmPrint installed on your Visor.

Collecting Database Files

HanDBase is something of an unofficial standard on the Visor for database applications. Many HanDBase-compatible database files are available on the Internet, which you can install on your Visor for a wide variety of applications. These include

CNS Drugs	Database of common medicines
Home Tracker	Records details about homes you've walked through when you're in the market to buy
PhotoProtocol	Records essential information during a photo shoot—for professional photographers
Horse Racing	Database of winners for all the Triple Crown races
Baseball Stats	For baseball fans: League leaders and top 50 performers in eight different categories

NOTE *This is only the tip of the iceberg; there are dozens more. You can find all these database files at www.palmgear.com.*

Print from Your Visor

The ultimate handheld PC would probably look a lot like the Visor, but with one important difference: it would have a paper-thin printer embedded inside, enabling you to print anything you see on the screen. While that's mere science fiction for the time being, it doesn't mean you can't print stuff from a Visor. The answer lies in a product called PalmPrint.

PalmPrint is a small program, as seen in Figure 17-3, that enables you to print memos, To Do lists, Address Book entries, e-mail, and other data, wirelessly using an IrDA-enabled printer.

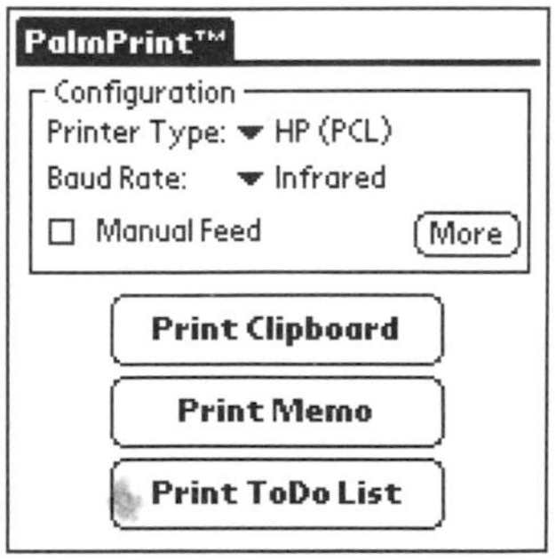

FIGURE 17-3 PalmPrint enables you to print data from the core apps, but it also hooks into many third-party programs like SmartDoc and HanDBase

17

What Is IrDA?

Technically, *IrDA* stands for the *Infrared Data Association,* which is just a bunch of companies that make IR-enabled products. More importantly, though, IrDA represents the industry-standard infrared port you can find on most laptops, handheld PCs, and printers with IR ports. If you find a printer with an IrDA port, chances are excellent it'll work with PalmPrint.

Right out of the box, PalmPrint works with the Memo Pad, the To Do List, and even the contents of the Visor clipboard. Printing the clipboard is a particularly powerful option because it enables you to print almost anything, even data from applications that don't support PalmPrint.

On the other hand, an increasing number of applications come with built-in support for PalmPrint. The program has become something of an unofficial standard among Visor app developers, and if you see a Print command in the program, it's almost certainly designed to work with PalmPrint.

Print to an Infrared Printer

If you have access to an IR printer, printing is pretty simple. Just select the printer type from PalmPrint's Printer Type list menu and choose Infrared from the Baud Rate list menu.

Then choose the appropriate print option and point your Visor at the printer.

TIP   *If your Visor and the printer don't communicate properly, try slowing the connection by choosing Infrared (slow). If that doesn't solve the problem, try an alternate Printer Type. Of course, you might also be too close or too far away. Try to get within six to twelve inches of the printer for best results.*

IR Printers for Your Visor

A small handful of IR-enabled printers are around. If you like the idea of printing wirelessly from your Visor, or if you travel frequently and want to print from wherever you happen to be, look into one of these:

Manufacturer	Printer	Comments
Canon	BJC-50, BJC-80	Lightweight mobile printers
Citizen	PN-60I	Point-of-sale printer
Hewlett Packard	LaserJet 6P, LaserJet 6MP	Desktop laser printers
Pentax	PocketJet 200	Lightweight mobile printer, compatible with IrDA adapter

Where to Find It

Web Site	Address	What's There
Stevens Creek	www.stevenscreek.com	PalmPrint
Think Outside	www.thinkoutside.com	Stowaway keyboard
DataViz	www.dataviz.com	Documents To Go
Cutting Edge Software	www.cesinc.com	SmartDoc Quicksheet, Quickchart
Iambic Software	www.iambic.com	TinySheet
DDH Software	www.ddhsoftware.com	HanDBase
Consult US GmbH	www.consult-us.cc/default_usa.htm	HanDJet
Screen Envy Software	www.screenenvysoftware.com	Palm Journal
Aportis	store.yahoo.com/pilotgearsw/aportis.html	AportisDoc
TealPoint Software	www.tealpoint.com	TealDoc
Visionary 2000	www.visionary2000.com	QED
Konstantin Klyatskin	www.geocities.com/SiliconValley/Platform/1527	Screen40x25
Alexis Lorca	www.thinkchile.com/alorca	PalmDocs

17

Chapter 18

HackMaster and Other Utilities

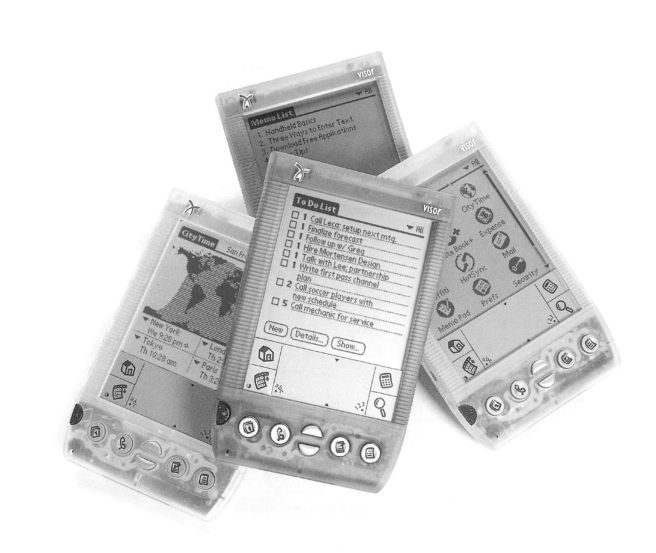

How to...

- Back up your entire Visor
- Restore your entire Visor
- Install and use HackMaster
- Make capital letters the easy way
- Access menus without having to tap the Menu button
- Automatically correct spelling errors
- Write anywhere on the screen, instead of just in the Graffiti area
- Drag and drop text
- Use the Visor buttons to load multiple applications
- Automatically remove duplicate entries from your databases
- Expand the Visor's clipboard
- Create your own Visor software
- Make your Visor run faster (or slower)
- Change the HotSync ID name on your Visor

When you hear the word "utilities," you probably think of your monthly electric bill or those four worthless Monopoly properties (hey, $150 isn't gonna break anybody's bank). In the world of computers and Visors, however, utilities are software programs that add capabilities and fix problems. They're power tools, though not necessarily limited to power users.

In this chapter, we tell you about some very cool and worthwhile Visor utilities. When we're done, you'll find yourself with a reliable backup that can overcome any data-loss disaster, a time-saving way to write capital letters, the newfound capability to drag and drop text, and lots more. Utilities may sound boring and technical, but they're actually fun, easy to use, and extremely practical.

HackMaster

The mother of all Visor utilities, HackMaster is what separates the men from the boys, the women from the girls. HackMaster is a tool Tim Allen would love, as it allows Visors to reach beyond their limits, to achieve "more power!" (ah, ah, ah). And it's a tool many users come to find indispensable.

What HackMaster Does

Technically speaking, HackMaster is an "operating system extension manager." By itself, HackMaster serves no function. But it enables the use of *Hacks*—little programs that extend the capabilities of your Visor. Forget the negative connotations usually associated with "hacking"—these programs are here to help, not harm.

And, if you want to run them, you must first download and install HackMaster. (See Chapter 4 for information on installing programs like this—it's also applicable to the Hacks you'll be downloading.)

CAUTION *Because Hacks tinker directly with the Visor's Palm OS, they can create the occasional glitch. And the more Hacks you have installed and running, the greater the likelihood of some sort of problem. The most common is your Visor crashing, which is usually more of an annoyance than anything else. But we encourage anyone who's working with HackMaster to perform regular backups, using either the Handspring Backup Module (discussed in Chapter 16) or a utility like BackupBuddyNG (discussed later in this chapter). That way, if the unthinkable happens (such as a total loss of data), you're protected.*

Where to Get It

HackMaster comes from a little company called DaggerWare (www.daggerware.com). You can download the program from there, or from Palm software sites like Handango and PalmGear H.Q.

HackMaster is shareware, meaning it's free to download but should be registered (and, hence, paid for) if you continue to use it. How much for this marvel of modern programming? A paltry five dollars. Thus, before you go any further, surf on over to PalmGear H.Q. (the only site where you can officially register HackMaster) and pay the piper. It's the honorable thing to do.

How to Use It

Launching HackMaster is no different from launching any other program—you just tap its icon. But, as we noted previously, HackMaster is useless without any Hacks loaded. Therefore, to help you learn to use this utility, we're going to walk you through the installation of one of our favorite Hacks.

It's called MiddleCaps, and it saves you having to write the Graffiti upstroke every time you want to create an uppercase letter. Instead, you simply write the letter so it crosses the invisible line between the alpha and numeric sides of the Graffiti area. We find that this enables us to write much more quickly and naturally.

MiddleCaps is freeware, as are many Hacks, so you can download and use it free of charge. (A note of appreciation e-mailed to the author is always nice.) You can find it at Handango and PalmGear H.Q., among other sites. Let's get it running on your Visor.

18

1. Download MiddleCaps and install it on your Visor. Note that you won't see an icon for it in the Applications screen; the only real evidence of Hacks appears within HackMaster itself.

2. Tap the HackMaster icon to run the utility; you see MiddleCaps is listed.

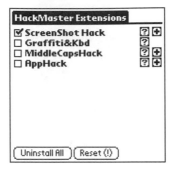

3. Notice that there's an empty box to the left of the name. Tap it with your stylus and you see a check mark appear. This means the Hack is now enabled. If you want to disable it, tap the box again. (For purposes of our tutorial, please leave it enabled.)

4. Notice the two symbols on the right-hand side of the screen: a question mark and a plus sign. Tapping the question mark brings up information about the Hack, usually consisting of the author's name, the version number, and an e-mail or Web site address. Tapping the plus sign (not all Hacks have them) takes you to the options screen for that particular Hack. Tap the plus sign next to MiddleCaps.

5. You're now in the MiddleCaps Preferences screen, where you can tweak a few of the program's settings. For now, check the box marked Caps on Crossing. This means a capital letter will appear whenever you write a character that crosses between the alpha and numeric sides of the Graffiti area. You can test it by placing your cursor on the line near the bottom of the screen (tap anywhere on the line), and then doing some sample writing.

6. Tap OK to return to the main HackMaster screen. That's it! MiddleCaps is now enabled and will work in all applications—even third-party ones.

What about those two buttons at the bottom of the HackMaster screen? When you tap Uninstall All, it simply disables all the Hacks—a timesaver if you're trying to troubleshoot a problem (see Chapter 25). When you tap Reset(!), your Visor resets. It's rare that you'd ever need to use this button.

Important Notes About HackMaster

You need to abide by a few rules of thumb when using HackMaster on your Visor, all of them intended to keep things running smoothly:

- ■ If you ever decide to delete a Hack, make sure you disable it first! If you try to delete a Hack while it's still running, it could cause errors, crashes, or even data loss.

- ■ If you install two or three Hacks on your Visor, don't enable them all simultaneously. Instead, enable one at a time, making sure it works properly before enabling the next one.

- ■ If you have to reset your Visor for any reason, a message will pop up asking if you want to "reinstall your formerly active collection of system Hacks?" Tap Reinstall (the equivalent of "yes") only if you're sure it wasn't a Hack that forced you to have to reset in the first place. Otherwise, tap Cancel. Then you can go back into HackMaster and manually enable your Hacks again.

World's Greatest Hacks

If you were impressed by what MiddleCaps did for your Visor, wait till you get a load of some of our other favorites. Rather than list them by name, which doesn't always express what they do, we're going to list them by function. You can find all these Hacks at the aforementioned Palm-software Web sites.

Automatically Correct Spelling Errors

Giving Graffiti a helping hand, CorrectHack works like the AutoCorrect feature in Microsoft Word, automatically correcting words you frequently misspell. Alas, it doesn't have a database of its own; you have to supply both the words and their correct spellings. But as you compile your list over time, you'll wind up with far fewer mistakes. And you can also use CorrectHack as shorthand for commonly used words. For instance, if you write your initials, the software would automatically plug in your full name.

Access Menus Without the Menu Button

On a computer, you access pull-down menus by clicking at the top of the screen—*where the menus are*. On a Visor, however, you must tap the Menu button, which is all the way down at the bottom of the Graffiti area. Horrors. MenuHack makes menus appear when you tap the title bar of any open application (although it doesn't work with a few).

18

Use the Entire Screen as a Graffiti Area

Many users find the Graffiti area a bit confining. If you're one of them, pick up ScreenWrite, which turns the entire screen into one big Graffiti area. Thus, you can write anywhere you want. Even better, ScreenWrite leaves a trail of "digital ink" beneath your stylus, so you can see your strokes as you enter them.

Drag-and-Drop Text

While you can select snippets of text by tapping and dragging your stylus, you can't drag that text to another spot and drop it in (as you can with any word processor). TextEditHack adds that capability to text-oriented applications like Memo Pad and even makes it easier to select text. You can double-tap to select a single word, triple-tap to select a sentence, and quadruple-tap to select all the text on the screen. Very handy.

Launch More than Four Programs with the Application Buttons

The more software you have loaded on your Visor, the harder it becomes to hunt for the desired program icon. Enter AppHack, which uses two sequential presses of the application buttons to launch up to 24 programs. You needn't remember the combinations you set up—AppHack displays a cheat-sheet when you press the first button, so you can see which program will load when you press the second one. This Hack is a little confusing to work with, especially because no instructions are provided, but it sure can save time.

Enhance the Find Feature

FindHack turbocharges the Visor's Find function, remembering the last six searches you performed and enabling you to define up to four default searches. What's more, you can choose whether to search all installed applications, just the core apps, or only the currently loaded program. It even supports the use of *wildcards*—searching for book* would return book, bookmark, bookstore, and so forth.

Look Up a Contact Without Switching Programs

While the Visor makes it easy to switch back and forth between programs, it can be a hassle to have to quit what you're doing to look up, say, a phone number or address. PopUp Names pulls up your Address Book "on top" of the program that's currently running—and with a handy two-paned window. Thus, it's not only a timesaver, it's also a more practical way of accessing your contact list.

Other Utilities

HackMaster works minor miracles, but it isn't the only tool you should consider owning. There are no Hacks that create reliable backups of your data, or give you greater flexibility in beaming software to other users, or remove duplicate entries from your databases. So read on to learn about some of the other highlights of the Visor utility world.

> **NOTE** *All the utilities listed here can be purchased and downloaded from PalmGear H.Q. at www.palmgear.com.*

BackupBuddyNG

One of the most important Visor utilities you can own, BackupBuddyNG does one thing and does it well: create a backup of every bit of data on your Visor, programs included, every time you HotSync. As you may recall, the Palm OS automatically backs up the databases for the built-in programs, but it doesn't back up all third-party software, files, e-books, and so forth. If your Visor happens to get wiped out, you'd lose all this stuff. Certainly you could reinstall most of it, but there's still the risk of losing valuable data.

18

BackupBuddyNG eliminates that risk. And it's a piece of cake to use, an install-and-forget program that works behind the scenes. Every time you HotSync, the software adds any new or changed programs and databases to the backup directory on your computer's hard drive. If the worst befalls your Visor, all you do is drop it into the cradle and HotSync again—everything is restored, effectively returning the Visor to its predisaster state.

> **NOTE** *The one hitch is HotSync times tend to be a little longer when BackupBuddyNG is running. In fact, your first HotSync after installing BackupBuddyNG can take several minutes, as it's archiving everything for the first time. After that, things should proceed more quickly.*

> **NOTE** *It's worth mentioning that you can accomplish the same goal with the Handspring Backup Module discussed in Chapter 16. Because it's a module, it goes where you go—so you can execute a backup (or a restoration) while traveling, something you can't do with BackupBuddyNG.*

While the software is highly automated, you can delve into some options if you want. This is done by choosing Start | Programs | BackupBuddyNG | BackupBuddy Configuration, which brings up the configuration screen shown in Figure 18-1. Here's a quick rundown of the various options:

- **Archive files deleted on handheld**   If checked, this option creates a backup of any files (programs, databases, and so forth) that you've deleted from your Visor—kind of a fail-safe procedure in case you someday decide you need something you pitched.

- **Exclude modified DOC files from backup**   When you read a Doc file on your Visor (as discussed in Chapter 22), the Palm OS considers it "modified"—and, therefore, it gets backed up by BackupBuddyNG. This just makes for longer HotSync times, so check this option if you're looking to shorten them.

- **Backup applications and data in Flash-ROM**   This option is not applicable to Visor users and should be left unchecked.

- **Backup databases mapped to conduits**   Many third-party programs have their own conduits, meaning their data already gets backed up when you HotSync. As such, BackupBuddyNG ignores it. But if you're an advanced user and have a reason for wanting to make an additional backup of these programs' data, check this box.

- **Skip Quicksheet files**   Cutting Edge Software's Quicksheet works directly with Microsoft Excel on your PC and backs up its own files. Thus, you can check this box and tell BackupBuddyNG to ignore Quicksheet files, thereby decreasing HotSync times.

- **Verbose output to HotSync log file**   Creates a lengthy HotSync report file, useful if you're contacting the company with a tech-support issue.

- **Exclude changes from the following from backup**   There may be certain programs or databases that you don't need to have archived on every HotSync. By putting check marks next to those items, you can decrease HotSync times.

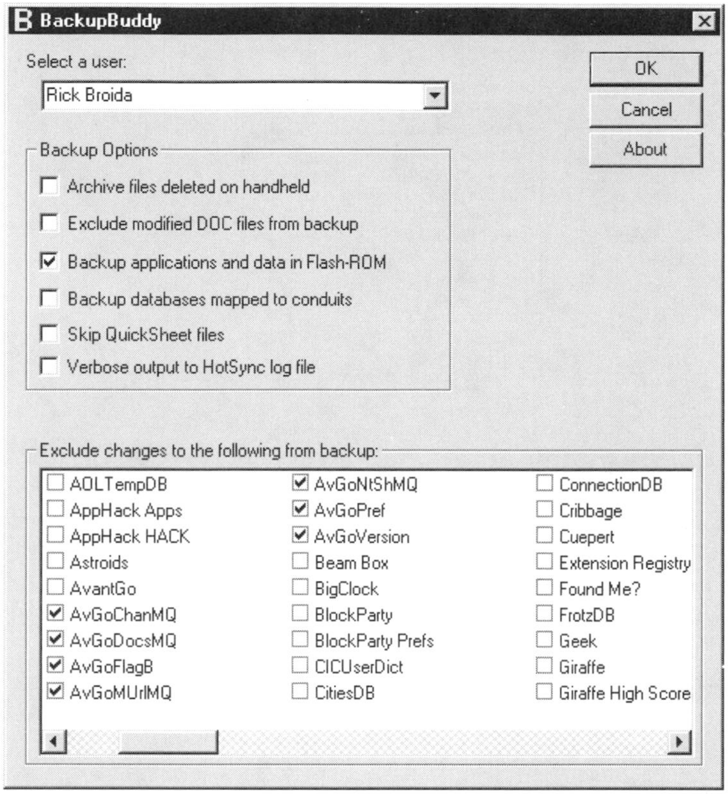

FIGURE 18-1   Although BackupBuddyNG is highly automated, you can tweak a few key options by visiting this configuration screen

> **TIP**
>
> *If you use the AvantGo Web browser (see Chapter 14), you could be in for fairly lengthy HotSyncs. That's because AvantGo imports new data almost every time you HotSync, which is, in turn, archived by BackupBuddyNG. There's really no need to back up these AvantGo channels, however, because they're stored on the Web anyway. Therefore, you can trim many seconds off your HotSyncs by telling BackupBuddyNG to ignore AvantGo databases. As shown in Figure 18-1, just click the box next to every item that begins with "AvGo."*

BeamBox

Beaming programs and data to other Visor users (see Chapter 4) is not only practical, it's just plain fun. But the Palm OS is a bit limited in what it can beam. Specifically, it can't beam Hacks or e-books or certain kinds of databases. That's where BeamBox comes in. This invaluable

18

utility lets you beam just about anything that's installed on your Visor. It's exceptionally easy to use and even enables you to designate certain files as "favorites," so you have an easier time finding them. Better still, BeamBox costs just five dollars to register.

```
┌──────────────────────────────────┐
│ ┌─────────────┐  ┌─────────┐     │
│ │Beam Box     │  │Hacks    │     │
│ └─────────────┘  │Apps     │     │
│ Address Book 3.0 │Data     │     │
│ AmusePak 1.1b    │E-books  │     │
│ AOLMail 1.0      │All      │     │
│ Astroids 1.00    │PQA's    │     │
│ AvantGo 3.0.81   │Other    │     │
│ Beam Box 1.15    │Favorites│     │
│ BigClock 2.2      ──JIK─── │     │
│ BlockParty 1.0      16K   │     │
│ Calculator 3.0      15K   │     │
│ Cribbage 1.0.0      17K   │     │
│                           ▼     │
│ ┌──────┐  ┌──────────────┐      │
│ │ Beam │  │ Add favorite │      │
│ └──────┘  └──────────────┘      │
└──────────────────────────────────┘
```

TIP
Interestingly, you can't use BeamBox to beam BeamBox to other users. (Yes, that sentence does too make sense. Go back and read it again.) But you can beam BeamBox using the stock Palm OS beaming utility, which is accessible from the Applications screen by choosing Menu | Beam.

How to ... Beam Software to Another Visor User

Suppose you're enjoying a game of Vexed (one of our favorites), and a fellow Visor user says, "Hey, I'd like to try that!" Generous sort that you are, you agree to beam a copy of the game (which is perfectly legal, as Vexed is freeware). To do so:

1. Return to the Applications screen, and then choose Menu | App | Beam.

2. Find Vexed in the software list, tap it to highlight it, and then tap Beam.

3. Point your Visor's IR transceiver at the other Visor's IR transceiver, and then wait a few seconds for the transfer to complete.

Presto! You've just shared some great software—wirelessly!

By the way, you're not limited to beaming with Visor users; the Visor is compatible with all Palm OS devices. So, you can share programs and data with a Palm V, an IBM WorkPad, or any handheld that employs the Palm OS.

Clipper

Like most computers, Visors make use of a "clipboard" for copying and pasting text. And, like most computers, Visors can hold only one selection of text at a time in that clipboard. But Clipper turns it into a repository for multiple selections, thereby expanding your copying and pasting capabilities. Everything you copy is retained in Clipper (where you can even go in and edit the text). When you want to paste something, you just make a special Graffiti stroke to bring up the Clipper window, and then choose which snippet of text to paste.

This can come in extremely handy if you frequently write the same lengthy words or phrases. Doctors could use Clipper to create a little database of diagnoses, lawyers to maintain a selection of legal terms. Sure, you could use the Visor's own ShortCuts feature (see Chapter 2) to do much the same thing, but you'd still have to remember the shortcut keys.

UnDupe

If you routinely work with ACT!, Outlook, or some other third-party contact manager on your computer, it's not uncommon to wind up with duplicate entries on your Visor. This can also happen if you import additional databases into Palm Desktop. Whatever the cause, the last thing you want to have to do is manually delete these duplicates from your records. UnDupe does it automatically, ferreting out duplicate entries in Address Book, Date Book, Memo Pad, and To Do List, eliminating them in one fell swoop.

> **TIP** *When you eliminate the duplicates from your Visor, they're eliminated from your desktop PIM as well the next time you HotSync.*

Create Your Own Visor Programs

Ever wonder why there's so much third-party software available for Palm OS devices like the Visor? Maybe because it's so easy to write programs for the platform. While the more sophisticated applications do require programming experience and professional development tools, utilities are available that enable you to design basic Palm OS software with ease. Indeed, if you're willing to tackle a short learning curve, you can create customized applications for your personal or business use.

Use PDA Toolbox to Design Simple Software

Like to tinker? Want to get your software-design feet wet without spending any money? If so, check out PDA Toolbox. This inexpensive programming environment employs a graphical interface and makes software design as easy as dragging and dropping elements onto a simulated Visor screen. You can even create your own icons for your programs.

18

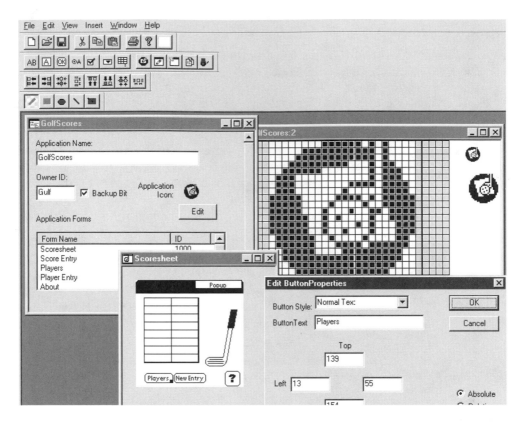

Use Satellite Forms to Develop Business Software

Suppose you have an idea for a Visor program and want to create a prototype before hiring a programmer. Or you want to design a special order form for your outside-sales team, one that links to your company's inventory database. Puma Technology's Satellite Forms can handle all this and more; it's a robust software-development package that can create sophisticated Palm OS programs. It uses a simplistic graphical environment similar to PDA Toolbox's, but it's a much more robust and sophisticated package.

Satellite Forms is not inexpensive: $795 for the Standard Edition and $995 for the Enterprise Edition (which supports enterprise-oriented databases like Oracle and Lotus Notes). And it's worth noting that the programs generated from it won't run on Visors unless accompanied by a special "runtime" program. Said program can be freely distributed from the Standard Edition, but the Enterprise Edition comes with only ten runtime licenses—meaning only ten people can use your Satellite Forms programs (unless you purchase additional licenses).

Use HotPaw Basic to Create Programs on Your Visor

The ubiquitous programming language BASIC is alive and well, as evidenced by HotPaw Basic, which enables you to create and run programs right on your Visor. Indeed, whereas tools like PDA Toolbox and Satellite Forms chain you to a desktop PC, HotPaw Basic is accessible "in the field." Thus, you could whip up a simple program to accommodate a need that arises while traveling or working. If you're fluent in BASIC, you'll definitely want to check out this $20 utility.

Use Programming Tools to Create Programs on Your Visor

If you have some programming experience and you really want to get serious about developing software for the Palm OS, you can find a wealth of resources on the Palm, Inc., Web site (www.palm.com/devzone). It has information for developers who are just getting started, listings of technical and marketing resources, and lots more. Anyone who's the least bit interested in programming for the Palm OS should start here.

Make Your Visor Run Faster

Like any computer, a Visor runs only as quickly as its microprocessor will allow. If you're working with a particularly large database or spreadsheet, or you're running a search and have a large number of records, you may find your Visor a bit more sluggish than you'd prefer. Oh, well, not much you can do about it, right?

Wrong. Thanks to so-called "overclocking" software, it's possible to turbocharge your device. A popular pastime among speed-hungry computer users, *overclocking* is the technique of forcing a processor to run at faster-than-rated speeds. Assuming all goes well, the result can be a significant speed boost.

CAUTION   *Overclocking is a try-at-your-own-risk technique, one that can result in crashed Visors, lost data, possibly even a fried processor. One guaranteed side effect is shortened battery life. Overclocking is not recommended by Handspring, nor by the authors of this book.*

Given the possible disasters associated with overclocking, why bother with it? Shaving a few seconds off certain operations is certainly a plus, but the more likely answer is that some users just like to tinker, to push the envelope. If you're one of them, you should check out three programs: BackupBuddy Software's Cruise Control, Jean-Paul Gavini's Afterburner 2.0, and IS/Complete's Tornado V, all available from PalmGear H.Q.

TIP   *If you're going to run the risk of overclocking, at least do it sensibly. Don't just jack up the clock speed to maximum; increase it gradually, starting with a small increment, and then using your Visor for a few days to see if any adverse effects result.*

Make Your Visor Run Slower

Why would you want your Visor to run slower? Glad you asked. As previously noted, increasing the processor's clock speed causes the batteries to drain more quickly. It stands to reason, then, that decreasing the clock speed would extend battery life. That's exactly what happens, hence, the "underclocking" capabilities of Afterburner and Tornado V. If you're taking a long trip, try cranking the Visor's clock speed down a notch or two. You're not likely to notice much of a performance hit, but you may get a couple extra days from your batteries.

Change the HotSync ID (a.k.a. User Name) on Your Visor

The very first time you HotSync your Visor, you're asked to supply a user name. This name is stored on your Visor, thus allowing HotSync manager to correctly identify it before actually synchronizing anything. While it's unlikely you'd ever need to change this user name, the only innate way to do so is by performing a hard reset (done by holding down the power button while pressing the reset button).

The problem with this method is it wipes out every trace of data and third-party software—a less-than-ideal solution. Fortunately, there's a freeware utility that gets the job done without returning your Visor to factory condition. It's called PalmName and it's available from PalmGear H.Q.

Where to Find It

Web Site	Address	What's There
PalmGear H.Q.	www.palmgear.com	HackMaster and virtually every other utility under the sun
BackupBuddy Software	www.backupbuddy.com	BackupBuddyNG and Cruise Control
Handango	www.handango.com	Utilities and other Palm OS software
Inkverse	www.inkverse.com	BeamBox and ScreenWrite
PDA Toolbox	www.pdatoolbox.com	PDA Toolbox
Puma Technology	www.pumatech.com	Satellite Forms
HotPaw	www.hotpaw.com/rhn/hotpaw	HotPaw Basic
IS/Complete	www.iscomplete.com	Tornado
Gavini Dot Com	www.gavini.com	Afterburner

Chapter 19

Time and Money Management

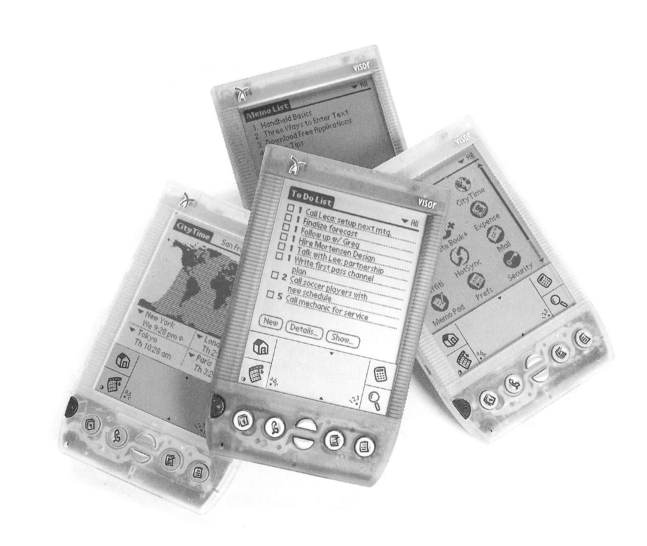

How to...

- Track your finances with the Visor
- Keep up with Quicken data entry on your Visor
- Calculate loans using your Visor
- Calculate restaurant tips and divide dining bills with the Visor
- Track your investments on the Visor
- Get stock price updates via the Internet
- Get wireless stock quotes with your Visor
- Manage projects and clients with the Visor
- Keep up with time zones
- Calculate the time between any two dates

There's a saying where Dave grew up: you can never have enough time or enough money. Actually, we're pretty sure this expression is common to most places, but Dave tends to ramble on and on about New Jersey on occasion. And because there's no reasonable way to discuss authentic New York pizza in this book, we're covering this topic instead.

No device in the world—at least not yet—is going to give you more time or money just as a happy consequence of owning it. But many programs for the Visor are designed to maximize what time and money you have by helping you manage it better. There are project management systems for tracking your jobs and clients, financial programs for keeping track of your checkbook, and portfolio systems for staying on top of your investments. In this chapter we rounded up a few of the best of each.

Manage Your Money with the Visor

"Money," the Swedish rock band Abba once said. "Money, money," they continued. In all, they said it three times, as in, "money, money, money." We couldn't agree more. Your Visor is an ideal pocket-sized tool for keeping track of your money. You can use it as an extension of your desktop financial management program or as a stock tracker—and a lot of little applications in between.

Keep Up to Date with Quicken

You know who you are. As soon as you get home from dinner and a movie, you rush to the PC and enter your receipts in Quicken. It's a habit, it's an addiction. Well, your Visor and the right software can now save you the agony of waiting until you get home: relax and enjoy the movie, because Pocket Quicken enables you to enter your expenses into your Visor as they happen.

Rock Bands to Live By

We need to make a strong caveat at this point: neither Dave nor Rick is particularly fond of Abba anymore (though Rick danced to "Fernando" every night through his formative years). Because you're relying on this book for advice anyway, we humbly give you our top choices for music to listen to as you troubleshoot your PC or surf the Web with your Visor:

Dave: The dual art forms of Electric Blues and '60s Rock really constitute the height of Western culture. For the most part, it has all been downhill since then, made painfully obvious by whatever that stuff is Rick forces me to listen to when I visit his office or ride in his car. No, I say, stop the madness. Listen to the Beatles, Pink Floyd, Velvet Underground, Kristin Hersh, Throwing Muses, and The Call, and you're pretty well set. If you have a few dollars left over, pick up some Peter Himmelman, BB King, Dire Straits, and Eric Clapton. You won't be disappointed. And whatever you do, don't buy anything that Rick is about to recommend.

Rick: Not unless you have good taste and want to *enjoy* what you're listening to. With the exception of the Beatles, Dave feels all music should be weird or depressing—or both, ideally. Give me Billy Joel, Green Day, Fiona Apple, Simon and Garfunkel, Alanis Morrissette, or Big Bad Voodoo Daddy. Yes, that's right, I don't listen to artists or bands just because they're unpopular or unknown. That's Dave's job. Oh, and for the record, Dave doesn't even like jazz—proof positive that he's a few sandwiches short of a picnic.

Pocket Quicken is not a Visor-based replacement for the entire Quicken application on your desktop. Instead, it's a handheld companion that lets you store payments, deposits, and account transfers in your Visor and synchronize the transactions with Quicken on the desktop at your next HotSync. You can also review your account balances and analyze old transactions. If you're a Quicken user and methodically enter all your receipts into the program, then this is a program you should try out.

CAUTION   *Pocket Quicken only handles 15 accounts. That sounds like a lot, but many serious Quicken users can easily exceed that limit. The first 15 accounts from the desktop are transferred to the Visor in alphabetical order, so you might need to rename some accounts to be sure they make it onto the handheld. In addition, the software doesn't handle your investment accounts, so you can't use Pocket Quicken as a way to track your stocks.*

Before you begin using Pocket Quicken, you should perform a HotSync. This transfers your accounts and categories from the desktop version of Quicken to your Visor. Be sure to do this before you take your Visor on the road expecting to enter any transactions!

Once you have a chance to synchronize the apps and get Pocket Quicken configured with your desktop settings, take a look at the Pocket Quicken interface. Pocket Quicken has two views: the display toggles between the Accounts view (which lists your accounts and current balance, Figure 19-1a) and the Register view, where you enter and review transactions (Figure 19-1b).

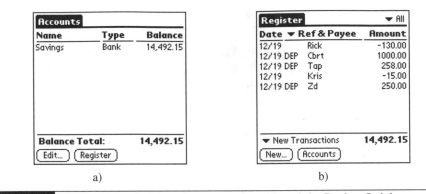

a)   b)

FIGURE 19-1 The Pocket Quicken Accounts view (a) and the Pocket Quicken Register view (b)

When you want to enter a new transaction, tap the New button at the bottom of the screen and choose whether you're creating a payment, deposit, or cash transfer. Then fill out the resulting dialog box as appropriate. Pocket Quicken includes Quicken's AutoFill tool (which completes the transaction for you when it recognizes what you're entering). You can also choose to use a "memorized" transaction from a pick list to speed entry.

You can lock prying eyes out of your records with a four-digit PIN. To protect your Quicken data, start Pocket Quicken and choose Options | Security from the menu. Then create your PIN.

If you use your Visor frequently to store transactions, the data can add up. It's easy to keep it in check, though, and preserve your Visor's memory. To trim your transactions to a manageable size, choose Actions | Trim History. Then delete old transactions based on date or by the oldest set of entries. Remember, though, not to delete any entries that haven't yet been HotSynced.

Use Other Cash Management Tools

If you aren't a Quicken user, or you don't want the capability to synchronize your Visor with a desktop finance program, you still might want to try some other applications out there. Specifically, take a look at some of these:

■ **Personal Money Tracker**   This is a popular finance package for your Visor that is ideal for non-Quicken users. It has a conduit that synchronizes the Visor data with a standard CSV file on the desktop. You can then import that data into a spreadsheet or personal finance software.

```
┌──────────────────────────────────┐
│      PMT Edit Transaction         │
│                                   │
│ Date:      12/19/1999             │
│ Repeat:    None                   │
│ Transfer to    ▼ Cash             │
│ From Account   ▼ Equity           │
│ Description:   ▼ none             │
│ Check Num:     129  □ Cleared     │
│ Amount:        1.29 ▼ $           │
│ Note:                             │
│           ..................      │
│           ..................      │
│                                   │
│ ( Done )( Cancel )( Nxt Check )   │
└──────────────────────────────────┘
```

■ **Accounts and Loans**   This program enables you to track your bank account balances and loan information in one application. The program is easy to use and lets you export your financial data to the Memo Pad.

```
┌──────────────────────────────────┐
│ Accounts & Loans                  │
│                                   │
│  ┌────────────────────────────┐   │
│  │       Quick Entry          │   │
│  └────────────────────────────┘   │
│  ┌────────────────────────────┐   │
│  │     Account Statements     │   │
│  └────────────────────────────┘   │
│  ┌────────────────────────────┐   │
│  │          Loans             │   │
│  └────────────────────────────┘   │
│  ┌────────────────────────────┐   │
│  │    Regular Transactions    │   │
│  └────────────────────────────┘   │
│  ┌────────────────────────────┐   │
│  │     Acct/Loan Balances     │   │
│  └────────────────────────────┘   │
│                                   │
└──────────────────────────────────┘
```

Streamline Your Day with Other Financial Tools

What is the Visor if not convenient? That's why we love to load Visor up with tools that make it easier to do mundane tasks like pay bills and calculate loans. Here are a few programs you might want to install on your Visor:

■ **LoanUtil**   This small application is handy when you're trying to figure out if you can afford that house or new car. It's a loan calculator that tells you the monthly payments, total amount of loan, or interest rate depending on what data you enter. Tap the icon marked three at the bottom of the screen and you are taken to a Compare screen that lets you directly compare two different loan offers based on the same principal.

```
┌─────────────────────────────────────┐
│  LoanUtil – Primary Loan    ❶        │
│ First Pay Date:   ( 12-1999 )        │
│ Last Pay Date:    ( 11-2003 )        │
│ # of Payments:      48.00            │
│ Amount Borrowed:  $ 12943.00         │
│ Interest Rate:    19.000 %           │
│ Monthly Payments: ................   │
│ ▉2 3   (Calculate)  [        ]       │
└─────────────────────────────────────┘
```

■ **HandyShopper**   This quirky little program is designed to help you shop. It lets you maintain lists of products you want to buy, and you can even tell HandyShopper in which store (and what aisle) you found it, so you can later go back and track the products down more easily. For us, one of the most interesting features is its capability to compare the actual price of two similar products. Suppose you're buying tissue paper that costs $4.99 for 10 ounces and another brand sells 12 ounces for $5.49. Which is the better deal? Find out by choosing Record Best Buy from the menu, and then enter the price and quantity in the Best Buy dialog box. For the record, you should buy the second item because it's cheaper by about 4 cents per ounce.

```
┌─────────────────────────────────────┐
│ Untitled ▼           ▼ All ❶         │
│ ▼ All Stores         Q ( $ )         │
│ ┌─────────────────────────────────┐ │
│ │          Best Buy               │ │
│ │            Product              │ │
│ │           A        B            │ │
│ │ Price:   12.99    14.49         │ │
│ │ Quantity:  10       12          │ │
│ │                    ( Go! )      │ │
│ └─────────────────────────────────┘ │
│ ( Done )                             │
└─────────────────────────────────────┘
```

■ **EZTip**   Do you go out for meals with friends and have a hard time divvying up the bill? Try EZTip, which enables you to enter the total amount of a bill, add a tip, and then evenly divide the total among a number of diners.

```
┌─────────────────────────────┐
│ EZTip                       │
│                             │
│      Bill Amt: ____69.49    │
│          Tax: ____5.73   8.25 % │
│    Sub-Total: ____75.22     │
│  ▼ Tip (BTax): ___10.42  15.00 % │
│        Total:    85.64      │
│     Divide by: _____3 Payers │
│                             │
│   Per Person: 28.55         │
│                             │
│  (Clear)(Total)(Itemize)    │
└─────────────────────────────┘
```

■ **MoneyChanger** This program is designed to convert currencies for you when you're on the road. If you travel to foreign countries, this program is handy for figuring out what your money is worth without having to stop at a currency exchange. The rates of exchange are automatically updated whenever you HotSync, so this program works best if you have the capability to HotSync while you're traveling.

Track Your Investment Portfolio

One of the Internet's biggest killer apps, it turns out, seems to be investment Web sites. Whether you're using E*Trade, Microsoft Investor, the Motley Fools, or one of a hundred other locations in cyberspace, everyone wants to deliver you a stock quote or graph your portfolio. And as great as those sites are, they have one major weakness: you can't carry them around town in your pocket.

That's where your Visor comes in. You can use any one of a number of portfolio management packages to watch your investments climb or, if you're not so lucky, plummet every day—all from the convenience of your Visor. Most investment programs for the Visor enable you to check your portfolio's health from anywhere, any time. Suppose you don't get a chance to check the paper's business pages until you get on the subway in the morning. You can update your portfolio right from your seat on the train and instantly know your new positions.

If you like the idea of using your Visor for portfolio management, give some of these programs a shot.

How to ...   Track Stocks with Portfolio Manager

Portfolio Manager is one of our favorite tools for tracking the profit and loss of our investments. On the other hand, it isn't perfect; you can only create a single portfolio with no more than ten individual stocks. That eliminates any chance of tracking your IRA, SEP-IRA, and personal investments separately.

Getting the hang of Portfolio Manager takes a bit of practice. There are three steps to using the program to track your stock's net worth. Do this:

1. Start by entering a new stock. Tap the New button and you can enter your stock details, including its current value on the Price field. Tap the Done button to save the entry.

```
┌─────────────────────────────┐
│ Details                     │
│ Code      MMM               │
│ Name      3m................│
│ Quantity  0                 │
│ Price     129.......  0      │
│ Lot Size  0.................│
│ Dividend  0.................│
│ Tot Cost  0                 │
│ Tot Value 0                 │
│ P/L       0                 │
│ (Done)(Cancel)(Delete)      │
└─────────────────────────────┘
```

2. Now you need to enter your first purchase of stock. Tap the Trans button to switch to transaction mode, and then tap the stock in the Portfolio list. Because we're in transaction mode, this time we enter a stock purchase instead of a new stock detail. You should see the Transaction view for the stock.

```
┌─────────────────────────────┐
│ MMM                         │
│ Date    Qty  Price  Amount  │
│                             │
│                             │
│                             │
│                             │
│                             │
│ Qty on hand            0    │
│ Total P/L              0    │
│ (Done)     (Buy)(Sell)      │
└─────────────────────────────┘
```

3. Tap the Buy button to enter purchase details. Enter the quantity of shares you've bought and the price per share.

```
BUY
Code      MMM
Name      3m
Date      12/19/99
Quantity  10
Price     129
Comm      0
Amount    1290

(Done) (Cancel) (Delete)
```

4. To see the current value of your stock, you need to tap the Details button, tap the stock, and update the Price field with the current share price. Tap Done, and you see your profit or loss on the Portfolio view.

```
Portfolio
Code      Qty   Price    P/L
MMM       10    131.50    25




Total Value          1315
Total P/L              25
(New)    Details Trans
```

> **TIP** *Portfolio Manager understands commission. You can input a number directly—such as if you pay a flat fee of $35 per transaction—or let Portfolio Manager calculate your commission as a percentage of the sale. This is controlled by choosing Options | Preferences from the menu.*

StockHand

We're big fans of StockHand because it does two important things: it connects to the desktop and it retrieves stock prices via the Internet. On the downside, the desktop component is for Windows only—Mac users can't use this program.

The desktop component is actually where most of the action occurs. You can organize your holdings into multiple portfolios (called Categories in StockHand) and view your positions by a single portfolio or everything at once. Adding stocks is easy with a single dialog box. Enter the transaction and StockHand automatically uses your existing Internet connection to check the latest stock prices. As a consequence, the desktop component of StockHand gives you a real-time snapshot of your market positions.

You can view your portfolio in a number of ways, including total value, today's profit and loss, and total realized gains or losses. An icon in the Windows System Tray shows a happy or sad face depending on whether your position is up or down today. If you'd like, StockHand can even notify you about price changes by pager.

Of course, this is a Visor application. HotSync your Visor and all the data currently stored in the StockHand desktop app is synchronized with your Visor. That way, if you HotSync right before you leave the office (as you might usually do anyway), you can then evaluate your portfolio while you're on the go. Everything in the desktop component also appears in the Visor.

StockPilot

Do you love to see your holdings in lots of different ways? Then you'll love StockPilot. This program is a serious competitor—all that it lacks is the capability to update prices automatically, like StockHand does, and perhaps some graphing features, like you'll find in StockWatch. Nonetheless, we love the way this program displays our data. Supporting just a single portfolio, the shareware version enables you to enter any number of stocks. The Personal version, which is free, limits you to a serviceable nine securities.

StockPilot tracks a lot of details about your holdings, including dividends, profits, fee as a percentage of stock value, and total value. StockPilot is the only program in this group that lets you "watch" a stock instead of owning it. And if you deal in European markets, you'll appreciate the unique Euro conversion tools.

The elegant display shows your portfolio in three columns, each of which is customizable to show different details, like stock symbol, shares, profit, and more. A comprehensive set of menus also enables you to export data to the Memo Pad and rearrange the display of your securities in any order you like.

TIP   *Add Stock Manager SP to your Visor and your StockPilot application is suddenly Web-enabled—it'll retrieve the latest stock prices from the Internet and update your Visor at each HotSync. Stock Manager is an important addition to StockPilot.*

Mange Your Time

In addition to your money, your time is also pretty valuable. In previous chapters, we talked about programs that make it easier for you to manage your time (the To Do List in Chapter 9 springs to mind). Here, though, we'd like to focus on a few tools for people whose livelihood revolves around the effective use of time. If that's you, you probably already use project management and job tracking software. The Visor has its own collection of these tools as well, and they may be more useful if you work away from the office, because you can take them with you and use them while you work.

PdaProjects

One of the simplest project management tools available for the Visor, PdaProjects is by no means limited or underpowered. The program lets you track multiple clients and projects, and log hours spent for each.

To get started with PdaProjects, you need to create some clients and some projects. Then you can log hours for projects as they occur. Start PdaProjects and follow these steps to create a simple project database:

1. Begin by making a list of the clients you usually work with. Tap the Jump To list menu and choose ClientEntry.

2. Enter information about this first client. Make sure you enter information in each of the four fields, or PdaProject won't let you save your work. When you're done, tap the check mark icon to save your entry. If you want to, enter a second client in the resulting blank form.

3. Now we'll create a project. Tap the Jump To list menu and choose ProjectEntry.

4. Enter information about the project. Because we already created at least one client, you can tap the Client list menu to choose the name from the list. Finish filling out the form and save it by tapping the checkmark icon.

19

Project Entry

Client:
Tap Magazine
Pr
Ac
De
Stylus feature

▼ Jump To?   ◀ X ✓ ▶

5. Now it's time to record time spent on the project we just created. Tap the Jump To list menu and choose HoursEntry. Choose a project from the list menu, and then fill in the rest of the form, including the date and hours spent.

Hours Entry   *TRIAL*

Project: ▼ feature-101

Date: ▼ 19.12.99

Hours: ▼ 2:00

Auto Timer: ☐ Off

▼ Jump To?   ◀ X ✓ ▶

6. When you've entered one or two hour logs for a project, you can tap the Jump To list menu and view the HoursSheet View. This lists your projects and hours committed to each.

Hours Sheet   ▼ View

Date	Project	Hours
19.12.99	feature-101	2:00
20.12.99	feature-101	1:00
23.12.99	feature-101	5:00

▼ Jump To ?   🕐 8:00   ◈

If you want to export these numbers to the Memo Pad, tap the Memo Pad button at the top of the screen.

TimeCard

This is about as simple as it gets. If you don't need sophisticated project tracking tools, but, instead, just need to know the hours you've worked, then give TimeCard a try. You tap the In button when you start and the Out button when you stop—and export the results to the Memo Pad for a log of all your work hours.

Streamline Your Day with Time Management Tools

Time management is about getting that spreadsheet to your client on time or tracking how many hours you were on the road delivering two tons of fertilizer to a nearby town. Time management can be little things—like knowing how many days are between two project milestones. Here is a small collection of utilities we think you might appreciate having on your Visor:

- **Time Traveler**   This program is a fairly comprehensive time zone manager that lets you find the time difference between your current location and major cities around the world. One of its most interesting features is in the Time Travel screen, where you can specify your flight itinerary (including your departure location and time followed by your arrival location and time), and the program calculates the actual travel time, taking time zone changes into account. That way, you know how many magazines to buy for your upcoming place flight.

```
┌─────────────────────────────────────┐
│ Edit Itinerary        ▼ Unfiled     │
│ Ship/Flight # UA1229                │
│ (Depart Port) Denver                │
│ Depart Date  12/19/99               │
│ Depart Time  12:00                  │
│ (Arrival Port) La                   │
│ Arrival Date  12/19/99              │
│ Arrival Time  15:02                 │
│   ▼ Duration ___0Days __3Hrs ⚡Mins  │
│ (Done) (Note) (Delete...)           │
└─────────────────────────────────────┘
```

Other Time-Tracking Apps

The Visor has a veritable wealth of time-tracking apps available for download. Here are a few others you can investigate:

- **TimeTrack**   This program is a more comprehensive project manager in the style of PdaProject.
- **PalmTask**   This is a project manager that is group-ware enabled; you can track and delegate projects using a local area network (LAN) and HotSyncing.
- **Project@Hand**   This sophisticated project manager actually synchronizes with Microsoft Project, enabling you to take Project files on the road in your Visor.

19

■ **BigClock** We've mentioned this program elsewhere in the book, but it's a winner and deserves mention here as well. Use BigClock to display the time, to play up to four different sets of alarms, and to serve as a counter or countdown timer.

■ **BlueMoon** When was the last time you changed the filter in the furnace, checked the oil in your car, or called your mom? These are tasks that don't always lend themselves to regular To Do List or Date Book entries, largely because they happen infrequently and not always on a predictable schedule. But BlueMoon is designed to accommodate just those kinds of recurring tasks.

■ **Timeout** Do you take enough breaks during the day? If not, you might be heading down the road to stress and heart failure, like our friend Rick. Timeout is a simple program that pops a reminder on the Visor screen randomly throughout the day to tell you to take a short break and relax.

■ **Date Wheel** This clever program lets you calculate the number of weeks, days, or business days between any two dates. You can also specify a duration, like ten business days, and find the necessary start or end date. This program is essential for any manager who needs to assign deadlines or determine if there's enough time between two dates to get a job accomplished.

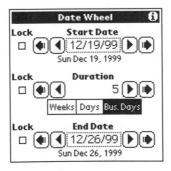

Chapter 20 Playing Games

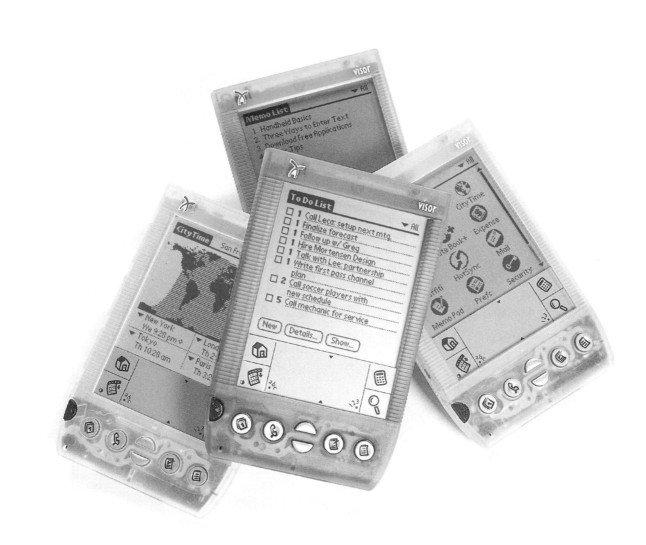

How to...

- Configure the sound on your Visor for gaming
- Enable IR games
- Install new games
- Control games on your Visor
- Install and play the bundled Visor games
- Play interactive fiction games
- Use the interactive fiction player
- See adventure game maps
- Use the Visor as a substitute for dice
- Find great games for your Visor

Of course, spreadsheets, databases, document readers, and memos are well and good. If that's all you ever plan to do with your Visor, that's fine—you're just unlikely to ever get invited to one of Dave or Rick's parties.

Your Visor is a miniature general-purpose computer—and, as a result, it can do almost anything your desktop PC can do. That includes playing games. Sure, the display is smaller and the processor isn't as fast, which can limit the kinds of games you play, but the fact remains that your Visor is a great game machine for passing the time in an airport, on the train, in a meeting (while you look like you're taking notes) or any other place you are bored with doing productive activities. In this chapter, we discuss what you need to know to get the most out of your Visor as a gaming machine and recommend some of the best games for you to try.

Turning Your Visor into a Game Machine

No, playing games isn't exactly rocket science, but before you get started with them, you should learn a few things that'll come in handy. You should know, for instance, how to control your Visor's volume, install applications, and control beaming—after all, some games out there enable you to multiplay using the IR port.

Control the Visor's Game Sound

At the top of the list is the Visor's sound system. The Visor has a control for how loud to play game sounds. Logic dictates that you'll want to set this loud enough to hear what's going on in your game, but this may not always be the case. As much as we like to play games, we don't always want others to know that's what we're doing—so we recommend you set the game sound level low or even off completely. That means you'll play your games without sound but, if you're at work, we think you'll agree this is a wise decision.

To tweak game sounds, do this:

1. Tap the Prefs icon to open your Preferences application.

2. Switch to the General category by tapping the category menu at the top right and choosing General.

3. Find the Game Sound entry and choose the volume level you want.

Enable Beaming

If you know other Palm OS device users, you might want to try your hand at some head-to-head games via the Visor's IR port. It's fun and addictive, and very nearly sociable. For two games on different Palm devices to find each other, though, you need to set your Visor to receive beams from other handhelds automatically. The control for this option is in the same place as game sounds—do this:

1. Tap the Prefs icon to open your Preferences application.

2. Switch to the General category by tapping the category menu at the top right and choosing General.

3. Look for the entry called Beam Receive and make sure it's set to On.

20

Leaving Beam Receive on is handy, too, so your friends can beam you games they've recently downloaded from the Internet.

Install Games

Installing games is a snap. We discussed how to install applications on your Visor in Chapter 4, and working with games is really no different. After all, a game is just another kind of Visor app.

If you're new to downloading applications from the Internet, you need to know that most apps come compressed in one of two popular formats:

- **Zip**   This is the standard way of managing files in Windows. To install a zipped file, you need a program capable of unzipping it first. Typically, this means using WinZip 7.0.

- **Sit**   Macintosh files are compressed in the Sit format, which can be uncompressed with Aladdin Stuffit Expander 5.0 (Stuffit works with Zip files as well).

Once expanded, you'll probably have several files to work with: text files that include installation instructions and, possibly, a file in PDF format that needs to be opened with a program called Adobe Acrobat (see Figure 20-1). Acrobat files are typically the user manual information. Finally, there should be one or more files with a PRC extension. These are Visor apps that need to be installed on the Visor to play the game.

Open the Install Tool and use the Add button to set these files for installation at the next HotSync.

If you use WinZip 7.0, a faster way to install apps in the Install Tool is simply to drag the PRC files from the WinZip window into the Install Tool dialog box (they'll dynamically expand as you drag them, meaning you needn't unzip the files into a folder on your hard disk at all).

Control the Games

You're all set to start playing some games. But where's the joystick? There is none, silly. Most action games on the Visor use the buttons on the Visor case to control the action (see Figure 20-2). While the game is running, the Date Book, Address Book, Memo Pad, and To Do List buttons are diverted to game controls and won't switch you to the usual apps. To find out which buttons do what in a given game, you can experiment (our favorite way, actually) or check the game documentation. In most games, you can find basic instructions by checking the game's Help option on the menu.

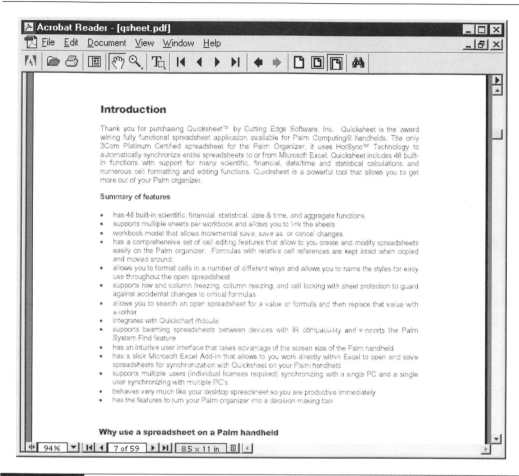

FIGURE 20-1   Acrobat enables you to view fully formatted documents on your PC or to print them for reference. Many programs ship their manual in Acrobat format

 TIP   *Need to pause a game? Turn off your Visor. The game remains frozen until you turn it on again. In many cases, though, switching to another app will end the game, so don't do that unless you want to start from scratch later.*

20

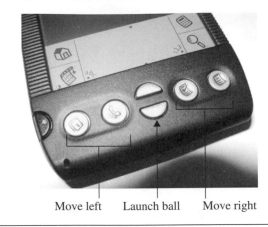

Move left   Launch ball   Move right

| FIGURE 20-2 | The arcade game HardBall uses the four buttons on the case to move the paddle left and right |

Installing the Bundled Games

If you're not a big fan of reading manuals, you may not have noticed that several games come with the Visor, right out of the box. They're found on the Palm Desktop CD-ROM, but they're not automatically installed on your Visor itself. Handspring must assume you're too busy to play games.

Whatever the reason the games aren't on your Visor yet, you can easily rectify that problem. Open the Install Tool application on the desktop and click the Add button. The Open dialog box opens automatically in the Add-on folder, which contains all five stock Visor games. Select one or more, and then HotSync.

> **TIP** *If, for some reason, you can't find those games in the Add-on folder of your hard disk, you can install them from the CD-ROM.*

The five games that come with your Visor are:

- **Giraffe** This is the Graffiti training game we discussed in Chapter 4. Giraffe is like the classic Tetris, in which objects fall from the top of the screen. In this case, though, the falling objects are actually letters and numbers. Correctly write the falling symbol before it hits the ground.
  Controls: Use your stylus to write the characters in the Graffiti area.

- **HardBall** Like the classic game of Breakout, this game combines Ping-Pong and a destructible brick wall. Actually, HardBall is extremely addictive. Keep hitting the ball to break away bricks. Certain bricks deliver extra balls or extra paddles, and you win by eliminating all the bricks from each screen.

Controls: Use either of the left buttons to move the paddle left and either of the right buttons to move the paddle right. The scroll button launches new balls.

■ **MineHunt**   Find all the mines hidden in the grid using your powers of logic and deduction. Each empty square reveals how many mines it is touching. Win by finding all the mines without getting blown up.
Controls: Reveal a square by tapping it; if you suspect a mine is under a square, mark it by pressing the scroll button and tapping.

■ **Puzzle**   This is like the annoying moving-square puzzle that you always won at school carnivals. Win by changing the order of the squares into the proper pattern.
Controls: Tap the square you want to move into an empty spot.

■ **SubHunt**   This game requires you to sink a vast armada of submarines by dropping depth charges overboard, all while avoiding their torpedoes. Win by sinking those subs without getting sunk yourself.
Controls: Move your ship left or right (to dodge torpedoes and get a better bead on subs) with the Date Book and Memo Pad buttons for left and right, respectively. Drop depth charges off the left and right end of your ship using the Address Book and To Do List buttons.

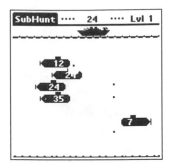

Playing IR Games

As we've already mentioned, infrared-capable games are a cool way to pass the time when you are traveling with another person who uses a Palm OS device. A variety of IR games are available in a variety of genres—action and board games being the most popular. To connect two handhelds, start the game on both handhelds and tap the Connect or Start button. You need to follow ordinary beaming rules—that is, you must be close enough to receive the beam, but not too close.

If your opponent doesn't have a copy of the game you want to play, beam it. Many IR games can be beamed, even if they're commercial products. If they're commercial, then the beamed copy will often work in conjunction with the one from which it was beamed or it'll work for a short period of time, like two weeks.

Here are some common IR games:

■ **PalmGun** This silly little game is more of a test for your IR port than anything else. Shoot your Visor opponent four times before he shoots you by pressing the scroll button while aiming the Visor.

■ **IR Pong** This is a modern version of the old Ping-Pong game with annoying obstacles in between the two players to obstruct the ball's travel. A great way for two people to pass the time.

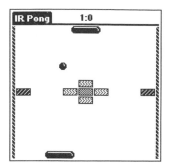

- **CodeFinder**   Remember Mastermind? CodeFinder is akin to that old tabletop game. Two players play via IR to crack each others' code.
- **IRBattleship**   The classic battleship game is available in IR format. Try to sink your opponent's ships and your torpedoes are sent to the other Palm device via IR. If you don't have an IR opponent available, you can also play this game in single player format.

NOTE   *All these games are available from www.palmgear.com.*

Playing Text Adventures

Remember Zork? How about Douglas Adams's *Hitchhikers Guide to the Galaxy* text adventure? Trinity? All these games were popular 15 years ago, at the dawn of the modern personal computer age. Text adventures put you in a text-based world, with flowing narratives and extensive text-based descriptions of your surroundings. When it was time to make your hero do something, you typed instructions into your PC at a text prompt. The computer then moved you along through the story based on your decisions. These games were often fiendishly clever, composed largely of logic puzzles and intellectual challenges.

So why are we telling you all this? Text adventures are long-lost icons for the museum, right? Not quite. Text adventures have made something of a comeback in the last few years, largely because handheld PCs like the Visor are an ideal format for playing them. And though their name has changed with the times—they're now often called Interactive Fiction instead of Text Adventures—they are still a lot of fun to play. No gamer would consider her Visor complete without one or two interactive fiction games installed for a rainy day at the airport (see Figure 20-3).

Enabling Interactive Fiction Files

You can find dozens, if not hundreds, of interactive fiction titles on the Internet. But these files are not playable all by themselves—they usually come encoded in something called *Z-Code*. Like a spreadsheet or document file, a Z-Code file is useless without the appropriate reader app. In this case, you need a program called Pilot-Frotz (or Frotz for short). Install Frotz, and you can play any interactive fiction games you find and transfer to your Visor.

Frotz essentially gives you the same experience as if you had played these text adventures 15 years ago. It displays the game's text on the screen and provides you with a text prompt in which to enter your next move. When you start the game, you see the Frotz list view, along with any games you currently have installed. To play a game, tap its name, and then tap the Play button.

```
Endless Stair
>look
Endless Stair
You are at the bottom of a seemingly
endless stair, winding its way upward
beyond your vision. An eerie light,
coming from all around you, casts
strange shadows on the walls. To the
south is a dark and winding trail.
Your old friend, the brass lantern, is at
your feet.

>
```

FIGURE 20-3   Interactive fiction combines good old-fashioned story telling with a need to solve puzzles and help the protagonist win the game

From there, you are taken to the game view, where you actually play the game. Unlike those early text adventures, Frotz gives you a few graphical tools that make these games easier to play. Here's how to use Frotz:

■   If the game displays a long text description, you might see the word MORE to indicate more text is after this pause. Tap the screen to continue.

> **"Detective"**
> An Interactive MiSTing
> By C.E. Forman
> (ceforma@rs6000.cmp.ilstu.edu)
> Created using Unix Inform 5.5
> Original AGT version by Matt Barringer
> Release 101 / Serial number 950814 /
> Inform v1502 Library 5/11
>
> **<< Chief's Office >>**
> You are standing in the Chief's office.
> He is telling you
> **<MORE>**

■   To enter your text command, write it in the Graffiti box.

■   You can display a list of common verbs and nouns by tapping the right-half of the Visor screen (not the Graffiti area) in any spot where there is no text. Instead of writing **Look**, for instance, tap for the menu and tap the word "Look."

> **<< Chief's Office >>**
>
> TOM: Tonight, on "The X-Files!"
>
> "Yessir!" You reply. He han | USER LIST
> sheet of paper. | Look
> Once you have read it, go | Examine
> west. | Read
> | Inventory.
> | Take
> It is a white sheet of paper | Take all
> | Drop
> MIKE: Thanks for clearing | Drop all
> | Put
> >|

20

■ You can tap any word in the story and that word appears on the text prompt line. Thus, you can assemble your command from the menu and words already onscreen instead of writing it all from scratch with Graffiti.

■ If you want your character to move, tap any blank space on the left half of the Visor screen. You'll see a map window. Tap the desired compass direction. You'll also see icons to Enter, Exit, and to go up or down stairs.

You can add custom words and phrases to the word list. Enter the desired word or phrase on the text prompt and select it with your stylus. Then choose List | Add from the menu. To see custom words, open the list menu, and then tap the first entry, User List.

When you finish playing a game, your position in the game is automatically saved when you leave the app. If you want to switch to another title, choose File | Force Quit to go back to the list view to choose another game. If you do that, though, your position in the current game will be lost.

Cheating with Maps

Some interactive fiction titles come with extras—like maps of the game area or walkthroughs of specific puzzles. These can be handy to have, but you need another tool to use them—an image viewer. Several image viewers are around, and it doesn't matter much which one you use. See Chapter 23 for a look at image-viewing software but, for the time being, we recommend a program like FireViewer. Any images on your Visor (including ones associated with a specific game) appear in the FireViewer list view when you start the program.

Finding Interactive Fiction Titles

Interactive Fiction titles aren't hard to find. In fact, one Web site has done an outstanding job of amassing all the most popular titles currently available. Visit www.fortunecity.com/underworld/rpg/22 for a fairly comprehensive list of games available for download.

Getting Started with Text Adventures

So, you want to try your hand at interactive fiction, but that text prompt is a little too intimidating? What on Earth are you supposed to write in there? How will the Visor know what you're trying to say? Fear not, because entering commands in a text adventure isn't too hard. You can enter only a verb—like **Look**—or a complete sentence, like **Pick up the compass**. Each game has something called a *parser* that's designed to decrypt your input. If the parser can't figure out what you meant, it says so. Here's a list of common commends you can use in almost any game.

Directions

- Compass points are frequently used. North, south, east, west, or any combination, like northeast or southwest. You can also use one and two-letter abbreviations, like *n* and se.

- Also: Up, down, in, out, enter, and exit.

Looking Around

- The old-reliable command is simply "look."

- You can combine "look" with anything that makes sense: Look up, look down, look inside, look through.

Action Verbs

- Push, pull, open, close, take, pick up, pump, give, swim, turn, screw, burn . . .dozens, if not hundreds, of working verbs are out there.

- When you deal with more than one object, you can use the word All, as in "Take all the coins."

Make sentences

You have to combine nouns and verbs into complete sentences to accomplish much in these games. Manipulating objects is the name of the game and the way to solve the puzzles. Try:

- Take the money
- Pick up the compass
- Read the book
- Put the pickles in the jar

- Look in the box
- Open the envelope
- Close the gate with the red key

Using the Visor as Dice

If you like to play board games in the real world, you might be interested in using your Visor as a virtual pair of dice. After all, the Visor is harder to lose (we always misplace the dice that go with our board games). Several apps are available, but one of the best is called DicePro. This program has pages and pages of dice available onscreen—you can configure different dice with any number of sides from 4 to 100, and you can roll dice in any combination. The program also has templates for a large number of role-playing games.

Games Worth Trying

The best part about the Visor is it's so easy to try out new software. Most programs are just a download away and they're easy to uninstall later if you get tired of them. Even if you download a commercial application, you can probably still try it out—the vast majority of commercial software has a trial period or simply annoys you with reminders to register. If you like it, buy it. If not, delete the game to make room for something you really do want. In the following section, we've assembled our picks of entertainment software you should try out for yourself.

NOTE   *Every one of these games can be found at www.palmgear.com. To look for more games on the site, search by keyword (type a term like "golf" into the search field). Or, find the Software section in the site's navigation bar and click the browse link. From there, you can select one of the gaming categories and search there. The site has perhaps five alternate games for every example listed here, so go wild and have fun with your Visor!*

How to ... Download Games from PalmGear

All of the games in this chapter can be downloaded from their author's Web site (listed at the end of the chapter) or found at our favorite Web site, PalmGear H.Q. To download and use a game from PalmGear, do this:

1. Visit PalmGear.com on your computer's Web browser.

2. Enter the name of the game in the PalmGear search box and click the Search button. Alternately, you can browse for games by clicking the Browse link under the Software heading in the navigation bar.

3. Click the Zip or Sit button to download the file.

4. Extract the game (PRC) file from the Zip or Sit file and drag it into the Install Tool.

5. HotSync to add the program to your Visor.

Card and Board Games

Card and board games are the most basic and often the most fun entertainment apps to have on the road. They are easy to play, don't require quick reflexes, and are easy to figure out. These games also make the best transition to the small Visor screen. They're like having a deck of cards in your pocket all the time.

- ■ **Blackjack**   Play traditional games of 21 with this rendition for the Visor. The game knows several variations of Blackjack and can keep you happily entertained for quite a while. The best part is you won't go broke playing it.

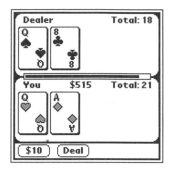

- ■ **Crosswords**   This is a Visor version of Scrabble, complete with a scoreboard and timer. This game is quite flexible—you can play with a basic English dictionary or, for a more challenging computer opponent, use larger dictionaries to give the Visor more options. You can also play against up to four humans.

- ■ **Vexed**   This infuriatingly addictive game is about as good as puzzle games get. The premise is simple—move blocks around to get identical ones to touch and annihilate each other, thus clearing the board. The execution is fiendishly difficult, though, and that's what makes this game so cool. There are 60 levels in this game, and neither Dave nor Rick could get past the halfway point.

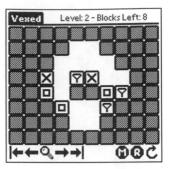

- **YahtC** Every computer has a version of YahtC, and the Visor is no different. This game is a good implementation of a parlor game classic.

- **Golf Solitaire** Like the game of golf (the one with the clubs and balls), the goal of Golf Solitaire is to get the lowest score. Clear cards from the columns at the top of the screen by playing them in sequence on the pile. The number of cards left at the end is your score and the lower, the better. This addictive game features nifty sound effects, a leaderboard to show the ten best scores, selectable pro/amateur rules, and commendable graphics.

■ **Pocket Chess**   Play chess against the Visor or another human. The game has several levels of difficulty and an 80-move opening library. If you want to, you can even watch the Visor play itself. Great for beginner and intermediate players.

Arcade-Style Games

If you're looking for something to do with your trigger finger, arcade games are the answer. These include old standbys like PacMac, Asteroids, and Graviton. The key to remember, though, is that your Visor isn't a Game Boy. Take care of the buttons or you'll be buying a new Visor.

■ **CuePert**   Q*Bert was a coin-op classic, a nonviolent game in which you made a little green guy hop around a pyramid for points. We never really understood it, but it was fun. Anyway, CuePert is the Visor equivalent, minus the quirky green guy—now he's just a little ball.

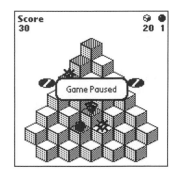

■ **PacMan**   No Visor is complete without the game that made coin-ops popular. The Visor implementation of PacMan is quite good, a faithful reproduction of the original game.

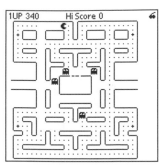

■ **Mulg**   Although it has a strange name, Mulg is one of the best Visor games we've ever seen. Guide a ball through a trap-infested maze. It comes with lots of levels and a level editor, and you can find about 50 new levels online to add to your collection.

■ **Fire!**   Can you catch the falling people? There's a raging fire and you're holding the net as civilians flee skyscrapers the hard way. It's entertaining in the style of old 1980s arcade games.

■ **Pipeline Perils**   This is an addictive time waster based on an old game for Amiga and Atari PCs. You play a plumber who has to lay pipe from one end of the screen to the other before the water starts flowing. It becomes challenging when you realize you have essentially a random assortment of pipes and connectors.

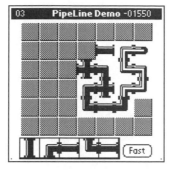

■ **Graviton**   If you played games like Oids or Thrust, you'll feel right at home with Graviton. You have a ship that's being yanked around by gravity forces. Control your ship, shoot enemy forces, and collect energy blobs. It's that simple. Oh, that's right— don't hit the walls and obstacles that appear onscreen.

Action and Strategy Games

The Visor may not be a great platform for strategy games (the screen is awfully small) but there are a few games around that can keep you planning and strategizing while you're sitting in the airport.

■ **Galactic Realms**   This game is a must-see. Graphically one of the most advanced games for the Visor as this book was being written, Realms is a real-time strategy game in which you need to mine asteroids for materials, build a space fleet, and fight an alien enemy. The game uses transparency and dour shades of gray for a very cool look.

20

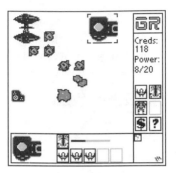

■ **Doomling**   Wolfenstein 3-D was the game that essentially started the first person shooter action game craze on the PC—from there we've seen Quake, Duke Dukem 3-D, Half Life, and a million others. Doomling is Wolfenstein 3-D ported to the Visor. If you enjoyed Wolfenstein, you definitely need to try out Doomling.

■ **Dragon Bane**   If you liked D&D graphical adventures from the early days of DOS, you'll love this. Dragon Bane is a 3-D graphical adventure in which you travel from towns into dungeons. You have puzzles to solve and bad guys to kill in four-shade graphics.

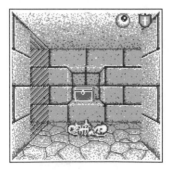

- **RayGin**   RayGin is a first-person shooter for the Visor that features 3-D graphics and fast frame rates. The graphics aren't amazing, but it is a rather unique game for this handheld format. Worth a look.

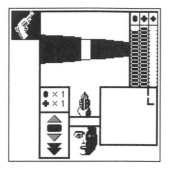

- **Tiger Woods PGA Tour Golf**   A golf game on the Visor? You bet—and it's from Electronic Arts, a major game company. This game includes three courses and most of the basic features you've seen in desktop-based golf games. Graphically, it's impressive (for a Visor) and it's good enough that you'll want to have it with you for those long plane flights. (For more information, see Chapter 15.)

- **Ancient Red**   If you like games like Dragon Bane (listed earlier in this section), you need to try Ancient Red, one of the "next wave" of Visor games. It's a large game with excellent four-shade graphics, a huge world (with over 20,000 screens), and wonderful action and animation.

■ **SimCity**   Build a town from scratch, complete with roads, buildings, utilities, and recreation facilities. It's just like the original SimCity, except this one fits on your Visor. It's the official version from Electronic Arts.

Where to Find It

Web Site	Address	What's There
Nico Mak Computing	www.winzip.com	WinZip compression/uncompression tool for Windows
Aladdin Systems	www.aladdinsys.com	Stuffit Expander compression/ uncompression tool for the Mac
PalmGear H.Q.	www.palmgear.com	Games for the Palm
Alien Hunter	www.geocities.com/ SiliconValley/Way/2367	Frotz, the Z-Code interpreter for interactive fiction games
FirePad	www.firepad.com	Image Viewer III
Interactive Fiction	www.fortunecity.com/ underworld/rpg/22	Interactive fiction titles
Rival Game Labs	www.geocities.com/ TimesSquare/Realm/9565	DicePro

Chapter 21

Graffiti Enhancements and Alternatives

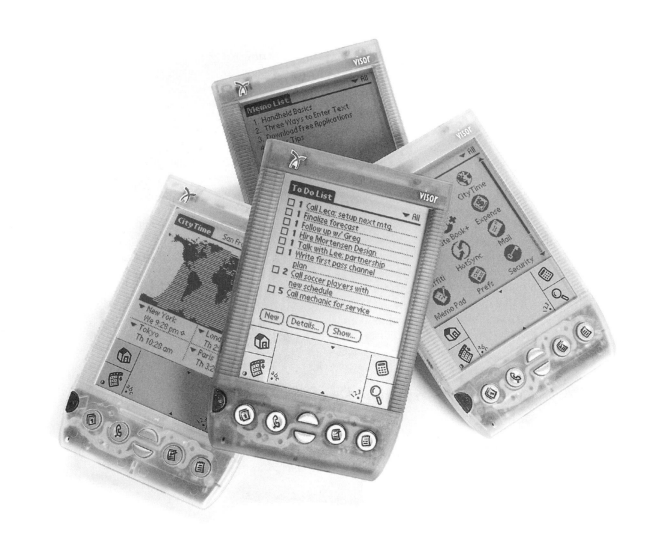

How to...

- Enter data using your thumbs
- Turn the Graffiti area into a keyboard
- Make the Graffiti area more functional
- Replace Graffiti with a different handwriting recognition engine
- Replace the built-in keyboard with other keyboards
- Write anywhere on the Visor's screen
- Take advantage of "digital ink"
- Write faster with word-completion software
- Tweak Graffiti so it's more responsive to your handwriting
- Improve Graffiti recognition without third-party software

Many of us have a love/hate relationship with Graffiti, the handwriting-recognition software used by Visors and other Palm OS devices. Some users take to it right away, finding it a speedy and convenient method for entering data. Others just plain don't like it or can't get the knack. It is for those folks (who have absolutely nothing to be ashamed of, really) that we present this chapter on Graffiti enhancements and alternatives.

Suppose you don't mind Graffiti, but find it too slow to keep up with your thought processes. Or too inflexible to recognize your particular style of handwriting. The answer could lie in one of many available "Graffiti assistants," which not only can speed data entry, but also make your handwriting more recognizable.

Maybe you've been using the onscreen keyboard as an alternative to Graffiti, but find it too small or cumbersome. There are keyboard alternatives as well, some of them quite radical. And maybe you're just ready to give Graffiti the heave-ho and try some other means of data entry. Full-blown replacements are out there, and they let you say good-bye to Graffiti forever.

We've divided all these products into four categories: overlays, which actually cover the Graffiti area; assistants, which give Graffiti a helping hand; keyboards, which substitute for the stock onscreen keyboard; and replacements, which send Graffiti packing.

Overlays: Wallpaper for the Graffiti Area

One of our favorite tips for Visor users is to apply a piece of Scotch 811 Magic Tape to the Graffiti area. It not only protects it from scratches, but adds a tackier writing surface that many people find preferable to the slippery screen. A new breed of plastic overlays takes this idea several steps further, redefining the Graffiti area's functionality and protecting it at the same time.

How Overlays Work

The entire Graffiti area—buttons and all—is sensitive to pressure. That's why when you tap a button or write something with your stylus, your Visor responds. The overlays simply take advantage of this fact, using special software to reprogram the Visor's responses to your taps and strokes. The products take different approaches to this, as you see in our overview of each.

An Introduction to FitalyStamp

Before we discuss Textware Solutions' FitalyStamp, we have to tell you about Textware Solutions' Fitaly Keyboard—a replacement for the built-in keyboard that's discussed later in this chapter. It's a fairly unusual product, but with practice it can increase your data-entry speed.

The problem with onscreen keyboards like Fitaly (and the standard keyboard) is they occupy a major chunk of the viewable area of the Visor's screen. FitalyStamp offers a solution: an overlay that moves the keyboard from the screen to the Graffiti area.

As you can see from this photo, the key layout is quite unusual. The idea is to minimize the distance your stylus needs to travel (more on that later in this chapter, when we look at the Fitaly Keyboard). But FitalyStamp also provides cursor-control buttons, numbers, symbols—even the Visor's ShortCut and Command functions. Thus, while there's a learning curve involved with the keyboard itself, there's also a lot of convenience. And FitalyStamp is a colorful, attractive addition to your Visor—an important consideration for those who prize aesthetics.

Put Your Thumbs to Work

ThumbType is a Japanese import that not only does away with Graffiti, but also does away with your stylus. This original and inventive overlay uses a Braille-like keyboard that responds to thumb-presses, effectively enabling you to type with your pollices. It also makes for a very different handheld computing experience (see Figure 21-1).

As you can see in Figure 21-1, ThumbType uses a QWERTY-style layout. Each letter has a little raised nub that you press lightly with a finger (thumbs aren't mandatory—if you place your Visor on a flat surface, you may prefer to use your index fingers). As with a traditional keyboard, pressing SHIFT activates each key's secondary function (usually a number or symbol). Pressing SHIFT a second time lets you produce a capital letter, and pressing it a third time activates the Caps-Lock.

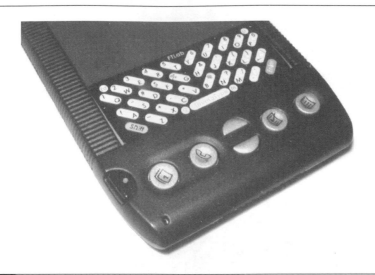

FIGURE 21-1 The revolutionary ThumbType keyboard covers the Graffiti area with a Braille-like overlay

Notice that ThumbType has no Applications, Menu, Calc, or Find buttons, despite the fact that it covers them. Indeed, what if you need access to the Graffiti area to enter a ShortCut or a copy/paste command? Must you pull off the overlay and disable the software driver? Nope: ThumbType has a smarter solution. When you tap the little '*g*' next to the space bar, a "virtual" Graffiti area appears on the screen:

Now you can access the Applications screen, calculator, and so forth, or even write with Graffiti strokes like you normally would. Clever!

Installing ThumbType is a simple matter of loading a software driver onto your Visor, and then pressing the self-adhesive overlay onto the Graffiti area. After four simple presses to calibrate the keyboard, it's ready to run.

It's normal to be dubious about ThumbType, which looks too small and awkward to actually work. But it does, and not at all badly. We found we could type a bit faster with ThumbType than with the built-in keyboard—but we were a bit faster still with Graffiti. Nevertheless, this is an innovative and practical alternative, one that Graffiti detractors may find preferable.

Have Your Keyboard and Graffiti, Too

If you often find yourself hopping between Graffiti and the built-in keyboard, and wishing there was an easier way to do so, Softava's Silkyboard is the answer. This overlay covers the Graffiti area with a large, easy-to-read QWERTY keyboard that enables full-time tap-typing, but also lets you use Graffiti without having to change modes.

Silkyboard's key advantage is that it provides access to a keyboard without sacrificing any screen estate. Its secondary advantage is protection of the Graffiti area. Working with the overlay is as simple as tapping the letter or number you want to enter, and holding down your stylus for a "long tap" when you want a capital letter or punctuation mark. Accessing Applications, Menu, Calc, and Find requires a stroke instead of a tap, but that's just a matter of simple memorization. Indeed, Silkyboard's learning curve is slight. And, if you get mixed up, you can go back to using Graffiti just by drawing the strokes on top of the letters. (The overlay even has the two little arrows that divide the letter and number areas.)

A simple calibration routine is all that's required to set up the driver software, and a handy applicator strip is provided to make sure the overlay is applied without any air bubbles. If you prefer to write with a keyboard but don't want to give up Graffiti entirely, Silkyboard is a great best-of-both-worlds solution.

Make Graffiti Smarter

One of the most promising new overlays is TapPad, which doesn't try to replace or revamp Graffiti, but merely gives it a boost. As you can see in Figure 21-2, TapPad doesn't extend the

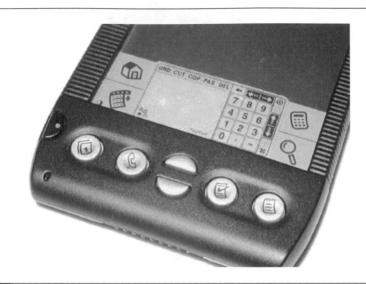

FIGURE 21-2   TapPad is one of our favorite overlays, leaving Graffiti alone for the most part but adding some much-needed shortcuts

full length of the Graffiti area—it covers only the input area, leaving the four buttons visible. This in itself is a plus, as it doesn't force you to learn a new way of accessing these very important buttons.

TapPad's benefits can be summed up thusly:

- Protection of the Graffiti area and a tackier surface that makes handwriting more comfortable.

- The addition of a keypad in the numeric section, thus enabling you to enter addresses and phone numbers much more quickly (and more easily, in our opinion).

- One-tap buttons for six commonly used commands: undo, cut, copy, paste, delete, and backspace. (Interestingly, Graffiti doesn't even have a delete stroke, which erases characters to the right of the cursor. It only offers backspace, which erases characters to the left.) The undo button alone is worth the price of admission.

- Left-right and up-down scroll buttons for easier cursor movement and document navigation. If you've ever tried to place your cursor in between two letters, you know what a struggle it can be. The left-right buttons move your cursor one space at a time, greatly simplifying its placement. And the up-down scroll buttons are a major improvement over the Visor's skinny scroll bars and tiny arrows.

Our Favorite Graffiti Aids

Rick: Of all the Graffiti alternatives and assistants in this chapter, I'm quite partial to TapPad. That's because I'm already quite adept with Graffiti and, therefore, don't want to learn a new system of data entry. TapPad protects the handwriting area, provides a rougher writing surface (which I quite like), and adds one-tap shortcuts for functions like undo and copy. It's the perfect Graffiti enhancement.

Dave: Graffiti alternatives? Why? The Visor is pretty much defined by Graffiti, and I can't imagine trying to tack on some other kind of input system—it's like wearing cleats to tap dancing class (not that I'd know anything about that . . .). Graffiti works pretty well all by itself, and you won't catch me writing with the TapPad, T9, or any of those other add-ons. Oh, and stop kicking your ball into my backyard.

Graffiti Replacements: A Software Solution

Love the idea of Graffiti, but don't like Graffiti itself? We understand—some of those special characters are just plain tough (Dave can't make a "*j*" to save his life, and who can remember the stroke for "%"?). CIC's Jot, born for Windows CE devices but eventually ported to the Palm OS, replaces Graffiti with a more natural—and familiar—character set.

And that's just one of Jot's advantages. It also frees you from the Graffiti area, enabling you to write anywhere on your Visor's screen. Even better, it leaves a trail of "digital ink" beneath your stylus tip, so you can see what you're writing as you write, as with a pen and paper. Finally, Jot recognizes a variety of cursive characters, handy for those who mix script with print. Tricky Graffiti letters like "*q*," "*v*," and "*y*"are much easier to make with Jot.

The problem with Jot is the way it handles punctuation. Like Graffiti, it has an "extended mode" that you access by drawing a vertical line. Then you write the desired symbol (such as a period or an exclamation point), and another vertical line to return to letter mode. This is a rather slow and awkward method, especially for frequently used punctuation like the period. In Graffiti, all it takes is a double-tap.

Still, Jot's more traditional character set makes writing easier, particularly for new Visor users who won't have to unlearn all of Graffiti's special strokes. Not sure this is the Graffiti alternative for you? Then try before you buy. As with most Palm OS software, there's a demo you can download for a test drive.

Keys, Please

Like to tap-type? Many users prefer the built-in keyboard to Graffiti, if only because there's no real learning curve to it. Of course, there are software developers who think they can do the keyboard one better, as evidenced by Tegic Communications' T9 and Textware Solutions' Fitaly Keyboard.

T9 Is Fine (for Some)

Born a data-entry system for cellular phones, the T9 keyboard (short for "text on nine keys") supplants the built-in keyboard with a telephone-like letter pad (see Figure 21-3). While it might seem unlikely that you could construct words with such a setup, the software makes it possible. And because the keys are so large, the T9 is a boon for those with poor eyesight.

So, how does tapping these oversize, multiletter keys make words? A linguistic database that's part of the software helps to guess the word you're typing. To write "palm," for instance, you tap the "pqrs" key, then "abc," then "jkl," and then "mno." If a particular combination of keys results in multiple acceptable choices (as with "ball" and "call," for instance), you simply tap the desired word from a displayed list.

As you can see in Figure 21-3, you can switch to numeric, symbol, and international key sets by tapping the appropriate button at the bottom of the screen. When you tap Done, the T9 hides itself just like the built-in keyboard. Thus, it's not a Graffiti replacement, but a keyboard replacement. In fact, the Graffiti area remains "live" even while the T9 is running, so you can easily switch to handwriting if you want.

While the T9 certainly works as advertised, we're not convinced too many users will want to switch to it. For one thing, punctuation is a major pain—you have to switch modes just to enter a comma. But practice makes perfect, and users who have trouble seeing the standard keyboard's tiny keys may find the T9 a welcome alternative.

QWERTY, Meet Fitaly

The Fitaly Keyboard (so named for the layout of its keys, like QWERTY) proceeds from the assumption that the Visor's own built-in keyboard requires too much hand movement. Because it's so wide, you have to move your stylus quite a bit, leading to slow and often inaccurate data

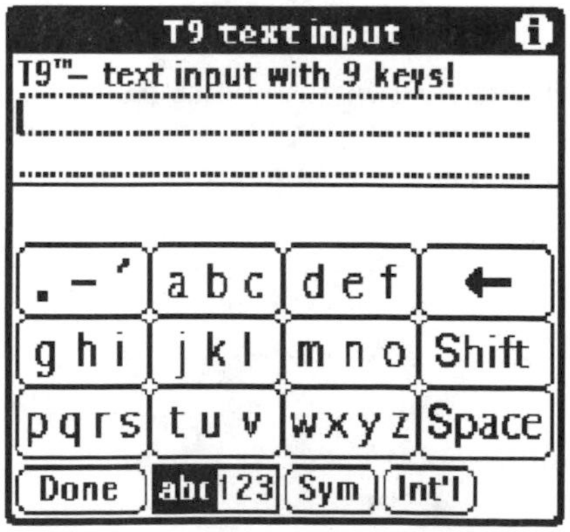

FIGURE 21-3   The T9 keyboard—remind you of any telephones you've seen lately?

entry. The Fitaly Keyboard arranges letters in a tightly knit group designed to minimize stylus travel. Hence, you should be able to tap-type much more quickly.

Clearly, Fitaly represents a radical departure from the standard QWERTY keyboard and, therefore, has a high learning curve. Make that a high practice curve: it could take you several days to master the layout, and even then you may decide you don't like it. The moderate speed gain may not offset the difficulty in learning an entirely new keyboard.

On the other hand, Fitaly is much more practical than the stock built-in keyboard, in part because it makes most common punctuation readily available, without the need to shift modes (or even tap the SHIFT key). And when you do access the numeric mode (done simply by tapping the "123" button), you gain access to a number of extended characters (including fractions, the Euro symbol, and more):

If you like the idea of Fitaly but hate sacrificing a big chunk of the screen, you might want to check out FitalyStamp—a plastic overlay that moves the keyboard right on top of the Graffiti area. It's covered in "An Introduction to FitalyStamp," earlier in the chapter.

What About a Real Keyboard?

Thumbs, overlays, styluses—whatever you use to enter data on your Visor, it won't be as fast as an actual keyboard. Fortunately, actual keyboards do exist for Visors, in the form LandWare's GoType and Think Outside's Stowaway. To find out all about them, see Chapter 24.

Give Graffiti a Helping Hand

Here's a novel idea: rather than try to built a better Graffiti than Graffiti, why not just cut down on the number of letters necessary to write a word? Or, make it so you can write anywhere on the screen, instead of just in the Graffiti area? How about tweaking the recognition engine so it's more accommodating to your handwriting? These are among the goals of Graffiti assistants: software tools that make life with Graffiti a little easier.

Was This the Word You Were Looking For?

Remember the old game show *Name That Tune*? The host would describe a song, and the contestant would say, "I can name that tune in *X* notes." Imagine if Graffiti could adopt that precept, guessing the word or phrase you're writing as you write it. By the time you'd entered, say, the "*e*" in "competition," the software would have figured out the rest of the word, thereby saving you six additional pen-strokes.

That's the appeal of CIC's WordComplete, a utility that helps you write faster by helping you write less. As you enter characters, a box containing possible word matches appears—if you spy the word you're after, just tap it. The more letters you enter, the closer you'll get to the correct word (if it's in the software's database).

Obviously, for little words like "the" and "to," the software won't help much. But for longer words, they can indeed save you some scribbling. And WordComplete lets you add your own words and/or short phrases to its database, which can definitely save you time in the long run. Let's take a look at its features and operation.

WordComplete

Once you install WordComplete on your Visor, run the program and tap the Enable WordComplete check box. A number of options appear:

■ **Suggest words after**   After how many letters should the software start suggesting words? The default is two, but you can make it anywhere between one and four.

■ **Display at most**   How many matches should the software display at a time? You have to experiment to decide your preference. Obviously, more matches means a greater likelihood of your desired word appearing, but it takes a tiny bit longer to glance through a longer list.

■ **Show word box near**   Where should the suggestion box pop up—next to the cursor or near the bottom of the screen? We think the former is the most practical, as it cuts down on stylus travel.

■ **Words with at least**   What's the minimum word length that WordComplete should attempt to guess? Three letters? Four? You can make your selection here.

■ **Insert a space after word**   Leave this box checked if you want the software to automatically add a space after you tap a word. Most of the time this is helpful, except when you're about to end a sentence with a punctuation mark. Then you have to draw a backspace stroke.

■ **Add words by double tap**   WordComplete supports the use of a custom dictionary to which you can add your own words. With this option checked, it's as simple as double-tapping a word with your stylus, and then tapping the "Add" option from the little box that appears. (You hear a beep confirming that the word has successfully been added.)

■ **Custom Dictionary**   Tap this button to manually add words to the software's dictionary. Although the aforementioned double-tap method limits you to adding one word at a time, here you can add multiple words (such as proper names) or even short phrases.

NOTE   *If you do add proper names to the dictionary, take note that they're case-sensitive. That means if you add "Rick Broida," you have to use a capital "R" if you want WordComplete to show the name while you're writing.*

Goodbye, Graffiti Area!

Ever notice that the Graffiti area is kind of, well, small? Most of us aren't used to writing in such a confined space, and that alone can be a source of Graffiti contention. Fortunately, a pair of virtually identical utilities can liberate your stylus from that tiny box, effectively turning the entire Visor screen into one big Graffiti area.

CIC's RecoEcho and Inkverse's ScreenWrite (see Figure 21-4) enable you to write—using Graffiti characters—anywhere on the screen. What's more, they leave a trail of "digital ink" beneath your stylus tip, which goes a long way toward helping you produce more accurate characters. You see what you write as you write it, just as you would with a pen on paper.

Although they function similarly, RecoEcho and ScreenWrite are different in a few key ways. The former, for instance, is a standalone utility, while the latter requires HackMaster (see Chapter 18). Let's take a look at how each one works.

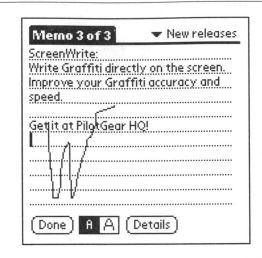

FIGURE 21-4   ScreenWrite, shown here, shows your pen-strokes in "digital ink" (which disappears after you complete the stroke)

RecoEcho

The easier-to-use and more polished of the two programs, RecoEcho is probably the best choice for novices and mainstream Visor users. After you launch the program, you simply tap a check box to enable it. Then there are just three simple options to set:

- **Write in full screen**   If, for some reason, you don't want to write on the screen itself (but just in the Graffiti area), uncheck this box. You still see your pen-strokes as you write, provided the next option is still checked.

- **Show ink**   If you prefer not to see the trail of "ink" as you write, uncheck this box.

- **Ink width**   Choose 1 for a thin trail of ink, 2 for a thicker trail. This is just a matter of personal preference.

When RecoEcho is activated, you see a large arrow at the top of the screen. This designates an invisible line separating the letter and number sides, just like in the standard Graffiti area. Now, write on the screen as you normally would, and presto: you're free to write as large as you like.

ScreenWrite

As previously noted, ScreenWrite is a Hack, meaning it's accessed and activated via HackMaster (see Chapter 18). As such, and because it offers more sophisticated options than RecoEcho, we recommend it as the better tool for power users. It also comes with very little documentation; the included *readme* file barely scratches the surface of installation and use.

To activate the software, simply load HackMaster, check the box next to ScreenWrite, and then tap the plus sign to bring up the setup and options screens. Unlike RecoEcho, ScreenWrite lets you adjust the delay time for handwriting versus screen-related functions. For instance, if you want to select a few words of text or put a check mark in a box, you must hold the stylus on the screen for an extra second, so ScreenWrite processes the action normally (instead of interpreting it as a handwriting gesture). Using the Delay slider, you can alter the length of time before ScreenWrite relinquishes control of the screen.

TIP *If you find the delay is too short, meaning you're unable to write your characters fast enough, increase the delay by moving the slider to the right.*

When you tap the Options button at the bottom of the setup screen, you're taken to two subsequent screens where you can tweak various settings. A few words about the most important ones:

```
ScreenWrite options

 W  Options (1 of 2)

 ☐  Auto-capitalize letters in middle
 ☑  Auto-capitalize big letters
 ☑  Learn application preferences
 ☐  SelectHack workaround
 ☐  Japanese OS workaround
 Ink: ▼ 2 pixels wide

 ( Prev )        ( Next )
```

■ **Auto-capitalize letters in middle**   When this is checked, any letters that cross the invisible dividing line between the letter and number sides of the screen are automatically capitalized, thus saving you having to draw the Graffiti upstroke every time. This is handy and works just like a Hack called MiddleCapsHack (see Chapter 18).

■ **Auto-capitalize big letters**   Similar to the previous option, this one capitalizes any letter you write "big" (almost the full height of the screen).

■ **ScreenWrite on/off graffiti shortcut**   There will undoubtedly be times when you want to turn ScreenWrite on or off, but going back to HackMaster every time is a major hassle. Fortunately, you can set up a Graffiti shortcut stroke that acts as an on/off toggle. First, tap the menu next to Start to choose where the stroke should begin (the Calc button, a corner of the screen, and so forth), and then the End menu to choose where the stroke should end (same set of choices). Our preference: start with the Calc button and end with Find. Now, whenever you draw a line between the two, ScreenWrite is turned on or off.

ScreenWrite doesn't leave as thick or dark an ink trail as RecoEcho, and it doesn't come with the support of a big company (the author has a Frequently Asked Questions page on his site, but that's about the extent of the help you'll find). But it is the more powerful of the two tools, and registration is a mere $5.

Graffiti, Your Way

Finally, we come to the one product that really manhandles Graffiti, that says, "Look, can't you learn to understand *my* writing?" It is TealPoint Software's TealScript, a utility that lets you tweak Graffiti so it's more responsive to your hand, or replace it altogether with a customized character set.

If you're willing to battle one of the steepest learning curves we've encountered in a piece of Visor software, the benefits are truly worthwhile. TealScript works its wizardry through the use of custom profiles, which contain the Graffiti character set as you define it. In other words, you teach TealScript how you like to write, and it teaches Graffiti to accommodate your penmanship.

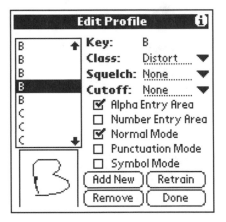

The letter *v* is a good example of how this works. Your profile can include the standard character—the one with the little tail we always forget to add—and a regular *v* that you added yourself. Similarly, instead of having to always write capitalized versions of letters like *R* and *B,* you can add lowercase versions.

As confusing as TealScript can be to work with, it's not totally out of the question for novice users. That's because it comes with an already-built profile that helps you overcome the most commonly miswritten Graffiti characters. So, right out of the box it's useful. And while TealScript may not be the friendliest program around, it's by far the best way to make Graffiti an ally instead of an obstacle.

How to ... Improve Graffiti Recognition

For all its quirks, Graffiti is actually an excellent handwriting-recognition tool. If you plan to stick with it, you can use these tips to improve accuracy:

- Write big. If your characters fill up the bulk of the Graffiti area, they're more likely to be accurately recognized.

- Don't write on an angle. Many of us do just that when writing with pen and paper, but that's poison to Graffiti. Keep your strokes straight.

- Take advantage of the built-in Graffiti Help application, which provides a graphical cheat-sheet for all Graffiti strokes. Go to Prefs | Buttons | Pen, and then choose Graffiti Help from the list of available options. Now, whenever you draw a line from the Graffiti area to the top of the Visor's screen, the Help applet appears.

- Having trouble with the letter *V*? Draw it backwards, starting from the right side and ending with the left. You needn't add the little tail (as with the standard Graffiti *V*), and the letter comes out perfectly every time.

- Having trouble with *B*? Forget trying to draw it Graffiti's way—just write the number 3 instead. Similarly, writing the number 6 gives you a good *G* every time.

- Start your *R* at the bottom of the letter instead of the top. That initial downstroke often produces the ShortCut symbol instead of an *R*.

Where to Find It

Web Site	Address	What's There
Textware Solutions	www.fitaly.com	Fitaly Keyboard, FitalyStamp
Softava	www.silkyboard.com	Silkyboard
MicroBurst	www.mburst.com	ThumbType
Brochu Shareware	www.tappad.com	TapPad
CIC	www.cic.com	Jot, RecoEcho, WordComplete
Tegic Communications	www.tegic.com	T9
Inkverse	www.inkverse.com	ScreenWrite
TealPoint Software	www.tealpoint.com	TealScript

Chapter 22

Building E-Book Libraries and Photo Albums

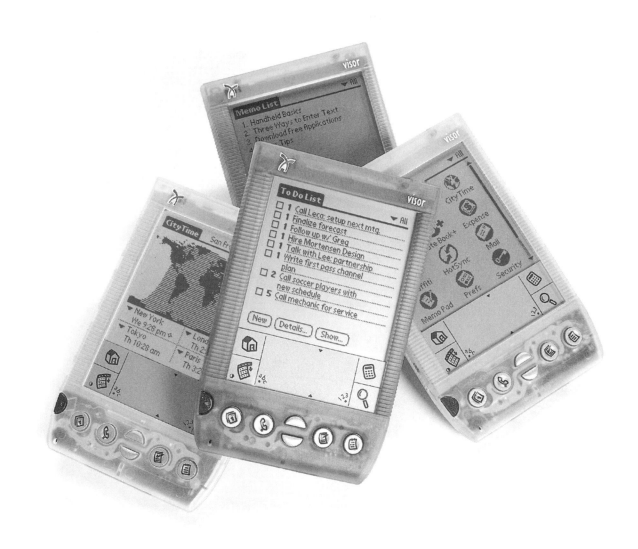

How to...

- Find electronic books (a.k.a. e-books)
- Make sure you have enough RAM for them
- Read e-books on your Visor
- Read in bed without disturbing your bunkmate
- Distinguish between public domain and commercial e-books
- Choose a Doc viewer
- Convert text files to the Doc format
- View photos and other images on your Visor
- Convert photos and image files to a Visor-viewable format
- Find street maps for your Visor

You know the future has arrived when a device the size of a Pop Tart can hold an entire Stephen King novel or the full contents of a photo album. Now that you've seen some of the minor miracles Visors can perform, it should come as little surprise that they're great for reading books and viewing images as well. No more must you overstuff your wallet with pictures of the kids and cats. Never again must you suffer through a coast-to-coast flight without a good book by your side.

Indeed, many users find that electronic books (a.k.a. e-books) are a major Visor perk. You can pay nothing at all and read hundreds of literary classics, or pay discounted prices for mainstream titles. And image-viewing software has become something of a hot property, now that Palm OS devices like the Visor have 16-grayscale screens. In this chapter, you learn everything you need to know about e-books and, for lack of a better term, e-photos.

An E-Book Love Affair

A while ago, Rick found himself on a train with nothing to do for several hours. Then he remembered he'd loaded an e-book on his Visor just before leaving home. He started reading, found the novel totally engrossing, and passed the time as happy as a clam. From that day forward, he vowed never to travel anywhere without an e-book. And when people ask him to explain what that little gadget is he's holding, he says it's a handheld PC—and an electronic library.

Build a Library of E-Books

Before Palm devices like the Visor came along, there existed on the Internet a growing collection of electronic books—mostly public-domain classic literature like Voltaire's *Candide* and Sir Arthur Conan Doyle's Sherlock Holmes stories. Because these works had already been converted to computer-readable text, why not copy them to Palm devices for reading anytime, anywhere?

In theory, one could simply paste the text into a memo. But users soon discovered a Memo Pad limitation that exists to this day: documents can be no larger than 4K (roughly 700 words), so even short stories were out. Hence the emergence of one of the very first third-party applications: Doc, a simple text viewer that had no length limitation (other than the amount of RAM in the handheld itself). Doc rapidly become a de facto standard, not just for e-books, but for documents created in desktop word processors and converted to Palm devices.

NOTE   *In this chapter, we mostly discuss the e-book aspect of Doc files. If you'd like to learn more about turning word processor documents into Doc files (and vice versa), see Chapter 17.*

Make Room for the Books

Before we delve into the details of finding, buying, and viewing e-books, we must alert you to the memory concerns associated with them. Specifically, e-books can be very large documents—one reason to consider buying the Visor Deluxe (which has 8MB of memory). Jules Verne's *The Mysterious Island,* for instance, takes a whopping 622K, while the infamous biography *Monica's Story* nabs 500K. If your Visor has only 2MB of RAM, you could wind up sacrificing a full 25 percent of it for just one e-book.

Fortunately, not all titles are quite so gargantuan. Most short stories are under 50K— even Stephen King's novel, *The Girl Who Loved Tom Gordon,* is a reasonable 226K. If you're particularly strapped for space, you can always try freeing some: delete infrequently used games and other applications; remove unwanted AvantGo channels; and clear out other e-books you've already read (no sense keeping them loaded).

TIP   *If, like many users, you find yourself totally enamored with e-books, you can turn to Springboard technology to build yourself an entire library of them—with no impact on the Visor's primary memory. Specifically, you could devote all or part of a Handspring 8MB Flash Module to your collection, thereby netting plenty of space for the books and leaving main memory free for other applications and data. Find out more about the Flash Module in Chapter 16.*

E-Books for Free, E-Books for Sale

There are dozens of online sources for e-books, both free and commercial. The former are works that are considered public domain: either their copyrights have expired (as in the case of classic literature), or they've been written and released by authors not seeking compensation. As you soon see, literally thousands of titles are available in the public domain, many of them already converted to the Doc format.

Commercial titles are not unlike what you'd buy in a bookstore: they've simply been converted to an electronic format and authorized for sale online. Notice we didn't mention Doc: most commercial e-books are created using a proprietary format, meaning that a special viewer is required. This is primarily to prevent unauthorized distribution—unlike actual books, commercial e-books aren't meant to be loaned out or given to others. When you buy one, you're effectively buying a license to read it on your Visor and only your Visor.

Find the Free Stuff

If there's one site that's synonymous with Doc files, it's MemoWare (www.memoware.com). Here you can find thousands of texts divided into categories such as business, history, travel, biography, sci-fi, and Shakespeare. Whether you're looking for a collection of Mexican recipes, a Zane Grey western, a sappy love poem, or a classic work by Dickens, this is the place to start. There's enough reading material here to last you decades, and the vast majority of it is free. (MemoWare is also affiliated with a few commercial sites that offer contemporary works for a small fee. More on those later in this chapter.)

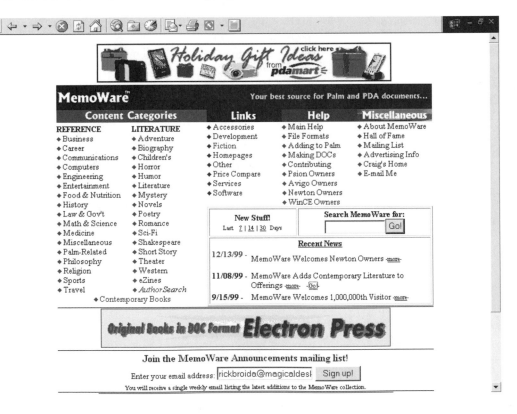

MemoWare offers a convenient search engine, so you can type in a title or keyword to quickly find what you're looking for. It also has links to other e-book sites, although none are as comprehensive. Finally, MemoWare provides numerous links to software programs (most for Windows, a couple for Mac) that turn computer documents into Doc files.

NOTE *As explained in Chapter 17, the Doc format is not to be confused with the ".doc" file extension used by Microsoft Word. The two are separate and not interchangeable (although utilities exist that will exchange documents between Visors and Word). To confuse matters further, Palm Doc files actually have a ".pdb" extension.*

Choose a Doc Viewer   Many people make this mistake: they download a bunch of nifty e-books from MemoWare (or wherever), load them onto their Visor, and then spend lots of time trying to figure out why they can't "see" their e-books. (Normally, when you install a piece of software, you see an icon for it.) The reason, of course, is they don't have a Doc viewer installed. Without one, there's no way to view Doc files.

Fortunately, there are plenty of Doc viewers out there, all of them reasonably priced (and a few of them free). How do you choose one? Well, they're all fairly similar, though some have features that others lack. We're partial to Cutting Edge Software's SmartDoc (see Figure 22-1), which lets you edit documents and compose new ones instead of just reading

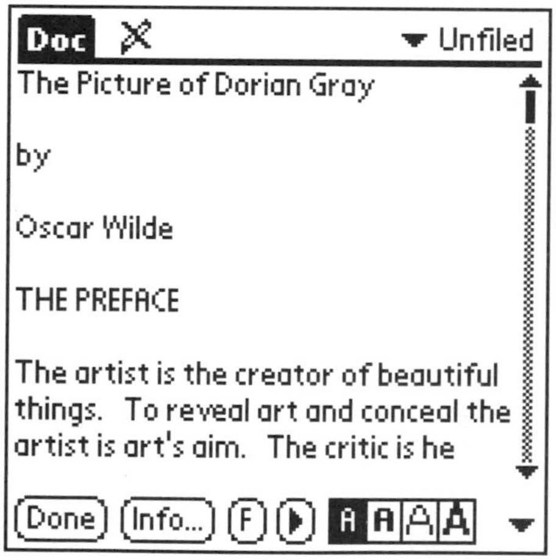

FIGURE 22-1   One of many available Doc readers, SmartDoc also lets you compose and edit documents

them. On the other hand, CSpotRun is free (and has a clever name). Here's a rundown of some of your other choices:

Doc Viewer	Noteworthy Features
CSpotRun	Free; supports auto-scrolling
iSilo	Supports HTML and text (.txt) files, as well as Doc files
QED	Doubles as a text editor; includes utility for converting Doc files back to Windows format
SmartDoc	Doubles as a text editor; supports autoscrolling and bookmarks; choice of four font sizes
TealDoc	Supports images and links between documents; advanced search options

NOTE   *All of these programs are available from sites like Handango and PalmGear H.Q.*

Make Your Own Docs   Not all e-books you find on the Internet will be in the necessary .pdb file format. Some may have filenames like *book.txt*, meaning they're just raw text. You can't install .txt files on your Visor, but you can convert them to .pdb files with relative ease. Here's how:

1. Download MakeDocW from PalmGear H.Q. or another Palm software site, and run the program. (Macintosh users should investigate MakeDocDD, which was still in beta testing at press time, but works much the same way.)

2. Choose the Conversion tab, and then click the Browse button.

3. Navigate to the text file you want to convert, click to highlight it, and then click Open.

4. If you want the converted file automatically installed on your Visor the next time you HotSync, make sure the Auto-Install box is checked and your Visor username appears in the pull-down menu next to it.

5. Click Convert.

Find the Commercial Stuff

The thing about public domain e-books is that most of them are, well, old. W. Somerset Maugham and Jack London are all well and good for catching up on the classics you promised yourself you'd read one day, but sometimes you just want a little Stephen King. Or Mary Higgins Clark. Or Captain Kirk. Fortunately, you can have them all on your Visor, provided you're willing to pay for them.

Peanutpress.com has long lead the charge in bringing contemporary, mainstream fiction and nonfiction to Palm OS devices. The company started in late 1998 with just a couple dozen lesser-known titles, but now offers hundreds of books from some well-known authors. Most of them are discounted by up to 30 percent, and you needn't take a special trip to the bookstore to get them (or wait a week for Amazon.com to deliver them). Here are some of the more prominent and popular titles available from Peanut Press:

Author	Title
Frank McCourt	*Angela's Ashes*
Stephen King	*The Girl Who Loved Tom Gordon*
Nicholas Sparks	*Message In A Bottle*
Diane Carey	*Star Trek: First Strike*
Laura Esquivel	*Like Water for Chocolate*
Robert Hartwell Fiske	*The Dictionary of Concise Writing*
Andrew Morton	*Monica's Story*
Piers Anthony	*Hope of Earth*
Tom Brokaw	*The Greatest Generation*
Seth Godin	*Unleashing the Ideavirus*
L. Ron Hubbard	*Battlefield Earth*

How to View Peanut Press Books   When you purchase a book from Peanutpress.com, you supply your name and credit card number, and then receive a Zip file to download. (If you need a utility that will let you expand Zip files, try downloading WinZip from www.winzip.com.) That file will contain not only the e-book itself (in an encrypted .pdb format), but also the Peanut Reader program. As with Doc files, you need this viewer to read Peanutpress.com books. Therefore, the first time you transfer a Peanutpress.com title to your Visor, be sure to install Peanut Reader at the same time. On subsequent occasions, you need to install only the books themselves.

NOTE *Shortly before this book went to press, Peanutpress.com updated Peanut Reader to support Doc files. Thus, you can use it for reading commercial and public domain works.*

You also receive, via e-mail, a code number that's used to "unlock" the e-book. You need to enter this number on your Visor the first time you open your e-book.

Other Sources for Contemporary E-Books Peanutpress.com may be the largest source for commercial e-books, but other Web sites offer contemporary works as well. Among them:

- **Books2Read** Touted as an Internet bookstore, this site has a small but growing collection of Palm OS-formatted titles—reminiscent of early Peanutpress.com.

- **Editio Online Publishing** A couple dozen original fiction and nonfiction titles, most priced at $5 or less.

- **Electron Press** A couple dozen original fiction and nonfiction titles, all priced at $5 or less.

- **Fictionwise** A growing catalog of short fiction titles from some renowned authors, most selling for just a dollar or two.

- **Mind's Eye Fiction** Dozens of original novels and short stories spanning numerous categories. You get to read the first part of any story free, and then pay a small fee if you want to buy the rest. (And we mean a really small fee: a novel might cost you three bucks; a short story, a quarter.) These titles are delivered to you in the standard Doc format, so you need a viewer like CSpotRun or SmartDoc.

Read in Bed Without Disturbing Your Bunkmate

Since the dawn of time, one seemingly insurmountable problem has plagued the human race: how to read in bed without disturbing one's bunkmate. Torches didn't work: they crackled too loudly and tended to set the bed on fire. Battery-operated book lights didn't work: they made books too heavy, leading to carpal reader syndrome. But, finally, there's an answer: the Visor. Just load up a novel from PeanutPress or MemoWare and turn on the backlight. You'll have no trouble seeing the screen in the dark, and your bunkmate won't even know it's on. Pocket-size PC or marriage saver? You be the judge.

Build an Electronic Photo Album

Factoring in inflation, cost-of-living increases, and so forth, a picture is now worth 1,256 words—a rather significant jump in value. All the more reason you should store your photos on your Visor. On a personal level, you'll never be without a picture of your spouse, kids, cats, and other loved ones. On a practical level—well, the possibilities are endless. Realtors can carry snapshots of available properties. Sales teams can show product photos to prospective buyers. Travelers can look at street maps of unfamiliar cities.

Thanks to new and improved third-party software, it's now possible to create cool photo albums on your Visor. The process is quite simple: electronic images on your desktop PC (whether scanned, transferred from a digital camera, or downloaded from the Web) are converted to a Palm OS-readable format, and then installed when you HotSync. Then you just load up your viewer and, well, view 'em.

Understanding Grayscales

If your first reaction to this whole idea is "Ugh, who wants to look at black and white photos?" we're not terribly surprised. But Visor screens are not technically black and white—they generate different levels of gray (called *grayscales*) by varying the intensity of each pixel. While photos may not look as sharp as on a computer screen, they're detailed enough to be practical. An example:

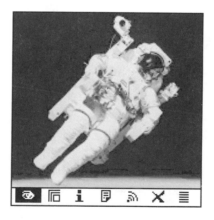

Understanding Electronic Images

As you may know, electronic images stored on your computer are usually in one of many different file formats. Photos downloaded from digital cameras and the Internet are often JPEGs, for instance, while scanned photos often wind up as BMPs or TIFs. The differences between these formats aren't important—what is important is that you can't simply transfer them directly to your Visor. Rather, you must use utility software (usually included with the viewer) to convert them to a Visor-compatible format.

NOTE *Not all these utilities support all kinds of graphics formats. The one bundled with ImagerX, for instance, supports only BMP, GIF, and JPEG—common formats, to be sure, but notably absent are PCX, TIF, and TGA. And Album To Go is limited to working with JPEG files. This won't present a problem for many users, but if you work with a wide variety of image files, you may want to seek a program that supports them all.*

Several programs enable you to view images on your Visor, most of them quite similar in their form and function. We're going to introduce you to two: Album To Go, which has the distinction of being available for both Windows and Macintosh; and FireViewer, one of the more robust programs.

Put Your Photos in an Album To Go

Album To Go is an offshoot of Club Photo, a Web site where you can share photos with friends and family. The software (touted as an "interactive album") consists of a Visor application that can create a slideshow of your pictures and a desktop utility—the latter compatible with both Windows and Macintosh. Everything's free, and you needn't register with Club Photo to get the software (although there are some advantages to doing so). Here's how to get started:

1. Visit the Club Photo Web site (www.clubphoto.com), and then choose the Tools option.

2. Locate Album To Go, and then click PC or Mac depending on which version of the software you want to download. (The conversion utility, Album To Go Desktop, is identical on both platforms. For purposes of this tutorial, we look at the Windows version.)

3. After you download and expand the Zip or SIT file (Windows and Mac, respectively), install the AlbumToGo.prc file on your Visor. Some sample photos are also included, which you can install on your Visor if you want. Next, find a home on your hard drive for the AlbumToGoDesktop application.

Now you're ready to pull some pictures into your Visor. There are two ways to do so: you can grab them directly from the Club Photo Web site or use the desktop application to convert any pictures already on your PC.

Import Pictures from Club Photo

Club Photo is a pretty neat Web site. It not only lets you set up online collections of photos for your personal use, it also offers showcases of amateur photos (some mighty good ones, in fact) you can peruse. And you can download any Club Photo photo into your Visor, by clicking the "Convert to Palm" link that appears when you're viewing the photo in your Web browser (see Figure 22-2).

After a few seconds, you're given the option of opening the file or saving it. If you open the file, it subsequently opens the Palm Install Tool, which gets it ready to load on your next

HotSync. If you save it to your hard drive, you then need to run the Palm Install Tool separately and select the file.

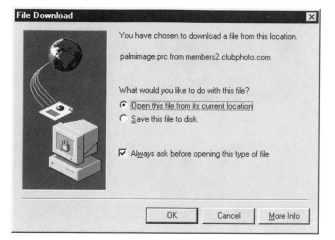

The "Convert to Palm" link

FIGURE 22-2   When you load a full-screen image in Club Photo, you can click the Convert to Palm/Gray-Scale link to convert it to Album To Go format

Convert Pictures on Your Computer

If you have a scanner, a digital camera, or just a collection of photos you downloaded from the Internet, you can easily convert those images to your Visor. Just fire up the AlbumToGoDesktop program and follow these instructions:

1. Click the Open button, and then navigate to the photo you want to convert and select it. Note that this utility supports only the JPEG format. If the file you're looking for doesn't appear in the Open window, it's because it isn't a JPEG. You may need a third-party program to convert it.

2. Notice the AlbumToGoDesktop window now shows many more options, including a preview of the photo as it'll appear on your Visor. You can adjust the brightness and contrast with the slider tools, and even attach a note by clicking the Note tab. Everything here is easy to understand, so tinker!

3. If it isn't checked already, be sure to check the box marked 16 Level Gray Scale. You'll immediately notice a difference in the smoothness of the preview photo.

4. Click the Send To HotSync button. When that happens, the converted photo is then added to your list of programs to install on the next HotSync.

5. HotSync! And then go on to the next section on viewing photos.

Viewing Your Photos in Album To Go

True to its name, Album To Go creates a photo scrapbook on your Visor. Its key feature is an automated slideshow that cycles through your pictures at a predetermined interval—complete with animated effects like fades and page curls. This can come in handy if you want to show someone your album, as it saves you having to manually hop back and forth between each picture and the menu.

After you load a couple photos, tap the AlbumToGo icon and let's take a look at the main screen (see Figure 22-3).

We have three pictures in our album. The check mark next to each indicates it will be included in the slideshow; you can uncheck any you don't want included. Photos are sorted alphabetically; tap Image Name to change the sort order. The Def option next to it is used to set the default transition effect.

What Are Transitions?   When the slideshow moves from one picture to another, it uses a *transition*: an effect that can range from simple to fancy. Album To Go includes seven such effects, though you can also choose not to use them at all (by selecting None). The Def option at the top of the screen lets you set a global transition effect (one that's applied to all pictures unless you change them manually), but you can also use the menus next to each photo to set individual effects. Thus, you could start with a fade, then do a mosiac, and then a page curl. Have fun—experiment!

Use Album To Go Options   As shown in Figure 22-3, the bottom of the Album To Go screen sports two buttons and five icons. The About button brings up a simple information screen that includes Club Photo's Web address, and the Slide button starts your slideshow.

AlbumToGo	
Image Name ▲	Def: ▼ Random
☑ mvc-006l	▼ Line Up
☑ NIKON_TELECO	▼ Mosaic
☑ Race_car8381	▼ Fade
(About...) (Slide...)	👤 ▦ 🗋 📷 🗑

FIGURE 22-3   You can tap the name of a photo to view it individually or see a slideshow of selected pictures by tapping Slide

NOTE   *To stop a slideshow, you must tap and hold down the stylus in the Graffiti area (for just a second or two). No other action, including pressing the application buttons or even the power button, will stop the show!*

From left to right, the icons work as follows:

- ■ **View**   When this mode is selected, you can view any individual photo by tapping its name. When done viewing, tap and hold down the stylus in the Graffiti area to return to the main screen.

- ■ **Rename**   When this mode is selected, you can rename any photo by tapping its name.

- ■ **Note**   Want to attach a description or note to a photo? Tap this icon, and then the name of the photo. You see a memo-like screen into which you can write the information.

- ■ **Beam**   You can beam photos to other Album To Go users by tapping this icon, and then the name of the photo.

- ■ **Delete**   Remove photos from your album (and your Visor) by tapping this icon, and then the name of the photo.

Set Slideshow Options   When you tap Menu | App | Preference, you find two options for Album To Go. First, you can choose whether to loop the slideshow (so it runs indefinitely) or just run it once. Uncheck the box if you prefer the latter. Next, you can set the length of time each image is displayed before the next one appears. Options here range from 1–30 seconds—tap the arrow to select one.

One Important Limitation   Album To Go suffers from one unfortunate limitation: you can't scroll around pictures that are larger than the confines of the screen. If you convert a photo that's fairly wide, for instance, you see only the middle section of it. That's one reason Album To Go is useless for maps, for which scrolling is all but mandatory. And it's the reason we're going to introduce you to FireViewer, which isn't quite as polished, but has a lot more features.

How to ... Turn Your Visor into a Digital Camera

The most expedient way to get pictures into your Visor is with the eyemodule, a digital camera that plugs right into the Visor's Springboard slot. Actually, this nifty piece of hardware isn't really intended for creating Visor-viewable snapshots; rather, it's designed to take photos, and then transfer them back to your computer (for printing, uploading to the Web, and so forth). You can read more about the eyemodule in Chapter 15.

Work with FireViewer

While Album To Go is a nice tool for viewing snapshots and other personal photos, it's not nearly as capable as Firepad's FireViewer. The latter supports scrolling, categories. and zooming and can provide detailed information about each picture. It's not free, but it does provide greater flexibility in both converting your photos and viewing them.

Convert Photos from PC to Palm

After you download and install FireViewer, you should return to Firepad's Web site and download FireConverter—a Windows utility that makes photos ready for viewing on your Visor. (Sorry, Mac users, the company doesn't offer a Mac version, but a third-party program called GraphicConverter can do the job. A link to GraphicConverter is on Firepad's site.) Extract FireConverter to a folder on your hard drive, and then find and double-click *pimg.exe*.

Using FireConverter is as simple as selecting the image you want to convert, tweaking a few options (if desired), and clicking the Convert button. The latter adds the converted image to your Palm Install Tool so it automatically gets loaded the next time you HotSync.

The first step is selecting an image source. The utility supports a variety of image file types, including GIF, JPEG, PCX, TIF, and BMP. It can also convert images that have been copied to the Windows clipboard. It can even create an on-the-fly screenshot from within Windows and convert that to your Palm. Choose the option you want in the Image Source area, and then click Open.

Once you line up an image, you can get a rough estimate of what it'll look like on your Visor by clicking the Preview tab, shown next.

View Photos in FireViewer

It doesn't get much easier than this: tap the Viewer III icon in your Visor's Applications screen (FireViewer used to be called Image Viewer III, and at press time the developers still hadn't changed the icon), and then tap the name of the image you want to view (see Figure 22-4). If the image is too large to fit onscreen all at once, you can scroll to different areas of it by placing your stylus tip on the screen and slowly dragging it around. You'll see the image moves with your stylus. (You can also use the Visor's buttons to scroll around an image, but you need to configure that in the Menu | Options | Assign Buttons screen.) Tap the Visor's Menu button to access FireViewer's function bar, and then tap the right-most icon to return to the main screen.

Notice the icons along the bottom of the main screen, shown in Figure 22-4. These same icons appear when you tap the Menu button while viewing an image. They enable you to navigate within the program and perform various tasks. From left to right, their functions are

- **View** The little eye puts you into view mode, where you can tap the name of an image to view it.

- **Preview** This option zooms out to fit the entire image onscreen. This helps you navigate large photos, as you can tap anywhere on the preview to zoom into that point.

- **Info** When you tap the little *i*, you see a screen containing loads of information and options for the image. Here you can assign an image to a category (this works like all other Visor category functions); beam, rename, or delete the image, and attach a note to the image.

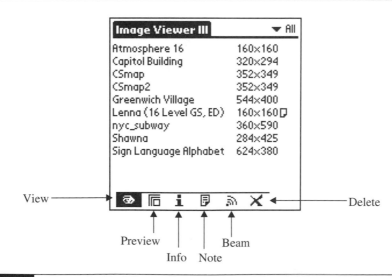

- **Note** You can write and link a note to an image by tapping this icon.
- **Beam** You can beam an image to another FireViewer user by tapping this icon.
- **Delete** Use this icon to delete an image (not just from FireViewer, but from your Visor as well).
- **Menu** This icon appears only when you're viewing an image; it takes you back to the main screen.

 These icons work differently depending on whether you're in the main screen or viewing an image. In the latter case, tapping any of them launches the respective function. If you're at the main screen, however, you first tap the icon, and then tap the image file.

FIGURE 22-4   The main FireViewer (formerly named Image Viewer III) screen displays the name and resolution of each image

Mapmaker, Mapmaker, Make Me a Map

Wouldn't it be cool if you could have a street map handy when you visit foreign cities? You can, and for free. Point your Web browser to Yahoo! Maps or one of the many other online cartography sources, generate the map you need, and then save it to your hard drive. Now run it through your image viewer's conversion software and load it onto your Visor. Of course, you need a viewer that supports scrolling, which leaves out Album To Go. For this task we recommend FireViewer.

Where to Find It

Web Site	Address	What's There
MemoWare	www.memoware.com	Thousands of books and articles, all formatted for the Palm
Cutting Edge Software	www.cesinc.com	SmartDoc
PalmGear H.Q.	www.palmgear.com	Doc viewers
Peanut Press	www.peanutpress.com	Commercial e-books for sale
Books2Read	www.books2read.com	Commercial e-books for sale
Mind's Eye Fiction	tale.com	Nonpublished fiction and nonfiction e-books for sale
Electron Press	www.electronpress.com	Small collection of e-books for sale
Club Photo	www.clubphoto.com	Album To Go
Firepad	www.firepad.com	FireViewer
Lemke Software	www.lemkesoft.de	GraphicConverter
Editio Online Publishing	www.editio-books.com	Commercial e-books for sale

Chapter 23

Creativity Software: Paint, Compose, and Organize

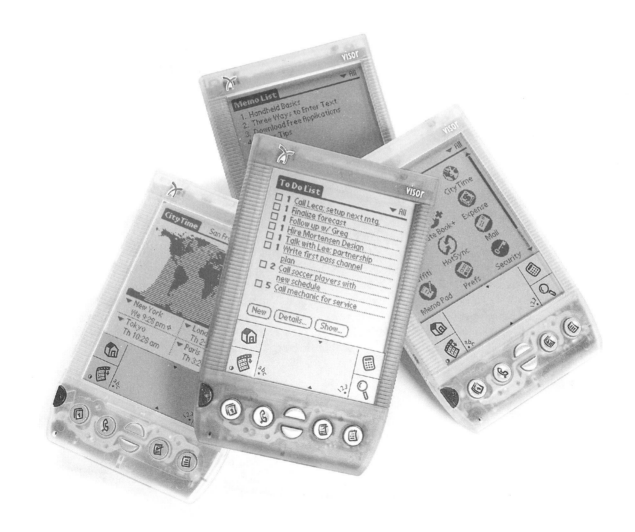

How to...

- Paint images on the Visor
- Use TealPaint
- Use Diddle
- Collaborate on a sketch using the Visor's IR port
- Create structured drawing on the Visor
- Use an Outliner to organize your ideas
- Make animations on the Visor
- Morph photographs on the Visor
- Create fractal images
- Capture Visor screenshots
- Use the Visor as a drum machine
- Learn piano and guitar chords on the Visor
- Use the Visor as a tuning fork
- Record music on the Visor
- Control WinAmp with the Visor
- Use the Visor as a MIDI controller

The Palm IIIc may have been the first color Palm OS device but, eventually, color Visors will also be everywhere. And thanks to developments by companies like Handspring, future Visors will probably have stereo sound for listening to audio. For the moment, though, pretty much any Palm device seems an unlikely tool for the arts—like painting and music.

You might be surprised at how handy the Visor is at being creative. A good smattering of drawing and painting apps is out there, and you can use them to sketch out ideas at meetings or create mini works of art. And the Visor might be the last place you'd look for music software, but a collection of that is available as well. In this chapter, we look at just what you can do with your Visor.

Paint on the Visor

You're probably wondering why you might want to paint on a handheld computer so small it fits in your pocket. Well, in the world of computers, the answer very often is "because you can." Programmers have never let something as silly as a technical limitation get in the way of doing something. And when Palm devices came out, it seemed like programmers literally scrambled to be the first to create a paint program for their favorite handheld PC.

But aside from that admittedly flippant answer, the ability to sketch things out on your Visor is a handy feature. You can draw a map to sketch the way to lunch, outline a process, or design a flowchart. You can also just doodle—use the Visor as a high-tech Etch-a-Sketch for those boring times when you're waiting for the train or pretending to take notes in a meeting.

Painting on your Visor is fun and productive, but you need to keep these limitations in mind:

- Some Visor paint programs enable you to make use of the later models' grayscale capability but, for the most part, you're stuck with black and white, two-color screens.

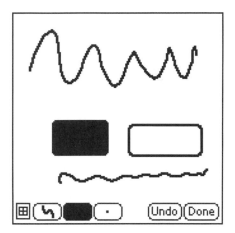

- The Visor has a resolution of 160×160 pixels. That's not a lot of room in which to draw, and you'll find that after being transferred to a PC, the images are very, very small (the smallest resolution in Windows is 640×480 pixels, and most people tend to run their display at $1,024 \times 768$ pixels). So it's generally not possible to draw something on the Visor that you later plan to export to, say, a PowerPoint presentation.

- Not all Visor paint programs support printing, which means, in some cases, what you draw on the screen pretty much stays on the screen. If you can print your work of art, it prints just as rough and jagged on paper as it looked onscreen. If you want to achieve high-resolution paper output, you should, instead, try a drawing program (as discussed later in this chapter).

As we mentioned, a plethora of painting tools exist for the Visor. So many, in fact, we decided to narrow the crop for you to only a pair of programs you should evaluate. We assembled the best of the litter for you to evaluate.

Paint with TealPaint

Perhaps the most full-featured paint program for the Visor, TealPaint seems to do it all. The program has a complete set of painting tools, including lines, shapes, fill tools, an eraser, and a variety of brushes. The main paint interface is shown next.

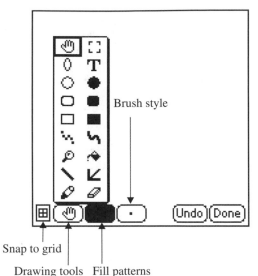

Brush style

Snap to grid

Drawing tools Fill patterns

Using TealPaint, you can copy-and-paste selections of your image, not just within the same picture, but in any picture in your database. To do this, tap the Tool button and choose the Selection tool. Drag a rectangle around some part of your image, and then choose Edit | Copy Selected from the menu. Then choose Edit | Paste Selected and a copy of the image appears, which you can drag around the screen to suit your taste.

TealPaint is also an animation tool. We talk about animation programs later in this chapter, but it's worth pointing out that you can use TealPaint to create animations by playing all the images in a particular database in sequence.

NOTE *TealPaint comes with a PC-side utility for viewing and saving images within Windows. A MacPac is also available for using TealPaint files on the Macintosh.*

Doodle with Diddle

Diddle is a neat little drawing program that enables you to sketch with a minimum of clutter to get in the way of your drawing. The interface is composed of a set of graphical menus at the top of the screen—you can choose from among various drawing styles, line thickness, and text. For the most part, the program is easy to explore on your own.

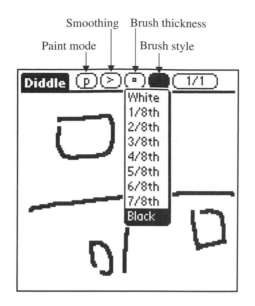

Smoothing   Brush thickness

Paint mode   Brush style

Collaborate on a Sketch

Drawing on a Visor is usually a solo affair, but what if you're in a meeting trying to lay out office furniture with your business partner? What then, huh? Okay, there are better examples, but work with us for a moment.

If both of you own a Palm OS device, you can sketch your ideas on your Visor and your partner can edit and contribute to your drawing in real-time. This is done via the IR port and a program called JchalkIR. The program is actually intended only as a technology demonstration, but it's darned useful nonetheless. Once you experience the power of collaborating with someone else via his handheld, you'll want to use this program all the time.

Unfortunately, JchalkIR is a Java app that requires the Palm OS Java Virtual Machine called Kjava, and that isn't easy to locate. So start by finding and installing this program before you do anything else. Many Web sites on the Internet purport to have the files, but we could only locate one that actually had them. The Kjava program is composed of two files:

- KjavaVM.prc
- KjavaVM.pdb

The Kjava program files can be found at: members.xoom.com/pilot_will/PiLotto.html.

Once you install the Kjava app, install JchalkIR on both Visors that need to communicate.

NOTE   *The Kjava app is locked and can't be beamed. As a result, you need to make sure everyone has the files installed before arriving at lunch with the intent of collaborating on a sketch.*

To use JchalkIR, start the app and draw. When you want to update the other person's drawing, tap the Beam button.

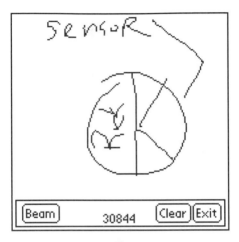

NOTE   *If you clear the screen to make a fresh drawing, the erased information is not transferred during a beam. So you may have a clean screen, but your collaborator still has all the data from the previous sketches. Everyone needs to tap the Clear button to work from a clean slate.*

What Is Java?

Glad you asked. Ordinarily, of course, a program only works on one kind of computer. But Java is a machine-independent programming language developed by Sun Microsystems, which is used extensively on the Web. Java is used on the Internet because, with the right interpreter, it can work on almost any kind of computer—PC, Mac, Linux, and so on.

The Visor can run certain kinds of Java apps, thanks to Java interpreters like Kjava. If you install Kjava, then you can find other programs written in Java that run on the Visor—this beam-enabled drawing program isn't the only one.

Draw on the Visor

Paint? Draw? What's the difference? Not a lot, unless you're talking about computer software—then the difference is significant. In computer lingo, drawing programs differ from paint programs in that drawing applications are *resolution independent*. In other words, when you print a drawing, it comes out at the printer's highest resolution, often without the jagginess you might see onscreen. A painting looks the same on paper as it does onscreen, complete with all the pixels and jaggies.

The reason for the difference is, when you paint, you are specifying exactly which pixels to change. In a drawing program, on the other hand, you are telling the program, for instance, to "add a circle that is 50 units in diameter." The difference is important when you print or display the image in another resolution.

Traditionally, drawing programs on the PC are CAD/CAM apps (drafting programs used by engineers), floor plan and blueprinting software, and business drawing programs used to draw flowcharts and organizational charts. On the Visor, you can make some of the same kinds of images, though the software is obviously not going to have quite as many features:

■ **QDraw** This program is an impressive demonstration of what you can do with your Visor in the graphics arena. It supports images up to four times the size of the Visor screen, and it has a full complement of tools including lines, boxes, circles, and text. More impressive, though, is QDraw's selection of fill styles. You can create objects filled with patterns like brick walls and various dot patterns, which should make you feel right at home if you've used drawing programs on the Mac or PC.

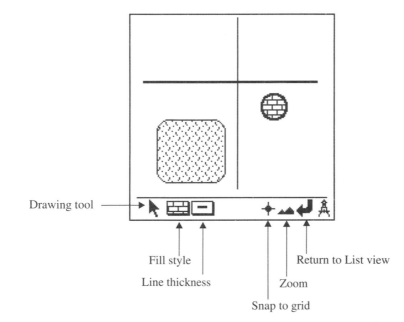

Drawing tool

Fill style

Line thickness

Snap to grid

Zoom

Return to List view

■ **PalmDraw**   The program enables you to draw large images, many times bigger than the Visor screen, and you can zoom in and out at will. A basic set of drawing tools exists—like text, lines, boxes, circles, and arcs. Images can be exported as PostScript files for printing on high-resolution printers or sent directly to the serial port for printing on an attached printer.

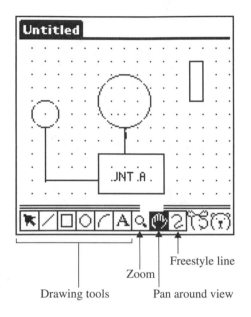

Drawing tools   Zoom   Freestyle line
                            Pan around view

■ **ToDo PLUS and Memo PLUS**   We mentioned these programs way back in Chapters 9 and 10, but we thought it was worth reminding you about them here. These two apps can replace your core To Do List and Memo Pad programs, and they add drawing features akin to PalmDraw. This enables you to create memos and To Dos with drawings—and sometimes a picture is worth a thousand words.

Outline Your Ideas

Outliners are an interesting class of software. Not quite a memo pad or a to do list, not quite a drawing program, they help you organize your thoughts into a logical and manageable order.

Typically, outliners use a hierarchical approach to data management. This might sound imposing, but the basic idea is your ideas are generally related to each other. So start with a single note, and then nest subnotes within it, as if you had a data tree with branches that grew off the main topic. By grouping related ideas together, it's easier to stay organized and arrange your data in a format that works for you.

The Visor has several excellent idea organizers with which you can experiment:

■ **BrainForest**   This program is perhaps the most complete organizer for the Visor and serves as an action item tracker, checklist manager, outliner, idea keeper, and project planner. BrainForest uses Tree, Branch, and Leaf metaphors to enable you to nest notes within each other, thus grouping items in a logical manner. Items are numbered using traditional outlining notation (like 1.2.3, for the third leaf in the second branch of the first tree of data). You can also export specific items to the Visor's To Do List and Memo Pad. BrainForest also enables you to prioritize, sort, and rearrange items by dragging-and-dropping.

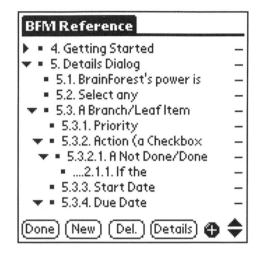

■ **Hi-Note**   Hi-Note is a simple organizer with a very cool feature: you can include both text notes and images in the program's hierarchy. No restriction exists on the way this program uses text and images, so you can create a text note, and then create a sketch as a subnote underneath it—or vice versa.

■ **ThoughtMill**   ThoughtMill is a simple, but powerful, outliner that looks and acts like the built-in Memo Pad. The program uses drag-and-drop to move entries around, and has a clever temporary folder for storing individual items you are moving around as you organize your outline.

Animate Images

Your Visor is certainly no Pixar Animation Studio graphic workstation, but you can create simple animations with it. This sort of thing probably has no practical application, but you have to admit it's a lot of fun. Animations can be completely pointless or, if you're a really proactive worker bee, we're sure you can come up with a reason to create animations on your Visor that complements your business duties.

Animate with Flip

The best of the animation bunch is a program called Flip. This program works like traditional onion-skin animation techniques. You can sketch a design on one cell of the animation and move to the next page, where you can see the previous page peeking through. The program also includes a "morphing" tool that enables you draw keyframes—like the start and end of the animation—and let Flip draw all the images in between. The Flip screen looks like this:

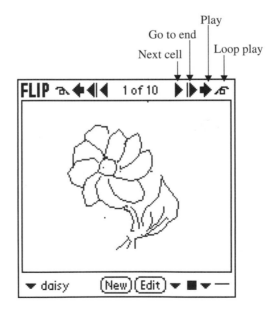

How to ...   **Create a Simple Animation**

To create a simple animation, follow these steps:

1. Tap the New button and give your animation a name on the Create New Flipset dialog box, and then tap Begin.

2. Draw your first cell of the animation. You have different line styles available in the list menu in the bottom-right corner, and you can erase by selecting the hollow box from the other list menu.

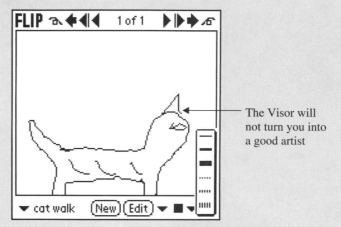

The Visor will not turn you into a good artist

3. When you are ready to draw your next cell, tap the Next Cell Arrow. To see the underlying drawing from cell 1, tap the Edit button and choose Trace Previous. You can, thus, base your cell on the contents of the previous cell.

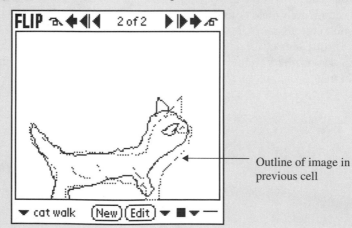

Outline of image in previous cell

 *If you want to duplicate the contents of cell 1 in cell 2, display cell 1, tap the Edit button, and choose Copy Slide. Then switch to cell 2, tap the Edit button, and choose Paste Slide(s).*

4. When you have made all the cells in your animation, tap the Play button to see your creation.

If you want Flip automatically to render an animation based on a start and end cell using morphing technology, draw two slides, and then tap the Edit button. Choose Morph Slides and tell Flip on which two slides to base the animation. You also need to designate how many slides to draw—the more slides you draw, the longer the animation will run.

> **Morph Slides...**   ⓘ
>
> Total Slides: **2**
> Range Available: **[1 to 2] inclusive**
>
> **Morph Control:**
>
> **Start Slide:** 1
>
> **End Slide:** 2
>
> **Num Between**
> **(Max 100)** 10
>
> **Insert After Slide** 1
>
> (Cancel)   (Begin Morph!)

Morph Images with PalmSmear

Even if you manage to come up with a decent excuse to use Flip around the office, you're going to have to admit defeat and consider PalmSmear as nothing more than a toy. This program enables you to create morph-based animations of pictures you've imported from the PC (sorry, no Mac version exists of the desktop component).

PalmSmear is pretty simple to use. The main interface has four buttons: to delete, beam, and play the current image, plus a fourth button to return to the image List view.

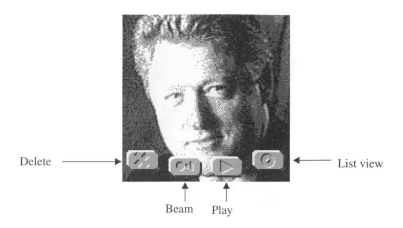

Delete ⟶   ⟵ List view

Beam   Play

Tap the Menu button and your view changes. You can select the smear mode and brush size. Just smear the image around a little, and then tap the keyframe to which you want to assign the image. There are four keyframes, which means you can do up to four distinct things to your image, in sequence.

Brush size

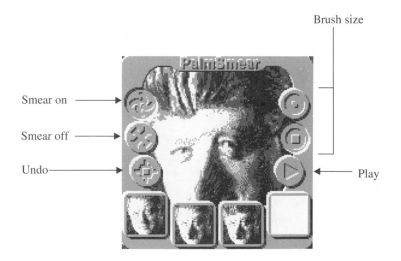

Smear on ⟶

Smear off ⟶

Undo ⟶

Play ⟵

Experiment with Fractals

If you're somewhat new to computing, you may have missed the fractal craze of the 80s. That was when it seemed everyone and her cousin was writing a graphics program for the PC that generated fractal images.

What's a fractal, you ask? A *fractal* is a class of mathematics invented in the 1970s by a mathematician named Benoit Mandelbrot. It's more interesting than it might sound—a fractal is concerned with reproducing infinitely repeating structures, both mathematically and visually. Consider a mountain, for instance—you can zoom in on the structure and no matter how far you zoom, the structure remains essentially the same, all the way down to the rocks that make up the mountain. Another example: think of a fiord. On the surface, it seems easy to calculate the total perimeter of the shoreline, but as you enlarge the fiord, you find there's a virtually infinite amount of structure to the shore, as it weaves back and forth in tiny jagged edges. All this has practical applications, though, because fractal equations do a darned good job of drawing computer-rendered natural objects like trees, mountains, snowflakes, and flowers. The perceived reality is stunning.

All this is great, but what about the Visor? Well, you can use your Visor to draw fractal sets that are beautiful in their own right, and you can experiment with them by zooming in and letting the Visor render the new scene. No matter where you zoom, you get an interesting picture and you can always zoom in further.

A few fractal programs are available for the Visor. You won't get stunning, full-color results like you can on a Mac or a PC, but you can have fun, nonetheless. Try PalmFract, available at www.palmgear.com.

One word of warning: the Visor's processor isn't as fast as the Pentium III and PowerPC chips in today's desktop computers. As a result, the time your Visor takes to draw a fractal onscreen may very well remind you of drawing fractals on 486's and Amigas in the 80s. It can take several minutes to render each image.

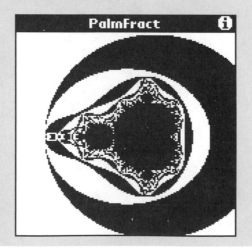

Capture Screenshots of the Visor Display

Perhaps you've thumbed through this book, some Palm Web sites, or a magazine like *Tap* and wondered how everyone else seems to be able to capture screenshots of the Visor display and publish them, apparently through a PC or Mac. Turns out capturing Visor screens isn't that hard to do because several tools are available to automate the process for you, at least partially.

The easiest way to capture a screen from your Visor is by using ScreenShot Hack, one of the many Palm OS extensions that work with HackMaster (see Chapter 18).

NOTE   *ScreenShot tools like ScreenShot Hack only work with Windows, so Mac users are unfortunately left out in the cold, at least for now.*

ScreenShot Hack is a great general-purpose tool because you don't have to do anything special to activate it. No countdowns till the screen is captured, no menu selections. Just display the screen you want to capture and draw the screen capture gesture in the Graffiti area. ScreenShot Hack responds to any of three gestures: Next Field, Previous Field, or Numeric Keyboard. Be sure, though, that you activate the Hack in HackMaster after you install it, and select the gesture you want to trigger the screenshot.

```
┌─────────────────────────────────────┐
│ ScreenShot Hack            ⓘ         │
│            Registered.               │
│ Activate Stroke                      │
│ ┌──────────┬──────────┬──────────┐   │
│ │Next Fld ⋎│Prev Fld ⋏│Numeric ⌐ │   │
│ └──────────┴──────────┴──────────┘   │
│                                      │
│ Screenshots stored: 14( View )       │
│ ( OK )( Erase last )( Erase all )    │
└─────────────────────────────────────┘
```

TIP   *We think the Numeric keyboard gesture (just a tap on the 123 dot on the Graffiti area) is the easiest to use because the Field gestures can be tricky to remember.*

After you have taken one or more screenshots, you need to HotSync the Visor to transfer the images to the PC. Make sure you set the System conduit to Handheld Overwrites Desktop. Then use the conversion utility that comes with ScreenShot Hack to transform the images into Windows bitmap files.

Capture Hard-to-Get Screens

ScreenShot Hack can't capture some screens—specifically, grayscale screens. These come out looking like you have double vision after a long night of playing Quake on the PC. For those, you need to resort to the less-friendly, but more compatible, Snapshot program.

Snapshot captures any screen on the Visor, including grayscale ones, and uses a timer to automate the image-taking process.

Snapshot

1. Click on the "Do It!" button below. This will start a **10** -second timer.

2. Switch to the screen you wish to capture. Wait for the double beep.

3. Find the screen shot as an ImageViewer file called "Screen Shot", "Screen Shot 2", etc.

(Do It!)

Once you have taken a screenshot, though, the procedure to make use of the image is a bit more involved. The problem is the images are saved in the Palm ImageViewer format, which is alien to the PC. What you need is to transfer the images to the desktop via the HotSync procedure (with the System conduit set to Handheld Overwrites Desktop), and then use a utility to convert the images to an appropriate format for the desktop. The easiest solution is to download the Image Preview Utility III, a program designed to work with Image Viewer (which, in its newest incarnation, is called FireViewer) by showing and saving Image Viewer files in Windows. You can find this program at www.firepad.com/web/iv_download.html. This site is the home of FireViewer.

Make Music on the Visor

Believe it or not, you can use the Visor for a number of music applications. It has a built-in speaker for creating (admittedly, very basic) sounds, and the display is perfectly suited for music notation in a small space. If you're a musician, be sure to check out some of these applications.

Metronome and Drumming Software

It doesn't take a rocket scientist to figure out that the Visor's sound capabilities aren't exactly symphonic in nature. So one obvious application for your Visor is to keep time, either as a drum machine or a metronome. In fact, this would have come in handy a long time ago—Dave used to carry a guitar around wherever he went, and having a metronome or a minidrum machine in a box as small as the Visor would have been really cool.

■ **Meep** Meep is your standard metronome. It has a slider for choosing any tempo from 40 to 280 beats per minute, and you can also select up to 8 beats per measure. You can work from onscreen counts or add an audible beep to each beat.

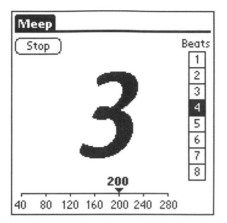

■ **Responsive Metronome** Another simple metronome tool, this program enables you to choose any tempo from 35 to 300 beats per minute, and both see (via a pulsing quarter note) and hear the beat. This program is quite simple. In fact, there's no on/off switch for the beat—to shut it off, you have to disable both the audio and video filters.

■ **PocketBeat** This app simulates a drum kit right on your Visor. It can remember two distinct tempos and you can switch between them easily by using onscreen controls or the scroll button. It can also play straight or shuffle beats, and can vary between 40 and 196 beats per minute. The best part, though, is you can tap out your own meter on the Visor screen—PocketBeat will memorize the tempo and play it accordingly.

Portable Music Lessons

Here are a few applications that budding musicians can carry around with them to bone up on notes, keyboard positions, and fingering:

- **MusicTeacher** This program can be used as an aid to learning to sing *prima vista*—that is, by reading sheet music by sight. Several tunes are stored in the MusicTeacher database, and you can also enter your own using the onscreen keyboard.

NOTE *This program is interesting because it is written in Java and uses a Java interpreter to run on the Visor. Because MusicTeacher is just a Java app, it can also be found on the Web and runs from within a Web browser window. You can find MusicTeacher at http://mathsrv.ku-eichstaett.de/MGF/homes/grothmann/java/waba/index.html.*

- **GTrainer** If you're learning to play guitar and don't want to be forever tied to "tab" sheet music, try GTrainer. This app displays a note onscreen and you need to tap the correct place on the guitar fretboard. It isn't enough just to choose the right note—you have to tap the correct octave as well.

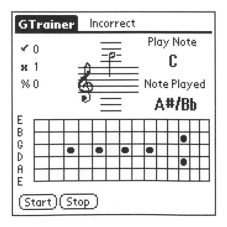

■ **McChords**   If you are learning piano, this program is an essential portable tool for working through chord fingerings. It shows you which keys to press to form the majority of chords you need to master basic piano playing.

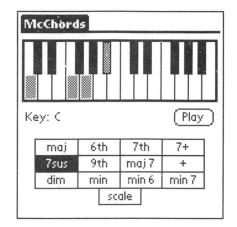

■ **Fretboard**   This program is indispensable for anyone trying to get the hang of the guitar. In fact, it also supports mandolin, banjo, violin, and other stringed instruments. Just choose a chord and the fretboard displays a variety of ways to finger it. Fretboard includes every chord we could think of, including obscure (minor 9th and stacked fourths) chords you might play only once in a great while. As such, it's a good memory jogger even for experienced players.

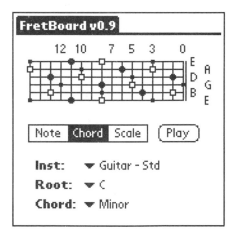

Tools for Musicians

Several programs around can help you tune your instruments. We're not sure we'd rely on the Visor for instrument tuning, but you can certainly try these apps and see if they do the job for you.

■ **Tuning Fork**   This program produces a tone that corresponds to *A*. You can fine-tune the tone to any frequency between 20 and 20,000 KHz, and play the tone for three, six, or nine seconds.

■ **Musician Tools**   This application is easily one of the best all-around utilities for all the Visor-wielding musicians out there. Musician Tools combines three utilities into a single interface and does them all well. You'll find a metronome that varies in tempo from 40 to 210 beats per minute and one to eight beats per measure. The output is both audible and visual. (Other metronome tools are described earlier in this chapter.) There's also an excellent tuning fork that emits a tone for various notes and a number of base frequencies. Finally, the program includes a circle of fifths.

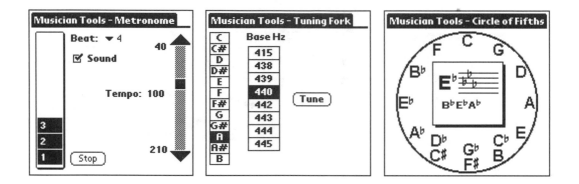

Music Annotation and Recording

You may have experimented with (or frequently use) applications on the Mac or PC that enable you to compose and play music. Those programs generally enable you to drag notes onto musical staffs or play an onscreen keyboard to construct musical compositions. Well, you can do the same thing on the Visor—the screen is just a bit smaller, and you don't have multiple voices to hear your multitimbral creations. Here are a few applications you can try:

■ **Noter**   This unusually named program is an online favorite because it's so good at helping you create music. Noter features a staff, as well as a set of tools for placing notes and rests. When you create your song, you can save it, play it, or even export it as an alarm for the Visor's Date Book. The program also has a built-in metronome.

■ **miniPiano**   This program enables you to play an onscreen keyboard while the notes you strike get added on a staff. You can then play back your creation. miniPiano has a "Free Play" mode in which the keys are duration-sensitive—the longer you hold the stylus on the key, the longer it plays.

■ **Palm Piano**   This simple program records the notes you tap out on a four-octave keyboard and it can play back the results. Palm Piano has some simple editing tools built in, but it has neither rests nor any way to select note lengths—they all play back at the same timing.

- **PocketSynth**   Like Palm Piano, this program enables you to create music by tapping on an onscreen keyboard. PocketSynth enables you to select note lengths and rests, though, which gives you more composing flexibility. Unfortunately, you must select the length of the note, and then tap it on the keyboard, which makes the composition process less than entirely fluid.

Play MP3s

If you've read Chapter 15, you know the Visor has the capability to play MP3 music files using an optional Springboard module. Snap in the module, and you can play music at near-CD-audio quality and listen to it with a pair of headphones.

If you're not interested in using your Visor as a portable music player, it can still help you listen to MP3s on your desktop PC. A clever program called Busker lets your Visor act as a tethered control panel for the popular WinAmp MP3 player as long as it's in the HotSync cradle.

Here's how it works: your Visor displays a control panel for the WinAmp program that shows all the songs in the queue and track controls for pausing and advancing through the track list. As long as the Visor is connected to the HotSync cradle, it can send commends to WinAmp.

Why would you want to use Busker? That's easy—instead of cluttering your desktop monitor display with the WinAmp interface, you can access WinAmp from your Visor. It's both easy to get to and kind of like having a remote control for your MP3 player.

Important MP3 Sites

Interested in trying Busker? First of all, you need WinAmp—other MP3 players for your desktop won't work. Get WinAmp from www.winamp.com.

Busker itself is available from www.palmgear.com or directly from www.hausofmaus.com/busker.html. And once you're configured, you need some music to listen to. Check out some of these Web sites for downloadable music:

- www.mp3.com
- www.emusic.com
- www.ubl.com
- www.rollingstone.com
- www.cductive.com

Use the Visor as a MIDI Controller

The Visor—a little personal organizer that stores phone numbers—can act as a MIDI controller? Bah, you say. It's true, though. After all, you've seen that many developers have created music applications for the Visor and it does, in fact, have a serial port. That's the same port the Mac and PC typically use to communicate with MIDI instruments. So it's possible—and many people use their Visors for this very, if somewhat unusual, purpose.

What Is MIDI?

MIDI stands for *Musical Instrument Digital Interface* and it has been used for well over a decade as a common language for electronic instruments to communicate with each other. Many keyboards are MIDI-enabled, which means if you connect a PC to the keyboard, it can control the music and play complex patterns without human intervention. Likewise, you can even connect a MIDI interface to an electric guitar and use the guitar to record music directly to a PC. You could also use the guitar to control a MIDI keyboard, thus giving the guitar a range of voices and sounds impossible to get any other way. MIDI cables are available that connect a PC's serial port to MIDI devices like keyboards.

You can build your own MIDI interface for your Visor and connect it to a keyboard. You can find instructions for such a device at fargo.itp.tsoa.nyu.edu/~gsmith/Pilot/PilotMidi.htm. Here are a pair of interesting MIDI applications for the Visor:

- **Palm MIDI Desktop** The sound files that constitute the alarms on your Visor are actually written in the MIDI language. This means they're easily edited. Using this program, you can change the alarms on the PC and save them back to your Visor.

- **Theremini** Familiar with the sound of a theremin? It's how Jimmy Page got that distinctive sound on so many classic Led Zeppelin albums. Well, you don't have to bring a small science lab on stage with you anymore because now you can use Theremini. Connect your PC to a synthesizer and reproduce theremin-like sounds. The Visor's theremin interface is very clever—just move the stylus around the screen: one way for amplitude and the other way for frequency. The control lends itself to improvisation. If you don't have a MIDI interface, you can play the theremin sounds through the Visor speaker.

Where to Find It

Web Site	Address	What's There
PalmGear H.Q.	www.palmgear.com	Virtually all the applications found in this chapter
TealPoint Software	www.tealpoint.com	Home of TealPaint and other Teal products
Pilotto Web Site	members.xoom.com/pilot_will/PiLotto.html	The files for the Visor's Java Virtual machine, needed for a number of Palm OS Java apps
MusicTeacher Home Page	mathsrv.ku-eichstaett.de/MGF/homes/grothmann/java/waba	MusicTeacher
Haus of Maus	www.hausofmaus.com	Busker, a WinAmp controller for Palm devices
Pilot MIDI Pages	fargo.itp.tsoa.nyu.edu/~gsmith/Pilot/PilotMidi.htm	MIDI information, including how to create an interface for the Visor
Image Viewer Web site	www.firepad.com/web/iv_download.html	Image Viewer (FireViewer) utilities

Chapter 24

Cases, Keyboards, and Other Accessories

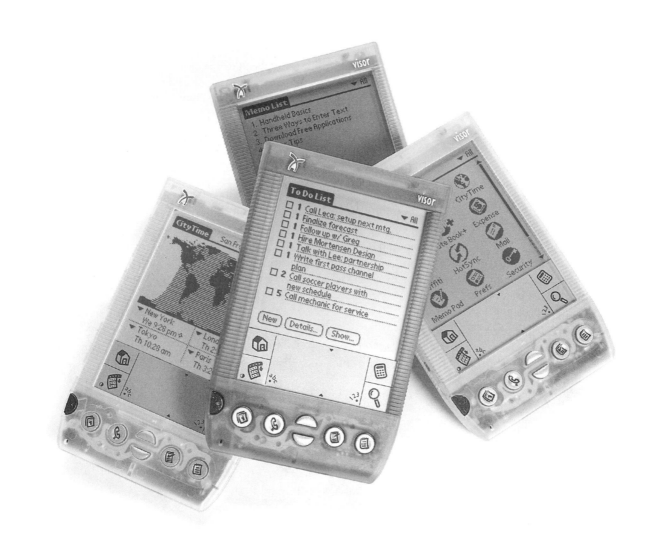

How to...

- Choose a case
- Choose a stylus
- Turn any pen into a stylus
- Choose a keyboard
- Protect your screen from dust and scratches
- Extend your Visor's battery life
- Decide between alkaline and rechargeable batteries
- Mount your Visor in your car

There's more to Visors than just software. We're talking gadgets, gear, accessories—the stuff that not only makes your Visor your own, but extends its capabilities beyond what mere software can accomplish. In this chapter, we look at accessories both nifty and practical. For starters, let's tackle cases—a subjective category if ever there was one.

Pick a Case, Any Case

As a new Visor owner, one of the first things you need to determine is how you plan to convey the device. In your pocket? Briefcase? Purse? Clipped to your belt? Backpack? Dashboard? Your answer will help determine the kind of case you should buy.

Picking one can be a tough call indeed. Do you opt for practical or stylish? (The two are often mutually exclusive.) Do you look for lots of extras like card slots and pen holders, or try to keep it as slim as possible? Do you shell out big bucks for a titanium shell that can withstand being run over by a car? (This happens quite a bit, believe it or not.)

Because so many varieties are out there, and because everyone's case needs are different, we're going to start by steering you to the case manufacturers themselves, and then offering a few general tips and suggestions.

> **NOTE** *Although most of the products in this chart are, indeed, cases, a few are better described as holders. The CM220 Universal Car Mount, for instance, connects to your car's windshield or dashboard and holds your Visor at a convenient viewing angle.*

Company	Phone	URL	Cases Offered
Arkon Resources	626-358-1133	www.arkon.com	CM220 Universal Car Mount
Devian	800-388-9709	www.devian.com	Various
E&B Company	800-896-2273	www.ebcases.com	Slipper
Handspring	888-565-9393	www.handspring.com	Value, Matching, Premier
Inferno Industries	800-733-0088	www.incipiodirect.com	Incipio Visor Case
MarWare	954-927-6031	www.marware.com	SportSuit, C.E.O.
RhinoSkin	307-734-8833	www.rhinoskin.com	ShockSuit SportCase, Ti Slider
Rhodiana	800-338-8759	www.rhodiana.com	Rhodiana for Visor

Here are some things to keep in mind as you shop for a case:

- **Style**   If you're an executive-minded person, you probably want a case to match. That means leather. If you're planning to tote the Visor in a suit pocket, look for something that doesn't add much bulk, like E&B's form-fitting Slipper.

- **Portability**   In the summer, when the tight clothes come out and the jackets get stowed, pockets are hard to come by. That's when something like RhinoSkin's ShockSuit SportCase can come in mighty handy—it hangs from your belt via a detachable plastic clip.

- **Screen Protection**   When your Visor is bouncing around in a pocket, purse, or briefcase, the last thing you want is for some piece of flotsam to gouge or scratch the screen. That's one of the main reasons behind getting a case in the first place.

- **Drop Protection**   Gravity—it strikes without warning (especially if you're a klutz like Rick), and it can fatally wound a Visor in a matter of milliseconds. A case made of neoprene, like MarWare's SportSuit, can save the day if your Visor gets knocked or dropped to the floor.

- **Moron Protection**   We've heard more than a few stories of people driving over their Visors. Why they're being left in the driveway in the first place is beyond us, but there's one case that's better suited to handling such punishment than any other: RhinoSkin's Ti Slider (see Figure 24-1). Made of durable titanium, this thing could survive a missile strike.

- **Velcro**   A few cases out there (usually ones designed to fit a wide variety of handheld devices) rely on Velcro to keep your Visor secured. While we look upon this as a necessary evil (who wants a big square of the stuff stuck to the back of their Visor?), we try to avoid such cases when possible.

- **Leveraging the Visor's Screen Cover**   As you've probably discovered, your Visor came with a plastic screen cover that snaps onto the front of the device. But did you know it's reversible? That is, it can snap onto the back just the same. Some cases, like those made by Handspring and Inferno Industries (see Figure 24-2), leverage that screen cover to lock a Visor in place, thereby obviating the need for Velcro. These are excellent solutions, as they keep your Visor secure while allowing it to snap in and out with ease.

The Stylus Decision

Many Visor users are perfectly happy with the stylus that came with their Visor—until they get a look at some of the alternatives. Indeed, while those bundled plastic pens do get the job done, they're not as comfortable or versatile as they could be. For instance, wouldn't a thicker or heavier stylus feel better in your hand? And wouldn't it be nice if it doubled as an ink pen? These are just some of the options available to the discriminating Visor user.

FIGURE 24-1   If you're really clumsy, you may want a heavy-duty case like RhinoSkin's titanium Ti Slider

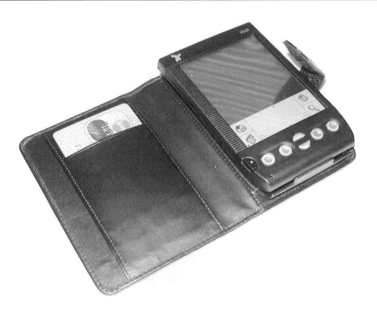

FIGURE 24-2   The Handspring-made cases are among a select few that use "screen cover technology" to lock the Visor inside—a clever and practical solution

24

As with cases, we wouldn't presume to pick a stylus for you. That's a matter of personal preference. So, here's a look at some of the stylus makers and their offerings.

Company	Phone	URL	Product(s)
Autopoint	608-757-0021	http://emerald.jvlnet.com/~autopt/stylus.htm	Stylus+
Cross	800-722-1719	www.cross.com	DigitalWriter
Handspring	888-565-9393	www.handspring.com	Visor Pen Stylus, Visor Stylus 5-Pack
PDA Panache	800-270-7196	www.pdapanache.com	Custom Visor Stylus
Pilot Pentopia	800-637-0004	www.pentopia.com	Various

There are basically two kinds of styluses: those that are too large to fit in a Visor's stylus holder and those that aren't. The former we'd classify as "executive" styluses: they seem right at home in a suit pocket or briefcase. The Autopoint Stylus+ and Cross DigitalWriter are in this category; they're big, comfy, and have that classy business look.

Replacement styluses, on the other hand, supplant the stock Visor pen. These include the PDA Panache Custom Stylus "Nail" (so nicknamed for its nail-like top, which makes for easy extraction; see Figure 24-3) and Handspring Pen Stylus (which doubles as a ballpoint pen).

> **TIP** *If your Visor happens to crash, the last thing you want is to have to hunt down a toothpick or a paper clip to press its reset button. Thus, look for a stylus that hides a reset pin, like the aforementioned PDA Panache Nail.*

FIGURE 24-3   The PDA Panache stylus includes not only a nice bright orange tip, but also a hidden reset pin for those untimely crashes

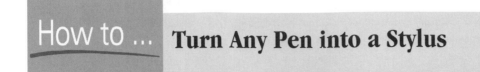

How to ... **Turn Any Pen into a Stylus**

A lot of users find that they don't care for the stock Visor stylus, which is too thin and light for comfort. One affordable alternative is Concept Kitchen's PenCap, a plastic accoutrement that fits over the end of any ordinary ballpoint pen and turns it into a stylus. Thus, if you're more comfortable writing with a Bic, this might be the perfect accessory for you. A pack of four PenCaps costs $9.99.

Keyboards

If you typically enter a lot of data into your Visor—memos, e-mail messages, business documents, novels—you've probably longed to replace your stylus with a keyboard. After all, most of us can type a lot faster than we can write by hand. Fortunately, there are two excellent keyboards now available for Visors, both of them priced under $100. Here's the skinny:

Company	Phone	URL	Keyboard
LandWare	800-526-3977	www.landware.com	GoType! Pro
Targus	877-482-7487	www.targus.com	Stowaway

GoType! Pro

LandWare's GoType! Pro has a built-in dock: your Visor plugs into the base of the clamshell lid that folds open when you use the keyboard. Thus, it's a fairly compact solution, and it doesn't require batteries (instead drawing a negligible amount of power from the Visor).

The trade-off is that the keys are smaller than average. They're big enough to accommodate touch-typing, but ultimately less comfortable than most keyboard keys. Ham-handed users will likely find themselves striking the wrong keys by mistake.

The GoType has two key advantages over the Stowaway, which we discuss next. First, it features a USB port that allows it to double as a HotSync cradle. Second, it comes with two pieces of software not found with other keyboards: TakeNote, a text editing program; and WordSleuth, a 210,000-word thesaurus. Best of all, it costs less.

Stowaway

Forgive us for using a hackneyed old phrase like "marvel of modern engineering," but that's exactly what the Stowaway keyboard is. This amazing piece of hardware folds up to a size barely larger than the Visor itself, and unfolds to produce a set of keys as large as a notebook's. Thus, it's more compact and comfortable than the GoType, and more practical as well.

Like the GoType, the Stowaway features a special cradle for the Visor. Its keys are extraordinarily comfortable, on par with most notebooks, and it includes special keys designed to quick-launch the core Visor apps. The Stowaway should be at the top of the list for anyone seeking a Visor keyboard. Its only hitch is that it requires a hard, flat surface—it can't really be used on a lap. If that's a key consideration for you, the GoType makes more sense.

Protect Your Screen

Keeping your screen pristine is the first rule of Visor ownership. Why? One word: scratches. A scratch in the Graffiti area can result in inaccurate handwriting recognition. A scratch on the main screen can impair its visibility. Fortunately, it's relatively simple to forestall such disasters.

What causes scratches? If your Visor is flopping around unprotected in a purse or briefcase, any loose item—a key, paper clip, pen, or pencil—can create a scratch. That's why we highly recommend a case (see the first section of this chapter). More commonly, however, little specks of grit and other airborne flotsam accumulate on your screen, and when you run your stylus over one of them—scratch city.

Therefore, we recommend you buy a lens-cleaning cloth, the kind used to wipe dust from camera lenses. Every day, give your screen a little buff and polish to keep it free of dust and grit.

Protecting with WriteRight

If you want serious screen protection, you need something like Concept Kitchen's WriteRight. These plastic overlays cover your screen from top to bottom, thus ensuring your stylus causes no damage. They also provide a tacky surface that makes for easier handwriting, and they cut down on glare. The only drawback? WriteRights cut down on contrast, too, making the screen a little tougher to read. If you consider that a small price to pay for total screen protection, then these plastic sheets are the way to go.

Protecting with Scotch Tape

The Graffiti area is where most stylus contact occurs, and therefore it's where scratches are most likely to result. You could cut a WriteRight sheet to fit just the Graffiti area—or you could buy yourself a roll of 3M's Scotch Magic Tape 811. It's exactly the right width for the Graffiti area, and one roll will last you a lifetime. Plus, its slightly rough surface makes for less-slippery handwriting—always a plus. Just cut a piece to cover the input area and replace it every month or so. You'll never see a single scratch.

Decide Between Alkaline and Rechargeable Batteries

Although a pair of alkaline batteries can last the average Visor user upwards of two months, it can get expensive to keep replacing them. And for heavy users, it can become a hassle to have to swap out batteries every two weeks or so.

For the latter segment, we recommend Duracell Ultras, which last about 25 percent longer than standard alkalines (based on some informal testing we conducted). They cost about $1 more per package, but you needn't replace them as frequently.

Many users also wonder about rechargeable batteries, which result in fewer used alkalines being dumped into landfills and can save some money over the long term. While Handspring doesn't recommend the use of certain kinds of rechargeables (specifically, NiCads, which don't supply sufficient voltage and may not properly trigger low-battery warnings), we've had good luck with newer nickel metal-hydride (a.k.a. NiMH) batteries. They cost about $10 per pair; a charger costs about $20 more. If you do plan to use rechargeables, keep a closer watch on the Visor's battery gauge and swap in a freshly charged pair on a regular basis.

How to ... **Extend Battery Life**

If you find you're getting only a couple weeks out of each pair of batteries, consider the things that impact battery life. Using the backlight for extended periods, for instance, creates a bigger power drain, as does using the infrared port for beaming. Also, if you frequently leave your Visor on until it turns itself off, that can shorten overall battery longevity. In the Prefs | General screen, adjust the "Auto-off after" setting to one minute.

Mount Your Palm Device in Your Car

Is your car your office? Your home away from home? If so, your Visor deserves a place of honor—and a place where you can access it while keeping at least one hand on the wheel. Arkon Resources' CM220 Universal Car Mount puts your Visor at arm's reach (see Figure 24-4). It can hold any model and comes with hardware for attaching to your car's windshield or dashboard.

FIGURE 24-4   The Arkon CM220 Universal Car Mount uses suction cups to attach to your windshield, but also comes with dashboard mounting hardware

In all seriousness, you should never, ever try to use your Visor while driving. If you must look something up or write something down, wait until you're stopped at a light. Or, ask a passenger to do it for you.

Where to Find It

Web Site	Address	What's There
Concept Kitchen	www.conceptkitchen.com	WriteRight, PenCap Stylus
Arkon Resources	www.arkon.com	CM220 Universal Car Mount

Chapter 25

Dealing with Problems

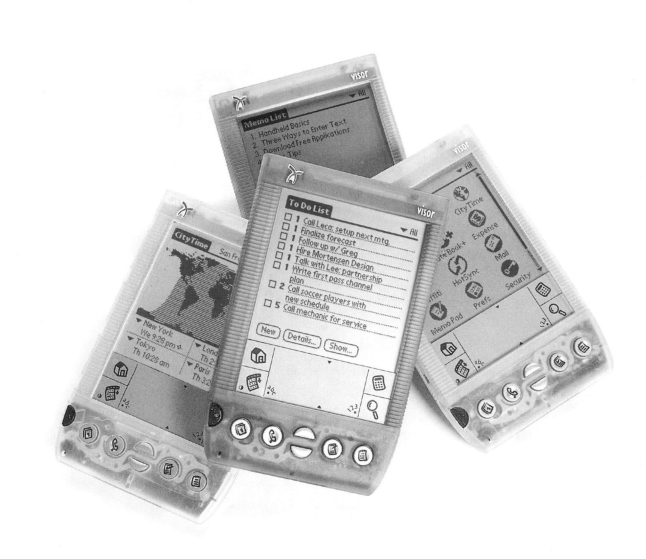

How to...

- Reset your Visor
- Avoid battery-related problems
- Fix a scratched screen
- Fix a screen that no longer responds properly
- Free some extra memory
- Resolve Hack conflicts
- Clean your Visor's contacts
- Avoid broken buttons
- Fix alarms that don't "wake up" your Visor
- Deal with a Visor that suddenly won't HotSync
- Obtain nonwarranty or accident-related repairs
- Troubleshoot HotSync glitches
- Manage two Visors on one PC
- HotSync one Visor on two PCs
- Solve software problems on the desktop

No computer is perfect. Windows is about as far from the mark as you can get, Macs have problems of their own, and even Visors suffer the occasional meltdown. Usually it's minor: an alarm that fails to "wake up" the unit, a wayward Hack that causes the occasional crash. But sometimes something downright scary happens, like a sudden and inexplicable lockup that wipes the Visor's entire memory. In this chapter, we help you troubleshoot some of the most common Visor maladies, and hopefully prevent the worst of them.

NOTE *Many common problems are addressed on Handspring's Web site (www.handspring.com). We won't rehash them here, but we do suggest you check the site if you have a problem we haven't addressed. Chances are good you can find a solution or at least get in touch with Handspring technical support.*

Save the Day with a Reset

Just as rebooting a computer often resolves a glitch or lockup, resetting your Visor is the solution to many a problem. And it's usually the first thing you need to do if your Visor crashes.

Just What Is a "Crash," Anyway?

When a computer crashes, that generally means it has plowed into a brick wall and can no longer function. Fortunately, whereas a car in the same situation would need weeks of bump-and-paint work, a computer can usually return to normal by being rebooted. In the case of Visors, a "reset" is the same as a "reboot."

When a Visor crashes, one common error message is "Fatal Exception." Don't be alarmed; this isn't nearly as disastrous as it sounds. It simply means the Visor has encountered a glitch that proved fatal to its operation. Quite often, an onscreen Reset button will appear with this error, a tap of which performs a "soft reset" (as we describe in the following section). Sometimes, however, the crash is so major that even this button doesn't work. (You know because when you tap it, nothing happens.) In a case like this, you have to perform a manual reset.

Different Ways to Reset a Visor

On the back of every Visor is a little hole labeled RESET. Hidden inside it is a button that effectively reboots the unit. When that happens, you see the startup screen that says "Palm Computing Platform," followed a few seconds later by the Preferences screen. That's how a successful reset goes 99.9 percent of the time. Everything is exactly as you left it—your data, your applications, everything.

Technically speaking, there are three kinds of resets: soft, warm, and hard. (Mind out of the gutter, please.) The details:

- ■ **Soft**   Only in rare instances do you need to perform anything other than a soft reset, which is akin to pressing CTRL-ALT-DELETE to reboot your computer. You simply press the reset button, and then wait a few seconds while your Visor resets itself.

- ■ **Warm**   This action, performed by holding the Up scroll-button while pressing the Reset button, goes an extra step by deactivating any system patches or Hacks you may have installed. Use this only if your Visor fails to respond to a soft reset (meaning it's still locked up or crashing).

- ■ **Hard**   With any luck, you'll never have to do this. A hard reset wipes everything out of your Visor's memory, essentially returning it to factory condition. In the exceedingly rare case that your Visor is seriously hosed (meaning it won't reset or even turn off), this should at least get you back to square one.

> NOTE   *Any time you reset your Visor, you run the risk of losing data. And with a hard reset, you lose everything. That's why we strongly recommend a utility like BackupBuddyNG (see Chapter 18) or a module like the Handspring Backup Module (see Chapter 16), which automatically restores not only your data, but your third-party files and applications as well.*

25

How to ... Press the Reset Button (The Toothpick Story)

A couple years ago, Rick was having lunch with some buddies when he pulled out his PalmPilot to jot a few notes. To his shock, it wouldn't turn on (a problem he later attributed to the extremely cold weather, which can indeed numb a pair of batteries). A press of the reset button was in order, but Rick didn't have the right tool—namely, a paper clip. So he asked the waitress to bring him a toothpick—the other common item that's small enough to fit in the reset hole. Presto: the Palm sprang back to life.

The moral of the story is, be prepared. If your Palm crashes and you need to reset it, the last thing you need is a desperate hunt for a paper clip or toothpick. Fortunately, many styluses have "reset tips" hidden inside them (see Chapter 24 for information on the third-party styluses that do).

And now, two tips about reset tips:

TIP   *Some replacement styluses, like the PDA Panache "Nail" (see Chapter 24), have a built-in reset tip. Where's it hiding? Unscrew the top from the barrel to find out.*

TIP   *If your stylus doesn't have a tip and you don't want to have to hunt for a paper clip whenever you need to do a reset, we have a solution. Using a pair of wire cutters, snip off the straight end of a paper clip and stow it in the battery compartment between the two batteries. (Just let it rest on top, in the groove between them.) Now you'll always have a reset tip.*

Avoid Battery Problems

Batteries are the lifeblood of any Visor. When they die, they take your data with them, effectively returning your Visor to factory condition. That's why it's vital to keep a close eye on the battery gauge shown at the top of the Applications screen (see Figure 25-1), and to take heed when the Visor notifies you the batteries are low.

Of course, if you HotSync regularly (and especially if you use a backup utility like BackupBuddyNG), a wiped Visor isn't the end of the world. Once you replace the batteries, a HotSync is all it takes to restore virtually everything. Still, there's no reason to let things reach that point. Following are some tips to help you avoid most battery-related incidents.

Battery gauge

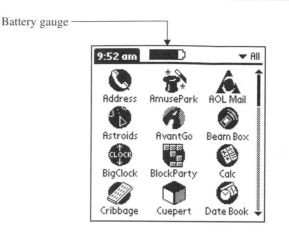

| FIGURE 25-1 | All Visors have this handy—and reasonably accurate—battery gauge at the top of the Applications screen |

Keep 'em Fresh

Suppose you head off to Bermuda for a two-week getaway (you lucky vacationer, you), leaving your work—and your Visor—behind. When you return, you find the Visor dead as a doornail. That's because it draws a trace amount of power from the batteries even when it's turned off, in order to keep the memory alive. If the batteries were fairly low to begin with, the long period of inactivity might polish them off.

The obvious solution is to keep your Visor with you as much as possible. (It's great for games, e-books, and other leisure activities, remember?) Or, if you know you're going to be away from your Visor for a while, put in a pair of new batteries before you leave.

Swap 'em Quick

The documentation for the Visor says that when replacing batteries, you shouldn't leave them out for more than 60 seconds (lest data loss occur). This is true, to a point. Near-dead batteries aren't supplying much power to the memory, so when you remove them, the memory can indeed fade fast. On the other hand, if you're replacing batteries that are still reasonably healthy, it can be half an hour or more before the memory gets wiped.

Of course, it can be difficult to gauge the batteries' remaining strength, so follow this rule of thumb: swap them fast. Pop the old ones out, pop the fresh ones in, and you're done. It's exceedingly rare to lose data when you adhere to this method—but you should always do a HotSync first anyway, just to be safe.

25

TIP *If you use rechargeable batteries, be aware the battery gauge might not accurately reflect remaining power. We recommend keeping a second set of fully charged batteries on hand at all times and swapping them at regularly scheduled intervals.*

Fix a Scratched Screen

Scratches happen. As discussed in Chapter 24, they happen most often when your stylus hits a piece of dust or grit. That's why it's important to keep your screen as clean as possible (we recommend a daily wipe with a lint-free, antistatic cloth). If you do incur a scratch, however, here are some steps you can take to repair it:

- **Tape**   A piece of Scotch Magic Tape 811 placed over the Graffiti input area (where most scratches occur) not only makes scratches less tangible while you're writing, it also prevents future scratches and provides a tackier writing surface.
- **WriteRight sheets**   As discussed in Chapter 24, Concept Kitchen's WriteRight sheets are plastic overlays that protect the entire screen. They won't remove scratches, but they do prevent them and, like the tape, make them less pronounced.
- **Screen Clean**   Creator Tim Warner says this bottle of goo—which closely resembles car wax—will remove 99 percent of all screen scratches. Basically, you wipe it onto the screen, wait five minutes, and then buff it off. Make no mistake: Screen Clean won't fix a really deep scratch, but it does work as advertised on light ones. And it leaves your screen as bright and shiny as the day you unpacked it.

Fix a Screen That No Longer Responds Properly

As noted in Chapter 2's discussion of the Pref's | Digitizer option, it's not uncommon to experience some "drift" in the screen's response to your stylus taps. An example: you have to tap just a bit to the left or right of your desired target for the tap to be recognized. This occurs over time as the accuracy of the digitizer (the hardware that makes the screen respond to your input) degrades.

Unless the digitizer has gotten so off-kilter that you can no longer operate your Visor, the solution is to hit the Prefs icon, and then choose Digitizer from the right-corner menu. Here, you can reset the digitizer, effectively making your Visor as good as new. If you can't even manage to tap Prefs, you can do a soft reset (as described earlier in this chapter). This gets you to the Prefs screen, at which point you should at least be able to select the Digitizer option.

Make Room for More Software and Data

A common problem among Visor users—especially those who discover games and e-books—is running out of memory. As we discussed in Chapter 16 (among other places), there are easy ways to increase the available RAM in your Visor. Of course, those are long-term solutions. If you suddenly find yourself in a memory crunch and need space for something important (say, a work-related spreadsheet), you need to do some housekeeping and clear a little space.

To delete software from your Visor, tap the Applications button, and then choose Menu | App | Delete.

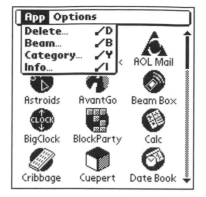

In a few seconds, you see a list of all the applications, utilities, games, and so forth installed on your Visor (see Figure 25-2). What you won't find here are e-books, Doc files, image files, individual spreadsheets, and other kinds of data. For items like those, you need to use their respective applications to delete them. Say you've imported some documents into SmartDoc or some photos into FireViewer; the only way to delete those documents or photos is from within those two programs.

As shown in Figure 25-2, the Delete screen tells you the size of each item, so you know just how much space you free up with each deletion. To remove something, tap it to highlight it, and then tap Delete.

FIGURE 25-2   The Delete screen lists all your installed programs, but not necessarily all your data

25

What to Delete

Don't bother culling through your contact list, appointment calendar, and so forth. Though they may be large, deleting a handful of entries will have a negligible impact on the Visor's total memory. Programs, on the other hand, can add up quickly. Here's a list of items to consider ditching:

- **Games**   Although many of them are relatively small, some, like SimCity, can eat up a pretty large chunk of memory. If you don't play it anymore or can live without it for a while, ditch it.

- **E-books**   No sense keeping books you've already read, especially if they occupy several hundred kilobytes of RAM.

- **Data files**   Spreadsheets, photos, Doc files, and databases can be quite large. Eliminate the ones you no longer need.

Resolve HackMaster Conflicts

This bears repeating (see Chapter 18 for the first time we said it): as marvelous as Hacks are, they can wreak havoc on your Visor. This is especially true if you run more than two or three simultaneously, as these little bits of code often conflict with one another. If you find your Visor is crashing on a regular basis, you may have to investigate your Hacks. Here's what you should do

1.   Start HackMaster, and then tap the Uninstall All button at the bottom of the screen. This disables (but does not delete) all Hacks.

```
┌──────────────────────────┐
│ HackMaster Extensions    │
│ ☑ ScreenShot Hack    ? ⊞ │
│ ☐ Graffiti&Kbd       ?   │
│ ☐ MiddleCapsHack     ? ⊞ │
│ ☐ AppHack            ? ⊞ │
│                          │
│                          │
│                          │
│                          │
│                          │
│                          │
│  ( Uninstall All )( Reset (!) ) │
└──────────────────────────┘
```

2. Go back to using your Visor. If you find the crashes no longer occur, then a Hack is the likely culprit. To help pin down which one, go on to Step 3.

3. Launch HackMaster again, and then enable just one Hack. Use your Visor normally and see if the crashes return. If not, enable a second Hack. Through this process of elimination, you should be able to determine which one is causing the problem. When you do, stop using it.

NOTE   *Power users pride themselves on running five, eight, even ten Hacks simultaneously. It can be done, but occasional crashes are almost guaranteed. If you can live with them, you can do likewise. We recommend running no more than five Hacks at a time and making sure to use a utility like BackupBuddyNG, just in case.*

25

Clean Your Visor's Contacts

After a few years' use, the metal contacts on your Visor's HotSync port can get a bit dirty or corroded. If you're experiencing HotSync problems and you discover wiggling the Visor while it's in the cradle helps remedy them, cleaning the contacts may be the solution. Because they're sunk in-between plastic grooves, they can be difficult to reach. Try cutting an eraser (preferably on the head of a pencil, so you have a "handle" to go with it) to fit the grooves.

Avoid Button Problems

With so many great action games out there, it's no surprise to find users pounding on their Visors like they were Game Boys. Don't. The application and scroll buttons have a rated life span, and if you overuse them, you run the risk of breaking them. And, while they are covered under warranty, you probably don't want to wait several days (or longer) for a repair or replacement.

If you absolutely must play games that require a lot of button pressing, at least try to vary which buttons get used. Many games let you configure their controls, so it might be possible to, say, use the Date Book and To Do List buttons one day and the Phone List and Memo Pad buttons the next. Or, there's a little program called Auto Fire Hack (see Chapter 18 for information on using Hacks) that can save wear and tear on your buttons; it enables automatic firing in games that support it.

Whatever you do, don't press too hard. Those buttons are fairly sensitive, so try to develop a light touch.

Fix a Visor That Won't "Wake Up" for Alarms

It's easy to fall out of love with your Visor when an alarm you set fails to go off (meaning the Visor doesn't "wake up" and beep). This can happen for several reasons: low batteries, a corrupted alarm database, or a conflict with third-party software. The first is easy to resolve: make sure your Visor has fresh batteries. For the other two problems, try a soft reset, which often does the trick.

If you're using a third-party program that has anything to do with alarms (such as ToDo PLUS, Snoozer, and so forth), it's possible this is causing the snafu. To troubleshoot it, try doing a warm reset (holding the up scroll-button while pressing the reset button). This disables any Hacks or third-party applications that tie into the operating system. Set an alarm in Date Book and see if it works; if so, then another program is likely to blame. A process of elimination should help you determine which one. In any case, you may have to discontinue using that program if it keeps fouling up your alarms.

If none of these options work, it's possible your Visor is damaged. Contact Handspring for service.

Deal with a Visor That Will No Longer HotSync

A known glitch with some Visors is they occasionally refuse to HotSync. You push the HotSync button on the cradle and nothing happens. If you were able to successfully HotSync previously, try a soft reset of the Visor. This should fix the problem; if it doesn't, try unplugging the HotSync cradle (assuming you're using the standard USB version), waiting a few moments, and then plugging it in again. If all else fails, see Handspring's Web site for other troubleshooting advice.

Obtain Service and Repairs

Visor problems, while relatively infrequent, come in all shapes and sizes. Yours may be as simple as an alarm that won't go off or as dire as a device that won't turn on. Fortunately, technical support and repair services are readily available from Handspring. Here's the pertinent info:

	Tech Support	Customer Service	Web Site
Handspring	716-871-6448	716-871-6442	www.handspring.com

Obtain Nonwarranty or Accident-Related Repairs

Right down there with the awful sound of your car crunching into another is the sound of your Visor hitting the pavement. A cracked case, a broken screen, a dead unit—these are among the painful results. And, unfortunately, if you drop, step on, sit on, or get caught in a rainstorm with your Visor, your warranty is pretty much out the window.

All is not lost, though. If your Visor is damaged or develops a problem after the warranty has expired, call Handspring to see what options are available. You may be able to pay for repairs or buy a refurbished one for less than the cost of a new unit.

Problems on the PC Side

For the most part, you can count on your Visor to be trouble-free. We use ours almost nonstop and rarely experience any kind of trouble.

The desktop computer to which we HotSync is another matter entirely. Most of the time, HotSyncing happens on a Windows PC—and that explains most of the trouble all by itself. Windows is cranky, belligerent, complicated, and annoying. Unlike the Palm OS, it crashes often and has a lot of interrelated technologies that only begrudgingly work together. Mac owners, you're not off the hook either. The iMac we used to HotSync has its share of troubles, too, despite the mantra of most Apple fans ("Windows crashed? You should have bought a Mac!").

In reality, you probably won't need a whole lot of troubleshooting help. The Visor/PC combination is a pretty stable one with few potential problems. Nonetheless, in this section, we look at the most common problems you might encounter with your desktop computer and offer solutions on how to solve them. Good luck!

Solve HotSync Problems

One of the few major hassles people encounter with the desktop computer is with HotSync sessions. After all, this is really the only time your desktop interacts with the Visor, so that's when problems arise.

Resolve USB Issues

As you already know, the Visor and Visor Deluxe come with a USB HotSync cradle. The beauty of USB technology is its plug-and-play simplicity: you needn't fiddle with complicated serial-port COM settings, or even power down your computer when you connect or disconnect the cradle.

USB doesn't always work perfectly, however. For one thing, it's important that you follow the installation instructions outlined in Chapter 3. If you plug the cradle into your computer before you've installed the Palm Desktop software, that can foul things up. What's more, some computers just have difficulty working with USB peripherals. If yours proves to be one of them (that is, you've worked with Handspring's technical support and simply can't get the HotSync cradle working), you may need to purchase Handspring's optional serial cradle, which plugs into a standard serial port.

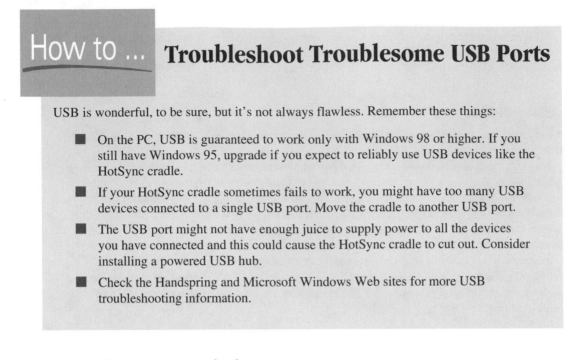

How to ...   Troubleshoot Troublesome USB Ports

USB is wonderful, to be sure, but it's not always flawless. Remember these things:

- On the PC, USB is guaranteed to work only with Windows 98 or higher. If you still have Windows 95, upgrade if you expect to reliably use USB devices like the HotSync cradle.

- If your HotSync cradle sometimes fails to work, you might have too many USB devices connected to a single USB port. Move the cradle to another USB port.

- The USB port might not have enough juice to supply power to all the devices you have connected and this could cause the HotSync cradle to cut out. Consider installing a powered USB hub.

- Check the Handspring and Microsoft Windows Web sites for more USB troubleshooting information.

Troubleshoot HotSync Glitches

If you can't get your Visor to talk to your computer, there are a number of likely causes. Consider the following checklist for resolving the issue:

- Close the HotSync Manager and restart it. Also, try a soft reset on the Visor itself (see the beginning of this chapter to learn how).

- An application you tried to install might have been too big for your Visor's memory and now it's forever interfering with HotSyncs. You need to manually delete the app from the install queue. To do this, open your username folder in the C:\Palm directory and open the Install folder. Delete anything you find in there, and then try to HotSync.

- Upgrade to the newest Palm Desktop software. See Handspring's Web site for upgrade information.

- If none of those things work, your Visor or the HotSync cradle may be defective. If possible, test them with another computer.

Solve the Most Common HotSync Problems

While the checklist we provided earlier in the chapter can get you through all kinds of HotSync issues, the fact remains that a few pesky problems account for about 90 percent of all the HotSync issues we've ever encountered—and they're all pretty easy to diagnose and solve.

The Visor Reports a COM Port Conflict   A device or application is probably just hogging the port (this usually happens when you're using a serial-port cradle). Communication software like fax programs and remote-control software are designed to grab and hold a COM port, so they might interfere with the HotSync Manager. Disable those programs before HotSyncing.

NOTE   *HotSync Manager hogs the COM port as well. If you disconnect the HotSync cradle and plug something else in—like a modem—the new device won't work unless you shut down HotSync Manager.*

The Visor Aborts a HotSync Immediately   If you press the HotSync button on the cradle and the Visor insists the COM port is in use immediately—so fast it doesn't seem possible for the Visor even to have checked—then the solution is to perform a soft reset on your Visor. After it resets, the HotSync should work fine.

When HotSyncing, the Visor Displays the HotSync Screen but Absolutely Nothing Else Happens
Frequently, this problem is the result of either HotSync Manager not being active or one of its dialog boxes being open. If you open the Custom dialog box to change conduit settings, for instance, and then fail to close it, the HotSync won't run and you won't get an error message—so look on the desktop for an open dialog box.

When HotSyncing, this Message Appears: "An Application Failed to Respond to a HotSync"
This one is easy to fix. When you started the HotSync, an Address Book or Date Book entry was probably left open. Your Visor can't successfully HotSync with one of those entries open for editing, so you should close the entry and try again.

The HotSync Conspiracy

This may sound ominous, but we just wanted to get your attention. Don't leave your Visor sitting in the HotSync cradle for an extended period of time. That's because the cradle gradually drains the batteries. Thus, after you finish your HotSync, make a point to remove the Visor from the cradle.

Manage Multiple Visors or Computers

Palm Desktop makes it simple to HotSync the same Visor to more than one PC or to HotSync several Visors to the same PC. For some reason, many Visor owners are reluctant to try this out. ("I was always kind of afraid to HotSync two Visors to my PC," Rick once told Dave in a particularly confessional moment.)

Two Visors, One Computer

If you have two Visors and only one computer, you're not alone. It's a pretty common scenario—spouses, for instance, often have their own Visors and want to HotSync to the household computer.
Here's what you need to do

1. Be absolutely sure both Visors have different user names (a.k.a. HotSync ID). Check this by tapping the HotSync icon on each Visor and looking at the name in the upper-right corner. Identically named Visors, HotSynced to the same computer, will thrash the data on the PC and both Visors. When you did your very first HotSync on each Visor, we hope you chose different user names. (If you didn't, check out the PalmName utility mentioned in Chapter 18.)

2. Put the Visor in the HotSync cradle and go. The first time the second Visor is synchronized, your Visor asks if you want to create a new account for the new Visor. Click Yes.

CAUTION *If, for some reason, both Visors have the same HotSync ID, don't attempt to HotSync them to the same PC! In fact, change their names before you HotSync at all to prevent accidentally HotSyncing the Visors in the wrong PC. Check Chapter 18 for information on how to change a Visor's HotSync ID.*

Two Computers for a Single Visor

No problem—the Visor can keep two different computers straight just as easily as one computer can keep a pair of Visors straight. When you HotSync, the Visor updates the second PC with whatever data it previously got from the first PC, and vice versa. This is a great way to keep your office PC and your home computer in sync, or a PC and a Mac—the Visor can serve as a nonpartisan conduit for keeping all the data in agreement.

TIP *While not essential, we recommend you have the same version of the Palm Desktop on both PCs. If you're using a PC and a Mac, you can't do this, but you should keep up with the latest release of the Mac Palm Desktop.*

CAUTION   *Your data can get damaged if you use different information managers on the various PCs, such as the Palm Desktop at home, but Outlook in the office. If you HotSync different computers to the same Visor, be sure to use the same contact management software on all the systems.*

Desktop Software Issues

Your Visor is a robust little device and software for it rarely causes any trouble. In months of working with a Visor on a daily basis, it's rare to encounter any crashes or software glitches at all. The desktop is a different matter entirely, though.

Using the HotSync Manager After Windows Has Crashed

Windows crashes. This is a sad fact of life and there's little we can do to solve it. Sometimes when Windows crashes, it recovers and you can keep working—but the icons in your System Tray vanish. If the HotSync Manager was one such icon, you have two choices: you can reboot your PC (which then restarts all the System Tray apps for you) or you can keep working without the icon. You can still HotSync just fine, but you won't be able to adjust any of the conduits.

Fix a Broken Conduit

If you discover a particular conduit—like the one that controls Desktop To Go or TrueSync, for instance—suddenly ceases working, the easiest and often only solution is to reinstall the corresponding application. The conduit is then reinstalled and whatever Windows silliness that made it stop working is corrected.

Upgrade the Palm Desktop Software

Handspring occasionally introduces updated versions of the Palm Desktop software. While we firmly believe that if it ain't broke, don't fix it, it makes sense to investigate these upgrades to see if they might prove beneficial to you. Check the Handspring Web site periodically to see if a new version of Palm Desktop is available. If so, you can usually find corresponding information that tells what features have been added or what problems were corrected.

Find Technical Support on the Web

You might encounter additional problems with your Visor. Many problems, in fact, are specific to Microsoft Office, like broken macros, apps not starting properly when you drag items in the Palm Desktop, and other issues. Handspring has a growing technical support area with problems and solutions—you can get there by visiting www.handspring.com.

25

In addition, several sites offer tips, tricks, hints, and technical solutions. If you're looking for answers that aren't in this book or on the Handspring Web site, try some of these Web sites:

www.palmgear.com	Look for both the Tips/Tricks section and Calvin's FAQ.
www.palmpower.com	This site has a message board area in which you can post questions and read answers to common questions. There's an extensive set of discussions on HotSync and desktop-related topics.
www.pdabuzz.com	The Tips & Tricks page has information divided by PDA device and there's a section just for the Visor. Also try the Discussion Forums, in which you can ask questions and get answers fairly quickly from actual Visor users who may have had the same experience.
Alt.comp.sys.palmtops.pilot Comp.sys.palmtops.pilot	These newsgroups are available to anyone with a newsreader like Outlook Express. They are threaded message boards that contain questions and answers about Palm device issues. You can post your own questions, respond to what's already there, or just read the existing posts.

Where to Find It

Web Site	Address	What's There
BackupBuddy Software	www.backupbuddy.com	BackupBuddyNG
PalmLife	www.palmlife.com	Screen Clean
Concept Kitchen	www.conceptkitchen.com	WriteRight
Till's PalmPilot Programs	www.ibr.cs.tu-bs.de/~harbaum/pilot/	Auto Fire Hack

Index